Economics of Labor and Employment Law
Volume I

Economic Approaches to Law

Series Editors: Richard A. Posner
*Judge, United States Court of Appeals for the Seventh Circuit
and Senior Lecturer, University of Chicago Law School, USA*
Francesco Parisi
*Professor of Law, University of Minnesota Law School, USA
and Professor of Economics, University of Bologna, Italy*

A full list of published and future titles in this series is printed at the end of this volume.

For a list of all Edward Elgar published titles visit our site on the World Wide Web at
www.e-elgar.com

Economics of Labor and Employment Law
Volume I

Edited by

John J. Donohue III

Leighton Homer Surbeck Professor of Law
Yale Law School, USA

ECONOMIC APPROACHES TO LAW

An Elgar Reference Collection
Cheltenham, UK • Northampton, MA, USA

Published by
Edward Elgar Publishing Limited
Glensanda House
Montpellier Parade
Cheltenham
Glos GL50 1UA
UK

Edward Elgar Publishing, Inc.
William Pratt House
9 Dewey Court
Northampton
Massachusetts 01060
USA

A catalogue record for this book is available from the British Library.

Library of Congress Control Number: 2007927950

ISBN 978 1 84542 706 1 (2 volume set)

Printed and bound in Great Britain by MPG Books Ltd, Bodmin, Cornwall.

Contents

Acknowledgements

The editor and publishers wish to thank the authors and the following publishers who have kindly given permission for the use of copyright material.

American Economic Association for article: James Peoples (1998), 'Deregulation and the Labor Market', *Journal of Economic Perspectives*, **12** (3), Summer, 111–30.

Michigan Law Review for article: Kenneth G. Dau-Schmidt (1992), 'A Bargaining Analysis of American Labor Law and the Search for Bargaining Equity and Industrial Peace', *Michigan Law Review*, **91** (3), December, 419–514.

MIT Press Journals for articles: Timothy Besley and Robin Burgess (2004), 'Can Labor Regulation Hinder Economic Performance? Evidence from India', *Quarterly Journal of Economics*, **119** (1), February, 91–134; Juan C. Botero, Simeon Djankov, Rafael La Porta, Florencio Lopez-de-Silanes and Andrei Shleifer (2004), 'The Regulation of Labor', *Quarterly Journal of Economics*, **119** (4), November, 1339–82.

University of Chicago Law Review, University of Chicago Law School via Copyright Clearance Center, Inc. for article: Richard A. Posner (1984), 'Some Economics of Labor Law', *University of Chicago Law Review*, **51** (4), Autumn, 988–1011.

University of Chicago Press for article: Thomas J. Holmes (1998), 'The Effect of State Policies on the Location of Manufacturing: Evidence from State Borders', *Journal of Political Economy*, **106** (4), August, 667–705.

Virginia Law Review via Copyright Clearance Center, Inc. for article: Cass R. Sunstein (2001), 'Human Behavior and the Law of Work', *Virginia Law Review*, **87** (2), April, 205–76.

Every effort has been made to trace all the copyright holders but if any have been inadvertently overlooked the publishers will be pleased to make the necessary arrangement at the first opportunity.

In addition the publishers wish to thank the Library of Indiana University at Bloomington, USA, for their assistance in obtaining these articles.

Introduction

John J. Donohue III

Labor law encompasses a broad and amorphous body of rules and regulations that govern an enormous array of features of the working lives and the economic welfare of workers and their families. Around the world and within countries, there is dramatic variation in the rules that govern unionization and the work relationship, as well as the process and permissible bases for hiring and firing workers. On the one hand, many countries in Latin America – Brazil is one good example – regulate the work relationship in minute detail. Judges are permitted to determine whether even minor changes in working conditions are consistent with humanist principles of fairness. The outcome – reminiscent of Grant Gilmore's line that 'in hell, there will be nothing but law, and due process will be strictly observed' – has been a disaster for the economic well-being of Brazilian workers that has only been mitigated by a substantial flight to the unregulated black market in labor. On the other hand, countries such as the United States have had relatively fewer restrictions on labor contracting, and have enjoyed immense growth in their labor markets over time.

In the last decade, a strong theme of writing on labor markets in the Organization for Economic Cooperation and Development (OECD) and the International Monetary Fund (IMF) has been that labor institutions are a major source of unemployment in advanced countries. Inflexible, overregulated markets are clearly bad, but the goal of policy is to determine optimal levels of regulation, which requires judgment about where in the large spectrum between the mercantile approach of some Latin American countries and the completely laissez-faire lies the appropriate degree of regulation. Michael Mussa, former chief economist at the IMF, wrote in 2002 that the collapse of the Argentinean economy at that time could have been avoided with greater flexibility in its economic system, particularly in its labor markets.[1]

At the same time, the International Labor Organization issued a report stating that it

> takes issue with the view that labour market rigidity has been the major cause of unemployment and that greater labour market flexibility is the solution … jobless rates appear to have risen independently of levels of labour market regulations … trade union power was reduced in many countries, together with unemployment benefits and in some cases minimum wages, producing little if any positive employment effect. (www.jobsletter.org.nz/jbl05210.htm).[2]

Some also point out that labor regulations and union-imposed standards for work time (as well as high marginal tax rates) enable Europeans to enjoy significantly greater leisure than Americans: the French, Germans, and Italians work about 400 hours less than the 1800 yearly hours worked by the average American worker.[3]

Volume I, Part I. Overview: A Cross-Country Comparison of the Regulation of Labor

The first paper in this volume takes a very comprehensive look at the regulation of labor across 85 countries in order to understand the origins and consequences of varying regulatory approaches – Botero, Djankov, La Porta, Lopez-de-Silanes and Shleifer (2004; Chapter 1). Botero *et al.* focus their inquiry on three theories of institutional design. The efficiency theory posits that governments choose institutions in order to maximize some social welfare function or at least that institutions adjust to that end. The political power theory assumes that the ruling classes make decisions that benefit themselves and their patrons. The legal traditions theory traces the development of institutions to the country's core legal tradition, which is typically inherited from colonial powers. This theory predicts differential outcomes for countries with civil versus common law traditions, and one of the authors' primary aims is to distinguish this effect from purely political forces.

Botero *et al.* divide the broad expanse of labor law into three categories: employment protection, collective bargaining, and social security. Their empirical agenda begins with the coding of the laws of 85 countries as of 1997 for the three categories, at which point they explore which institutional theories best explain the legal outcomes. Their worker protection index seeks to capture the marginal cost to employers of departing from standard contract provisions by, for example, hiring temporary workers or dismissing employees. Their coding of collective bargaining laws focuses on the power of labor unions and the balance of power between firms and unions enshrined in procedural protections. Their index of social security is based on old-age pensions, coverage for illness and unemployment insurance. The authors create their indices so that higher values will reflect greater protections of and benefits for workers. For example, as Table 1 illustrates, Portugal had one of the highest index values in the sample, while the United States and New Zealand ranked nearer the bottom because of their relatively low values for employment and collective bargaining protections. But one could query whether these indices can be taken as having more than ordinal significance. Is the regulation of employment law in Portugal really five times more stringent than that of New Zealand, and what does that really mean?

In their regression models based on these indices, Botero *et al.* find, contrary to the efficiency theory, that prosperous countries tend to provide more generous social security systems but that employment regulation is unrelated to income. Civil law countries mandate greater worker protection than common law states in the areas of employment and collective bargaining law. Support for the political theory emerges with evidence that longer experience with centrist or leftist governments and higher levels of union density lead to heavier labor market regulation. When the legal and political determinants are included in the same regression, the authors find that only the former generate robustly significant effects on regulatory regimes.

In order to bolster further the findings in favor of legal tradition, Botero *et al.* report relatively high correlations between their labor law indices and economic entry regulations, which the authors quantify by counting the number of steps or number of days it takes to start a business in a particular country. The authors conclude from their analysis that stronger labor regulation leads to worse economic outcomes, including lower levels of labor force participation, higher levels of youth unemployment, and a larger underground economy. Thus, their work is deemed to undermine the efficiency theory and support the view that legal tradition substantially influences labor regulation, with the common law leading to the lowest level of regulation.

Table 1: Employment Law Index Values and Rankings (Portugal, United States, New Zealand)

Countries	Aggregate Index Values Shown in Bold Ranking within 85 Countries shown in Parentheses		
	Employment Laws	Collective Relations Laws	Social Security Laws
Portugal	**0.809** (3rd)	**0.649** (4th)	**0.735** (27th)
United States	**0.218** (77th)	**0.259** (76th)	**0.646** (46th)
New Zealand	**0.161** (84th)	**0.25** (77th)	**0.719** (32nd)
Mean	0.488	0.445	0.569
Median	0.475	0.455	0.677
No. of Countries	85	85	85

Source: Botero *et al.*, Table III, pp. 1362–4.

Obviously, there is a high degree of distillation involved in the attempt to quantify such a large body of law into index numbers. Many questions can be raised about whether the authors have been sufficiently attentive to differences between the law on the books, which is their main focus in coding, and the law in practice, which is obviously harder to identify for so many laws in countries all across the globe. Moreover, their various index scores represent averages of subindices, so that two countries with identical values on, say, the social security index might have very different protections for the subcomponents of old-age benefits, health benefits, and unemployment compensation benefits. Taking the US as an example, one can imagine ways in which federal labor regulation may sensibly be captured in a single index, but this would mean that the broad variation in regulation across the states would be missed. Finally, critics of Botero *et al.* have charged that their analysis may simply be picking up correlations that have no causal significance. But even the critics have conceded that this is very provocative work raising important questions that need further exploration, particularly as aging populations in the developed world will put increasing pressure on the old-age benefit programs of many countries.

Volume I, Part II. The Economics of American Labor Law

While Botero *et al.* try to examine the broad contours of labor regulation across the globe, important papers by Richard Posner, Ken Dau-Schmidt, and Cass Sunstein evaluate the elements of American labor law from the perspectives of the Chicago School, progressive law and economics, and behavioral economics and come to strikingly different conclusions on the value of certain features of the legal landscape. In a characteristically provocative essay –

Posner (1984; Chapter 2) – Posner depicts labor unions as cartels whose primary function is to elevate the firm wage beyond competitive levels. Posner argues that the consequences of such anticompetitive pricing tend to be socially harmful, and therefore he laments the fact that federal labor law has encouraged the emergence of cartels.

Posner states that labor law does not passively manage the collective bargaining environment, but rather facilitates the organization of firm employees while narrowly setting the rules of the game. During the interwar period, Posner concedes that labor markets often did not generate competitive wages due to informational asymmetries. In the absence of organizations, employers could exploit workers' lack of outside options or their investment in firm-specific human capital to keep wages artificially low. Therefore, one might consider the Wagner Act and the subsequent unionization movement as a means of reducing wage distortions since it codified the right of employees to redress grievances over pay and working conditions. Without such protection, the classic free rider problem would surely prevent workers from mounting successful resistance to the 'predatory' actions of employers.

Posner describes the collective bargaining system from the birth of a union to the strike phase while highlighting the likely motives of employers and employees. He observes that the two sides in a labor dispute effectively find themselves in a situation of bilateral monopoly. The union has only one 'customer' for its services, and the firm may only negotiate with the union representatives. In the event of a strike, the union must weigh lost income against future wage concessions, while the employer must balance the reputation gains from standing firm against the cost of lost production. Posner claims that labor law ultimately determines the nature and extent of costs borne by both parties. By specifying the terms under which the firm may hire replacement workers, for example, labor law slightly shifts the cost balance in favor of the employer.

Posner rejects the claims most famously advanced by Freeman and Medoff (1984), that unions actually enhance the productivity of the labor force, finding union support for the minimum wage or federal oversight regarding working conditions to be better explained by his cartel theory. He argues that government intervention through the National Labor Relations Act helps employees overcome the large-numbers difficulty that hampers cartelization efforts. Specifically, labor law (1) reduces competition between union sympathizers and workers who would accept the competitive wage, (2) restricts free riding among the labor force, thereby increasing the wealth and power of the union, and (3) establishes picketing as a method for detecting cheating among the cartel's ranks.

A decidedly more optimistic assessment of unions and labor laws underlies the work of Dau-Schmidt (1992; Chapter 3). His paper argues against the view that unions are barriers to efficiency that lead to rising prices, as well as declining output and labor employment, and therefore should not be encouraged by federal labor law. According to Dau-Schmidt's formulation, union wage benefits derive from employer rents and productivity boosts rather than cartelization, and the generated surplus becomes the focus of Coasean collective bargaining. As a result, unions provide wage gains for their employees without imposing attendant inefficiencies in hiring levels or consumer prices by squeezing employer rents and increasing productivity. Dau-Schmidt observes that because bargaining players may resort to strategic behavior such as strikes or lockouts in order to obtain greater shares of the surplus, federal labor law can play a socially beneficial role by establishing the 'rules of the game' in order to discourage such strategic behavior.

Dau-Schmidt begins by identifying three sources of union wage increases: (1) rents from the cartelization of labor markets; (2) employer product market rents and quasi-rents generated by the capital stock; and (3) increases in productivity. He then discusses how employers might respond to the union's wage demands regardless of the source of surplus. The first hypothesis posits that employers 'move up' their demand curve, that is, employ fewer workers at the higher wage. Yet, this suboptimal outcome is unlikely to ensue as long as employers and workers can bargain over employer rents. For, under certain assumptions about the employees' utility functions and the employer's profit function, there exists a set of Pareto-improving wage–employment points off the demand curve. Turning to the costs of collective bargaining, Dau-Schmidt distinguishes between the transaction costs associated with strikes and the propensity of both sides to resort to collectively irrational strategic behavior – in accord with the predictions of the well-known prisoner's dilemma.

Dau-Schmidt's assessment of American labor law conflicts with the monopoly model that conceives union activity as an adverse force on economic activity, one that achieves inequities between organized workers on the one hand and consumers and laid-off employees on the other. Dau-Schmidt notes that the goal of federal labor law has been to facilitate collective bargaining and 'industrial peace', and he argues that theory and empirical evidence refute the claims that wage increases are obtained solely through cartelization, and that employers do not bargain in response to union demands. If the size of the pie can be increased through bargaining, the parties have an incentive to reach the efficient solution if bargaining costs can be lowered. Consequently, labor law can therefore lower bargaining costs as a way to achieve more efficient outcomes than the cartel model anticipates.

Dau-Schmidt offers his preferred set of assumptions that yield conditions under which unions may actually generate efficient and equitable outcomes, especially when one allows for productivity increases as a source of wage increases. However, mindful of strategic motivations, Dau-Schmidt contends that governments can and should adjust negotiation costs in order to direct parties to the set of efficient bargaining solutions. In his view, the bargaining model also matches the public policy goals of labor law and the empirical activities of employers and unions. Nevertheless, he identifies several suboptimal aspects of labor law that cannot be explained by the promise of the bargaining model. These include the lack of stricter penalties for violating the National Labor Relations Act (which would help align bargaining costs more efficiently), delays in the union certification process, the ability of employers to permanently replace striking workers, and the problem of bad faith bargaining just after organization. Dau-Schmidt also effectively marshals accessible game theory concepts to stress the strategic underpinnings of wage negotiations. One can think of Posner and Dau-Schmidt as offering the polar positions in the law and economics literature on the costs and benefits of unions and American labor law.

Along with his coauthors Christine Jolls and Richard Thaler, Cass Sunstein has been on the forefront of the effort to incorporate concepts of cognitive psychology and behavioral economics into the analysis of law.[4] In a specific application of this broad theme – Sunstein (2001; Chapter 4) – Sunstein analyzes the structure of employment law in the hope of enriching previous law and economics work by being attentive to areas in which actual human behavior seems to depart from the standard neoclassical assumptions.

Sunstein makes two major claims. First, traditional employment law runs astray when it is not based on workers' actual values and behavior.[5] For example, a standard economic analysis might begin with the Coase Theorem, which states that with zero transaction costs the initial allocation of rights does not matter since the parties will negotiate to the same, efficient solution regardless of the initial allocation – what I have referred to as the identity prediction.[6] While Sunstein accepts the theorem's validity with respect to efficiency – thus implicitly accepting Dau-Schmidts's point and rejecting Posner's thesis – he doubts that the solution would be *the same* depending on who gets the right first. His assessment is based on the 'endowment effect', a behavioral finding that people tend to value something more highly when it is initially allocated to them rather than allocated to someone else. The endowment effect creates a spread between a person's willingness to buy a right that they lack and their willingness to sell a right that they were allocated. So contrary to the conventional analysis, for Sunstein the initial allocation matters because it determines the optimal outcome. The real question then becomes: who should initially be assigned the right? By ignoring behavioral findings – such as the endowment effect – the traditional analysis overlooks the importance of alternative approaches to employment law.

The second major claim that Sunstein makes is that waivable workers' rights are currently underutilized but are a promising approach for future employment law reforms. More specifically, Sunstein suggests a two-tiered system, in which the first tier is made of non-waivable statutory minimal safeguards, and the second tier is made of waivable workers' rights. These waivable workers' rights would come in two forms, constrained and unconstrained. The constrained rights would be subject to government regulation and possible price floors, while the unconstrained ones would be subject only to market forces and free contracts between employers and employees. The underlying motivation for the waivable workers' rights is that it is often unclear what a 'market mimicking' employment law rule would look like so waivable workers' rights are the best way to elicit information. They compel employers to be very specific in contracts about the rights they want the employee to waive and thus allow employees to be better informed about the rights that they have.

This information eliciting requirement is important to Sunstein because, contrary to the premise of conventional analysis, workers often don't know their rights, as Pauline Kim's work has underscored.[7] For example, Kim found in Missouri that a large majority of employees (80 percent or more) were quite ignorant of the laws concerning wrongful discharge. Many thought it was unlawful to be fired if the employer merely wanted to hire someone else or if he personally disliked them. However, all are lawful grounds for discharge in Missouri. Similar results were found in California and New York. Kim also notes that such worker ignorance is independent of a number of variables, including geography, age, work experience, and union experience. While there are many causes for this lack of understanding, behavioral economics and cognitive psychology provide insight into at least some of them. As Sunstein outlines, people like to align their beliefs about how things are with how they think things should be to reduce cognitive dissonance, thus making themselves subject to self-serving bias. So their understanding of fair laws is mediated by their biased beliefs in fairness, which in turn makes them believe that they cannot be fired without cause. Ultimately, the lack of information on the side of the workers undermines the traditional explanation for an at-will doctrine, namely that it reflects the shared understanding of the parties.

Sunstein's analysis sweeps across many important areas of employment law including unionization, occupational safety and health, discrimination, vacation and parental leave time, and workers compensation. He repeatedly applies the behavioral insights with the intention of finding criteria to distinguish waivable from non-waivable rights. In his opinion, important criteria for determining whether rights should be non-waivable are: whether third parties are affected, whether workers have inadequate information (even if information eliciting procedures are in place), and whether the rights involve the establishment of norms that are not acceptable to society at large (for example, the decision to waive discrimination rights). Ultimately, Sunstein prefers waivable rights because they provide less 'rigidity, inefficiency and potential harm to workers and consumers' than are created by non-waivable 'one-size-fits-all' rights.

Sunstein's article is important in that it: (1) incorporates new behavioral findings into debates over controversial doctrines and institutions, such as employment at will and unionization; and (2) recommends a two-tiered system where there is a minimum floor of workers rights below which no employer may go and a number of waivable rights above this floor that are subject to negotiation. In the area of the contract at will, he suggests that 'legislatures should experiment with waivable for-cause rules, and also that courts should move in this direction by penalizing employers who lead employees to believe that they have protection against at-will discharge'.

Volume I, Part III. The Impact on Economic Welfare of the Regulation of Labor in the US and the World

Thomas Holmes tries to determine empirically whether state right-to-work laws stimulate business activity – Holmes (1998; Chapter 5). Such laws outlaw the union shop, the hiring structure in which all the firm's employees must belong to the union. Presumably, if unions dampen business activity in the way that Posner's analysis would suggest, then laws that decrease the extent of union penetration should encourage business expansion.

Holmes notes that the cross-section data are not supportive of the 'unions tax business' thesis in that the states traditionally known as manufacturing centers in the United States do not have right-to-work laws. But such cross-section data cannot readily reveal the causal impact of the law. Even a panel data analysis that regresses manufacturing growth on a legal indicator variable may not reveal the causal impact of a right-to-work law if other unrelated characteristics of right-to-work states, for which these models do not account, lead to geographic shifts in manufacturing activity, while the passage of right-to-work laws coincidentally correlates with these features.

Holmes develops a theoretical model that illuminates why policy differences at state borders should matter. Holmes describes the manufacturing entrepreneur's decision as one between remaining in the firm's current location and moving to a more pro-business locale, provided moving costs are not prohibitive. Based on his model, Holmes predicts there will be a discontinuous jump in manufacturing activity at the border but that the effect will dissipate as one moves farther from the border into the pro-business region. Because moving costs are positive, the farther from the border an entrepreneur finds himself, the less state policy matters and the less relocation occurs.

Holmes' empirical analysis assigns to each county a distance variable representing the minimum distance from the population centroid to the border. Holmes then explores the effect of right-to-work laws on two dependent variables: the employment share of the manufacturing sector and the post-war growth rate of manufacturing employment. Straightforward comparisons of means at various distances from the policy border reveal stark differences in both measures. On the antibusiness side, the mean employment share of the manufacturing sector is only 21.0 percent with a post-war growth rate in manufacturing employment of only 62.4 percent; on the pro-business side, the mean employment share is 28.6 percent with a growth rate of 100.7 percent. Moreover, the employment shares follow the patterns predicted by Holmes's model when one moves through the various anti- and pro-business 'layers'.

Holmes's regression analysis estimates a county's manufacturing employment share as a function of the state's business posture, its distance from the border and its position along the border (employing several functional forms for the latter two). Holmes's primary analysis uses data from states bordering right-to-work states, from which he conducts a county-level analysis on those counties whose population centroid is within 100 miles on either side of the border separating the 'pro-business' states from the 'antibusiness' states. In addition, Holmes conducts a state-level analysis looking at pairs of states that lie along the border – that is, he pairs a pro-business state on one side of the border with a corresponding antibusiness state on the other side of the border. In this side-by-side comparison of 17 pairs of such states, Holmes measures their mean manufacturing employment share in 1992 and their manufacturing employment growth rate between 1947 and 1992. He finds once again that there are noticeable differences in both variables when crossing from one side of the border to the other. The right-to-work law is found to increase the manufacturing share – which averages about 20 percent – by about 6.6 percentage points, or roughly by one-third. In addition, Holmes finds that manufacturing employment grew substantially faster between 1947 and 1992 in the pro-business counties relative to the antibusiness counties. Ultimately, Holmes has marshaled impressive evidence that a more pro-business industrial policy – proxied by the presence of a state right-to-work law – increases manufacturing activity.

Shifting focus from the effect on manufacturing of antiunion right-to-work laws in the United States (Holmes, 1998) to pro-worker legislation in states across India provides further support for the view that governmental solicitude for workers can come at a price – Besley and Burgess (2004; Chapter 6). At a time when many Asian economies experienced significant GDP increases tied to growth in the manufacturing sector, the share of manufacturing output in India only rose by 5 percentage points between 1960 and 1995. Besley and Burgess query whether state-level variation in labor policy explains the cross-state differences in manufacturing output and employment as well as the overall slow national manufacturing growth. Their primary conclusion is that pro-worker policies are associated with more depressed conditions and the growth of the informal economy.

Pursuant to the Regulation and Development Act of 1951, the central government in India established the national industrial policy. However, beginning in the 1950s, Indian states became more involved with industrial relations by amending another federal statute, the Industrial Disputes Act of 1947. Besley and Burgess code each of the 113 state amendments as pro-worker (1), pro-employer (-1) or neutral (0), which are then used to characterize the ten treatment states during the period 1958–92. Initial evidence suggests that the pro-worker states started out with higher productivity relative to pro-employer and control states and that this gap shrank considerably by 1990.

Besley and Burgess hypothesize that regulation might affect economic outcomes in two ways. If the price of labor relative to capital rises after regulation, one might expect to observe a substitution effect away from labor. Since regulation only covers registered firms in India, the unregistered sector may grow in size and productivity. If regulation leads to greater union expropriation of investment returns, however, the capital stock may decline in the face of holdup threats.

Their empirical strategy employs a panel data model in which a logged economic outcome measure is regressed on lagged regulation measures, a vector of controls, and state and year fixed effects. Besley and Burgess estimate this model with a variety of dependent variables, including total state, agricultural, nonagricultural and manufacturing output. The negative coefficient on regulation achieves significance only when the latter is used, which lends credence to their hypothesis because the regulations amending the 1947 Industrial Disputes Act were *sector specific* and should only impact the manufacturing sector. If, instead, the effect in another regression on a different sector such as agricultural output turned out to be negative, this would imply that the labor regulations for manufacturing were actually proxying for other (bad) government policies. Moreover, the estimate becomes more negative and statistically significant when only registered firms are included and becomes positive and significant when unregistered firms are analyzed, consistent with the hypothesized substitution effect to the informal sector.

The sensitivity analysis performed by Besley and Burgess generally supports these baseline findings. Adding several control variables for state infrastructure, health, education and political parties in power has little effect on the regulation coefficient. Only the addition of state-specific trends appears to dilute the effect of regulation on manufacturing output. Turning to alternative economic measures, Besley and Burgess report a negative effect of regulation on manufacturing employment, labor usage and capital formation but no discernible effect on wages. However, they consider the possibility of endogeneity through reverse causation from manufacturing performance to adoption of labor regulation measures. Using instruments such as union membership and patterns of land tenure (which is hypothesized to correlate with development and thus political power), Besley and Burgess again confirm the robustness of their original estimates.

Finally, the authors assess the effect of regulation on poverty, distinguishing between urban and rural effects. In line with their earlier estimates, labor regulation has a significant positive effect on urban poverty since most manufacturing firms are located in cities and regulation has a negative effect on manufacturing output. However, this effect disappears when state trends are added to the model. Besley and Burgess's overall conclusion is that pro-worker regulation policies, which are ostensibly designed to improve economic welfare for the worst off, adversely impact the poor.

Further insight into the impact and behavior of unions can be gained by looking at the circumstances in which unions thrive or are undermined. One major event in the US that substantially impacted the labor market was the deregulation of four major American industries that occurred in the 1970s and 1980s. This initiative led to the easing of governmentally imposed barriers to entry and the elimination of rate schedules in the trucking, railroad, airline, and telecommunications industries. A useful examination of the impact on labor markets of this important experiment in deregulation is provided by Peoples (1998; Chapter 7).

One might predict that the removal of barriers to entry to create an essentially competitive environment would have a dampening effect on unionization and reduce the capacity of unions to drive hard bargains for higher wages. Indeed, data from the trucking sector for the period

1978–96 indicate a fall in union membership from 46 to 23 percent, an extraordinary increase in the labor force, and a concomitant 28 percent decrease in earnings. The railroad industry, however, did not exhibit much of a decline in union participation due to its natural barriers to entry. Overall railroad employment did fall considerably, while weekly wages decreased only slightly. Among the airlines, union membership fell from 45 to 36 percent, as total employment trended upward. Telecommunications companies exhibited the largest weakening of union power: membership totals fell from 59 to 29 percent from 1973 to 1996. Although Peoples attributes this decline to the introduction of labor-saving technologies, he also notes that the skill required to implement them led to an upsurge in employment and wages over the observation period. The declines in union power in these four industries that was prompted by deregulation still left the four industries above the national average in terms of percentage union membership and earnings.

Peoples highlights the relationship between regulatory legislation and industrial organization in the four industries. He observes that the trucking industry most closely approaches the competitive paradigm in the absence of regulation because of low skill requirements and entry costs. The Motor Carrier Act of 1935, however, restricted entry and set rates for interstate commercial transport. The Teamsters union gained substantial power during this period only to see that strength weakened by the easing of barriers to entry following passage of the 1980 Motor Carrier Act. Regulation of the railroads, which tend to resemble natural oligopolies, began in the 1920s. This move eventually harmed the industry because the setting of rates above their competitive levels exposed it to competition from other shipping modes, namely trucking. The 1926 Railroad Labor Act spurred heavy yet disjointed unionization in this sector that kept crew numbers above their efficient level as technology made their services redundant. Legislation in the 1970s and 1980s allowed carriers to charge competitive rates and amend work rules in a more resourceful manner. The airline experience with respect to pricing behavior and union membership mirrored that of the railroads since regulation seemed a logical response to high start-up costs and fears of price wars. Finally, the history of deregulation in the telecommunications industry story is dominated by the initial privileged market position and eventual breakup of AT&T. After a period of extensive union growth, the dissolution of AT&T led to highly fractured – and weakened – collective bargaining.

Peoples concludes with some empirical evidence of deregulation's effect on wage premiums. Regressing log earnings on a variety of individual-level covariates and a dummy for employment in a deregulated industry using Current Population Survey (CPS) data, he presents separate graphs of the coefficient on the deregulation variable for each of the four industries. Trucking experienced the most extreme decrease in the wage premium after 1982 (the premium eventually transforms into a loss relative to non-transportation operatives). The railroad industry did not exhibit a noticeable trend in its wage premium, and airline employees experienced a short-lived increase by 1982 but an eventual decline by 1991. The telecommunications sector displays the clearest break in trend following deregulation: after six years of steady wage gains, changes in the collective bargaining environment led to an abrupt reversal of fortune. While deregulation generated many economic gains, it did impose some major costs on certain elements of the unionized workforce.

Volume II, Part I. Mandating Employee Benefits

A. Minimum Wage Laws

One of the most intriguing debates in labor economics was launched by David Card and Alan Krueger, who upended the world of price theory with an empirical paper that purported to show no disemployment effect from an increase in the minimum wage – Card and Krueger (1994; Chapter 1). Card and Krueger's heretical attack was based on their examination of the impact on employment in the low-skill service industry from the passage of a New Jersey bill that increased the state minimum wage (a classical example of a price floor) to $5.05 – 80 cents above the federal minimum wage level – in the early 1990s. They compared employment, wages and prices at fast-food restaurants in New Jersey to restaurants in eastern Pennsylvania, which serve as a natural control group given the economic and demographic similarities between the two areas.

Based on estimates by previous researchers of the elasticity of low-wage employment to the minimum wage, the scheduled 18 percent increase in the New Jersey minimum wage would be expected to cause the number of workers per fast-food restaurant to decline by from 0.4 to 1. Card and Krueger, however, find no indication that the rise in the minimum wage reduced employment. Indeed, nine months after the effective date of the minimum-wage increase in New Jersey, Card and Krueger found that, compared to Pennsylvania restaurants, New Jersey fast-food restaurants had *added* 2.7 full-time workers. The basic finding of an *increase* in employment held across specifications and was robust to a slew of sensitivity checks.

While such a finding contradicts the simple price theoretic prediction of an increased minimum wage under perfect competition, other theories are compatible with an increase in employment. Specifically, under monopsony, wages and employment are both suppressed below the competitive level, so a price increase that moves wages toward the competitive wage will expand employment. A similar result occurs in the general job-search model, where workers are actively searching employers for jobs. If the wage increases, that firm should have a larger steady state labor force because it can attract more new workers while losing fewer workers to other firms. In this case, if the minimum wage increased, one might expect employment in the fast-food industry to rise. But both of these noncompetitive models would predict that output prices should drop in New Jersey relative to Pennsylvania. In fact, prices for fast-food products increased faster in New Jersey than in Pennsylvania, apparently reflecting the employer's ability to pass at least some of the additional cost of the minimum wage onto the consumer. Thus, none of the models seem to lead to predictions that can be fully reconciled with the data.

Not surprisingly, Card and Krueger's findings spurred many critical responses. A mere six months after Card and Krueger's original publication, Neumark and Wascher published a working paper in which they concluded the opposite of Card and Krueger, namely that '…the New Jersey minimum-wage increase led to a relative decline in fast-food employment in New Jersey' if compared to the control group in Eastern Pennsylvania. In the final version of their 'comment' on Card and Krueger's original paper – Neumark and Wascher (2000; Chapter 2) – Neumark and Wascher conclude, based on a newly created data set, 'that the New Jersey minimum-wage increase led to a 3.9 to 4.0 percent decrease in fast-food employment in New Jersey relative to the Pennsylvania control group…'. Neumark and Wascher gathered firm payroll records from fast-food restaurants because they deemed the phone-survey data of Card and Krueger unreliable. In particular, Neumark and Wascher point to the high variability of employment changes in the Card and Krueger survey data which they interpret as a sign of extreme measurement error that marred Card and Krueger's estimates.

In a reply to Neumark and Wascher's reevaluation, Card and Krueger revisited their analysis while replacing their initial survey data with payroll data provided by the Bureau of Labor Statistics – Card and Krueger (2000; Chapter 3). They still find faster employment growth in New Jersey than in the control group – although in most specifications these results are not significant. Furthermore, Card and Krueger raise questions about the data utilized by Neumark and Wascher, which had been supplied to them by the Employment Policies Institute (EPI). Card and Krueger argue that the EPI collected this data from a small and unrepresentative group of restaurants. Overall, after evaluating all the available data, they conclude the following: 'The increase in New Jersey's minimum wage probably had no effect on total employment in New Jersey's fast-food industry, and possibly had a small positive effect.'

While the question of the true effect of the increase of the minimum wage in New Jersey is still debated, the importance of the original Card and Krueger paper is clear: it has sparked the reexamination of beliefs held by generations of economists and policy makers. Their general finding that a modest increase in the minimum wage does not necessarily reduce overall employment, while still in need of ultimate validation, has had an impact on minimum-wage legislation in the US and elsewhere. Of course, Card and Krueger's results can be harmonized with price theory if the increase in minimum wages stimulates the income of the class of individuals who like to patronize fast-food restaurants. In this case, it is the stimulus in the demand for the product that Card and Krueger evaluate that offsets the dampening effect on the quantity demanded of labor from the increase in the minimum wage (an important input in the fast-food industry).

B. Mandated Maternity Benefits

While the most common benefit that governments mandate for workers is probably a minimum wage, many other benefits can also be required by law. Jonathan Gruber focuses on the impact on wages of mandated maternity benefits – Gruber (1994; Chapter 4). Specifically, Gruber explores whether adoption of required maternal leave benefits led to a downward adjustment of the female relative wage, which would reflect a transfer of the benefits' cost to the group that values them most. In addition, Gruber estimates whether and how women respond in terms of their labor supply. Exploiting the natural experiments produced by variation in states' adopting mandated maternity benefits as well as the 1978 passage of the federal Pregnancy Discrimination Act (PDA), he finds that nearly all of the mandate's costs are borne by the target group and, therefore, these mandates have virtually no effect on female labor supply decisions.

Gruber estimates that in the late 1970s, nearly half of all women either did not receive maternity benefits or faced differential coverage relative to other health care needs. Gruber calculates the expected cost of giving birth ($767) as well as the expected cost to a firm of adding maternity benefits ($984) to establish the significant expense of expanding health care coverage. Gruber argues that if this government mandate does not lead to lower wages, then the mandates can be no more efficient than the distortionary taxes used to finance public benefits.

Relying on a differences-in-differences-in-differences (DDD) estimation strategy, Gruber's empirical model compares the labor market outcomes of 'treated' individuals against 'control' subjects within states that passed mandated benefits laws and then draws the same comparison between states that did and did not pass such laws. The treatment group is taken to be married women between the ages of 20 and 40, and the control population covers all persons over 40 and unmarried men aged 20–40. This nonparametric approach is supplemented by a finer measure of the mandate's expected cost using the estimates described above. Gruber used only Illinois, New Jersey and New York as the treatment states before adoption of the PDA (which become the controls in the second experiment) because of limitations in the CPS data.

Gruber's DDD estimate of the impact of mandated benefits (controlling for other demographic and experience characteristics as well as fixed and time-varying effects), suggests that the relative wage of married women of childbearing age fell by a statistically significant 4.3 percent. In addition, Gruber finds that a rise in hours worked, a fall in employment, and small overall changes to labor supply accompanied this wage decrease. When he considers individually estimated mandate costs, the resulting coefficients point to 100 percent cost shifting to wages without any demonstrable effect on net labor input. Finally, estimation of the DDD regression using federal passage of the PDA to identify the effects of mandated benefits confirms the state-level conclusions: wages fall by about 2 percent, hours worked increases, employment decreases and the net effect on labor supply is negligible. Gruber concludes that, despite legislation protecting against differential pay on the basis of sex, maternity benefits drive a wedge between male and female wages.

C. Mandating Accommodations

The third paper to examine the impact of governmental directives to provide workers with particular benefits is Jolls (2000; Chapter 5). Jolls tries to provide a comprehensive economic framework that can be used to systematically analyze the distributive effects of mandates on accommodated workers relative to non-accommodated workers. So, for example, Jolls uses her framework to predict that mandates that accommodate disabled workers will result in unchanged or increased relative wage levels but decreased relative employment. In the case of mandates that accommodate female workers, she predicts a decrease in relative wages along with an ambiguous effect on relative employment levels. Jolls then argues that the empirical evidence roughly supports her predictions.

Jolls's analytical framework builds upon Lawrence Summers' labor supply and demand model, which applies to mandates directed at workers as a whole. Jolls extends Summers' framework so that it models two distinct, yet interconnected, classes of workers – those who receive the accommodation and those who do not.

Critical to Jolls's framework is the fact that most groups to which accommodation mandates are directed are simultaneously protected by antidiscrimination laws designed to prevent discriminatory treatment in the payment of wages and in hiring and firing. Consequently, the effects of mandates will depend on how much employers' behavior is constrained by the wage and employment components of antidiscrimination law. When the wage and employment discrimination components are truly binding, mandates' costs are distributed over the entire labor market. This implies that some of the costs of mandates are carried by non-accommodated workers. Thus, the mandate might still prove distributionally advantageous to accommodated workers even if the mandate is not efficient, as the benefits to the accommodated workers are smaller than the costs imposed on the rest of the workforce.

If, however, *only* the equal wage component of antidiscrimination law is binding, the costs of mandates falls fully upon accommodated workers in terms of a decline in their relative employment. Importantly, this decrease in employment occurs regardless of whether a mandate's value exceeds its costs. On the other hand, when wage laws are *not* binding, the cost of the mandate will be shouldered by accommodated workers primarily through lower relative wages; the employment effects will be ambiguous (depending on the cost–benefit ratio). Jolls notes that the presence of occupational segregation influences the overall effectiveness of antidiscrimination law and therefore can be an important element in using her analytical framework. Specifically, she argues that in the case of female workers, strong occupational segregation prevents the equal wage component of antidiscrimination law from having bite, since equal wages need only be maintained within a narrow labor market. In contrast, disabled workers are generally occupationally integrated, which by itself makes wage antidiscrimination laws more easily enforceable. However, since disabled workers represent a relatively small fraction of the labor force, the small-numbers problem makes employment discrimination difficult to prove, undermining the power of antidiscrimination law for these workers.

Having laid out the theoretical model, Jolls proceeds to test the model's predictions about wages and employment against empirical evidence.[8] First, she selects three accommodation mandates: the Americans with Disabilities Act (ADA), state laws that require health insurance plans to provide for maternity-related expenses, and the Family and Medical Leave Act (FMLA). For each, she identifies the accommodated group targeted by the mandate's provisions, derives her model's predictions for each provision, and compares her predictions to the relevant empirical evidence. For those provisions that apply to female workers, her model predicts lower relative wages with unchanged employment levels, which she concludes is largely consistent with the findings of Gruber's 1994 study. In the case of mandates directed at workers with disabilities, Jolls's framework predicts approximately equal wages along with declines in relative employment, which is supported by both Acemoglu and Angrist's (1999) study of the effects of the ADA and Ruhm's (1998) study of European mandates.

D. Training

Human capital theory is one of the pillars of the neoclassical economic theory of labor. One major insight – first analyzed fully by Gary Becker – is the distinction between general and specific human capital. General human capital enhances productivity independent of the firm while specific human capital enhances productivity only in the firm in which an employee is currently working. Becker theorized that firms would never invest in general skill training because the worker would reap the complete benefit from his general training through higher wages. This claim follows directly from the assumption of competitive labor markets in which workers' wages are determined by their productivity.

While Becker's theory is broadly true – for example, law firms don't pay for smart undergraduates to go to law school – there are situations where firms seem to be paying for certain programs designed to enhance general human capital. In their 'Beyond Becker' paper,

Acemoglu and Pischke focus on the areas in which the predictions of conventional training theory based on Becker's general/specific skill model seem to be erroneous – Acemoglu and Pischke (1999; Chapter 6). In order to explain firm-sponsored general training of employees, they relax Becker's assumption of a competitive labor market. Acemoglu and Pischke argue that non-competitive models seem better suited to explain apprenticeships, temporary-help training and firms sending their employees to Master of Business Administration (MBA) programs.

Acemoglu and Pischke argue that labor market imperfections change what Becker would consider to be general skills into '*de facto* specific skills' and that in several non-competitive scenarios firms are willing to invest in the general training of their employees. The common feature in their examples is that wages are below productivity and the wage structure is compressed, which means that the gap between wages and productivity (firm rent) increases with increased general training.

According to Acemoglu and Pischke, the following factors allow firms to profit by providing general training to their workers:

1. High job search costs, which match specific surpluses that allow the firm to obtain – through bargaining – some of the workers' productivity as profit.
2. Asymmetrical information between the firm and outside firms about the employee and asymmetrical information between the firm and its employees.
3. Labor market institutions, such as minimum wages, unions, or progressive unemployment benefits. Minimum wages, for example, give firms incentive to train their subminimum wage productivity workers without having to pay them more.
4. If general and specific skills are complements – which according to Acemoglu and Pischke is most often the case – then an increase in general skills will also increase the value of specific skills.

While Acemoglu and Pischke concede that they do not yet have the necessary understanding to make sensible policy recommendations, they feel confident enough in their noncompetitive models to assert that Becker's recommendation – easing the liquidity constraints of workers – is not sufficient to ensure optimal training. Contrary to Becker and the standard theory built around his model, Acemoglu and Pischke see a potentially positive impact on investment in human capital from subsidies and regulations. In particular, they note that 'different training systems may make different labor market regulation regimes optimal'. They also conjecture that countries that subsidize the training of low-skilled workers have enabled them to take advantage of new technologies, thereby explaining why wage inequality did not increase in those countries as it did in most others.

E. Employment at Will and Wrongful-Discharge Laws

The endowment effect, or status quo bias, refers to a propensity to value something more highly if one possesses it initially than if someone else possesses it. This effect can explain why individuals are loss averse – they are far more unhappy to lose something they currently have than they are pleased to gain something they previously did not have. When it comes to the labor market, it would seem that these psychological effects are much more potent in

Europe than in the US and may explain the striking contrast between the US and Europe with respect to the issue of job security. Europeans tend to have much greater protections against discharge than American workers, who traditionally could be fired for any reason or no reason under the doctrine of employment at will. But the dramatic protections of European workers come at a price: Europeans who have jobs have great security but those who don't have a much lower chance of securing employment than, say, unemployed Americans would.

In the US, however, the trend to provide protections against certain unfair discharges has been growing for the last quarter-century in the form of a series of exceptions to the doctrine of employment at will. Richard Epstein has been unhappy with this direction of the law, and has attempted to revive support for the traditional US employment relationship – Epstein (1984; Chapter 7). Epstein reasons that the intended benefits ascribed to these exceptions actually impose more disorder in the legal system through increased complexity and litigation. Epstein argues that employment-at-will contracts actually serve the interests of both employers and employees rather than promote exploitation.

Concerning fairness, Epstein argues that both parties to a contract should be free to enter into an at-will agreement if they deem it to be the optimal contract. This libertarian argument rejects the need for intrusive governmental mandates over what types of economic arrangements individuals may devise. Citing the high frequency of at-will contracting, Epstein concludes that agents must be acting rationally in choosing such contracts. Moreover, he expresses faith in the ability of agents – especially employees – to protect themselves from predatory action, and assigns scant weight to reports of fraudulent or coercive behavior in litigation claims.

Epstein is persuaded that utility is enhanced by the employment-at-will doctrine as confirmed by the widespread adoption of at-will contracts when labor markets are free. He discounts cases in which the naïvete of one or both parties actually cuts against claims of rational behavior. Seeking to explain the empirical fact that agents freely enter into at-will contracts, he draws an analogy with simple partnerships and the mechanisms used by either side to prevent abuse of the relationship and rent seeking. The thrust of the comparison is that partners – like employers and employees – retain a bilateral monopoly over their contributions to the business venture. Consequently, the shared threat of withdrawal, which at-will contracts permit, serves as a check against exploitative behavior. With respect to the problem of bilateral monopoly, he maintains that the fluidity of at-will contracts offsets the 'holdup' that ensues when either party attempts to take the employment relationship as a hostage. In addition, employers may suffer reputation costs for capricious behavior, and Epstein argues that employees are free over the life cycle of employment to diversify their labor supply when free entry and exit from jobs exist.

Finally, Epstein claims that issues of redistribution should not (or cannot) inform the debate over at-will contracts. Epstein argues that the increased litigation engendered by the exceptions to employment at will soaks up social and firm-specific resources, overall levels of resources diminish and these losses are spread among both firm owners and their employees. In light of this consideration and in the absence of any clear gains from redistribution, Epstein counsels against relying on the abolition of at-will contracts to achieve such ends.

While Epstein defends the idea that employment at will should be the default rule, Stewart Schwab offers a justification for what he calls the current intermediate position of the courts that favors neither the at-will or for-cause default rule – Schwab (1993; Chapter 8). Schwab terms this background presumption the life cycle default rule. Focusing primarily on the case of the career employee, Schwab argues that this flexible stance is the optimal one for courts to take today as it minimizes the risk of opportunism for both employers and employees by considering how the incentives for opportunistic firing and shirking vary in magnitude over the career relationship.[9]

According to Schwab, at-will employment allows employers to easily fire bad or unproductive workers, but it fails to protect workers from opportunistic firings, such as being discharged before receiving a commission or before a pension vests. On the other hand, a just-cause employment rule, such as those specified in many union contracts, protects the employee from arbitrary firings, but does not do much to prevent shirking. In contrast to these polar, unvarying rules, the life-cycle default rule affords greater flexibility to accommodate the changing risks of opportunistic behavior throughout the career relationship. A just-cause background rule would seem most appropriate in the early- and especially late-career stage when the risk of opportunistic firing is arguably the greatest. On the other hand, an at-will default rule would work well in the mid-career stage when the risk of employees shirking on the job is highest. Schwab finds that courts have done this in practice: intervening to protect employees when the danger of employer opportunism is high, while upholding the presumption of at-will employment when the risk of an employee shirking is high.

Schwab argues that these interventions by the courts are essential for policing the opportunistic incentives created by factors such as efficiency wages, high monitoring and training costs, and vague contracts. For example, a firm might pay a worker a higher efficiency wage to induce higher levels of effort. However, as the worker ages and the value of his wage is perceived to exceed his productivity, the employer has an incentive to let him go. On the other hand, high monitoring and training costs prohibit employers from easily replacing current employees, making it easy for workers to shirk. Nevertheless, supporters of a simple default rule of either at-will or for-cause point out that there are a number of internal mechanisms and social norms that keep such opportunism in check. They argue that an employer's desire for a good reputation both within and outside the firm would keep him from firing a productive worker. Schwab acknowledges that such mechanisms do exist, but notes they are far from perfect. Young or new workers at a firm may have difficulty observing how an employer treats more senior workers. Additionally, while higher-level managers may want to keep productive employees, 'low-level supervisors' could become involved in petty disputes that could lead to the discharge of a productive worker.

Schwab's examination of common law cases supports his hypothesis of a life-cycle default rule. He cites several general examples of courts upholding the duty of good faith to protect employees against opportunistic behavior by an employer. For example, in the case of *Fortune v. National Cash Register Co.*, the courts imposed a duty of good faith on the employer to prevent the firing of a salesman who was about to receive a commission for equipment installed in his territory.[10] Schwab claims that courts have moved in the direction of a life cycle default rule by protecting early- and late-career employees from employer opportunism while generally not interfering in at-will cases involving mid-career employees. Schwab cites the case of *Grouse v. Group Health Plan, Inc.* as an example of the courts protecting a beginning-career employee from employer opportunism. A pharmacist had quit his job on the promise of a job offer from a health clinic, but upon his arrival, the clinic told him they had filled the position. The court determined that the pharmacist had 'reasonably relied on the job offer', and thus upheld his claim. Notably, despite such evidence, Schwab also acknowledges the ambivalence of courts in protecting early-career employees. The courts must consider both the new employee who incurs substantial moving costs and an employer who requires time to determine whether or not the new worker is actually a good hire.

Court interventions in late-career employment terminations seem more common as the employer has greater incentive to discharge an employee. In addition, the Age Discrimination in Employment Act or ADEA helps to protect employees from opportunistic discharge based on the employee's age. Cases such as *Foley v. Community Oil Co.*, where the court upheld the claim of an employee who was fired after 30 years of service, is one example where courts take into account the considerable personal and economic sacrifices an employee makes when he commits to a career relationship with a single firm.

Schwab's hypothesis that courts have indeed upheld the at-will doctrine during the mid-career stage is buttressed by his finding that 'mid-career employees have made the fewest contributions to the doctrinal erosion of at-will employment'.

In the end, Schwab concludes that the life-cycle default rule is the best rule for both parties. As its flexibility minimizes opportunistic risks on both sides of the bargaining table, it allows employers and employees to invest more in the career relationship, making it more productive. He also notes that it is easier to bargain away from the life-cycle rule (that is, to an at-will or a for-cause contract), than to move toward it. However, as Schwab acknowledges, an important limitation to his analysis is that it is focused on the life cycle of *men* who generally have the greatest job security in their mid-career years. In contrast, women often face the greatest risk of opportunism mid-career when they may take time off work to have or raise children.

While Epstein marshals a strong theoretical argument countering the trend against the doctrine of employment at will, it is important to examine the empirical evidence on the impact of the adoption of exceptions to this doctrine. Autor, Donohue and Schwab do just that in Autor, Donohue and Schwab (2006; Chapter 9). This paper notes that the exceptions to the doctrine of employment at will fall into three categories. The public policy exception, which has been adopted in 43 states, prohibits discharges that undermine an explicit public policy of the state. For example, an employee who was discharged because he or she would not commit perjury on behalf of the employer can sue for this violation of the public policy exception. The good faith exception, adopted by 13 states, is designed to protect an employee from being deprived of a major benefit by the bad faith conduct of an employer. For example, an employer who fires a worker just before a pension will vest purely to deprive the worker of this benefit violates the good faith exception. Finally, the implied contract exception, adopted in 43 states, says that language in employee handbooks and manuals can, under certain circumstances, create a contractual right to protect against discharges that are without just cause.

Autor, Donohue and Schwab analyze a panel of CPS data showing monthly employment rates (the ratio of employment to population) for all 50 states for the period 1978–99. Epstein's criticism of the implied contract doctrine does seem to have some force in that state employment rates appear to drop by between 0.8 and 1.7 percent when this exception is adopted. The initial impact is largest for female, younger, and less-educated workers – all of whom tend to change jobs frequently. The somewhat longer-term effect is greater for older and more-educated workers, who are the ones most likely to litigate. Epstein's fears about the other exceptions may be misplaced, as the adoption of the good faith and public policy exceptions, which admittedly have a more narrow scope than the implied contract exception, appear not to have any dampening effect on employment.

Autor, Donohue and Schwab find that despite the apparent backward shift in the demand curve that results from the adoption of the implied contract exception, there is no evidence of a drop in wages. Indeed, if workers value this exception, one would expect an outward shift in the supply curve that would further dampen wages. The lack of any wage effect may suggest that the employment protection that results from the implied contract exception may increase the bargaining power of incumbent workers, thereby offsetting any dampening effect on wages from a backward demand shift.

Volume II, Part II. Employment Discrimination

One important attribute of competitive markets is that they are supposed to ensure the rough equation of prices and value. Because capital markets are highly competitive and have relatively low transaction costs, the efficient capital markets hypothesis posits that stock prices will reflect all publicly available information that bears on the value of the firm. As Donohue (1994) discusses, labor markets have far higher transaction costs than capital markets, and the pressures moving wages to value are far less potent.[11] When one contemplates the history of labor markets in the US – and of course many other countries – discrimination has been an important factor in preventing workers from achieving wages that reflect their inherent productivity. The original goal of employment discrimination law in the United States was to eliminate this disparity by increasing the earnings of certain disadvantaged groups whose employment prospects were hampered by discrimination. Today, some argue that the goal of mimicking the outcome of perfectly competitive labor markets is insufficient and that employment discrimination law should more aggressively pursue broader goals of social fairness that will enhance the economic status of disadvantaged groups beyond what a perfect market would provide.

A. Racial Discrimination

The massive and indisputable employment discrimination against blacks and women became unlawful throughout the country in 1964 with the adoption of Title VII of the Civil Rights Act of 1964. Congress later broadened the coverage of this statute when it enacted the Equal Employment Opportunity Act (EEOA) of 1972, and then further expanded federal antidiscrimination law (primarily by providing greater damage remedies for successful sex discrimination plaintiffs and workers discharged because of their race) in passing the Civil Rights Act of 1991.

The 1964 Act has received the most scholarly attention for it was clearly the most momentous piece of antidiscrimination law ever enacted. Milton Friedman had been a strong opponent of such antidiscrimination law, arguing in part on the basis of Gary Becker's work that such laws would not be needed since competitive markets drive discriminators – and others that fail to maximize profits – out of the market. But when the federal law was passed, it appeared that Friedman was wrong: blacks enjoyed substantial economic gains, particularly in the South. Initially, James Smith and Finis Welch try to carry Friedman's banner by arguing that the Civil Rights Act of 1964 was not responsible for these gains in black economic welfare.[12] Instead, they contended, the gains were all the result of human capital enhancement, not of demand-side stimulation resulting from decreased discrimination: blacks had been adding to their low skill levels and modest levels of education, and as they secured more human capital their wages rose appropriately. Smith and Welch argued that the economic gains of blacks were no different during the period from 1940 to 1960 than they were in the following two decades. They took this as evidence against the view that Title VII generated any benefits for black workers.

The major response to Smith and Welch came in Donohue and Heckman (1991; Chapter 10). Donohue and Heckman argued that Title VII did indeed generate a decade of economic gains for blacks. As Donohue and Heckman note:

> the evidence of sustained economic advance for blacks over the period 1965–1975 is not inconsistent with the fact that the racial wage gap declined by similar amounts in the two decades following 1940 as in the two decades following 1960. The long-term picture from at least 1920–1990 has been one of black relative stagnation with the exception of two periods – that around World War II and that following the passage of the 1964 Civil Rights Act.

It is now widely accepted that in helping to break down the extreme discriminatory patterns of the Jim Crow South, Title VII did considerably increase the demand for black labor, leading to both greater levels of employment and higher wages in the decade after its adoption.[13]

Ken Chay wrote an important paper attempting to determine whether the EEOA, which broadened the coverage of Title VII in 1972, provided additional independent stimulus beyond that provided by the initial Civil Rights Act of 1964.[14] Chay used the fact that the EEOA had a predictably different impact across industries and between the South and the non-South as a way to estimate the economic consequences for blacks of this strengthening in the federal antidiscrimination law. Prior to 1972, Title VII's prohibition against employment discrimination only applied to firms with 25 or more employees. The Equal Employment Opportunity Act (EEOA) of 1972 lowered this threshold to include employers with 15 to 24 employees. Moreover, many states already had fair employment practice (FEP) laws that covered these employers, so if the legal prohibition in these states was as effective as the federal prohibition, then the EEOA would be redundant in those states. Of the nine states that did *not* have FEP laws before 1972, eight were in the South. Based on his careful empirical work, Chay concludes that the EEOA increased the demand for black workers among small employers not previously covered by FEP laws.

But if federal antidiscrimination laws adopted in 1964 and 1972 yielded important economic gains for blacks, the same cannot be said about the final expansion that occurred in 1991. In a series of papers, Paul Oyer and Scott Schaefer demonstrate that there is little support for the view that the strengthening of federal antidiscrimination law in 1991 stimulated black or female employment.[15] Indeed, James Heckman who was a major figure opposing the view that labor markets in the 1960s were fully protecting workers against discrimination has emphasized that the labor market is doing a much better job today at rewarding skills than it did a half-century ago. Heckman no longer believes that market discrimination substantially contributes to the black–white wage gap (as it once clearly did), and therefore he doubts that at present racial discrimination in the labor market is a first-order problem in the United States.[16] Rather, Heckman looks to other factors (that is, those that promote skill formation) to explain the black–white earnings gap – a theme that he builds on in Carneiro, Heckman, and Masterov (2005).[17]

An important paper that informs Heckman's analysis of the current reasons for the black–white wage gap is Neal and Johnson (1996; Chapter 11). If factors that exist prior to workers' entry into the labor market largely explain the black–white wage gap, then the contribution of racial discrimination to this wage gap is presumably small. Neal and Johnson note that many studies have examined the black–white wage gap and found that it could not be explained with standard measures such as age, years of education, marital status, and so on, creating the inference that the contribution of discrimination was sizeable. Neal and Johnson note that years of education may exaggerate the true skill level attained by blacks, given the poorer quality schools that many blacks attend. They argue that scores on the Armed Forces Qualification Test (AFQT) are a better measure of acquired skill (rather than innate ability) that one brings to the labor market.

The authors use a log-linear model that regresses the log of hourly wages on a number of demographic and educational variables. The *unadjusted* wage gap between black and whites is –24.4 percent for black men and –18.5 percent for black women. A significant proportion of the respondents to the National Longitudinal Surveys of Youth (NLSY) took the AFQT in 1980. Using this data for those who took the exam before entering the labor market, Neal and Johnson found that the unexplained wage gap in their regressions containing controls for race, age, and AFQT score is –7.2 percent for black men and +3.5 percent (although insignificant) for black women. In other words, the AFQT test score can explain a very large portion of the black–white wage gap for men, and all of the gap for women. One source of continuing debate in the literature is whether these wage regressions should include controls for years of education as well as AFQT score. Neal and Johnson say it should not since the test better captures ability, and so they exclude the education measure from their regressions. Others have included years of education and find that the unexplained wage gap reemerges when this control is added.

Of course, Neal and Johnson recognize that their analysis would be compromised if the AFQT were racially biased, but they cite a National Academy of Sciences report to negate this charge. Another potential problem with their conclusion that the impact of discrimination is small is the possibility that statistical discrimination could lead to black underinvestment in human capital. Neal and Johnson instead find that the return to higher AFQT scores is significantly higher for black men (although not for black women), so the incentive to invest in developing human capital seems to be high enough to undermine the argument based on statistical discrimination.

B. Sex Discrimination

As the now former President of Harvard University, Larry Summers, learned, few issues are as sensitive as the issue of sex discrimination in employment. After a largely (although not entirely) nuanced and sophisticated address to a National Bureau of Economic Research (NBER) Conference on Diversifying the Science and Engineering Workforce (14 January 2005), Summers closed with the following controversial summary about why one sees an underrepresentation of women in the most elite academic science and engineering positions:

> So my best guess, to provoke you, of what's behind all of this is that the largest phenomenon, by far, is the general clash between people's legitimate family desires and employers' current desire for high

power and high intensity, that in the special case of science and engineering, there are issues of intrinsic aptitude, and particularly of the variability of aptitude, and that those considerations are reinforced by what are in fact lesser factors involving socialization and continuing discrimination. I would like nothing better than to be proved wrong, because I would like nothing better than for these problems to be addressable simply by everybody understanding what they are, and working very hard to address them.

While Summers was criticized for his expressed opinion that sex discrimination was not the primary factor explaining the shortfall of women in science at elite institutions, he certainly would not have disputed that substantial discrimination against women was once widespread. As with the issue of race discrimination, however, there is greater debate about the extent of the problem today. Discrimination is always difficult to prove, but one landmark study of a design that provides credible evidence of sex discrimination in employment 20 to 30 years ago is Goldin and Rouse (2000; Chapter 12).

Goldin and Rouse examine labor market discrimination in the context of auditions and hiring of musicians for the major US orchestras. To test for sex discrimination in the hiring process, they exploit the changes in the audition process introduced by all major US orchestras in the 1970s and 1980s. Of particular interest for their study was the change to 'blind' auditions, which effectively hid the identity and gender of the applicant from the hiring committee for certain rounds of the audition process. Using audition and roster data spanning several decades and employing an individual fixed-effect strategy, they find that the likelihood of female hiring and advancement is increased by the introduction of blind auditions.

More specifically, using audition data from the late 1950s to 1995, Goldin and Rouse found that in blind audition rounds women were as much as 50 percent more likely to advance from preliminary to final rounds. Furthermore, the likelihood of women winning the finals increased by 33 percentage points if the final round was blind. Using official roster data from 1970 to 1996, they find that completely blind auditions – defined as auditions in which all rounds are conducted with a screen hiding the gender of the applicant – increased the likelihood of a women being hired by 25 percent. Based on the roster data, blind auditions explain 30 percent of the increase in female hiring and 25 percent of the increase in overall female representation in the orchestras. There are, however, some caveats with respect to these findings: first, some estimates are associated with relatively large standard errors that render them statistically insignificant; second there is one scenario – auditions with blind semifinals – in which the effect on females is persistently strongly negative.

This latter finding is potentially troubling to the Goldin-Rouse thesis. Some auditions in the study had a semifinal round, often held on the same day as the preliminary round. This gave judges another chance to hear the contestants before making the decision to advance them to the final round. In the study, having a blind audition in the semifinal round was found to have a strong *negative* effect on the probability of a female musician advancing to the final round. The authors offer one possible explanation: the non-blind semifinals may provide an opportunity for some form of affirmative action. If audition committees 'actively seek to increase the presence of women in the final round', and only do so if the woman is above a certain level of quality, then a blind semifinal round could actually have a negative effect on the probability of a female musician advancing to the finals.

To implement the fixed-effect strategy, Goldin and Rouse limit the original audition sample to musicians who competed more than once and entered both blind and non-blind audition rounds. The most extensive specification controls for automatic placement, the number of previous auditions, years since last audition, total number of musicians competing in the round, proportion of females in the round and the type of position. Also included are year and instrument fixed effects and a dummy for auditioning for one of the 'Big Five' orchestras.

Goldin and Rouse address several potential biases that arise from their fixed-effect strategy. First, they include time-varying individual covariates to deal with the fact that female musicians who improve over time faster than male musicians seem to be switching from non-blind to blind auditions. Second, the fixed-effect strategy excludes musicians who are hired (or discouraged) after their first audition. Goldin and Rouse point out that this is not an issue because so few musicians are actually hired in a given year. Nonetheless, they control for the number of auditions and show that the estimates are not significantly different when the sample is limited to musicians who compete in at least three auditions. Third, their results could potentially be biased because orchestras that introduce blind auditions may be intrinsically less discriminatory. To address this, Goldin and Rouse establish that orchestra fixed effects do not change previously established estimates. Fourth, potential bias introduced by measurement error due to sex misclassification is assessed. Goldin and Rouse document that their results remain intact when they rerun their estimation and employ the census probability distribution on the gender of names instead of their subjective labeling.

While the data is highly imperfect, another factor that undermines women in the labor market is the large percentage of working women who experience sexual harassment on the job.[18] The result of such harassment is reduced job satisfaction, higher absenteeism, adverse health outcomes, increased job turnover, and lower productivity. A recent study by Antecol and Cobb-Clark criticizes the existing literature for not being systematic enough and therefore making comparison of findings and general inferences difficult.[19] For example, there does not seem to exist an agreed-upon definition of sexual harassment and most studies rely on small, nonrepresentative samples. Antecol and Cobb-Clark try to rectify the sampling shortcomings by using a large-scale data set spanning 15 years and various federal agencies. They find unwanted sexual behavior is increasingly likely to be considered sexual harassment and attribute this change to structural changes in attitudes about what constitutes sexual harassment. Some other broad conclusions that Antecol and Cobb-Clark mention in their literature review include:

1. Sexual harassment is common across employment sectors and observed in many countries.
2. '[T]he incidence of sexual harassment is related both to demographic characteristics and to the nature of one's employment', in particular, organizational factors seem to be able to facilitate or inhibit sexual harassment.
3. Sexual harassment seems to be widely underreported – less then 5 percent of sexual harassment incidents are reported to anyone in authority. Formal complaints are even less frequent.

Overall, there is much room for additional research on the extent of work-related sexual harassment, and whether law has played a role in dampening such conduct.

But while the critics of Larry Summers argued that all the problems of women in the labor market came from discrimination in all its forms, a growing body of literature is focusing on attributes of the women themselves. For example, the issue of gender differences in aptitude, specifically aptitude in competitive environments, is explored in an article by Gneezy, Niederle and Rustichini (2003; Chapter 13).

The authors seek to understand the relative dearth of women in high-profile jobs as a major factor in the gender gap in earnings by looking at the performance of women and men in competitive environments. Unlike previous studies that tried to explain the gender gap either through occupational self-selection due to differences in abilities and preference or through employer discrimination, Gneezy *et al.* explore the possibility of gender-differentiated performance in competition. As the authors point out, such a difference in competitive performance could 'reduce the chance of success for women when they compete for new jobs, promotions, etc.' In a series of controlled experiments Gneezy *et al.* examine the performance of men and women in a computerized maze game as they vary the incentive schemes and group composition for different treatments. They find that while men receive a significant performance boost in competitive environments such as tournaments, the response of women in competitive environments is more nuanced: they do not significantly change their performance in mixed tournaments, but they do increase their performance in single-sex competitions.

In their experimental setup, the authors use the number of mazes solved as their measure of performance. Their subject pool is composed of male and female students at the Technion, a competitive engineering school in Israel. In their basic design, a group of six students, three men and three women, are each given 15 minutes to solve as many mazes as they can. Varying the payment schemes and the gender composition of the groups, the authors conduct five different treatments, each replicated ten times with different participants. In total, the authors conduct 51 sessions with 324 participants and compare the performance distributions of different treatment groups.

In their benchmark noncompetitive treatment, Gneezy *et al.* administer a piece rate payment scheme on a group of three men and three women. They find that while men perform slightly better than women on average, there is no significant gender difference in performance. The mean performance of men in the piece rate treatment is 11.23 while that of women is 9.73, resulting in a mean gender gap of 1.5. However, when the authors introduce their main competitive treatment of mixed tournaments they find that men increase their performance significantly, while women's performance remains relatively unchanged. The mean performance of men in mixed tournaments increases to 15 while that of women barely changes to 10.8. While this increase for men is highly significant ($p = 0.001$), there is no statistically significant difference in female performance under the piece rate and mixed tournament setups ($p = 0.62$). The increase in the gender gap when moving from the piece rate treatment to the mixed tournament treatment – a jump from 1.5 to 4.2 – is also significant ($p = 0.034$).

Refining their analysis, the authors also examine additional reasons why a woman who solves the same number of mazes as a man in a noncompetitive environment may not receive the same performance boost as the man would in mixed tournaments. Specifically, the authors test for gender differences in risk aversion, the competitiveness of women in a single-sex environment, and for different self-perceptions of competence across genders.[20] In the case of risk aversion, the authors recognize that the tournament structure has two big differences compared to piece rate payment. First, payment is uncertain, and second, the final outcome only depends on *relative* performance. If women are more risk averse than men and effort is costly, then women might not expend as much effort in a mixed tournament as men would. Using a random payment scheme, where a single winner is chosen at random and paid according to his output, Gneezy *et al.* introduce a noncompetitive game with uncertainty. The performance of men and women in the random payment scheme is not significantly different from their performances under the piece rate structure, leading the authors to conclude that the gender gap is *not* due to differences in risk aversion.

Next, the authors introduce single-sex tournaments to test whether women dislike competition in general or if they simply dislike competing against men. They find that women are indeed competitive, at least in the single-sex tournaments, experiencing a significant performance boost when compared to the noncompetitive treatments ($p = 0.0148$ when comparing it to piece rate and 0.0469 when comparing it to random payment). Men also experienced increased performance when competing in single-sex tournaments, but this increase was not significantly different from their increased performance in mixed tournaments.

Finally, the authors look at a few explanations of why women and men of similar ability might perform differently under competition.[21] Specifically, they test the hypothesis that women and men might not feel equally competent when presented with the task of solving mazes, which could affect performance in competition and contribute to the gender gap. Indeed, when the authors allow men and women to choose their level of difficulty (payment per maze solved increases with choice of difficulty), they find that men choose a significantly higher level than women do. The mean choice out of five levels of difficulty is 3.4 for males and 2.6 for females – a highly significant difference ($p = 0.0065$). Because the psychology literature has established clear links between 'task choice and feelings of competence', it would appear that men feel more competent than women when faced with the task of solving mazes.

This paper is significant in that it implies that a gender gap in wages may not only be caused by discrimination or individual differences in ability and preferences, but by differences in performance between men and women resulting from the nature of the competitive environment. In addition, their findings have been offered to provide support for the practice of single-sex schooling, as the women in this study demonstrate significant increases in performance in competitive, single-sex environments. A recent report by Goodman, Cunningham, and Lachapelle (2002) examining reasons for female attrition rates in engineering programs has found that women do not necessarily drop out because of poor performance, but rather many women cite 'negative aspects of their school's climate such as competition, lack of support, and discouraging faculty and peers'. Gneezy *et al.* suggest that changing the nature of the environment has the potential to improve the performance of female workers and students.

C. Statistical Discrimination

A number of theoretical articles have explored whether statistical discrimination can play an important role in explaining the black–white earnings gap. One reason for skepticism about such an effect is that if, say, blacks are on average treated as their productivity would warrant, then as a class there should be no earnings shortfall, apart from the issue of underinvestment that was discussed above with the Neal and Johnson paper. An informative and insightful paper that explores the impact on the hiring and productivity of minority workers of moving from a more informal worker selection process to one based on standardized testing is Autor and Scarborough (2004; Chapter 14). Many have speculated that job testing presents an intrinsic 'equity–efficiency trade-off': testing produces productivity gains but at the cost of adverse hiring effects on minorities. Given that minorities and underprivileged groups on average score lower on standardized tests, the potential of this equity–efficiency trade-off exists.

To explore this issue, Autor and Scarborough use employment data from a large, nationwide retail firm that instituted a standardized testing system in 1999. Before June 1999, the company used informal, paper applications to select candidates for line positions (entry-level positions). Starting in June 1999, the firm, throughout its outlets, began instituting a computer-based application system that included a personality test which the firm uses to select compatible and potentially productive candidates. Autor and Scarborough's sample of 34 257 observations contains information on test scores, worker demographics, termination date and termination reason (if applicable) for hires made between January 1999 and May 2000 in all of the firm's outlets. The question they address is how the introduction of testing and the ensuing improvement in the firms' applicant selection procedure affected minority hiring and productivity.

Autor and Scarborough illustrate that *pre*-testing hiring practices determine the effects of job testing. In other words, whether job testing has a negative impact on minority hiring depends on how hires where made in the absence of standardized testing. They argue that testing leads to reduced minority hiring if the pre-testing procedure is: (1) random and unsystematic or (2) the firm uses a systematic selection criterion *not* based on demographic characteristics. However, if employers statistically discriminate before the test is introduced – that is, if they already use demographic characteristics as a signal for expected productivity of the candidate – then adding testing to the model does not hurt minority hiring but still increases the average productivity of both minority and nonminority workers. The empirical evidence supports this last scenario – uniform increased productivity along with no negative effects on minority hiring.

Using various specifications and attempting to control for endogeneity concerns, Autor and Scarborough test for changes in productivity using two proxies, tenure length and the reason for job termination. The article finds a *uniform* increase in the productivity of all hires across demographic groups. Furthermore, although the data clearly shows that minorities' test scores were significantly lower, the authors find no statistically significant drop in the firm's hiring of minorities. Using a conditional logit model that controls for constant store-specific effects, the authors regress the probability of a hire being black (or, alternatively, being Hispanic) on a dummy variable that equals 1 if the hire was tested (in addition to several other controls). They find that, in all specifications, the coefficient on the job testing dummy is statistically insignificant, leading them to reject the hypothesis that testing reduces the odds of minority hiring.

In addition to the conditional logit model, the article further supports its conclusions by looking at the relationship between a store's hiring and the store's neighborhood demographics. The authors find that, for each store, there exists a close link between minority hiring patterns and minority presence in the surrounding neighborhood. Using a pooled cross section (across tested versus non-tested applicants) with several different specifications, they conclude that the neighborhood–store relationship was not significantly changed by the introduction of testing. Importantly, these empirical results imply that before testing was introduced, employees must have already statistically discriminated in their informal screening based on visible demographic characteristics. Nevertheless, since testing measurably increased overall productivity, the authors conclude that testing raised productivity by 'improving selection *within* observable race groups'.

As the authors recognize, 'standard human capital variables such as age, education and earnings' are not included in their analysis. Nevertheless, they point out that applicants for line positions – the focus of their study – tend to be young, have little schooling, and are usually paid a minimum wage, such that the exclusion of these variables would not significantly alter their results. Even if one accepts this explanation, an important question remains: can the article's conclusions be extrapolated to higher-end labor markets where education, age and wages significantly vary? In any event, finding the presence of statistical discrimination in a major retail employer provides evidence that employers do in fact take race into account in making their hiring decisions. While Autor and Scarborough suggest that this may have been an efficient hiring practice, such conscious race-based decision making clearly violates federal antidiscrimination law.

Notes

1. Freeman, Richard (2005), 'Labour Market Institutions without Blinders: The Debate over Flexibility and Labour Market Performance', *International Economic Journal*, **19** (2), 129–45.
2. Quoted by Freeman, at p. 133.
3. Alesina, Alberto (2006), 'Europe', *NBER Reporter*, Summer, p. 8.
4. Jolls, Christine, Cass R. Sunstein and Richard Thaler (1998), 'A Behavioral Approach to Law and Economics', *Stanford Law Review*, **50** (5), 1471–550.
5. Some important points of divergence between the conventional view of workers' values and behavior and the newer behavioral view are that workers are particularly loss averse, they greatly discount the future, and they care more about their relative economic position than their absolute economic position.
6. Donohue, John (1989), 'Diverting the Coasean River: Incentive Schemes to Reduce Unemployment Spells', *Yale Law Journal*, **99**, 549–609.
7. Kim, Pauline (1997), 'Bargaining With Imperfect Information: A Study of Worker Perceptions of Legal Protection in an At-Will World', *Cornell Law Review*, **83** (1), 105–60.
8. Jolls notes that the empirical analysis is complicated in that the most readily available data is aggregated across the accommodated groups as a whole, as opposed to accommodated groups *within* individual labor markets, which is what her theoretical framework assesses. This forces Jolls to treat a group as large as female workers as a homogenous entity. For example, her analysis is based on the assumption that female workers are in segregated markets. Although a majority are, a not insignificant percentage of females work in male-dominated and mixed labor markets. For these women, the effects of an accommodation mandate might be more evident in employment levels. Furthermore, the mandates she studies are often overlapping, which further complicates the empirical effort to disentangle their individual effects.
9. Schwab notes that career employment has been a relatively recent phenomenon, becoming much more common after World War II and the introduction of pensions. As such, he does not dispute Epstein's claim that at-will employment was the optimum for much of the previous century when it was not common for workers to stay with a single employer for their entire working career. However, he argues that as the employment relationship has moved toward career employment, the common law has changed along with it, approaching the 'life-cycle doctrine in employment law'.

10. Epstein has called this decision 'wrong in principle', and argues that this was not a case of employer opportunism as the money from the commission was instead used to pay an installations employee who installed the equipment. Schwab counters by saying that the Fortune decision may be 'wrong in application', but it is correct in principle, because it provides a precedent that 'courts should scrutinize opportunistic firings in which the employee has largely performed his side of the bargain but has yet to reap his reward'.

11. Donohue, John (1994), 'Employment Discrimination Law in Perspective: Three Concepts of Equality', *Michigan Law Review*, **92**, 2583–612.

12. Smith, James P. and Finis Welch (1989), 'Black Economic Progress After Myrdal', *Journal of Economic Literature*, **27** (2), 519–64.

13. See also Freeman, R.B., R.A. Gordon, D. Bell and R.E. Hall (1973), 'Changes in the Labor Market for Black Americans, 1948–72', *Brookings Papers on Economic Activity*, **1**, 67–131; Conroy, M. (1994), *Faded Dreams: The Politics and Economics of Race in America*, Cambridge: Cambridge University Press; and Orfield, G. and C. Ashkinaze (1991), *The Closing Door: Conservative Policy and Black Opportunity*, Chicago: University of Chicago Press.

14. Chay, Kenneth (1998), 'The Impact of Federal Civil Rights Policy on Black Economic Progress: Evidence from the Equal Employment Opportunity Act of 1972', *Industrial and Labor Relations Review*, **51** (4), 608–32.

15. See Oyer, P. and S. Schaefer (2000), 'Layoffs and Litigation', *Rand Journal of Economics*, **31** (2), 345–58; Oyer, P. and S. Schaefer (2002a), 'Litigation Costs and Returns to Experience', *American Economic Review*, **92** (3), 683–705; and Oyer, P. and S. Schaefer (2002b) 'Sorting, Quotas, and the Civil Rights Act of 1991: Who Hires When It's Hard to Fire?', *Journal of Law and Economics*, **45** (1), 41–68.

16. Heckman, James J. (1998), 'Detecting Discrimination', *Journal of Economic Perspectives*, **12** (2), 101–16.

17. Carneiro, Pedro, James Heckman and Dimitriy Masterov (2005), 'Labor Market Discrimination and Racial Differences in Premarket Factors', IZA Discussion Paper no. 1453, ftp://ftp.iza.org/dps/dp1453.pdf.

18. Fitzgerald, Louise F. and Alayne J. Ormerod (1993), 'Breaking Silence: The Sexual Harassment of Women in Academia and the Workplace', in Florence L. Denmark and Michele A. Paludi (eds), *Psychology of Women: A Handbook of Issues and Theories*, Westport, Conn.: Greenwood Press, pp. 553–82; Schneider, Kimberly T., Suzanne Swan and Louise F. Fitzgerald (1997), 'Job-Related and Psychological Effects of Sexual Harassment in the Workplace: Empirical Evidence from Two Organizations', *Journal of Applied Psychology*, **82** (3), August, 401–515.

19. Antecol, Heather and Deborah Cobb-Clark (2004), 'The Changing Nature of Employment-Related Sexual Harassment: Evidence from the US Federal Government (1978–1994)', *Industrial & Labor Relations Review*, **57** (3), April, 443–61.

20. Gneezy *et al.* also create hypothetical distributions of women's expected performance in mixed tournaments based on their performance in the noncompetitive treatment by comparing them to similarly ranked men in the noncompetitive treatment. For example, if a man solved 15 mazes in the noncompetitive treatment and ranked 12th–17th out of 60 (both piece rate and random pay treatments are combined here), then in the mixed tournament with 30 observations he would be expected to place between 6th–9th, and solve a corresponding 17–19 mazes. If women received a similar performance boost, a woman who solved 15 mazes in the noncompetitive treatment should be able to solve at least 17 mazes in the competitive treatment. But, in fact, the actual performance of women was much lower than projected, a difference that is significant at $p = 0.04$.

21. The authors also note the additional explanation that men and women actually face different sets of competitors which could be drawn from slightly different ability distributions and affect participants' choice of effort: men face three women and two men, while women face three men and two women. As noted previously, men consistently perform slightly better than women on average in both the noncompetitive treatments and single-sex tournaments and significantly outperform women in the mixed tournament. While they are not able to test this effect directly, the authors calculate that a man in a mixed group of three men and three women has a 0.07 to 0.1 greater probability of winning than a woman in the same group.

References

Acemoglu, D. and Angrist, J.D. (2001), 'Consequences of Employment Protection? The Case of the Americans with Disabilities Act', *Journal of Political Economy*, **109** (5), 915–57.

Freeman, R. and Medoff, J. (1984), *What Do Unions Do?*, New York: Basic Books.

Goodman, I., Cunningham, C.M., Lachapelle, C., Thompson, M., Bittinger, K., Brennan, R. and Delci, M. (2002), 'Final Report of The Women's Experiences in College Engineering (WECE) Project', Goodman Research Group Inc., Cambridge, MA.

Rhum, C.J. (1998), 'The Economic Consequences of Parental Leave Mandates: Lessons from Europe', *Quarterly Journal of Economics*, **113** (1), 25–317.

Part I
Overview: A Cross-Country Comparison of the Regulation of Labor

[1]

THE REGULATION OF LABOR*

JUAN C. BOTERO
SIMEON DJANKOV
RAFAEL LA PORTA
FLORENCIO LOPEZ-DE-SILANES
ANDREI SHLEIFER

We investigate the regulation of labor markets through employment, collective relations, and social security laws in 85 countries. We find that the political power of the left is associated with more stringent labor regulations and more generous social security systems, and that socialist, French, and Scandinavian legal origin countries have sharply higher levels of labor regulation than do common law countries. However, the effects of legal origins are larger, and explain more of the variation in regulations, than those of politics. Heavier regulation of labor is associated with lower labor force participation and higher unemployment, especially of the young. These results are most naturally consistent with legal theories, according to which countries have pervasive regulatory styles inherited from the transplantation of legal systems.

I. INTRODUCTION

Every country in the world has established a complex system of laws and institutions intended to protect the interests of workers and to help assure a minimum standard of living for its population. In most countries, in addition to some basic civil rights protections, this system encompasses three bodies of law: employment law, collective relations law, and social security law. Employment laws govern the individual employment contract. Collective or industrial relations laws regulate the bargaining, adoption, and enforcement of collective agreements, the organization of trade unions, and the industrial action by workers and employers. Social security laws govern the social response to needs and conditions that

* This research was supported by the World Bank, the Gildor Foundation, the National Science Foundation, and the International Institute for Corporate Governance at Yale University. We appreciate helpful comments from Daron Acemoglu, Gary Becker, Olivier Blanchard, Simon Deakin, Richard Freeman, Edward Glaeser, Peter Gourevitch, Simon Johnson, Lawrence Katz, Casey Mulligan, Mark Roe, Christopher Woodruff, and anonymous referees. We also want to thank Patricio Amador, Jose Caballero, Benjamin Chen, Ronald Chen, Eugenio De Bellard, Gabriela Enrigue, Manuel Garcia-Huitron, Eidelman Gonzalez, Magdalena Lopez-Morton, Camila Madrinan, Christian Pfirrmann, Alejandro Ponce-Rodriguez, Kumar Rakhi, Damian Rozo, David Stewart, Franco Tapia, and Deniz Yavuz for excellent research assistance. The complete data set and descriptions of all variables at the country level can be found at http://iicg.som.yale.edu//.

The Quarterly Journal of Economics, November 2004

have a significant impact on the quality of life, such as old age, disability, death, sickness, and unemployment.

In this paper we examine these laws in 85 countries through the lens of three major theories of institutional choice: the efficiency theory, the political power theory, and the legal theory. The *efficiency* theory holds that institutions adjust to serve the needs of a society most efficiently. Each society chooses a system of social control of business that optimally combines market forces, dispute resolution in court, government regulation, and corrective taxes and subsidies [Djankov et al. 2003a]. Under the *political power* theory, institutions are shaped by those in power to benefit themselves at the expense of those out of power. Both voting and interest group politics allow the winners to benefit at the expense of the losers, with checks and balances on the government limiting the extent of redistribution. Under the *legal* theory, a country's approach to regulation is shaped by its legal tradition. Most countries in the world have inherited their basic legal structures from their colonizers, such as the English, the French, the Germans, the Portuguese, or the Spanish, or their conquerors, such as Napoleon or the Soviets. The laws of the different colonizers and occupiers belong to different legal traditions, which significantly influenced the legal systems of conquered countries [Zweigert and Kotz 1998; La Porta et al. 1997, 1998]. In broad terms, common and civil law traditions utilize different strategies for dealing with market failure: the former relying on contract and private litigation, the latter on direct supervision of markets by the government. Under this theory, the historical origin of a country's laws shapes its regulation of labor and other markets.[1]

Our focus on labor laws might be particularly helpful in distinguishing political power and legal theories. Roe [2000] and Pagano and Volpin [2001] argue that the political power of labor has been central to legal and regulatory design of the twentieth century. Using data on OECD countries, these authors challenge the observation of La Porta et al. [1997, 1998] that the differences in financial development among common and civil law countries are best understood in terms of legal theories. Roe [2000] maintains that civil law is simply a proxy for social democracy. An

---

1. In footnotes, we also consider the cultural theory, under which regulations are shaped by a country's cultural history, such as the dominance of particular religious groups. The data do not support this theory, so we keep its discussion to a minimum.

analysis of labor laws gives these political theories their best shot, for two reasons. First, we expect leftist governments to regulate labor markets to benefit their supporters. Second, because labor laws are relatively recent, we would not expect a profound influence of legal tradition on their structure.

To assess these theories, we collect data on employment, collective relations, and social security laws as of 1997 for the Djankov et al. [2002] sample of 85 countries, and code them to measure worker protection. We combine these data with existing (and some newly collected) information on economic development, leftist orientation of governments, union power, political constraints on government action, and legal origins to examine the determinants of the regulation of labor. We also examine data on the unofficial economy, labor force participation, unemployment, and relative wages to consider who benefits and who loses from the regulation of labor.

The available research on labor regulations is more extensive than that on most other laws. The Organization of Economic Cooperation and Development has sponsored the creation of a database of labor regulations in member countries [Nicoletti, Scarpetta, and Boylaud 1999; Nicoletti and Pryor 2001]. The World Bank has assembled a database of International Labor Office certifications for 119 countries, which provide a partial view of the labor laws as well [Forteza and Rama 2000]. Heckman and Pages-Serra [2000] examine an extensive data set of job security regulation for Latin American and Caribbean countries. Mulligan and Sala-i-Martin [2004] assemble and analyze data on social security systems. What distinguishes our data from previous efforts is a combination of a significant coverage of countries and a comprehensive approach to labor market regulations.[2]

In the next section we briefly describe the theories of the determinants of labor regulations. In Section III we describe the data. In Section IV we illustrate the data by comparing New Zealand and Portugal. In Section V we examine the determinants of labor market regulations. In Section VI we compare patterns of labor regulation to those of other activities. In Section VII we look at the consequences of regulation. Section VIII concludes.

2. There is also an extensive literature on the consequences of regulation of labor, including Lazear [1990], Besley and Burgess [2003], Fonseca, Lopez-Garcia, and Pissarides [2000], Heckman and Pages-Serra [2000], and Ichniowski, Freeman, and Lauer [1989].

II. HYPOTHESES

II.A. Background

Why do governments intervene in the labor market? The theory underlying most interventions is that free labor markets are imperfect, that as a consequence there are rents in the employment relationship, and that employers abuse workers to extract these rents, leading to both unfairness and inefficiency. For example, employers discriminate against disadvantaged groups, underpay workers who are immobile or invest in firm-specific capital, fire workers who then need to be supported by the state, force employees to work more than they wish under the threat of dismissal, fail to insure workers against the risk of death, illness or disability, and so on. In response to the perceived unfairness and inefficiency of the free market employment relationship, nearly every state intervenes in this relationship to protect the workers.

Regulation of labor markets aiming to protect workers from employers takes four forms. First, governments forbid discrimination in the labor market and endow the workers with some "basic rights" in the on-going employment relationships, such as maternity leaves or the minimum wage. Second, governments regulate employment relationships by, for example, restricting the range of feasible contracts and raising the costs of both laying off workers and increasing hours of work. Third, in response to the power of employers against workers, governments empower labor unions to represent workers collectively, and protect particular union strategies in negotiations with employers. Finally, governments themselves provide social insurance against unemployment, old age, disability, sickness and health, or death. The basic question addressed in this paper is what determines these choices of government intervention in the labor market. We consider three broad theories along these lines.

II.B. Efficiency

Demsetz [1967] and North [1981] propose that the choice of institutions is dictated primarily by efficiency considerations. In the present context, this approach broadly implies that countries choose a combination of labor market interventions to maximize social welfare. The standard interpretation of this objective is curing market failures. More recent research has focused on identifying public interventions that are themselves cheapest and least vulnerable to subversion [Glaeser and Shleifer 2002, 2003; Glaeser, Scheinkman, and Shleifer 2003; Djankov et al. 2003b]. For example, countries would choose heavier intervention when employer abuse of employees in the market is greater (to cure market failures), and lighter intervention when distortions associated with government interference are more severe (to cut social enforcement costs).

By itself, the efficiency theory is too broad to have strong implications for the extent and consequences of regulation, and as such is difficult to reject. We examine two of its plausible, but not unambiguous, implications. First, if government intervention in the labor market in the form of worker protection is efficient, then it should not have *large* adverse consequences, such as unemployment, withdrawal of people from the labor force, and the growth of the unofficial economy. Of course, it is possible that the benefits of regulation to protected workers are higher than these distortions, making the overall welfare assessment indeterminate. Second, if efficiency is the correct model, political factors such as the power of the left or constraints on government would not shape regulatory choices. Again, it is possible that some divided societies efficiently require more regulations to preserve social peace, and efficiently pick leftist governments to enact them. We show, however, that, if anything, divided societies regulate less (see footnote 14). The relationship between efficiency and legal theories is even more complex, and we discuss it below.

II.C. Political Power

According to political power theories, institutions are designed to transfer resources from those out of political power to those in power, as well as to entrench those in political power at the helm [Marx 1872; Olson 1993; Finer 1997]. In the context of labor markets, these theories imply that labor regulations are more protective of workers when leftist governments are in power. Such protection can restore efficiency if in a free market workers are "abused," or in lower efficiency if government intervention leads to expropriation of capital by labor.

Political power theories come in two varieties. The first holds that the principal mode of political decision making is elections, and that the parties that win them shape laws. The second variety, which applies to both democracies and dictatorships, holds that laws are shaped by the influence of interest groups [Olson 1965; Stigler 1971; Posner 1974; Becker 1983].

Political power theories are by far the leading explanation of the choice of labor regulations. In the electoral version, they hold that regulations protecting workers (or at least employed workers) are introduced by socialist, social-democratic, and more generally leftist governments to benefit their political constituencies [Esping-Andersen 1990, 1999; Hicks 1999]. In the interest group version, these theories hold that labor regulations respond to the pressure from trade unions, and should therefore be more extensive when the unions are more powerful, regardless of which government is in charge.

Political theories also hold that the ability of those in power to use regulations to benefit themselves is limited by checks and balances on the government [Buchanan and Tullock 1962]. Dictatorships are less constrained than democratically elected governments, and therefore will have more redistributive laws and institutions. Constitutions, legislative constraints, and other forms of checks and balances are all conducive to fewer regulations. This theory found some empirical support in our previous work on the regulation of entry [Djankov et al. 2002].

II.D. Legal Theory

Legal theory has received considerable attention in the discussions of institutional evolution. This theory emphasizes the emergence of two very distinct legal traditions in Western Europe as far back as the twelfth century, namely common law and civil law, and the transplantation of these traditions both within Europe and to the new world through conquest and colonization. Importantly, because most countries in the world received their basic legal structures in this involuntary way, these structures are exogenous to their economies.

Common law emerged in England and is characterized by the importance of decision-making by juries, independent judges, and the emphasis on judicial discretion as opposed to codes. From England, common law was transplanted to its colonies, including Ireland, the United States, Canada, Australia, New Zealand, India, Pakistan, and other countries in South and East Asia, East Africa, and the Caribbean.

Civil law evolved from Roman law in Western Europe through the middle ages, and was incorporated into civil codes in France and Germany in the nineteenth century. Civil law is characterized by less independent judiciaries, the relative unimportance of juries, and a greater role of both substantive and

THE REGULATION OF LABOR   1345

procedural codes as opposed to judicial discretion. Through Napoleonic conquest French civil law was transplanted throughout Western Europe, including Spain, Portugal, Italy, Belgium, and Holland, and subsequently to the colonies in North and West Africa, all of Latin America, and parts of Asia.

In addition to common law and French civil law, three legal traditions play some role in parts of the world. The German code became accepted in Germanic Western Europe, but also was transplanted to Japan and from there to Korea, and Taiwan. Socialist law was adopted in countries that came under the influence of U.S.S.R. Finally, an indigenous Nordic or Scandinavian legal tradition developed in Sweden, Norway, Denmark, and Finland.

The legal theory holds that countries in different legal traditions utilize different institutional technologies for social control of business [Djankov et al. 2003b]. Common law countries tend to rely more on markets and contracts, and civil law (and socialist) countries on regulation (and state ownership).[3] As argued by Glaeser and Shleifer [2002], there were efficiency reasons for the choice of different legal systems in mother countries. However, since most countries in the world received their legal structures involuntarily, their approach to social control of business may be dictated by the history of transplantation rather than indigenous choice.

Legal theory may be consistent with efficiency when one recognizes enforcement costs. Suppose that a country inherits its broad legal tradition from its conquerors or colonizers. When it does so, its basic laws, the institutions for enforcing the laws, and human capital of the law enforcers, are all shaped by that legal tradition. Suppose that now a country decides to regulate a previously unregulated activity, such as work. Even if it does not wish to borrow the regulations themselves from anywhere in the world, the marginal cost of adopting an approach similar to that of the mother country is lower than starting from scratch, since both people and rules are shared across regulatory activities [Mulligan and Shleifer 2003, 2005]. It might then be efficient to

---

3. Legal theories have been tested in other areas. Compared with civil law and particularly French civil law countries, common law countries have better legal protection of shareholders and creditors [La Porta et al. 1997, 1998], lighter regulation of entry [Djankov et al. 2002], less formalized legal procedures for resolving disputes [Djankov et al. 2003b], and securities laws more focused on private contracting than regulation [La Porta, Lopez-de-Silanes, and Shleifer 2003].

adopt the same regulatory approach to the new area of regulation as is used elsewhere. In this way, path dependence in the legal and regulatory styles emerges as an efficient adaptation to the previously transplanted legal infrastructure.

The legal theory predicts that patterns of regulation of labor markets should follow the general styles of social control utilized by each legal system more generally. It implies that civil and socialist law countries would regulate labor markets more extensively than do common law countries, which preserve the freedom of contract to a greater extent [Deakin 2001]. The legal theory also predicts that common law countries should have a less generous social security system, because they are more likely to rely on markets to provide insurance. Finally, the legal theory predicts that patterns of regulation of different activities are correlated across countries.

Legal theories have been challenged by advocates of political power theories, such as Roe [2000] and Pagano and Volpin [2001], who argue that at least in Western Europe, the civil law tradition has often coincided with the political pressure to regulate, usually coming from the left. By combining extensive data on political orientation and legal origins for a sample of 85 countries, we attempt to distinguish the pure political power from the pure legal theory.

III. MEASURES OF LABOR REGULATION

We constructed a new data set that captures different aspects of the regulation of labor markets in 85 countries. Our measures of labor regulation deal with three broad areas: (i) employment laws, (ii) collective relations laws, and (iii) social security laws. In addition, we assembled some data on civil rights laws in different countries. We describe these data and summarize the results in footnotes, but do not treat this area of law as systematically as the others because there is extensive disagreement among the legal scholars as to what constitutes civil rights. For each of the three areas of law, we examine a range of formal legal statutes governing labor markets. We then construct subindices summarizing different dimensions of such protection, and finally aggregate these subindices into indices. We construct all measures so that higher values correspond to more extensive legal protection of workers.

As in our previous work, we measure formal legal rules.

There are two concerns with this approach. First, it has been argued that the quality of enforcement of rules varies tremendously across countries, and therefore formal rules themselves provide little information for what happens "on the ground" or outcomes. We cannot measure enforcement directly. However, here as elsewhere, we can roughly control for enforcement quality. In addition, despite the broad-brush criticism that formal rules do not matter, we show below that here, as elsewhere, formal rules matter a lot (see La Porta et al. [1997, 1998, 2003, 2004] and Djankov et al. [2002, 2003b]).

Second, it has been argued that the focus on formal rules is misleading because, *formally* distinct legal systems can and do achieve the same *functional* outcome, only through different means. In the extreme form, the argument holds that in the French civil law tradition, the practice is just to "write it down," leading to greater measured formalism and interventionism. In the present context, this argument would hold that the greater protection of workers in civil law countries that we might identify is fictitious—the common law countries regulate just as much through court decisions which are never "written down" in statutes.[4] For example, Autor [2003] and Krueger [1991] describe how common law courts in the United States have systematically deviated from the employment at will doctrine even absent a statutory basis for such deviations.

To us, this critique is not convincing. First, virtually all of labor law is statutory, even in common law countries, and deviations from statutes are an exception not the rule. Second, and more importantly, we construct several of our indices, such as the cost of raising working hours and the cost of firing workers, to reflect actual economic costs and not just statutory language. For these variables, the distinction between what is written down and what it actually costs to do something is minimized. At least with some key variables, then, we are measuring the economic costs of worker protection—*functional* differences—and not pure formalism.

To codify our measures of worker protection, we used a range of sources. Table I presents brief definitions and sources of the

---

4. Bertola, Boeri, and Cazes [2000] examine the enforcement of employment protection by courts in a few rich economies, and find that courts in the United States and Canada (common law countries) are less likely to rule for workers than courts in Spain and France (French civil law countries). This bit of data suggests that court enforcement, if anything, widens the differences between the French civil law and the common law that we document below.

TABLE I

THE VARIABLES

This table presents brief definitions of the variables used in the paper. For a full description of all variables and the data refer to the on-line appendix posted at ⟨http://iicg.som.yale.edu/⟩. Unless otherwise specified, the sources for the variables are the laws of each country. We also relied on secondary sources to confirm our data, including the *International Encyclopedia for Labor Law and Industrial Relations* [Blanpain 1977], the *International Handbook on Contracts of Employment* [Cox and Jeffers 1988], the ILO's *Conditions of Work Digest* [1994, 1995], and the U. S. Social Security Administration's *Social Security Programs Throughout the World* [1999]. Unless otherwise specified, higher values indicate higher worker protection. All dummy variables are equal to one or zero. All normalized variables lie between 0 and 1, where 0 (1) is the minimum (maximum) actual value in our sample.

Variable	Description
	Employment laws
Alternative employment contracts	Measures the existence and cost of alternatives to the standard employment contract, computed as the average of (1) a dummy variable equal to one if part-time workers enjoy the mandatory benefits of full-time workers, (2) a dummy variable equal to one if terminating part-time workers is at least as costly as terminating full-time workers, (3) a dummy variable equal to one if fixed-term contracts are only allowed for fixed-term tasks, and (4) the normalized maximum duration of fixed-term contracts.
Cost of increasing hours worked	Measures the cost of increasing the number of hours worked. We start by calculating the maximum number of "normal" hours of work per year in each country (excluding overtime, vacations, holidays, etc.). Normal hours range from 1,758 in Denmark to 2,418 in Kenya. Then we assume that firms need to increase the hours worked by their employees from 1,758 to 2,418 hours during one year. A firm first increases the number of hours worked until it reaches the country's maximum normal hours of work, and then uses overtime. If existing employees are not allowed to increase the hours worked to 2,418 hours in a year, perhaps because overtime is capped, we assume that the firm doubles its workforce and each worker is paid 1,758 hours, doubling the wage bill of the firm. The cost of increasing hours worked is computed as the ratio of the final wage bill to the initial one.
Cost of firing workers	Measures the cost of firing 20 percent of the firm's workers (10 percent are fired for redundancy and 10 percent without cause). The cost of firing a worker is calculated as the sum of the notice period, severance pay, and any mandatory penalties established by law or mandatory collective agreements for a worker with three years of tenure with the firm. If dismissal is illegal, we set the cost of firing equal to the annual wage. The new wage bill incorporates the normal wage of the remaining workers and the cost of firing workers. The cost of firing workers is computed as the ratio of the new wage bill to the old one.
Dismissal procedures	Measures worker protection granted by law or mandatory collective agreements against dismissal. It is the average of the following seven dummy variables which equal one: (1) if the employer must notify a third party before dismissing more than one worker, (2) if the employer needs the approval of a third party prior to dismissing more than one worker, (3) if the employer must notify a third party before dismissing one redundant worker, (4) if the employer needs the approval of a third party to dismiss one redundant worker, (5) if the employer must provide relocation or retraining alternatives for redundant employees prior to dismissal, (6) if there are priority rules applying to dismissal or layoffs, and (7) if there are priority rules applying to reemployment.
Employment laws index	Measures the protection of labor and employment laws as the average of (1) Alternative employment contracts, (2) Cost of increasing hours worked, (3) Cost of firing workers, and (4) Dismissal procedures.

Collective relations laws

Labor union power	Measures the statutory protection and power of unions as the average of the following seven dummy variables which equal one: (1) if employees have the right to unionize, (2) if employees have the right to collective bargaining, (3) if employees have the legal duty to bargain with unions, (4) if collective contracts are extended to third parties by law, (5) if the law allows closed shops, (6) if workers, or unions, or both have a right to appoint members to the Boards of Directors, and (7) if workers' councils are mandated by law.
Collective disputes	Measures the protection of workers during collective disputes as the average of the following eight dummy variables which equal one: (1) if employer lockouts are illegal, (2) if workers have the right to industrial action, (3) if wildcat, political, and sympathy/solidarity/ secondary strikes are legal, (4) if there is no mandatory waiting period or notification requirement before strikes can occur, (5) if striking is legal even if there is a collective agreement in force, (6) if laws do not mandate conciliation procedures before a strike, (7) if third-party arbitration during a labor dispute is mandated by law, and (8) if it is illegal to fire or replace striking workers.
Collective relations laws index	Measures the protection of collective relations laws as the average of (1) Labor union power and (2) Collective disputes.

Social security laws

Old-age, disability, and death benefits	Measures the level of old-age, disability, and death benefits as the average of the following four normalized variables: (1) the difference between retirement age and life expectancy at birth, (2) the number of months of contributions or employment required for normal retirement by law, (3) the percentage of the worker's monthly salary deducted by law to cover old-age, disability, and death benefits, and (4) the percentage of the net preretirement salary covered by the net old-age cash-benefit pension.
Sickness and health benefits	Measures the level of sickness and health benefit as the average of the following four normalized variables: (1) the number of months of contributions or employment required to qualify for sickness benefits by law, (2) the percentage of the worker's monthly salary deducted by law to cover sickness and health benefits, (3) the waiting period for sickness benefits, and (4) the percentage of the net salary covered by the net sickness cash benefit for a two-month sickness spell.
Unemployment benefits	Measures the level of unemployment benefits as the average of the following four normalized variables: (1) the number of months of contributions or employment required to qualify for unemployment benefits by law, (2) the percentage of the worker's monthly salary deducted by law to cover unemployment benefits, (3) the waiting period for unemployment benefits, and (4) the percentage of the net salary covered by the net unemployment benefits in case of a one-year unemployment spell.
Social security laws index	Measures social security benefits as the average of (1) Old-age, disability, and death benefits, (2) Sickness and health benefits, and (3) Unemployment benefits.

continued overleaf

TABLE I
(CONTINUED)

Variable	Description
	Political variables
Chief executive and largest party in congress have left or center political orientation	Measures the percentage of years between 1928 and 1995, and, alternatively, between 1975 and 1995, during which both the party of the chief executive and the largest party in congress had left or center orientation. If the country was not independent in the initial year of the period, we use the independence year as the first period. For countries that were part of a larger country in the initial year of the period and subsequently broke up, we include in calculations the political orientation of the political parties in the mother country in the prebreakup period. In the case of military regimes, where political affiliations are unclear, we classify the regime based on its policies. Source: *Authors' calculations based on: Political Handbook of the World, Europa Yearbook, World Encyclopedia of Political Systems and Parties, Cross-National Time-Series Data Political Parties of the Americas: Canada, Latin America, and the West Indies, Encyclopedia of Latin American Politics, Political Parties of Europe, Political Parties of Asia and the Pacific, Statesmen database: ⟨http://rulers.org/⟩, Country Reports History: ⟨http://www.countryreports.org⟩, Rulers database: ⟨http://www.worldstatesmen.org⟩, various regional and country sources.*
Union density	Measures the percentage of the total workforce affiliated to labor unions in 1997. Source: *ILO, Key Indicators of the Labor Market, Laborsta: ⟨http://laborsta.ilo.org⟩, and The World Bank [2001].*
Autocracy	This variable classifies regimes based on their degree of autocracy. This variable ranges from zero to two, where higher values equal a higher degree of autocracy. Democracies are coded as zero, dictatorships with a legislature are coded as one, and dictatorships without a legislature are coded as two. Transition years are coded as the regime that emerges afterwards. This variable is measured as the average from 1950 through 1990. Source: *Alvarez et al. [2000].*
Proportional representation	Equals one if legislators were elected based on the percentage of votes received by their party; equals zero otherwise. This variable is measured as the average from 1975 through 1995. Source: *Beck et al. [2001].*
Divided government	This variable measures the probability that two randomly chosen deputies will belong to a different party in a given year. It is missing if there is no parliament or if there are no parties in the legislature; and zero if there are no opposition party seats. This variable is measured as the average from 1975 through 1995. Source: *Beck et al. [2001].*
Democracy	A measure of the degree of democracy in a given country based on (1) the competitiveness of political participation, (2) the openness and competitiveness of the chief executive recruitment, and (3) the constraints on the chief executive. The variable ranges from zero to ten, where higher values represent a higher degree of institutionalized democracy. The starting period is either 1950 or the country's independence date, whichever is later. The variable is measured as the average from the initial period through 1995. For countries that are breakup nations, we include in the calculations the democracy score of the mother country in the prebreakup period. Source: *Authors' calculations using the data in Jaggers and Marshall [2000].*

THE REGULATION OF LABOR   1351

Outcomes

Size of the unofficial economy	Size of the shadow economy as a percentage of GDP (varying time periods). Source: *Authors' calculations based on averaging all estimates reported in Schneider and Enste [2000] for any given country, as well as Sananikone [1996] for Burkina Faso, Chidzero [1996] for Senegal, Turnham et al. [1990] for Indonesia and Pakistan, and Kasnakoglu and Yayla [1999] for Turkey.*
Employment in the unofficial economy	Share of the total labor force employed in the unofficial economy in the capital city of each country as a percent of the official labor force. Figures are based on surveys and, for some countries, on econometric estimates. Source: *Schneider and Enste [2000] and the Global Urban Indicators Database [2000].*
Male (Female) participation rate in the labor force 1990–1994	Male (Female) participation rate as a percentage of the total male (female) population aged 15 to 64. Based on population censuses or household surveys. Source: *Forteza and Rama [2000].*
Unemployment rate 1991–2000	Average unemployment rate as a percentage of the total labor force during 1991–2000. Source: *ILO, Key Indicators of the Labor Market, Laborsta ⟨http://laborsta.ilo.org⟩.*
Unemployed males (females) 20–24 years old/active males (females) 20–24 years	Unemployed males (females) aged 20 to 24 as a percentage of the total active male (female) population of the same age during 1991–2000. Source: *ILO, Key Indicators of the Labor Market, Laborsta ⟨http://laborsta.ilo.org⟩.*
Wages of machine operators/wages of clerks and craft and related trades workers 1990–1999	Ratio of the average wage of machine operators across industries to the average wage of clerks and workers in craft and related trades. This variable is measured as the average for the period 1990 to 1999. Source: *Authors' calculations based on data in Freeman and Oostendorp [2001].*

continued overleaf

TABLE I
(CONTINUED)

Variable	Description
	Other variables
Log of GNP per capita	Natural logarithm of GNP per capita in 1997, Atlas method, expressed in current US dollars. *Source: World Bank, World Development Indicators [2001].*
Legal origin	Identifies the legal origin of the company law or commercial code of each country (English, French, Socialist, German, or Scandinavian). *Source: La Porta et al. [1999].*
Court formalism index for the eviction of a nonpaying tenant	The index measures substantive and procedural statutory intervention in judicial cases at lower-level civil trial courts in a case for evicting a tenant who has not paid rent. Higher values represent more statutory control or intervention in the judicial process. *Source: Djankov et al. [2003a].*
Court formalism index for the collection of a bounced check	The index measures substantive and procedural statutory intervention in judicial cases at lower-level civil trial courts in a case for collecting on a bounced check. Higher values represent more statutory control or intervention in the judicial process. *Source: Djankov et al. [2003a].*
Log number of steps to start a business	Natural logarithm of the number of different procedures that a start-up business has to comply with to obtain a legal status, i.e., to start operating as a legal entity. *Source: Djankov et al. [2002].*
Log number of days to start a business	Natural logarithm of the number of days required to obtain legal status to operate a firm in 1999. *Source: Djankov et al. [2002].*
Log cost to start a business / GDP per capita	Natural logarithm of the cost of obtaining legal status to operate a firm as a share of per capita GDP in 1999. *Source: Djankov et al. [2002].*
Average years of schooling	Years of schooling of the total population aged over 25. Since there are no data for 1997, we use the average of 1995 and 2000. The only exception is Nigeria for which only 1992 data exist. *Source: Barro and Lee [2000]* ⟨http://www.cid.harvard.edu/ciddata/ciddata.htm⟩ and, for Nigeria, *Human Development Report [1994, 1997].*

variables used in the paper. The unpublished appendix, available at *http://iicg.som.yale.edu//*, describes all data sources and full details of variable construction (including civil rights[5]). To ensure comparability and consistency across countries, we consider a "standardized" male worker and a "standardized" employer.[6]

III.A Employment Laws

Employment laws regulate the individual employment relation, including the alternatives to the standard employment contract, the flexibility of working conditions, and the termination of employment. To capture all of these aspects, we calculate four subindices: (i) alternative employment contracts, (ii) cost of increasing hours worked, (iii) cost of firing workers, and (iv) dismissal procedures. Our index of employment laws, more so than other indices, reflects the incremental cost to the employer of deviating from a hypothetical rigid contract, in which the conditions of a job are specified and a worker cannot be fired. This index is thus an economic measure of protection of (employed) workers, and not just a reflection of legal formalism.

An employer can reduce his costs by hiring part-time labor or through temporary contracts if such practices reduce benefits or termination costs. The first subindex captures the strictness of

5. Civil rights laws seek to stop employment discrimination against vulnerable groups. Our index reflects five such mandates: prohibition of discrimination on the basis of a) race or b) gender, c) the statutory duration of paid maternity leave, d) minimum age of employment of children, and e) the existence of a statutory or broadly applied minimum wage determined by law or mandatory collective agreements. The ostensible logic behind the last variable is that the minimum wage protects disadvantaged persons against exploitation by those with more power.

6. The standardized male worker has the following characteristics: (i) he is a nonexecutive full-time employee who has been working in the same firm for twenty years; (ii) his salary plus benefits equal the country's GNP per worker during the entire period of employment; (iii) he has a nonworking wife and two children, and the family has always resided in the country's most populous city; (iv) he is a lawful citizen who belongs to the same race and religion as the majority of the country's population; (v) he is not a member of the labor union (unless membership is mandatory); and (vi) he retires at the age defined by the country's laws. We also assume a "standardized" employer with the following characteristics: (i) it is a manufacturing company wholly owned by nationals; (ii) its legal domicile and its main place of business is the country's most populous city; (iii) it has 250 workers; and (iv) it abides by every law and regulation, but does not grant workers more prerogatives than are legally mandated. Whenever both a standard duration or payment and a possible extended period of time or payment is provided by law, we choose the standard one. These assumptions ensure comparability across countries, but they are not critical for the results of the paper as variations in the overall level of labor protection are by far greater across countries than across industries within a country. We collected information for a worker who has been employed for three years, and the results do not change materially.

protection against such alternative employment contracts. We measure whether part-time workers are exempt from mandatory benefits of full-time workers and whether it is easier or less costly to terminate part-time workers than full-time workers. We also measure whether fixed-term contracts are only allowed for fixed-term tasks and their maximum allowed duration.

The second subindex measures the cost of increasing working hours. We assume that our hypothetical firm in each country has each employee working at 1758 hours per year initially (Denmark's maximum considering all regulations before overtime), and it wants to increase these numbers by 660 hours per year per worker due to increased demand (which would bring it to 2418 hours per year per worker, Kenya's legal maximum before overtime). We assume that the firm in each country meets the increased need for labor by first asking its workers to work up to the country's legal maximum, then asking them to work overtime at the statutory wage premiums. If neither proves sufficient, we assume that the firm must instead hire another complete duplicate set of workers each working the initial 1758 hours (i.e., workers are complements and each job must be filled with an extra worker to meet the increased demand). Under these assumptions, we can calculate the cost of accommodating increased demand relative to the firm's previous wage bill, a measure of how strictly employment laws protect workers from being "forced" to work more.

The third subindex captures the economic cost of firing workers. We construct a scenario where our standardized firm with 250 workers fires 50 of them: 25 for redundancy and 25 without cause. The cost of firing workers is computed as the equivalent in pay of the sum of the notice period, severance payment, and any other mandatory penalty directly related to the dismissal of the worker.[7] Because many rules govern when a redundancy or no cause dismissal is allowed, we make assumptions to make the scenario comparable across countries.[8] If the laws of a country do

7. For the cost of firing workers subindex, we report results for an employee with three years of seniority. We also calculated the relevant data for a worker with two and twenty years of seniority with no significant change in results.

8. In particular, we assume that (i) there is no discrimination and all procedures regarding notice periods and social conditions for firing are followed (this includes last-in first-out rules as well as seniority and "social need" criteria); (ii) the negative demand shock puts the firm in "manifest unprofitability" and therefore redundancy dismissal is allowed whenever the law permits it for economic reasons less stringent than outright bankruptcy; (iii) whenever permission from a

not allow the firm to fire a worker, the cost is set equal to his full year's salary.

The fourth subindex summarizes the restrictions on employers for firing workers; whether individually or collectively. These may include notifications, approvals, mandatory relocation or retraining, and priority rules for reemployment. Their effect is to raise the costs of dismissal of existing workers beyond those already captured in the previous subindex.

III.B. Collective Relations Laws

Collective relations laws seek to protect workers from employers through collective action. They govern the balance of power between labor unions and employers and associations of employers.[9] We deal with two subareas of these laws: (i) the power granted by the law to labor unions and (ii) the laws governing collective disputes.

The subindex of labor union power measures the power of labor unions over working conditions. Many countries protect by law the right to unionization, the right to collective bargaining, and the obligation of employers to engage in it. In some countries collective agreements are extended to third parties as a matter of public policy at the national or sectoral levels, whereas in others they only extend to nonsignatory workers at the plant level, or only bind the parties to the agreement. Laws in some countries mandate closed shops, and even give unions the right to appoint some directors of firms. Finally, many countries require by law the creation of workers' councils to look after the best interests of employees.

The second subindex measures protection of employees engaged in collective disputes. Some countries enshrine the right of workers to engage in collective action in their constitutions, and allow wildcat strikes (not authorized by the labor union), political strikes (to protest government policy on nonwork-related issues),

---

third party (courts, government regulators, worker councils, or labor unions) is required prior to dismissing a worker, third party consents to the dismissal; (iv) if permission from a third party is required for a dismissal without cause, the third party does not allow it; (v) if dismissal without cause is not allowed but the law establishes a clearly defined penalty for firing the worker (which does not include mandatory reinstatement), the employer fires the employee and pays the fine.

9. Some provisions aim to protect workers from other workers. For instance, "right-to-work" laws in the United States protect workers from unions by prohibiting the exclusive hiring of union labor. Such cases are rare, and the bulk of collective relations provisions protect workers from employers.

and sympathy strikes (to support the claims of workers other than the striking workers). Others do not. Procedural restrictions on the right to strike may include majority voting, advance notice requirements, prohibitions on strikes while a collective agreement is in force, and the obligation to go through conciliation procedures before the strike may take place. Employer defenses may include bans on lockouts and on employers' retribution against strikers, such as the termination of employment of striking workers and the hiring of replacement labor during a lawful strike. Finally, in many countries, one (normally the employer) or both of the parties may be subject to arbitration against their will.

III.C. Social Security Laws

The bulk of social security expenditure across countries addresses old-age pensions, sickness and health care coverage, and unemployment. Following the design of the decommodification index of Esping-Andersen,[10] our variables cover the risks of (i) old age, disability, and death; (ii) sickness and health; and (iii) unemployment. For each, we code four variables to measure the generosity of the social security system.

The construction of each subindex is slightly different, but all capture the generosity of benefits by measuring the percentage of the net previous salary covered by net benefits. This measure approximates the living standard a worker would enjoy considering the effects of the tax structure and the duration for which benefits are received.[11] A second driver of generosity is the cost borne by the worker for the privilege of social security coverage. We approximate this by measuring the required months of contribution or of covered employment required by law to qualify for a standard pension or to enjoy unemployment and sickness benefits as well as the percentage of the worker's monthly salary deducted by law to cover these. Finally, we consider the length of the waiting period before receiving benefits.

---

10. Esping-Andersen used the share of the relevant population covered as a weight for the variables in his index for eighteen developed countries. This information is not available for a large sample of countries, so we present the unweighted data. The correlation between the Esping-Andersen index and our index of social security laws for the eighteen countries in his sample is 0.38.

11. Countries vary in the type of pension system they have, including lump-sum systems, private systems, and systems that provide fixed benefits to everyone. Table I and Appendix 1 (available on-line at http://iicg.som.yale.edu//) describe the details of our calculations.

THE REGULATION OF LABOR   1357

III.D. Aggregation

For each of our three areas of law, we construct an aggregate index by averaging the subindices for the particular area. This is not the only possible aggregation procedure, but it is transparent. Table II presents the correlations between the various subindices and indices of labor regulation. The table shows, for example, that the four subindices of the employment laws index are highly correlated with each other, as are the two subindices of the collective relations law index, and the three subindices of the social securities law index. The correlations between employment and collective relations indices and subindices are high and significant as well, inconsistent with the notion of substitution between different kinds of regulation.

III.E. Independent Variables

We assemble data on a number of potential determinants of labor regulations, as well as some labor market outcomes. We measure development using the (logarithm of) per capita income in 1997 (the year the regulations are measured), and the average years of schooling of the population over 25 years of age from Barro and Lee [2000].

To measure politics, we expand back to 1928 the World Bank data recording the fraction of years between 1975 and 1995 that each country's chief executive or the largest party in the legislature or both was rightist, leftist, or centrist. We present results for the fraction of years during 1928–1995 and 1975–1995 when the chief executive AND the legislature were of left or centrist orientation (these variables yield the strongest results for the political theories). We use union density to proxy for the influence of labor interest groups. To measure political constraints, we take average "autocracy" between 1950 and 1990 from Alvarez et al. [2000], and the 1975–1995 averages of proportional representation and divided government from Beck et al. [2001].[12]

---

12. We have gathered additional variables that measure political orientation as well as political and economic constraints. Additional measures of political orientation include the fraction of years when the chief executive was of left and centrist orientation, the fraction of years when the legislature was of left or centrist political orientation, and the percentage of the labor force covered by collective agreements. Alternative measures of political constraints are the effectiveness of the legislature and constraints of the executive. We also used alternative measures of proportional representation and divided government from various sources including plurality rules in the legislature chambers, and the sum of the square of the total share of the congress controlled by each party. Finally, our measures for economic constraints are actual trade openness in 1985, geographic openness, and factor accumulation openness from Frankel and Romer [1999].

TABLE II

CORRELATION BETWEEN INDICES AND SUBINDICES

This table presents pairwise correlations between our various measures of regulation of labor. All the variables are described in Table I.

	Employment laws index	Alternative employment contracts	Costs of increasing hours worked	Cost of firing workers	Dismissal procedures	Collective relations laws index	Labor union power	Collective disputes	Social security laws index	Old-age, disability, and death benefits	Sickness and health benefits
Alternative employment contracts	0.4702[a]										
Cost of increasing hours worked	0.7948[a]	0.1411									
Cost of firing workers	0.6590[a]	0.2514[b]	0.3170[a]								
Dismissal procedures	0.6868[a]	0.1996[c]	0.2891[a]	0.3877[a]							
Collective relations laws index	0.4894[a]	0.2792[a]	0.2911[b]	0.2466[b]	0.5109[a]						
Labor union power	0.3772[a]	0.2160[b]	0.2859[a]	0.1336	0.3404[a]	0.7568[a]					
Collective disputes	0.3401[a]	0.1932[c]	0.1360	0.2321[b]	0.4125[a]	0.7100[a]	0.0770				
Social security laws index	0.2339[b]	0.1765	0.3011[a]	0.0931	−0.0165	0.2275[b]	0.2277[b]	0.1017			
Old-age, disability, and death benefits	0.1732	0.2206[b]	0.1749	−0.0238	0.0707	0.1338	0.0738	0.1246	0.5825[a]		
Sickness and health benefits	0.1432	0.1063	0.1313	0.1924[c]	−0.0283	0.1643	0.1172	0.1244	0.8443[a]	0.3742[a]	
Unemployment benefits	0.2382[b]	0.1475	0.3699[a]	0.0142	−0.0324	0.2232[b]	0.2863[a]	0.0321	0.8795[a]	0.3649[a]	0.5418[a]

a = significant at 1 percent level; b = significant at 5 percent level; c = significant at 10 percent level.

To test legal theories, we use legal origin of commercial laws from La Porta et al. [1999], which classifies close to 200 countries. Labor market outcomes include the size of the unofficial economy, labor force participation, unemployment including that of the young, and a crude measure of relative wages of protected and unprotected workers.

IV. A LOOK AT THE DATA

A comparison of New Zealand and Portugal, two countries of roughly similar income level can serve to illustrate our indices. In the area of employment laws, neither country exempts part-time workers from mandatory benefits of full-time workers, and neither makes it easier or less costly to terminate them. Fixed term contracts can be entered in New Zealand for any reason, and there is no maximum duration provided by the law. In Portugal, such contracts are allowed for a maximum of three years, are granted for specific situations (such as substitution for another worker or seasonal activity), and are therefore temporary in nature. The alternative employment subindex for New Zealand is 0.50, while for Portugal it is 0.91.

The Portuguese Constitution regulates working times and leaves, remuneration, and working conditions, matters that in New Zealand are normally regulated by collective bargaining or left to the individual employment contract. The premium for overtime work in Portugal is 50 percent for the first six hours per week and 75 percent for every hour thereafter; there are 24 days of paid annual leave; and there is a cap of 200 hours of overtime per year. New Zealand mandates no premium for overtime work, has no quantitative restrictions on night work, and grants only fifteen days of paid leave. The result of this is that the cost of increasing working hours in Portugal is equal to the maximum in our sample (1.00) while the cost in New Zealand is the lowest in our sample (0.00).

In New Zealand, notice period and severance pay are not regulated by statute, while in Portugal the minimum notice period and severance period that may be paid are strictly regulated; for example, a worker with three years seniority fired for redundancy in Portugal is entitled to one month of notice and three months of severance pay. Dismissal without cause is allowed in New Zealand, but constitutionally forbidden in Portugal. These factors explain why New Zealand has the lowest cost of dismissal in our sample (0.00), while Portugal has one of the highest (0.61).

In New Zealand, a reasonable advance notice is generally considered a fair reason for termination for redundancy. Portugal, on the other hand, has a public policy list of fair grounds for termination and stringent procedural limitations on dismissal, such as mandatory notification of the government, permission in the case of collective dismissal, and priority rules for reemployment of redundant workers. These differences are reflected in the dismissal procedures subindex, where New Zealand scores a 0.14 and Portugal a much higher 0.71.

These differences add up to the employment laws index of 0.16 for New Zealand (one of the lowest in the world), and 0.81 for Portugal (one of the highest).

In collective relations laws, the Portuguese Constitution guarantees the rights to form trade unions and to engage in collective bargaining. Employers have a legal duty to bargain with unions, collective agreements are extended to third parties by law, and workers' councils allowing workers to participate in management are mandatory. In New Zealand, these issues are not regulated by law. For example, once a bargaining agent has established its authority to represent an employee, the employer must recognize his authority, but there is no obligation upon the employer to negotiate with this agent. In New Zealand, as in Portugal, the law does not allow closed shops. These differences explain why the subindex of labor union power for New Zealand is 0, the lowest possible, while Portugal's is 0.71, the highest in our sample.

Regarding collective disputes, the two countries are similar. The right to strike is protected in both countries, but while it is a mere freedom in New Zealand, it is a constitutional right in Portugal. Employer lockouts are allowed in New Zealand, but not in Portugal. New Zealand does not mandate a waiting period or notification before strikes can occur, while Portugal requires employers to be notified before the strike. In both countries, employers are not allowed to fire or replace striking workers; there is no mandatory conciliation procedure before a strike; and compulsory third-party arbitration during a labor dispute is not mandatory. The overall collective disputes subindex is 0.58 in Portugal and 0.50 in New Zealand; the overall collective relations laws index is 0.65 for Portugal compared with 0.25 for New Zealand.

Although social security is regulated by the Constitution in Portugal but not in New Zealand, the two countries have similar—and generous—systems. In the case of old-age, disability, and death insurance, workers in New Zealand are not only obliged to contribute less to their retirement, but can also expect to enjoy their benefits for 13.4 years while those in Portugal only expect 10.5 years. The percentage of the previous net wage covered by net benefits is 76 percent in New Zealand and only 58 percent in Portugal. For the overall old-age, disability, and death benefits subindex, New Zealand scores a 0.84, and Portugal only 0.60.

Sickness and health benefits in Portugal require six months of contributions before benefits can be claimed, 3.17 percent of the workers' monthly pay is deducted to pay for insurance, and there is a waiting period of three days between the time the employee falls ill and payments begin. New Zealand has no minimum contribution conditions, no waiting period, and does not deduct pay from workers to cover for insurance. Net benefits in Portugal cover approximately 65 percent of the net previous wage, while benefits in New Zealand are income tested and our model worker falls above the threshold. These differences roughly cancel each other out: New Zealand has a sickness and health benefits subindex of 0.75, and Portugal of 0.70.

For unemployment benefits, New Zealand has no minimum contribution period, while Portugal mandates eighteen months. However Portugal has no waiting period from the time an employee is fired and when he can claim benefits, while a worker in New Zealand must wait for 70 days. The benefits received are also more generous in Portugal: the net benefit is 77 percent of net previous wages, while only 25 percent in New Zealand. The results of this are that the subindex of unemployment benefits is 0.56 for New Zealand and a much higher 0.90 for Portugal.

The three measures of social security translate into a slightly higher score in the social security laws index of 0.74 for Portugal than 0.72 given to New Zealand.

Table III presents, for each country, the indices of employment, collective relations, and social security laws, as well as the logarithm of GDP per capita in 1997, the fraction of years during 1928–1995 when the chief executive and the legislature were of left or centrist orientation, and the legal origin. The table also presents the means and medians of the data across income

TABLE III

MAIN INDICATORS BY COUNTRY

Panel A of this table shows the indices of employment laws, collective relations laws, and social security laws, as well as the log of GNP per capita for 1997, the percentage of years between 1928 and 1995 during which both the party of the chief executive and the largest party in congress had left or center orientation, and the legal origin of each country. Panels B, C, and D present summary statistics for the cross section of countries by GNP per capita, degree of left/center political orientation, and legal origin, respectively. All variables are described in Table I, and the data can be found at http://iicg.som.yale.edu/.

	Employment laws index	Collective relations laws index	Social security laws index	Log GNP per capita 1997	Chief executive and largest party in congress have left or center political orientation (1928–1995)	Legal origin
			Panel A: Data			
Argentina	0.3442	0.5774	0.7154	9.0070	0.4559	French
Armenia	0.6017	0.5179	0.7337	6.2538	1.0000	Socialist
Australia	0.3515	0.3720	0.7820	10.0110	0.3529	English
Austria	0.5007	0.3601	0.7139	10.2481	0.2353	German
Belgium	0.5133	0.4226	0.6240	10.1988	0.0882	French
Bolivia	0.3728	0.4613	0.3702	6.8773	0.4412	French
Brazil	0.5676	0.3780	0.5471	8.4638	0.2206	French
Bulgaria	0.5189	0.4435	0.7610	7.0648	0.7059	Socialist
Burkina Faso	0.4396	0.5268	0.1447	5.4806	0.9429	French
Canada	0.2615	0.1964	0.7869	9.9179	0.6912	English
Chile	0.4735	0.3810	0.6887	8.5112	0.3824	French
China	0.4322	0.3304	0.7643	6.5511	0.6765	Socialist
Colombia	0.3442	0.4851	0.8131	7.8241	0.3676	French
Croatia	0.4879	0.4524	0.6797	8.3802	0.6765	Socialist
Czech Republic	0.5205	0.3393	0.6981	8.5698	0.8382	Socialist
Denmark	0.5727	0.4196	0.8727	10.4406	0.7353	Scandinavian
Dominican Republic	0.5972	0.2715	0.4876	7.4384	0.1176	French
Ecuador	0.3966	0.6369	0.6542	7.3588	0.3971	French
Egypt	0.3683	0.4107	0.7550	7.0901	0.8382	French
Finland	0.7366	0.3185	0.7863	10.1511	0.7941	Scandinavian
France	0.7443	0.6667	0.7838	10.1601	0.3382	French
Georgia	0.7713	0.5685	0.4491	6.3456	1.0000	Socialist
Germany	0.7015	0.6071	0.6702	10.2608	0.2941	German
Ghana	0.2881	0.4821	0.1576	5.9662	0.7368	English
Greece	0.5189	0.4851	0.7386	9.4222	0.2059	French
Hong Kong	0.1696	0.4554	0.8050	10.1382	0.2794	English
Hungary	0.3773	0.6071	0.7275	8.4141	0.6618	Socialist
India	0.4434	0.3839	0.4003	6.0403	1.0000	English
Indonesia	0.6813	0.3929	0.1772	7.0121	0.1957	French
Ireland	0.3427	0.4643	0.7144	9.8924	0.0000	English
Israel	0.2890	0.3095	0.8068	9.7238	0.7660	English
Italy	0.6499	0.6310	0.7572	9.9311	0.3235	French
Jamaica	0.1628	0.2262	0.1677	7.5229	0.4242	English
Japan	0.1639	0.6280	0.6417	10.5545	0.0147	German
Jordan	0.6977	0.3810	0.2099	7.3840	0.0000	French
Kazakhstan	0.7796	0.6815	0.2778	7.2298	1.0000	Socialist
Kenya	0.3687	0.2262	0.3114	5.8579	1.0000	English
Korea	0.4457	0.5446	0.6774	9.3405	0.4000	German
Kyrgyz Republic	0.7459	0.4613	0.7678	6.1527	0.9412	Socialist
Latvia	0.7211	0.5327	0.7023	7.7407	0.7647	Socialist

THE REGULATION OF LABOR   1363

Lebanon	0.5024	0.4137	0.3948	8.1197	0.1923	French
Lithuania	0.6233	0.4970	0.7458	7.7053	0.7941	Socialist
Madagascar	0.4749	0.4643	0.2003	5.5215	1.0000	French
Malawi	0.1833	0.2470	0.0000	5.3471	0.1290	English
Malaysia	0.1885	0.1875	0.1950	8.4338	0.0000	English
Mali	0.6674	0.3929	0.1658	5.5607	0.3429	French
Mexico	0.5943	0.5774	0.5063	8.2188	1.0000	French
Mongolia	0.3256	0.2292	0.7383	6.0403	0.9706	Socialist
Morocco	0.2616	0.4881	0.5165	7.1309	0.0000	French
Mozambique	0.7946	0.5804	0.4452	5.1930	1.0000	French
Netherlands	0.7256	0.4643	0.6282	10.2128	0.2647	French
New Zealand	0.1607	0.2500	0.7188	9.6909	0.4559	English
Nigeria	0.1929	0.2054	0.3447	5.5984	0.5429	English
Norway	0.6853	0.6488	0.8259	10.5018	0.7059	Scandinavian
Pakistan	0.3433	0.3095	0.4714	6.2344	0.4375	English
Panama	0.6246	0.4554	0.7431	8.0163	0.5000	French
Peru	0.4630	0.7113	0.4167	7.7832	0.4265	French
Philippines	0.4762	0.5149	0.4941	7.1148	0.3469	French
Poland	0.6395	0.5655	0.6459	8.1775	0.9118	Socialist
Portugal	0.8088	0.6488	0.7352	9.3281	0.0882	French
Romania	0.3273	0.5565	0.7411	7.2442	0.9265	Socialist
Russian Federation	0.8276	0.5774	0.8470	7.8633	0.9412	Socialist
Senegal	0.5099	0.5744	0.3835	6.2729	1.0000	French
Singapore	0.3116	0.3423	0.4618	10.2198	0.3000	English
Slovak Republic	0.6571	0.4524	0.7284	8.2584	0.8824	Socialist
Slovenia	0.7359	0.4851	0.7755	9.1973	0.7353	Socialist
South Africa	0.3204	0.5446	0.5753	8.2134	0.0147	English
Spain	0.7447	0.5863	0.7660	9.6382	0.3088	French
Sri Lanka	0.4685	0.5060	0.1945	6.6720	0.8298	English
Sweden	0.7405	0.5387	0.8448	10.2306	0.8529	Scandinavian
Switzerland	0.4520	0.4167	0.8151	10.6782	0.6912	German
Taiwan	0.4534	0.3155	0.7478	9.2519	0.0000	German
Tanzania	0.6843	0.3244	0.0880	5.3471	1.0000	English
Thailand	0.4097	0.3571	0.4707	7.9302	0.0735	English
Tunisia	0.8158	0.3810	0.7063	7.6401	0.9744	French
Turkey	0.4026	0.4732	0.4777	8.0678	0.5441	French
Uganda	0.3530	0.3810	0.1088	5.7683	0.9697	English
Ukraine	0.6609	0.5774	0.8499	6.9177	1.0000	Socialist
United Kingdom	0.2824	0.1875	0.6915	9.9763	0.2794	English
United States	0.2176	0.2589	0.6461	10.3129	0.7059	English
Uruguay	0.2762	0.3542	0.6778	8.7641	0.5000	French
Venezuela	0.6509	0.5357	0.7299	8.1662	0.5441	French
Vietnam	0.5401	0.4821	0.5198	5.8290	1.0000	Socialist
Zambia	0.1480	0.2914	0.1055	5.9135	1.0000	English
Zimbabwe	0.2513	0.4435	0.1623	6.5793	0.5000	English
Sample mean	**0.4876**	**0.4451**	**0.5690**	**8.0213**	**0.5646**	
Sample median	**0.4749**	**0.4554**	**0.6774**	**8.0163**	**0.5441**	

Panel B: Data by GNP per capita

Below median:	Mean	0.4889	0.4408	0.4481	6.6285	0.6846
	Median	0.4657	0.4613	0.4471	6.6256	0.8120
Above median:	Mean	0.4862	0.4493	0.6872	9.3817	0.4473
	Median	0.5007	0.4554	0.7154	9.6382	0.4000

Panel C: Data by left / center political orientation

Below median:	Mean	0.4378	0.4345	0.5504	8.4929	0.2676
	Median	0.4277	0.4330	0.6350	8.4875	0.2971
Above median:	Mean	0.5361	0.4554	0.5873	7.5607	0.8546
	Median	0.5205	0.4732	0.7063	7.2442	0.8824

TABLE III
(CONTINUED)

		Employment laws index	Collective relations laws index	Social security laws index	Log GNP per capita 1997	Chief executive and largest party in congress have left or center political orientation (1928–1995)
Panel D: Data by legal origin						
English legal	Mean	0.2997	0.3313	0.4236	7.8045	0.5204
origin:	Median	0.2886	0.3170	0.4311	7.7266	0.4779
Socialist legal	Mean	0.5944	0.4925	0.6923	7.3650	0.8646
origin:	Median	0.6233	0.4970	0.7337	7.2442	0.9118
French legal	Mean	0.5470	0.4914	0.5454	7.9034	0.4484
origin:	Median	0.5161	0.4792	0.5855	7.9202	0.3750
German legal	Mean	0.4529	0.4787	0.7110	10.0557	0.2725
origin:	Median	0.4527	0.4807	0.6957	10.2545	0.2647
Scandinavian legal	Mean	0.6838	0.4814	0.8324	10.3310	0.7721
origin:	Median	0.7110	0.4792	0.8354	10.3356	0.7647

groups, degrees of leftist political orientation, and legal origins. At first glance, the data suggest that richer countries have more generous social security systems than poorer ones but otherwise similarly protective labor laws, that countries with more left-wing governments have more protective laws than those with less leftist ones, and that common law countries protect labor less than do those from the four civil law traditions. Below we examine these data systematically.

V. Testing the Theories

In Table IV we examine the relationship between the protection of workers and two of its potential determinants: income per capita and legal origin. There is no evidence that employment laws or collective relations laws vary with the level of economic development. This result is inconsistent with the implication of the efficiency hypothesis that rich countries should regulate less because they have fewer market failures. In contrast, there is clear evidence that richer countries have more generous social security systems, both as measured by the aggregate index and for old-age, health, and unemployment benefits separately.

The results in Table IV also show that legal origin matters for several areas of labor law. In employment laws, all categories of civil law countries have higher values of the index than do the common law countries, and the differences are quantitatively large for French, socialist, and Scandinavian legal origins. The explanatory power of legal origins is high: the R^2 of the regression is 44 percent. Differences among legal origins are also large for collective relations laws, with common law countries being less protective of workers than civil law countries. The R^2 here is 31 percent. With social security laws, the picture is more complex. Socialist, Scandinavian, and French legal origin countries, but not German legal origin countries, have more generous systems than do the common law countries. Since income is so important for social security laws, the R^2 of this regression rises to a somewhat unbelievable 64 percent. In short, legal traditions are a strikingly important determinant of various aspects of statutory worker protection, with French and socialist legal origin countries being most interventionist, consistent with the evidence on regulation of other aspects of economic life [La Porta et al. 1999; Djankov et al. 2002].

Panel D of Table IV focuses on Roe's [2000] hypothesis that civil law is a proxy for social democracy by rerunning the regressions for the three aggregate law indices using the subsample of nondemocracies during 1950–1995. Even in nondemocracies, legal origin remains an important determinant of employment, collective relations, and social security laws, inconsistent with the view that it proxies for social democracy. This result is robust to a variety of definitions of nondemocracy we have tried.

Table V examines the effect of politics on labor laws, holding per capita income constant. Countries with longer histories of leftist or centrist governments between 1928 and 1995, as well as between 1975 and 1995, have heavier regulation of labor markets, as measured by employment, collective relations, and social security laws (five out of six coefficients are statistically significant).[13] Higher union density is also associated with stronger worker protection. These results support political theories, which hold that worker protection comes from their political power, although the explanatory power of the political variables is

---

13. These results also hold mostly, although at lower levels of statistical significance, if we use the pure leftist government variables (rather than the combination of leftist and centrist governments), or if we use the executive or the legislative branch separately.

TABLE IV
REGULATION OF LABOR AND LEGAL ORIGIN

Ordinary least squares regressions of the cross section of countries. The dependent variables are (1) the employment laws index and its components (in Panel A), (2) the collective relations laws index and its components (in Panel B), and (3) the social security laws index and its components (in Panel C). In Panel D we repeat regressions for the three aggregate indices for countries classified as "nondemocracies" during the period 1950–1995. Using democracy scores from Jaggers and Marshall [2000], we classify as nondemocracies countries with the 1950–1995 average democracy score below 8. The 21 countries classified as democracies, and left out of the sample in Panel D are Australia, Austria, Belgium, Canada, Denmark, Finland, France, Germany, India, Ireland, Israel, Italy, Jamaica, Japan, Netherlands, New Zealand, Norway, Sweden, Switzerland, the United Kingdom, and the United States. Robust standard errors are shown in parentheses. All the variables are described in Table I and the data can be found in http://fieg.som.yale.edu/.

Dependent variables	Log GNP per capita	Socialist legal origin	French legal origin	German legal origin	Scandinavian legal origin	Constant	N [R^2]
Panel A: Employment laws and legal origin							
Employment laws index	−0.0010 (0.0116)	0.2943[a] (0.0453)	0.2474[a] (0.0381)	0.1553[b] (0.0702)	0.3865[a] (0.0462)	0.3072[a] (0.1038)	85 [0.44]
Alternative employment contracts	0.0123 (0.0095)	0.1219[b] (0.0536)	0.2514[a] (0.0351)	0.1490[c] (0.0824)	0.1404[c] (0.0810)	0.3728[a] (0.0840)	85 [0.31]
Cost of increasing hours worked	0.0436 (0.0299)	0.5935[a] (0.1012)	0.3335[a] (0.0901)	0.3515[c] (0.1896)	0.7746[a] (0.0713)	−0.2248 (0.2566)	85 [0.34]
Cost of firing workers	−0.0241 (0.0172)	0.2067[a] (0.0552)	0.2091[a] (0.0599)	0.0883 (0.1065)	0.2553[a] (0.0640)	0.5168[a] (0.1462)	85 [0.24]
Dismissal procedures	−0.0357[c] (0.0186)	0.2550[a] (0.0840)	0.1955[a] (0.0679)	0.0327 (0.0881)	0.3758[a] (0.1029)	0.5641[a] (0.1740)	85 [0.21]
Panel B: Collective relations laws and legal origin							
Collective relations laws index	0.0063 (0.0077)	0.1639[a] (0.0332)	0.1594[a] (0.0295)	0.1332[b] (0.0590)	0.1342[c] (0.0713)	0.2824[a] (0.0629)	85 [0.31]
Labor union power	0.0055 (0.0120)	0.1822[a] (0.0516)	0.1672[a] (0.0468)	0.2475[a] (0.0872)	0.3174[a] (0.0799)	0.2445[b] (0.0973)	85 [0.27]
Collective disputes	0.0070 (0.0124)	0.1456[a] (0.0477)	0.1517[a] (0.0416)	0.0189 (0.0589)	−0.0490 (0.1029)	0.3203[a] (0.1060)	85 [0.19]

Panel C: Social security laws and legal origin

Social security laws index	0.1029^a	0.3139^a	0.1116^a	0.0557	0.1488^a	−0.3798^a	85
	(0.0104)	(0.0470)	(0.0406)	(0.0512)	(0.0430)	(0.0865)	[0.64]
Old-age, disability, and death benefits	0.0489^a	0.0325	0.0449	−0.0026	0.1306^a	0.1529	85
	(0.0111)	(0.0381)	(0.0364)	(0.0386)	(0.0434)	(0.0980)	[0.38]
Sickness and health benefits	0.0977^a	0.3684^a	0.1817^b	0.0389	0.1943^a	−0.3049	85
	(0.0216)	(0.0940)	(0.0781)	(0.0904)	(0.0728)	(0.1986)	[0.34]
Unemployment benefits	0.1623^a	0.5409^a	0.1084	0.1307	0.1214	−0.9874^a	85
	(0.0152)	(0.0673)	(0.0698)	(0.0855)	(0.0790)	(0.0996)	[0.63]

Panel D: Regulation of labor and legal origin for nondemocracies

Employment laws index	−0.0043	0.2841^a	0.2217^a	0.1476^a	n.a.	0.3419^b	64
	(0.0164)	(0.0505)	(0.0459)	(0.0447)	n.a.	(0.1290)	[0.34]
Collective relations laws index	0.0138	0.1332^a	0.1212^a	0.0441	n.a.	0.2577^a	64
	(0.0099)	(0.0384)	(0.0354)	(0.0921)	n.a.	(0.0721)	[0.25]
Social security laws index	0.0964^a	0.3553^a	0.1653^a	0.1895^a	n.a.	−0.3727^a	64
	(0.0149)	(0.0545)	(0.0523)	(0.0647)	n.a.	(0.1024)	[0.63]

a = significant at 1 percent level; b = significant at 5 percent level; c = significant at 10 percent level, "n.a." not applicable.

TABLE V

REGULATION OF LABOR, LEFT POWER, AND POLITICAL CONSTRAINTS

Ordinary least squares regressions of the cross section of countries. The dependent variables are (1) the employment laws index, (2) the collective relations laws index, and (3) the social security laws index. Robust standard errors are shown in parentheses. All the variables are described in Table I, and the data can be found in http://iicg.som.yale.edu/.

Dependent variables	Log GNP per capita	Chief executive and largest party in congress have left or center political orientation 1928–1995	1975–1995	Union density 1997	Autocracy 1950–1990	Proportional representation 1975–1995	Divided government 1975–1995	Constant	N [R²]
Employment laws index	0.0189	0.1812[b]						0.2335	85
	(0.0149)	(0.0693)						(0.1419)	[0.08]
	0.0216		0.1934[a]					0.2088	85
	(0.0141)		(0.0553)					(0.1295)	[0.12]
	−0.0051			0.2275[b]				0.4545[a]	70
	(0.0150)			(0.0869)				(0.1140)	[0.08]
	0.0216				0.0295			0.2640	70
	(0.0198)				(0.0613)			(0.1913)	[0.02]
	−0.0136					0.1431[a]		0.5310[a]	84
	(0.0140)					(0.0486)		(0.1074)	[0.08]
	−0.0055						0.1892[b]	0.4354[a]	83
	(0.0153)						(0.0946)	(0.1116)	[0.06]

	(1)	(2)	(3)	(4)	(5)	(6)	(7)	(8)	Obs	[R²]
Collective relations laws index	0.0130 (0.0101)	0.0651 (0.0459)						0.3039^a (0.0941)	85	[0.03]
	0.0160^c (0.0093)		0.0908^b (0.0342)					0.2669^a (0.0810)	85	[0.07]
	−0.0002 (0.0110)			0.1091^c (0.0643)				0.4177^a (0.0862)	70	[0.04]
	0.0255^c (0.0131)				0.0586 (0.0404)			0.1875 (0.1266)	70	[0.05]
	−0.0124 (0.0099)					0.1436^a (0.0386)		0.4755^a (0.0719)	84	[0.16]
	−0.0001 (0.0105)						0.1052^c (0.0583)	0.3923^a (0.0748)	83	[0.04]
Social security laws index	0.1130^a (0.0108)	0.2311^a (0.0582)						−0.4680^a (0.1068)	85	[0.50]
	0.1115^a (0.0104)		0.1962^a (0.0519)					−0.4329^a (0.1020)	85	[0.50]
	0.0791^a (0.0135)			0.1871^c (0.0951)				−0.1142 (0.1146)	70	[0.43]
	0.0953^a (0.0191)				−0.0322 (0.0596)			−0.2027 (0.1944)	70	[0.52]
	0.0846^a (0.0134)					0.0549 (0.0541)		−0.1372^b (0.1076)	84	[0.41]
	0.0902^a (0.0124)						0.0709 (0.0981)	−0.1962^c (0.1016)	83	[0.43]

a = significant at 1 percent level; b = significant at 5 percent level; c = significant at 10 percent level.

sharply lower than that of legal origins, as reflected in the lower R^2 of these regressions.[14]

In addition, Table V presents mixed evidence on the importance of constraints on government. Countries with proportional representation have more protective employment and collective relations laws, suggesting that constraints on the executive lead to more protection. But the result does not hold for other variables. These results offer mixed support for the view that constraints on government lead to less intervention in markets. However, they do provide some support for the Alesina-Glaeser [2004] theory that proportional representation as a form of democracy is a reflection of labor power, as are the laws protecting labor.[15]

Table VI presents the results of a horse race between legal origins and politics. We exclude socialist legal origin countries from the sample because of extremely high correlations between leftist variables and socialist origin, but all the results hold on a larger sample as well. Legal origin wins out and accounts for the bulk of the R^2. In six out of nine regressions, the proxies for politics lose their consistent influence on the regulation of labor. In contrast, the difference between common law and French legal origin countries is always statistically significant. The average French legal origin country has employment and collective relations laws scores 50 to 100 percent higher than the average common law country. German and Scandinavian legal origin countries continue to be more protective than common law countries, although the results are not quite as consistent as in Table V for Scandinavian legal origin. We conclude that the effects of

14. We ran regressions with more variables that are related to the political view of regulation. The results show that the Gini coefficient has a significant *negative* effect on all but collective relations laws. Measures of ethnic, linguistic, and religious heterogeneity from Alesina et al. [2003] also have a *negative* effect, inconsistent with the theory that labor laws are efficiently more protective of workers when social divisions are greater. Tax efficiency affects negatively collective relations laws only. Finally, public old-age pensions/GNP (1960–1995) has significant positive effects on employment and social security laws. Once we control for legal origin, however, all these go away, except the effect of public pensions on employment and collective relations laws at the 10 percent significance level.

15. Other measures of political constraints impact labor regulation without legal origin control, but not once we control for legal origin. Economic constraints on government, measured by proxies for trade openness from Frankel and Romer [1999], have a weak impact on employment laws and collective relations laws, but do affect social security laws when controlling for legal origin.

legal origin on the regulation of labor are larger and different from those of politics.[16]

This evidence does not suggest that politics does not matter, but it is inconsistent with the extreme hypothesis that law is just a proxy for social democracy. The importance of legal origin—and the unimportance of per capita income—is also difficult to reconcile with the efficiency theory of regulation of labor, except for the version that sees the efficiency of regulatory schemes stemming largely from their compatibility with the country's broader legal framework.[17]

VI. REGULATION IN DIFFERENT DOMAINS

One of the strongest implications of the legal theory is that societies have regulatory styles shaped in part by their legal systems, and that therefore societies that regulate one activity are also expected to regulate others, which might be totally unrelated. We have already shown in earlier work that French civil law countries regulate entry of new firms, dispute resolution in courts, and other activities more heavily than do common law countries [La Porta et al. 1999; Djankov et al. 2002, 2003b]. The findings of this paper are broadly consistent with this research.

Table VII presents the correlations between our measures of regulation of labor and the measures of regulation of entry from Djankov et al. [2002] and of legal formalism from Djankov et al. [2003b]. The data show that all these aspects of regulation go together, even though the methodologies of data collection differ tremendously across the three studies. The correlation between the employment laws index and the judicial formalism index is 0.33 for one case, and 0.41 for the other. The correlation between the employment laws index and the logarithm of the number of steps required to start a business is 0.34. These correlations fall by about 0.05 if we exclude socialist countries, but remain highly statistically significant. The numbers are even higher for the

16. We also considered the effects of the religious composition of the population in 1900 and in 1980—our proxy for culture—on contemporary labor laws. There are no statistically significant effects of religious variables measured in 1900. For 1980 measures, we find that catholic countries have more protective collective relations and social security laws, but the significance is small and typically does not survive a control for legal origin.

17. Our index of civil rights laws, described in footnote 6, does not depend on income per capita, is higher in socialist countries, but does not otherwise depend on legal origins. It is strongly correlated with leftist government measures, even controlling for legal origin.

TABLE VI
REGULATION OF LABOR, POLITICAL VARIABLES, AND LEGAL ORIGIN

Ordinary least squares regressions of the cross section of nonsocialist countries. The nineteen countries excluded from this table are Armenia, Bulgaria, China, Croatia, Czech Republic, Georgia, Hungary, Kazakhstan, Kyrgyz Republic, Latvia, Lithuania, Mongolia, Poland, Romania, Russian Federation, Slovak Republic, Slovenia, Ukraine, and Vietnam. The dependent variables are (1) the employment laws index (in Panel A), (2) the collective relations laws index (in Panel B), and (3) the social security index (in Panel C). Robust standard errors are shown in parentheses. All the variables are described in Table I, and the data can be found in http://iicg.som.yale.edu/.

Left power variables	Log GNP per capita	Left power variables	French legal origin	German legal origin	Scandinavian legal origin	Constant	N [R²]
Panel A: The dependent variable is the employment laws index							
Chief executive and largest party in congress have left or center political orientation 1928–1995	0.0034 (0.0124)	0.0711 (0.0656)	0.2521ᵃ (0.0377)	0.1631ᵇ (0.0695)	0.3575ᵃ (0.0561)	0.2360ᵃ (0.1178)	66 [0.46]
Chief executive and largest party in congress have left or center political orientation 1975–1995	0.0090 (0.0121)	0.1196ᵇ (0.0554)	0.2525ᵃ (0.0368)	0.1542ᵇ (0.0694)	0.3395ᵃ (0.0502)	0.1729 (0.1118)	66 [0.49]
Union density	−0.0066 (0.0156)	0.0827 (0.1109)	0.2283ᵃ (0.0408)	0.1422ᵇ (0.0690)	0.3318ᵃ (0.0689)	0.3513ᵇ (0.1354)	57 [0.43]
Panel B: The dependent variable is the collective relations laws index							
Chief executive and largest party in congress have left or center political orientation 1928–1995	0.0079 (0.0093)	0.0384 (0.0495)	0.1617ᵃ (0.0302)	0.1380ᵇ (0.0601)	0.1212 (0.0760)	0.2512ᵃ (0.0914)	66 [0.33]
Chief executive and largest party in congress have left or center political orientation 1975–1995	0.0118 (0.0080)	0.0696ᶜ (0.0360)	0.1624ᵃ (0.0292)	0.1331ᵇ (0.0621)	0.1075 (0.7240)	0.2063ᵃ (0.0704)	66 [0.36]
Union density	−0.0001 (0.0104)	0.0649 (0.1015)	0.1608ᵃ (0.0326)	0.1337ᵇ (0.0626)	0.1025 (0.0936)	0.3253 (0.0843)	57 [0.33]

Panel C: The dependent variable is the social security laws index

Chief executive and largest party in congress have left or center political orientation 1928–1995	0.1242ª (0.0122)	0.1333ᵇ (0.0657)	0.1191ª (0.0399)	0.0408 (0.0546)	0.0615 (0.0481)	−0.6151ª (0.1230)	66 [0.72]
Chief executive and largest party in congress have left or center political orientation 1975–1995	0.1214ª (0.0122)	0.0928 (0.0604)	0.1146ª (0.0400)	0.0307 (0.0535)	0.0852ᶜ (0.0469)	−0.5675ª (0.1221)	66 [0.71]
Union density	0.1061ª (0.0127)	−0.0674 (0.1111)	0.0806ᶜ (0.0445)	0.0232 (0.0539)	0.1506ᵇ (0.0730)	−0.3582ª (0.1090)	57 [0.63]

a = significant at 1 percent level; b = significant at 5 percent level; c = significant at 10 percent level.

TABLE VII
CORRELATIONS BETWEEN REGULATION INDICES

The table shows pairwise correlations between various indices of regulation for the cross section of 85 countries. All the variables are described in Table I.

	Employment laws index	Collective relations laws index	Social security laws index	Court formalism index for the eviction of a nonpaying tenant	Court formalism index for the collection of a bounced check	Log (number of steps to start a business)	Log (number of days to start a business)
Collective relations laws index	0.4894[a]						
Social security laws index	0.2339[b]	0.2275[b]					
Court formalism index for the eviction of a nonpaying tenant	0.3292[a]	0.5134[a]	0.1283				
Court formalism index for the collection of a bounced check	0.4103[a]	0.4430[a]	0.0448	0.8506[a]			
Log (number of steps to start a business)	0.3439[a]	0.4041[a]	−0.2309[b]	0.5036[a]	0.5675[a]		
Log (number of days to start a business)	0.3335[a]	0.3663[a]	−0.2949[a]	0.5274[a]	0.5525[a]	0.8263[a]	
Log (cost to start a business/GDP per capita)	0.1722	0.1721	−0.4737[a]	0.3667[a]	0.4309[a]	0.6354[a]	0.6147[a]

a = significant at 1 percent level; b = significant at 5 percent level; c = significant at 10 percent level.

collective relations laws, although generosity of social security systems is negatively correlated with entry regulation (because income matters for both in opposite directions). Regulatory style is pervasive across activities—consistent with the legal theory.

VII. Outcomes

Finally, we consider some of the consequences of the regulation of labor. This is of interest for two reasons. First, efficiency theories predict that heavier regulation of labor markets should be associated with better, and certainly not worse, labor market outcomes. This prediction has been contradicted by a variety of empirical studies from Lazear [1990] to Besley and Burgess [2003], and here we confirm their findings. Second, if the regulation of labor is damaging at least to some workers, then who benefits from it? Put differently, is there political support for the heavier regulation of labor, or does legal origin simply provide a politically unsupported "technology" for the social control of labor markets?

We look at several potential consequences of labor regulation. These include the size of and the employment in the unofficial economy, male and female participation in the labor force, and unemployment computed separately for everyone, and for male and female workers aged 20–24. In addition, as a crude measure of relative wages of protected and unprotected workers, we consider the average wage of machine operators relative to that of clerks and workers in craft and related trades. All of these variables have measurement problems, particularly for the developing countries, where some employment is informal and not recorded in official statistics. Still, by looking at the various dimensions of the data, we hope to get a general picture.

Table VIII presents the results. In all specifications, we control for average years of schooling (which is less likely to be itself caused by regulations than income per capita) as a proxy for the quality of law enforcement.[18] The strength of the results varies across specifications, but in general they show no benefits, and some costs, of labor regulation. There is some evidence that more

18. As alternative enforcement measures, we used the length of court proceedings in collecting a bounced check and evicting a tenant from Djankov et al. [2003b], with no change in results.

TABLE VIII

REGULATION OF LABOR AND OUTCOMES

Ordinary least squares regressions of the cross section of countries. Robust standard errors are shown in parentheses. All the variables are described in Table I, and the data can be found in http://iicg.som.yale.edu/.

Dependent variables	Average years of schooling	Employment laws index	Collective relations laws index	Social security laws index	Constant	N [R²]
Size of the unofficial economy	−2.8030[a] (0.3665)	3.5502 (7.0070)			48.7084[a] (4.4941)	85 [0.31]
	−2.8685[a] (0.3763)		19.1262[c] (9.6501)		42.369[a] (5.0447)	85 [0.33]
	−2.3368[a] (0.5009)			−8.6085 (7.2730)	52.1915[a] (3.4650)	85 [0.31]
Employment in the unofficial economy	−3.7368[a] (0.8193)	−5.2811 (11.7934)			65.5531[a] (6.3751)	46 [0.37]
	−4.1016[a] (0.7008)		33.4761[b] (14.1319)		49.7917[a] (6.8795)	46 [0.42]
	−3.9765[a] (0.9858)			3.0795 (10.4304)	62.5621[a] (4.6112)	46 [0.37]
Male participation in labor force 1990–1994	−0.7144[a] (0.1519)	−6.1870[a] (1.8148)			91.3752[a] (1.4274)	78 [0.30]
	−0.6782[a] (0.1468)		−9.4694[a] (2.5269)		92.3725[a] (1.5015)	78 [0.31]
	−0.4918[a] (0.1774)			−4.2943[c] (2.3415)	89.3289[a] (1.1189)	78 [0.26]
Female participation in labor force 1990–1994	−0.2810 (0.7163)	10.4136 (10.0358)			52.7763[a] (6.8501)	78 [0.02]
	−0.2066 (0.7677)		−12.1189 (14.6474)		62.6992[a] (7.9967)	78 [0.01]
	0.1450 (0.9509)			−7.5902 (11.8392)	59.2293[a] (6.0495)	78 [0.01]

	(1)	(2)	(3)	(4)	(5)	N [R²]
Unemployment rate 1991–2000	−0.3530 (0.2511)	5.7617[b] (2.8478)			8.7263[a] (2.9019)	65 [0.11]
	−0.3864 (0.2402)		3.6447 (3.8279)		10.1519[a] (3.0622)	65 [0.06]
	−0.5299[b] (0.2536)			3.9441 (3.5397)	10.3762[a] (2.5577)	65 [0.06]
Unemployed males 20–24 years old/active males 20–24 years old 1991–2000	−0.0435 (0.4329)	14.6331[a] (4.4582)			7.9778[c] (4.5509)	52 [0.13]
	−0.1017 (0.4372)		11.4341[c] (6.6775)		10.4372[b] (5.1096)	52 [0.04]
	−0.5567 (0.5194)			11.5683 (10.2300)	11.7265[c] (6.2166)	52 [0.04]
Unemployed females 20–24 years old/active females 20–24 years old 1991–2000	−1.7850[b] (0.7247)	18.0146[a] (6.5874)			23.5590[a] (7.6256)	52 [0.21]
	−1.8788[b] (0.7552)		8.7493 (11.6417)		29.2557[a] (10.7692)	52 [0.14]
	−2.3658[a] (0.8754)			12.7964 (16.9366)	28.7286[a] (10.1868)	52 [0.14]
Wages of machine operators/wages of clerks and craft and related trades workers 1990–1999	0.0015 (0.0070)	0.2202 (0.1520)			0.8521[a] (0.0856)	52 [0.07]
	0.0021 (0.0073)		0.0418 (0.1756)		0.9357[a] (0.1056)	52 [0.01]
	−0.0208[c] (0.0110)			0.4084[a] (0.1343)	0.8789[a] (0.0537)	52 [0.15]

a = significant at 1 percent level; b = significant at 5 percent level; c = significant at 10 percent level.

protective collective relations laws (but not others) are associated with a larger unofficial economy, that more protective employment, collective relations, and social security laws lead to lower male (but not female) participation in the labor force, and that more protective employment laws lead to higher unemployment, especially of the young. Finally, there is some evidence that more generous social security systems are associated with higher relative wages of privileged workers. The evidence on the unemployment of the young is most consistent with the political view that the privileged and older incumbents support more stringent labor laws, a finding broadly consistent with other research [Blanchflower and Freeman 2000].

As an additional way to examine enforcement, we divide the sample into countries with per capita income above and below the median, and replicate the analysis in Table VIII. The results hold among the richer, but generally not the poorer, countries. This evidence is consistent with the view that labor laws have adverse consequences in countries where they are more likely to be enforced, namely the richer ones. This evidence sheds further doubt on the efficiency theory, since it confirms the damage from regulation precisely when the laws have a bigger bite.

We also reestimated the regressions in Table VIII with instrumental variables, using legal origins (either just the common law dummy or all of them) as instruments. The results for male labor force participation, and the unemployment rates, particularly of the young, remain statistically significant in most cases, and many coefficients rise in magnitude. The results on the relative wages of privileged and less privileged workers become stronger.

All of this evidence does not provide much support for the efficiency theory, namely that labor regulations cure market failures, although of course it is possible that the adverse outcomes we measure are unavoidable to alleviate capitalist abuse of workers. The results are consistent with the view that legal origins shape regulatory styles, and that such dependence has adverse consequences for at least some measures of efficiency.

VIII. Conclusion

There are three broad theories of government regulation of labor. Efficiency theories hold that regulations adjust to effi-

THE REGULATION OF LABOR   1379

ciently address the problems of market failure. Political theories contend that regulations are used by political leaders to
benefit themselves and their allies. Legal theories hold that the
patterns of regulation are shaped by each country's legal tradition, which is to a significant extent determined by transplantation of a few legal systems. We examined the regulation
of labor markets in 85 countries through the lens of these
theories.

As we indicated, the efficiency theory is difficult to reject,
but we do not find much support for conventional versions. In
particular, we find that heavier regulation of labor has adverse
consequences for labor force participation and unemployment,
especially of the young. There is some support for the view that
countries with a longer history of leftist governments have
more extensive regulation of labor, consistent with the political
theory. There is, finally, strong evidence that the origin of a
country's laws is an important determinant of its regulatory
approach, in labor as well as in other markets. Moreover, legal
origin does not appear to be a proxy for social democracy—its
explanatory power is both independent and significantly
larger. This evidence is broadly consistent with the legal theory, according to which patterns of regulation across countries
are shaped largely by transplanted legal structures.

These results do not mean that efficiency forces in regulation
are unimportant, and indeed our focus on a large sample of
developing countries, as opposed to just the rich ones where the
law evolves more quickly, predisposes our findings against the
efficiency hypothesis. These findings also do not mean that politics is unimportant, and indeed we find evidence that it matters.
Still, the main factor explaining labor laws in our data is legal
origin.

This evidence echoes our earlier results on the regulation of
entry and on the formalism of judicial procedures. Those findings
also showed that countries from different legal origins rely on
different institutional technologies for social control of business.
A key result in the present paper is the high correlation among
our measures of regulation of different activities across countries:
countries that regulate entry also regulate labor markets and
judicial proceedings. The bottom line of this research is the cen-
trality of institutional transplantation: countries have regulatory

1380   *QUARTERLY JOURNAL OF ECONOMICS*

styles that are pervasive across activities and shaped by the
origin of their laws.

YALE UNIVERSITY
THE WORLD BANK
DARTMOUTH COLLEGE AND NATIONAL BUREAU OF ECONOMIC RESEARCH
YALE UNIVERSITY AND NATIONAL BUREAU OF ECONOMIC RESEARCH
HARVARD UNIVERSITY AND NATIONAL BUREAU OF ECONOMIC RESEARCH

REFERENCES

Alesina, Alberto, Arnaud Devleeschauwer, William Easterly, Sergio Kurlat, and
    Romain Wacziarg, "Fractionalization," *Journal of Economic Growth,* VIII
    (2003), 155–194.
Alesina, Alberto, and Edward Glaeser, *Fighting Poverty in the U. S. and Europe:
    A World of Difference* (Oxford, UK: Oxford University Press, 2004).
Alexander, Robert, ed., *Political Parties of the Americas: Canada, Latin America,
    and the West Indies* (Westport, CT: Greewood Press, 1982).
Alvarez, Michael, Jose Cheibub, Fernando Limongi, and Adam Przeworski,
    "ACLP Political and Economic Database Codebook," in *Democracy and De-
    velopment: Political Institutions and Material Well-Being in the World, 1950–
    1990* (Cambridge, UK: Cambridge University Press, 2000).
Autor, David, "Outsourcing at Will: The Contribution of Unjust Dismissal Doc-
    trine to the Growth of Employment Outsourcing," *Journal of Labor Econom-
    ics,* XXI (2003), 1–42.
Barro, Robert, and Jong-Wha Lee, 2000, International Data on Educational At-
    tainment: Updates and Implications, ⟨*http://www.cid.harvard.edu/ciddata/
    ciddata/html*⟩.
Beck, Thorsten, George Clarke, Alberto Groff, Philip Keefer, and Patrick Walsh,
    "New Tools and New Tests in Comparative Political Economy: The Database
    of Political Institutions," *World Bank Economic Review,* XV (2001), 165–176.
Becker, Gary, "A Theory of Competition among Pressure Groups for Political
    Influence," *Quarterly Journal of Economics,* XCVIII (1983), 371–400.
Bertola, Giuseppe, Tito Boeri, and Sandrine Cazes, "Employment Protection in
    Industrialized Countries: The Case for New Indicators," *International Labour
    Review,* CXXXIX (2000), 57–72.
Besley, Timothy, and Robin Burgess, "Can Labor Regulation Hinder Economic
    Performance? Evidence from India," *Quarterly Journal of Economics,* CXIX
    (2003), 91–134.
Blanchflower, David, and Richard Freeman, eds., *Youth Employment and Job-
    lessness in Advanced Countries* (Chicago, IL: University of Chicago Press for
    the NBER, 2000).
Blanpain, Roger, ed., *International Encyclopaedia for Labour Law and Industrial
    Relations* (The Hague, The Netherlands: Kluwer Law International, 1977).
Buchanan, James, and Gordon Tullock, *The Calculus of Consent* (Ann Arbor, MI:
    University of Michigan Press, 1962).
Cahoon, Ben, ed., *Statesmen database,* ⟨*http://www.worldstatesmen.org*⟩.
Chidzero, Anne-Marie, "Senegal," in *The Informal Sector and Microfinance Insti-
    tutions in West Africa,* Leila Webster, and Peter Fidler, eds. (Washington, DC:
    The World Bank, 1996).
Council of Foreign Relations, *Political Handbook of the World* (New York, NY:
    McGraw-Hill Book Co., 1928–1960 and 1963–1970).
Constitution of the Portuguese Republic, ⟨http://oncampus.richmond.edu~jjones//
    confinder/const.htm⟩.
Cox, Tim, and R. Jeffers, eds., *International Handbook on Contracts of Employ-
    ment* (The Hague, The Netherlands: Kluwer Law International: 1988).
Cross-National Time-Series Data Archive, ⟨http://www.databanks.sitehosting.net/⟩.
Deakin, Simon, "The Contract of Employment: A Study in Legal Evolution," ESRC

Centre for Business Research, University of Cambridge Working Paper No. 203, 2001.

Demsetz, Harold, "Toward a Theory of Property Rights," *American Economic Review Papers and Proceedings*, LVII (1967), 347–359.

Djankov, Simeon, Edward Glaeser, Rafael La Porta, Florencio Lopez-de-Silanes, and Andrei Shleifer, "The New Comparative Economics," *Journal of Comparative Economics*, XXXI (2003a), 595–619.

Djankov, Simeon, Rafael La Porta, Florencio Lopez-de-Silanes, and Andrei Shleifer, "The Regulation of Entry," *Quarterly Journal of Economics*, CXVII (2002), 1–37.

Djankov, Simeon, Rafael La Porta, Florencio Lopez-de-Silanes, and Andrei Shleifer, "Courts," *Quarterly Journal of Economics*, CXVIII (2003b), 457–522.

Emulate Me, *Country Reports History*, ⟨http://www.countryreports.org⟩.

Esping-Anderson, Gøsta, *The Three Worlds of Welfare Capitalism* (Princeton, NJ: Princeton University Press, 1990).

——, *Social Foundations of Post-Industrial Economies* (Oxford, UK: Oxford University Press, 1999).

Europa Publications Limited, *Europa Year-Book* (London, UK: Europa Pub. Co., Ltd., 1960–1974).

Finer, Samuel, *The History of Government*, I–III (Cambridge, UK: Cambridge University Press, 1997).

Fonseca, Raquel, Paloma Lopez-Garcia, and Christopher Pissarides, "Entrepreneurship, Start-up Costs and Employment," *European Economic Review*, XLV (2000), 692–705.

Forteza, Alvaro, and Martín Rama, "Labor Market 'Rigidity' and the Success of Economic Reforms: Across More than One Hundred Countries," mimeo, World Bank, 2000.

Frankel, Jeffrey, and David Romer, "Does Trade Cause Growth," *American Economic Review*, LXXXIX (1999), 379–399.

Freeman, Richard, and Remco Oostendorp, "The Occupational Wages around the World: Data File," *International Labor Review*, CXL (2001), 379–402.

Glaeser, Edward, Jose Scheinkman, and Andrei Shleifer, "The Injustice of Inequality," *Journal of Monetary Economics: Carnegie-Rochester Series on Public Policy*, L (2003), 199–222.

Glaeser, Edward, and Andrei Shleifer, "Legal Origins," *Quarterly Journal of Economics*, CXVII (2002), 1193–1230.

Glaeser, Edward, and Andrei Shleifer, "The Rise of the Regulatory State," *Journal of Economic Literature*, XLI (2003), 401–425.

Heckman, James, and Carmen Pagés-Serra, "The Cost of Job Security Regulation: Evidence from Latin American Labor Markets," *Economia*, II (2000), 109–154.

Hicks, Alex, *Social Democracy and Welfare Capitalism* (Ithaca, NY: Cornell University Press, 1999).

Ichniowski, Casey, Richard Freeman, and Harrison Lauer, "Collective Bargaining Laws, Threat Effects, and the Determination of Police Compensation," *Journal of Labor Economics*, VII (1989), 191–209.

International Labor Organization, *Key Indicators of the Labor Market* (Geneva, Switzerland: 1999).

——, *Conditions of Work Digest* (Geneva, Switzerland: 1994 and 1995).

——, *Laborsta*, ⟨http://laborsta.ilo.org⟩.

Jaggers, Keith, and Monty Marshall, *Polity IV Project Dataset*, Center for International Development and Conflict Management, University of Maryland, 2000.

Kapiszewski, Diana, and Alexander Kazan, eds., *Encyclopedia of Latin American Politics* (Westport, CT: Oryx Press, 2002).

Kaple, Deborah, ed., *World Encyclopedia of Political Systems and Parties* (New York, NY: Facts on File, 1999).

Kasnakoglu, Zehra, and Münür Yayla, "Unrecorded Economy in Turkey: A Monetary Approach," in Tuncer Bulutay, ed., *Informal Sector in Turkey*, I (Ankara, Turkey: SIS, 1999).

Krueger, Alan, "The Evolution of Unjust-Dismissal Legislation in the United States," *Industrial and Labor Relations Review*, XLIV (1991), 644–660.

La Porta, Rafael, Florencio Lopez-de-Silanes, and Andrei Shleifer, "What Works in Securities Laws?" mimeo, Harvard University, 2003.

La Porta, Rafael, Florencio Lopez-de-Silanes, Christian Pop-Eleches, and Andrei Shleifer, "Judicial Checks and Balances," *Journal of Political Economy,* CXII (2004), 445–470.

La Porta, Rafael, Florencio Lopez-de-Silanes, Andrei Shleifer, and Robert Vishny, "Legal Determinants of External Finance," *Journal of Finance,* LII (1997), 1131–1150.

La Porta, Rafael, Florencio Lopez-de-Silanes, Andrei Shleifer, and Robert Vishny, "Law and Finance," *Journal of Political Economy,* CVI (1998), 1113–1155.

La Porta, Rafael, Florencio Lopez-de-Silanes, Andrei Shleifer, and Robert Vishny, "The Quality of Government," *Journal of Law, Economics, and Organization,* XV (1999), 222–279.

Lazear, Edward, "Job Security Provisions and Employment," *Quarterly Journal of Economics,* CV (1990), 699–726.

Lewis, D. S., and D. J. Sagar, eds., *Political Parties of Asia and the Pacific: A Reference Guide* (Essex, UK: Longman Current Affairs, 1992).

Marx, Karl, *Das Kapital* (London, UK: Lawrence and Wishart, 1974 [1872]).

Mchale, Vincent, and Sharon Skowronski, eds., *Political Parties of Europe* (Westport, CT: Greenwood Press, 1983).

Mulligan, Casey, and Xavier Sala-i-Martin, "Internationally Common Features of Public Old-Age Pensions, and their Implications for Models of the Public Sector," *Advances in Economic Analysis and Policy,* IV (2004), Article 4.

Mulligan, Casey, and Andrei Shleifer, "Population and Regulation," mimeo, 2003.

Mulligan, Casey, and Andrei Shleifer, "Conscription as Regulation," *American Law and Economics Review,* 2005, forthcoming.

Nicoletti, Giuseppe, and Frederic Pryor, "Subjective and Objective Measures of the Extent of Governmental Regulations," mimeo, OECD Economics Department, 2001.

Nicoletti, Giuseppe, Stefano Scarpetta, and Olivier Boylaud, "Summary Indicators of Product Market Regulation with and Extension to Employment Protection Legislation," OECD Working Paper No. 226, 1999.

North, Douglass, *Growth and Structural Change in Economic History* (New York, NY: Norton, 1981).

Olson, Mancur, *The Logic of Collective Action* (Cambridge, MA: Harvard University Press, 1965).

——, "Dictatorship, Democracy, and Development," *American Political Science Review,* LXXXVII (1993), 567–576.

Pagano, Marco, and Paolo Volpin, "The Political Economy of Corporate Governance," CEPR Discussion Paper No. 2682, 2001.

Posner, Richard, "Theories of Economic Regulation," *Bell Journal of Economics and Management Science,* V (1974), 335–358.

Roe, Mark, "Political Preconditions to Separating Ownership from Corporate Control," *Stanford Law Review,* LIII (2000), 539–606.

Sananikone, Ousa, "Burkina Faso" in Leila Webster and Peter Fidler, eds., *The Informal Sector and Microfinance Institutions in West Africa* (Washington, DC: The World Bank, 1996).

Schemmel, B., *Rulers database,* ⟨http://rulers.org/⟩.

Schneider, Friedrich, and Dominik Enste, "Shadow Economies: Size, Causes, and Consequences," *Journal of Economic Literature,* XXXVIII (2000), 77–114.

Stigler, George, "The Theory of Economic Regulation," *Bell Journal of Economics and Management Science,* II (1971), 3–21.

Turnham, David, Bernard Salome, and Antoine Schwartz, *The Informal Sector Revisited* (Paris, France: OECD, 1990).

United Nations, *Human Development Report* (New York, NY: Oxford University Press, 1994, 1997).

United Nations Human Settlements Programme, *Global Urban Indicator Database,* 2000 ⟨http://www.unhsp.org/programmes/guo/⟩.

U. S. Social Security Administration, *Social Security Programs Throughout the World* (Washington, DC: SSA, 1999), http://www.ssa.gov/.

World Bank, *World Development Indicators* (Washington, DC: The World Bank, 2001).

Zweigert, Konrad, and Hein Kotz, *Introduction to Comparative Law* (Oxford, UK: Oxford University Press, 3rd revised edition, 1998).

Part II
The Economics of American Labor Law

[2]

Some Economics of Labor Law

Richard A. Posner†

The law governing employment is of vast compass. Among the subjects it embraces are racial and sexual discrimination in employment, the liability of an employer ("master") for the torts of his employees ("servants"), the regulation of occupational health and safety, employees' rights under the pension-regulation law (ERISA), the emerging tort of wrongful discharge of an employee at will, and much else besides. But, to lawyers anyway, the most important subject in the law of employment, as measured by the number of cases, the density of legal doctrine, and other measures of legal activity, remains—even in a period of union decline—the regulation by the National Labor Relations Board of the process by which unions seek to bargain collectively on behalf of workers.[1] This regulation is conducted under the authority of the National Labor Relations Act,[2] which is the Wagner Act of 1935,[3] as amended, principally by the Taft-Hartley Act of 1947.[4] When I use the term "labor law" in this paper, I shall, unless otherwise indicated, be referring to this regulatory scheme, even though properly speaking it is just a part of a much larger field.

Whether defined broadly or, as I am doing, narrowly, labor law is as natural a field for the application of economics to law as one could imagine. It regulates explicit markets that have been a subject of continuous and fruitful economic study since Adam Smith's

---

† Judge, United States Court of Appeals for the Seventh Circuit; Senior Lecturer, University of Chicago Law School. This is the revised text of a paper given on April 27, 1984, at the Symposium on the Conceptual Foundations of Labor Law, held at the University of Chicago Law School, sponsored jointly with the Social Philosophy and Policy Center of Bowling Green State University. The author is grateful to William Landes, Douglas Leslie, Michael Lindsay, Bernard Meltzer, Melvin Reder, Ronald Schy, George Stigler, and James Talent for many helpful comments on a previous draft of this paper.

[1] Regulation by the NLRB is subject to review by the federal courts of appeals, 29 U.S.C. § 160(e) (1982), and on writ of certiorari by the Supreme Court, 28 U.S.C. § 1254 (1982).

[2] 29 U.S.C. §§ 151-169 (1982).

[3] Pub. L. No. 74-198, 49 Stat. 449 (1935) (codified as amended at 29 U.S.C. §§ 151-169 (1982)).

[4] Labor-Management Relations Act, Pub. L. No. 80-101, 61 Stat. 136 (1947) (codified as amended at 29 U.S.C. §§ 141-197 (1982)).

day.[5] And though in recent years the focus of labor economics has shifted from unions to other phenomena of labor markets,[6] such as human capital and employment discrimination, there is a rich—and reviving—contemporary literature on the economics of unions.[7] Moreover, as I shall argue in this paper, a well-developed field of economic analysis outside of labor economics—the economic analysis of cartels—can yield to the student of the legal regulation of unionizing many insights.

Yet despite abundant opportunity, there has been relatively little writing in an economic vein about the particulars of labor law, especially—and especially surprisingly—of labor law as I am narrowly defining it.[8] There are, I conjecture (a word used advisedly), two reasons for this situation. The first is that because labor law is doctrinally complex (much more so than antitrust, the economists' favorite field of law), economists have not found it accessible in the way they have found antitrust law, and more recently

---

[5] For a summary of the economics of labor, see R. EHRENBERG & R. SMITH, MODERN LABOR ECONOMICS: THEORY AND PUBLIC POLICY (1982); *see also* THE ECONOMICS OF TRADE UNIONS: NEW DIRECTIONS (J. Rosa ed. 1984); F. MARSHALL, A. KING & V. BRIGGS, LABOR ECONOMICS: WAGES, EMPLOYMENT, AND TRADE UNIONISM (4th ed. 1980). A notable contribution, highly pertinent to the theme of this article, is MANCUR OLSON, THE LOGIC OF COLLECTIVE ACTION 66-97 (1965). The current periodical literature is well-illustrated by Lazear, *A Competitive Theory of Monopoly Unionism*, 73 AM. ECON. REV. 631 (1983).

[6] *See* Johnson, *Economic Analysis of Trade Unionism*, 65 AM. ECON. REV. PAPERS & PROC. 23 (May 1975).

[7] *See, e.g.,* NEW APPROACHES TO LABOR UNIONS (J. Reid ed.) (Research in Labor Economics Supp. 2, 1983); ALBERT REES, THE ECONOMICS OF TRADE UNIONS (2d rev. ed. 1977); sources cited *supra* notes 5-6.

[8] Some exceptions to this generalization should be noted. There is an economically informed literature on the application of the antitrust laws to the union activities that are not exempt from those laws. *See, e.g.,* Leslie, *Right to Control: A Study in Secondary Boycotts and Labor Antitrust*, 89 HARV. L. REV. 904 (1976); Meltzer, *Labor Unions, Collective Bargaining, and the Antitrust Laws*, 32 U. CHI. L. REV. 659 (1965). There is, of course, an extensive economic literature on the effects of laws regulating wages and hours, industrial health and safety, and employment discrimination. Wrongful discharge is a new area of labor law that has received interesting economic treatment recently. *See* Epstein, *In Defense of the Contract at Will*, 51 U. CHI. L. REV. 947 (1984); Harrison, *The "New" Terminable-at-Will Employment Contract: An Interest and Cost Incidence Analysis*, 69 IOWA L. REV. 327 (1984). But economic analyses of specific provisions of the National Labor Relations Act appear to be rare, although I do not pretend to have made a complete search of the literature. I have found a few brief analyses of such provisions by economists. *See* JACK HIRSHLEIFER, PRICE THEORY AND APPLICATIONS 380-82 (3d ed. 1984); Alchian, *Decision Sharing and Expropriable Specific Quasi-Rents: A Theory of First National Maintenance Corporation v. NLRB*, 1 S. CT. ECON. REV. 235 (1982). Some contributions of economically minded lawyers are cited *infra* notes 9 & 21. The legal community is not unaware of the economic literature on unions—quite the contrary. *See, e.g.,* BERNARD D. MELTZER, LABOR LAW: CASES, MATERIALS, AND PROBLEMS 37-94 (2d ed. 1977). But for the most part that literature has not yet been brought to bear on particular provisions of the NLRA.

tort law, accessible. The second reason is that because labor law is (as we shall see) founded on a policy that is the opposite of the policies of competition and economic efficiency that most economists support, the field is unlikely to attract, as a subject for teaching and scholarship, the lawyer who is deeply committed to economic analysis; it is likely to repel him. Of course, you don't have to agree with the normative premises of a field to find it a worthwhile subject for teaching and scholarship. But the fact is—I suppose it reflects the lawyer's training in advocacy—that it is rare for a law professor to make a sustained commitment to a field for whose premises he feels no sympathy at all.

Nevertheless, and somewhat ironically since unions have been in decline in the United States, England, and other countries in recent years, the last few months have seen the appearance of several interesting papers in which economic analysis is brought to bear (in very different ways) on specific problems of labor law in my narrow sense of the term.[9]

One task I have set myself in this paper is simply to make labor law less mysterious to economists, in the hope that they will be encouraged to overcome a natural resistance to immersion in complex legal doctrine. I shall begin therefore with a brief sketch of the American system of labor law and then propose a simple economic model of that system. My basic thesis will be that American labor law is best understood as a device for facilitating, though not to the maximum possible extent, the cartelization of the labor supply by unions. Lest this seem an impolitic (especially for a judge) condemnation of the union movement, I emphasize that I am using the word "cartelization" in a nonpejorative, technical sense: it is the cooperative endeavor of competing sellers to raise the prices of their goods or services (here labor services) above the level that would prevail under conditions of unregulated competition. I take no position on whether it is socially preferable for the price of labor to be determined on a competitive or on a cartelized basis. My analysis is positive, not normative.

---

[9] *See* Epstein, *A Common Law for Labor Relations: A Critique of the New Deal Labor Legislation*, 92 YALE L.J. 1357 (1983) [hereinafter cited as Epstein, *Common Law*]; Epstein, *Agency Costs, Employment Contracts, and Labor Values*, in THE AGENCY RELATIONSHIP (J. Pratt & R. Zeckhauser eds. forthcoming); Leslie, *Labor Bargaining Units*, 70 VA. L. REV. 353 (1984). Professor Epstein's papers sound themes very similar to those that I develop in this paper. It may be significant that neither of us is a specialist in labor law.

I. AMERICAN LABOR LAW

Professor Richard Epstein has conducted a very useful survey of the position of the common law with regard to labor unions.[10] Although that position is typically and not inaccurately described as "anti-union," Professor Epstein shows that it could just as well be called "pro-competitive," or, as some economic analysts of the common law would have it, "pro-efficiency."[11] At common law, labor unions were recognized for what they were: worker cartels designed to raise the price of labor above the competitive level.[12] Picketing, too, was recognized for what it was: an attempt to interfere, by means inherently intimidating, with contractual relationships between the picketed firm and its customers and suppliers, including new workers hired to replace the strikers.[13] So-called "yellow dog" contracts (under which workers agreed not to join unions during the term of their employment) were enforced on the assumption, congenial to classical economic thinking, that the worker was compensated for giving up his right to join a union.[14] If he was not *generously* compensated, that was nothing to worry about; compensation for not combining with other workers to create a labor monopoly is itself a form of monopoly rent.

It can of course be argued that this picture of an efficient common law of labor relations rests on unrealistic premises about the nature of labor markets, especially in the years prior to the revolution in labor law brought about by the Wagner Act in 1935. If many workers were ignorant of their alternative employment opportunities, wages would frequently have been below the competitive level. If many workers (especially, perhaps, older workers) would have incurred heavy costs by changing jobs, maybe because they had become specialized to a particular employer's methods or had developed close social and family ties to a particular community or region, employers would have monopsony power, and the workers might be paid less than a competitive wage.[15] If, as Adam Smith believed, conspiracies among employers to depress wages

---

[10] *See* Epstein, *Common Law, supra* note 9, at 1358-86.

[11] This finding provides additional support for the thesis, which I have expounded elsewhere, that the common law is on the whole efficiency-promoting. *See, e.g.,* RICHARD A. POSNER, ECONOMIC ANALYSIS OF LAW 25-191 (2d ed. 1977).

[12] *See* SELIG PERLMAN, A HISTORY OF TRADE UNIONISM IN THE UNITED STATES 147 (1922).

[13] *See, e.g.,* Vegelahn v. Guntner, 167 Mass. 92, 97-98, 44 N.E. 1077, 1081 (1896).

[14] *See generally* Epstein, *Common Law, supra* note 9, at 1370-75, 1382-85.

[15] This description is not wholly accurate; the situation would be one of bilateral monopoly since specialization would also tend to give the workers monopoly power.

were common,[16] this would be another source of monopsony power.

These conditions *may* have been common in the nineteenth and early twentieth centuries in this country, when there were low levels of worker education, a great deal of immigrant labor, a limited number of employers in some markets, no serious enforcement of antitrust laws against employer cartels, and some obstacles to labor mobility (though Americans have always moved around a lot).[17] But against all this must be set the facts that in the great era of immigration between the Civil War and the end of unrestricted immigration after World War I, America had a chronic labor shortage, which was the main reason for the great immigration; that wages were much higher in the United States than in the rest of the world; and that competition for workers must have been intense and should have limited the extent of monopsony power in labor markets.[18]

Even assuming that American labor markets were substantially distorted from the competitive norm in ways that unions might have alleviated,[19] by 1935 these distortions must have been largely in the past (they certainly have a quaint ring today). But whether economically justified or not, the Wagner Act brought about a revolution in the American law of labor relations. The common law was displaced by a system of federal regulation administered by a new agency, the National Labor Relations Board, and designed—as its sponsors and supporters made clear[20] and as is anyway obvious from the structure of the Act—to foster unionization. In the Taft-Hartley Act in 1947, Congress redressed the Wagner Act's tilt toward unions somewhat. Legislative and judicial

---

[16] ADAM SMITH, THE WEALTH OF NATIONS 66-67 (Mod. Lib. reprint 1937, E. Cannan ed. 1904) (1st ed. London 1776).

[17] *See generally* DON D. LESCOHIER, 3 HISTORY OF LABOR IN THE UNITED STATES, 1896-1932, at 15-47, 293-302 (1935).

[18] *Id.*

[19] But not cured: the negotiations between monopolistic unions and monopsonistic employers, a situation of classic bilateral monopoly, will result in fewer employees than under competition because both sides are trying to restrict the supply of labor. *Cf.* GEORGE J. STIGLER, THE THEORY OF PRICE 207-08 (3d ed. 1966).

[20] *See, e.g.,* 78 CONG. REC. 3443 (1934) (statement of Sen. Wagner); 78 CONG. REC. 3679 (1934) (address by Sen. Wagner); *Hearings on S. 2926: Hearings Before the Senate Comm. on Education and Labor,* 73d Cong., 2d Sess. 59 (1934) (statement of Dr. Sumner Slichter, Professor of Economics, Harvard Business School, and William Green, President, AFL); 79 CONG. REC. 267 (1935) (address by Donald Richberg, Executive Director, National Emergency Council); *Hearings on S. 1958: Hearings Before Senate Comm. on Education and Labor,* 74th Cong., 1st Sess. 151 (1935) (statement of Charlton Ogburn, counsel for AFL), *reprinted in* 1 NLRB LEGISLATIVE HISTORY OF THE NATIONAL LABOR RELATIONS ACT OF 1935, at 15, 20, 95-99, 1291-92, 1531 (1949).

innovation since 1947 has greatly expanded the scope of labor law, so that today, as I said at the outset, it extends beyond the regulation of union-organizing activities to embrace the internal governance of unions, racial and other discrimination in labor markets, the regulation of pension plans, and much else besides. But the core of modern labor law remains the NLRB's regulation, under the Wagner Act as amended by the Taft-Hartley Act, of unions' efforts to organize employees and bargain with the employers on their behalf.[21]

Rather than attempt to summarize the relevant statutory provisions and interpretive doctrines, I will try to convey the essential features of the NLRB's regulation through a description of the process of union organizing and bargaining as it might occur in a small industrial plant.[22] The process begins with an employee of a union ("business agent," he is usually called) approaching a friendly employee of the plant (sometimes the plant employee initiates the contact) and giving him union authorization cards to hand out to his fellow employees; when signed, these cards authorize the union to represent the employees who sign them.[23] The importance of union authorization cards lies in the fact that if a majority of the workers in the bargaining unit (of which more presently) sign them, the employer may decide to recognize the union as the workers' exclusive representative for collective bar-

---

[21] Two other statutes complete the core: the Norris-LaGuardia Act, 29 U.S.C. §§ 101-115 (1982), which among other things greatly restricts the authority of the federal courts to issue injunctions in labor cases, and the Railway Labor Act, 45 U.S.C. §§ 151-188 (1982), which imposes a form of compulsory arbitration on the railroad and airline industries. Compulsory arbitration is also a common legal regime for labor relations in the public sector, which is exempt from the federal labor laws and will not be discussed in this paper, in part because it is already the subject of a rich, and economically well-informed, literature. *See, e.g.,* H. WELLINGTON & R. WINTER, THE UNIONS AND THE CITIES (1971); Meltzer & Sunstein, *Public Employee Strikes, Executive Discretion, and the Air Traffic Controllers,* 50 U. CHI. L. REV. 731, 738-44 (1983). On the economics of compulsory arbitration, see Ashenfelter & Bloom, *Models of Arbitrator Behavior: Theory and Evidence,* 74 AM. ECON. REV. 111 (1984).

[22] The reader who wants greater detail and citations to cases is advised to begin with ROBERT A. GORMAN, BASIC TEXT ON LABOR LAW: UNIONIZATION AND COLLECTIVE BARGAINING (1976). This is a lucid, compact, and relatively nontechnical introduction to the field. No extensive knowledge of law is required to be able to read it with understanding and profit. Also very good and more up-to-date, though longer, is the two-volume THE DEVELOPING LABOR LAW (C. Morris 2d ed. 1983). For a brief, serviceable description of the federal labor statutes for nonlawyers, see F. MARSHALL, A. KING & V. BRIGGS, *supra* note 5, at 426-52.

[23] *See* R. GORMAN, *supra* note 22, at 41. The reason the business agent will work through one or more plant employees, rather than distribute the cards himself, is that the Board allows the employer to forbid union solicitation on his premises. The Board's position rests on the practical ground that a stranger's presence on the premises can disrupt work discipline and in some cases can be a hazard to the employees' safety.

gaining without the formality of a representation election.[24] More important, if at least thirty percent of the workers sign authorization cards and the employer refuses to recognize the union, the Board will order a representation election.[25]

The efforts of an employee to induce his fellows to sign union authorization cards would often, in the absence of legal protection or of successful concealment by the employee of his activities, be set at naught by the employer's firing him. This would be an example of rational predatory action.[26] It is true that the employer would impose a cost on himself by firing the worker, assuming that he was a satisfactory worker (and if he were not, he probably would have been fired already). But the cost would be small compared with the benefit to the employer of signaling to the remaining employees that if any one of them stepped forward to take the place of the fired employee as the union's organizer, he would be fired too. True, if the workers hung together and struck in support of the fired employee, the balance of costs would be altered and the employer might back down. But since the workers would be unorganized (for I am speaking of how an employer might try to thwart an organizational drive), a strike might be difficult to arrange: the workers would face classic free-rider problems. Those problems, however, should not be exaggerated. There were independent unions (as well as "company unions," which the Wagner Act forbade[27]) long before the Wagner Act was passed.[28] But the fraction of workers who were unionized rose very rapidly after the Act was passed, and this is some evidence that it was indeed difficult to organize workers without the protections that the Act extended to union-organizing efforts.

The key protections are in the sections of the Act that entitle employees to engage in concerted activities and that make it unlawful for the employer to interfere with those activities.[29] Firing an employee because he is trying to organize the plant presents a

---

[24] *See id.* at 230.

[25] *See* 29 C.F.R. § 101.18(a) (1983).

[26] For an alternative characterization, see *infra* notes 52-55 and accompanying text.

[27] *See* National Labor Relations Act § 8(a)(2), 29 U.S.C. § 158(a)(2) (1982).

[28] For an interesting, if dated, treatment of independent unions, see S. PERLMAN, *supra* note 12. Incidentally, chapter 7 contains some interesting discussion of common law attitudes toward labor unions.

[29] *See* National Labor Relations Act §§ 7-8, 29 U.S.C. §§ 157-58 (1982); *see also* Inter-Collegiate Press v. NLRB, 486 F.2d 837, 845 (8th Cir. 1973) ("Conduct having even a 'comparatively slight' impact on employee rights may be a violation of § 8(a)(3), unless the employer has established a legitimate and substantial business justification." (citation omitted)).

clear case of unlawful interference, as do much milder forms of retaliation—even something as trivial as not inviting the employee to
a company party.[30] The employer is thus denied the natural advantage that he would have, as one facing many, in fending off organizing activities. In addition, "yellow dog" contracts are forbidden by section 3 of the Norris-LaGuardia Act.[31]

Let us assume that the union organizer has gotten signatures
from thirty percent of the employees. The next step chronologi-
cally is the election campaign, but before getting to that I must
pause briefly to discuss the electoral unit, or the "bargaining unit"
as it is called. It is not a synonym for the firm, or even for the
plant. Rather, it is any group of employees that the Board decides
is sufficiently homogeneous, and sufficiently distinct from other
employees, to be allowed to form its own bargaining unit.[32]
Ordinarily, though not always, the unit will be limited to one plant
even if the firm owns other plants as well. Often there will be more
than one unit in the plant or facility. For example, a single hospital, whether or not part of a chain, might contain separate units for
doctors, for registered nurses, for nurses' aides and other maintenance employees, and perhaps for technical employees such as X-
ray technicians. The Board's discretion in determining the appropriate bargaining unit for a particular type of firm is broad, but
there are some restrictions on it; most important, the Taft-Hartley
Act denies protected status to supervisory employees, from fore-
men on up, unless their supervisory responsibilities are incidental
(e.g., a doctor supervising his secretary).[33]

Only one question is put to the electorate—the members of
the bargaining unit—in the representation election: whether to
make the union that is trying to organize the unit the exclusive
agent of the unit employees for purposes of bargaining with the
employer over wages and working conditions.[34] The outcome of the
election is determined by majority vote of the employees in the
unit, voting by secret ballot.[35] The election is preceded by a campaign that in some ways is like a political campaign. But it is
shorter, and the voting is on whether to unionize rather than on
candidates for office. Furthermore, the contending parties—union

---

[30] *See* NLRB v. Village IX, Inc., 723 F.2d 1360, 1366-67 (7th Cir. 1983).
[31] 29 U.S.C. § 103 (1982).
[32] *See* National Labor Relations Act § 9(b), 29 U.S.C § 159(b) (1982).
[33] *See id.* (as amended by Taft-Hartley Act) §§ 2(3), 2(11), 7, 29 U.S.C. §§ 152(3), 152(11), 157 (1982).
[34] *See id.* § 9(a), 29 U.S.C. § 159(a) (1982).
[35] *See id.* § 9(c)(1), 29 U.S.C. § 159(c)(1) (1982).

and employer—are more limited in what they are allowed to say than are candidates and supporters in political elections: not only must the employer refrain from firing union adherents or otherwise interfering with the union's campaign, but he may not threaten retaliation if the union wins or promise specific benefits if the union loses;[36] promises of benefits if the candidate wins are of course a staple of true political campaigns.

If the union loses a valid representation election, the Board will not direct another election for a year,[37] and then only if the union again gets at least thirty percent of the employees to sign union authorization cards.[38] If the union wins the election the consequences are more complicated. First, all the employees in the bargaining unit, whether or not they voted for the union and whether or not they want to belong to it, are forbidden to bargain individually with the employer;[39] the union is as much the exclusive bargaining representative of the dissenters as of the employees who voted for it. Second, all the employees, again regardless of their personal sympathies, must, if the collective-bargaining agreement between the employer and the union so provides (and it is a provision for which unions press very hard in negotiations), pay union dues and often must actually join the union.[40] Third, the employer must negotiate with the union in good faith for a collective-bargaining agreement that will specify the terms and conditions of employment of the members of the unit[41] for a specified period, usually one to three years.

But the employer is not required to yield to the union's demands even in part (which makes one wonder whether the duty to bargain in good faith has much bite), and often he will not. In that event the union may decide to call a strike in an effort to win at least partial agreement to its demands. If it does not call a strike, even though the employer has made no significant concessions to its demands, the union may lose the workers' support: they will see that they are getting nothing in exchange for union dues that are

---

[36] *See* NLRB v. Exchange Parts Co., 375 U.S. 405, 409 (1964) ("We have no doubt that [the NLRA] prohibits not only intrusive threats and promises but also conduct immediately favorable to employees which is undertaken with the express purpose of impinging upon their freedom of choice for or against unionization and is reasonably calculated to have that effect.").

[37] *See* National Labor Relations Act § 9(c)(3), 29 U.S.C. § 159(c)(3) (1982).

[38] *See* 29 C.F.R. § 101.18(a) (1983).

[39] *See* National Labor Relations Act § 9(a), 29 U.S.C. § 159(a) (1982).

[40] *See* NLRB v. General Motors Corp., 373 U.S. 734, 740-44 (1963).

[41] *See* National Labor Relations Act § 8(d), 29 U.S.C. § 158(d) (1982).

not trivial.

The economic function of the strike requires consideration at this point. It is related to the bilateral-monopoly character of labor-management negotiations. When a nonlabor market becomes cartelized, members of the cartel raise their price and, anticipating some substitution away from their product by consumers, reduce output, but not to zero. But if there were only one consumer for the cartel's product, he might say to the cartel, "I won't buy from you at the higher price," and they would then face the choice of either backing down or not selling to him. This happens occasionally in nonlabor markets, but in labor markets it happens often. The union deals with a single employer (or several employers bargaining as one in a multi-employer bargaining unit), who may be tempted to refuse to accept the union's demands (i.e., may threaten to buy nothing rather than come to terms), and then the union must either strike in order to enforce its terms or else back down. The union cannot just write off this "customer" as marginal, as a product monopolist often can when he raises his price; for each employer's work force will be represented by its own local union (often more than one), and if the union ignores the workers' interests they will vote the union out and the employer will be free to go his own way. Thus we have a classic example of bilateral monopoly: the union and employer can deal only with each other and a refusal to deal, by imposing costs on the other party, makes him more likely to come to terms. The strike imposes costs on both parties: on the employer, by forcing him to reduce or cease production, and on the workers, by stopping their wages. The balance of those costs will determine the ultimate settling point between the union's initial demand and the employer's initial offer.

Labor law affects these costs. For example, the Board allows the employer, if there is a strike, to hire replacements for the striking workers.[42] He is even allowed to offer the replacement workers permanent jobs—and to do so even if such an offer would not be necessary to induce them to work for him. It would never be necessary if the employer were permitted to pay a wage high enough to induce a replacement to work temporarily, without promise of a permanent job. But the employer is not permitted to pay replacement workers a higher wage than he paid the workers who have struck. This rule shifts the balance the other way; it limits the em-

---

[42] *See* NLRB v. Mackay Radio & Tel. Co., 304 U.S. 333, 345 (1938) ("Nor [is] it an unfair labor practice to replace the striking employes with others in an effort to carry on the business.").

ployer's ability to hire replacements, permanent or temporary.

Although, subject to this qualification, the employer may hire permanent replacements, he may not fire the striking workers who have been replaced.[43] True, unless the strike was provoked by an employer's unfair labor practice, the employer does not have to reinstate all of the strikers as soon as the strike ends or pay any of them their back wages. But when the strike is over, those strikers whose places have been filled by permanent replacements must be put at the head of the queue, to be reinstated as vacancies appear, and those strikers whose places have not been filled must be reinstated immediately.[44]

Attempts to defeat strikes by hiring replacement workers are less common than one might expect; more common is the use of supervisory personnel to replace the striking workers temporarily (hence the importance of the National Labor Relations Act's exclusion of such personnel from the Act's protections). The problem with using replacement workers is that in order to get to the workplace they will have to cross the picket line thrown up by the striking workers' union. Even though picketers are not legally privileged to use force to prevent the crossing of picket lines, whether by replacement workers or by customers or suppliers of the picketed establishment, there is often a latent threat of violence (which cannot, however, be used as a ground for firing or enjoining a picketer[45]), especially against replacement workers ("scabs"). And in pro-union communities the police may not have the desire or ability to control this threat effectively (though they may come down hard on any effort by the employer to hire "goons" to intimidate the picketers). Usually the picketing workers can at the very least identify the replacement workers, who may therefore fear eventual retaliation even if the picketing itself is completely peaceful. Their fear will be enhanced by the Act's provision forbidding the employer to fire striking workers. When the strikers eventually return to work, they will be working side-by-side with the permanent replacements, who may entertain fears for their own safety or at least for the continued congeniality of the workplace.

[43] 29 U.S.C. § 152(3) (1982) preserves the strikers' status as "employees" protected by the NLRA. *See also* NLRB v. Fleetwood Trailer Co., 389 U.S. 375, 378 (1967) ("[U]nless the employer who refuses to reinstate strikers can show that his action was due to 'legitimate and substantial business justifications,' he is guilty of an unfair labor practice." (citation omitted)).

[44] *See* NLRB v. Fleetwood Trailer Co., 389 U.S. 375, 379 (1967).

[45] *See, e.g.,* Chevron U.S.A., Inc. v. NLRB, 672 F.2d 359, 360-61 (3d Cir. 1982); NLRB v. W.C. McQuaide, Inc., 552 F.2d 519, 527-28 (3d Cir. 1977).

If a collective-bargaining contract between union and employer is signed, with or without a strike, it will be judicially enforceable in accordance with a federal common law of collective-bargaining contracts.[46] Often such contracts contain no-strike clauses, and if such a clause is violated, the employer may be able to get an injunction against the strike and an award of damages against the union.[47] Whether or not there is a no-strike clause, a "wildcat" strike—a strike not authorized by the union—is not protected activity if it has a tendency to interfere with the union's role as exclusive bargaining representative;[48] and if a strike is unprotected, the employer can fire the wildcat strikers with impunity.

Unlike an elected public official, a union that is elected to be the collective-bargaining representative of some unit does not serve a fixed term. But upon a showing that the union probably has lost majority support the employer can file an election petition or can refuse to bargain with the union and thus force the union to file such a petition.[49] In such a case the Board will order a new election if at least one year has elapsed since the union was certified as the unit's bargaining representative.[50]

II. Unions as Labor Cartels

Cognoscenti of labor law will recognize the preceding discussion as but a crude thumbnail sketch of the law of collective bargaining. But it will serve to frame an inquiry into the economic logic of that law. My discussion will be illustrative rather than exhaustive: multi-employer bargaining, secondary boycotts, and antitrust restrictions on union activity are among the relevant topics that I have omitted in the interests of time and space.

If unionization is a means of cartelizing labor markets, the National Labor Relations Act, which even with the Taft-Hartley amendments plainly fosters unionization, is likewise a means to cartelize such markets. Economists have long treated unions as labor cartels,[51] though alternative explanations have been ad-

---

[46] Textile Workers Union v. Lincoln Mills, 353 U.S. 448, 456-57 (1957).

[47] Boys Mkts., Inc. v. Retail Clerks' Local 770, 398 U.S. 235, 252-54 (1970).

[48] *See* Emporium Capwell Co. v. Western Addition Community Org., 420 U.S. 50, 70-73 (1975) (unauthorized strike by minority employees to protest discrimination not protected by NLRA).

[49] *See* National Labor Relations Act § 9(e)(1), 29 U.S.C. § 159(e)(1) (1982).

[50] *See id.* § 9(e)(2), 29 U.S.C. § 159(e)(2), (1982).

[51] *See, e.g.,* J. Hirschleifer, *supra* note 8, at 380-82; G. Stigler, *supra* note 19, at 268-70; Friedman, *Some Comments on the Significance of Labor Unions for Economic Policy,* in The Impact of the Union 204 (D. Wright ed. 1951); Lazear, *A Microeconomic Theory of*

vanced.[52] One is that the way in which unions benefit their members is not by reducing the supply of labor (and hence forcing up the price, i.e., wages), but by increasing the productivity of the work force.[53] This they are said to do in various ways. One is by providing a vehicle for collecting, and communicating to the employer, workers' complaints about wages and working conditions.[54] In the absence of such a vehicle, it is argued, workers might be afraid to voice their complaints, and the employer would learn of them only indirectly and belatedly, by observing a higher quit rate. Another example: unions invariably press for inclusion, in any collective-bargaining contracts that they negotiate, of a provision forbidding management to fire workers except for good cause, and requiring it, when it lays off workers because of an economic downturn, to lay them off in reverse order of seniority (i.e., juniors first). When such job security is lacking, as is usually the case in nonunion firms, the older, more experienced workers may—it is argued—be reluctant to share their know-how with the younger, newer employees, fearing that if they do the younger employees will then be competing for their jobs. As a result of this reluctance, productivity is thought to suffer.

Although some empirical support has been marshaled for this productivity-enhancement theory of unionization,[55] the theory is extremely hard to accept. It is inconsistent with the fundamental assumption of economics: that people, in this case employers, are rational profit or utility maximizers. Although this assumption may not hold true in all settings, the behavior of business employers towards their employees is one setting where it probably does.

Labor Unions, in NEW APPROACHES TO LABOR UNIONS, *supra* note 7, at 53; Machlup, *Monopolistic Wage Determinations as a Part of the General Problem of Monopoly*, in CHAMBER OF COMMERCE OF THE UNITED STATES, ECONOMIC INSTITUTE ON WAGE DETERMINATION AND THE ECONOMICS OF LIBERALISM 49 (1947); Reder, *Unionism, Wages, and Contract Enforcement*, in NEW APPROACHES TO LABOR UNIONS, *supra* note 7, at 27; Simons, *Some Reflections on Syndicalism*, 52 J. POL. ECON. 1, 6-9 (1944); Viner, *The Role of Costs in a System of Economic Liberalism*, in CHAMBER OF COMMERCE OF THE UNITED STATES, *supra*, at 15.

[53] *See, e.g.*, Brown & Medoff, *Trade Unions in the Production Process*, 86 J. POL. ECON. 355 (1978); Freeman, *Individual Mobility and Union Voice in the Labor Market*, 66 AM. ECON. REV. PAPERS & PROC. 361 (1976); Freeman & Medoff, *The Two Faces of Unionism*, 57 PUB. INTEREST 69 (1979); Lester, *Reflections on the "Labor Monopoly" Issue*, 55 J. POL. ECON. 513 (1947); and for an able summary, Leslie, *supra* note 9, at 910-20.

[53] *See, e.g.*, Brown & Medoff, *supra* note 52, at 356-59; Freeman, *supra* note 52, at 365.

[54] *See, e.g.*, Freeman, *supra* note 52, at 366 (unionism is a "market mechanism for imparting information, aggregating preferences, [and] altering authority relations"); *see also* Freeman & Medoff, *supra* note 52, at 70-74.

[55] *See* Brown & Medoff, *supra* note 52, at 362-69; Freeman & Medoff, *supra* note 52, at 78-87.

If granting his employees tenure will increase their productivity, the rational employer will do so, for this will reduce his costs of production. Even if the whole productivity gain is paid to the employee in the form of a higher wage, the employer will be better off. He will have lower total costs than his competitors and will therefore be able to expand his output relative to theirs and increase his profits. Even if only a single employer in a competitive industry tumbled to the advantages of granting tenure, competition would force the others to follow suit.[56] And so with encouraging workers to complain rather than waiting for them to quit: the rational employer will encourage them to complain, by cash rewards or whatever it takes, if worker turnover is costly to him.

The proposition that unions enhance productivity also flies in the face of massive, if unsystematic, evidence pointing to the opposite conclusion. Featherbedding seems a more common attribute of unionized than of nonunionized work forces (at least in the private sector); many industries that are heavily unionized are notable for their low productivity; and for every older worker whom job security encourages to share his know-how, casual observation suggests that there is at least one other older worker, and probably several, whom job security protects at the expense of a more efficient younger worker. Most important of all, for many generations now employers have expended substantial resources to prevent unionization of their plants—expenditures that would be irrational if it were true that unions enhanced labor productivity. Such *persistent* irrationality by American businessmen is very hard to credit, but it is a proposition entailed by the productivity-enhancement theory of unionization.

It seems far more plausible to assume that the intended and actual effect of unionization is to raise the price of labor above the competitive level, and to depress the supply of labor below the competitive level, in the unionized sector (about twenty percent of the American work force is unionized[57]). This view not only is commonsensical but explains a wide range of phenomena. It explains the support of unions for the minimum wage, which has the effect of raising the price of substitute nonunion labor, and for government regulation of workplace safety, which reduces competition from nonunion employers. It also explains the pattern of unioniza-

---

[56] These points are neglected by Freeman & Medoff, *supra* note 52, at 91-93, in their attempt to explain management opposition to independent unions.

[57] BUREAU OF THE CENSUS, U.S. DEPT. OF COMMERCE, STATISTICAL ABSTRACT OF THE UNITED STATES 408 (103d ed. 1982-1983).

tion in the American economy, which is about what one would predict from differences in the ability to cartelize the labor supply in different industries. Thus we predict that we will find, and do find, the most effective unions in industries where competition among employers is weak (often because of government regulation), the cost of the organized work force is a small part of the employer's total costs, and the employer produces a nonstorable commodity, so that a strike will impose heavy costs on him. Excellent examples of all three factors (all of which are different aspects of labor-supply inelasticity) are found in the airline pilots' union before the deregulation of the airline industry and in the railroad industry in its heyday, where unionization took hold long before government came directly to its aid. Finally, as we will now see, the cartel theory of unionization explains better than any alternative theory the dominant features of the regulation of labor relations by the National Labor Relations Board.

The theory of cartels[58] teaches that cartelization of a market is a very difficult, perhaps hopeless, endeavor if there are a large number of competitors. And that is the typical situation in labor markets. It is not only that the work force of all but the smallest employers will contain far more members than has been thought the limit for effective cartelization without government assistance (a critical qualification in the present context, obviously); in addition, the relevant market includes workers employed by other firms (or unemployed) who, for a slightly higher wage, would go to work for an employer facing a strike.

These workers are an important part of the relevant market. In the theory of cartels, potential entrants are important only when the number of firms actually selling in the market—a number corresponding in the labor market to the number of employees actually selling their services to the employer in question—is small. If the number of significant firms is large (the qualification being added to exclude the case where a few firms have most of the sales and there is an unimportant fringe of tiny firms), cartelization probably will fail because each firm can expand its output and will be irresistibly tempted to do so if others reduce their output. (If none could expand its output, then a reduction in output by even a single firm would push the market price above the competi-

---

[58] For a discussion of the theory of cartels, see RICHARD A. POSNER, ANTITRUST LAW: AN ECONOMIC PERSPECTIVE 39-77 (1976); GEORGE J. STIGLER, THE ORGANIZATION OF INDUSTRY 39-63 (1968); McGee, *Ocean Freight Rate Conferences and the American Merchant Marine*, 27 U. CHI. L. REV. 191, 196-201 (1960).

tive level because the market's total output would be smaller as a result of that reduction.) Now it is easier for a firm to expand its output than for an individual worker to do so. The firm can add to its work force or to its capital; the individual worker would have to work harder or work longer hours. Of course this is possible within limits, especially for a short time. And a short time may sometimes be good enough: since a strike is costly to the striking workers, keeping the firm operating for a short time may be sufficient to break the strike even if the firm is forced to contract its operations—provided it is not forced to shut down completely. But if the strikers have more staying power than this, their strike may be effective though far fewer than all the workers join it, for the remaining workers may not be able to take up the slack by working harder, or for longer hours, for as long as it would take to break the strike. The strike might last too long for nonstriking workers or supervisors to be able to keep the plant operating and too long for the employer to substitute capital inputs for the labor inputs no longer available to it. In either case the firm's ability to hire replacement workers from other employers or from the pool of unemployed workers could determine the success or failure of the strike.

The large number of potential competitors of the striking workers is such a large obstacle to cartelizing labor markets without governmental assistance that most union-organizing efforts probably would be ineffectual without such assistance, provided the government enforced against unions as against the rest of society the basic laws protecting rights of property, contract, and personal safety (so that unions could not use force or the threat of force to achieve their ends). We now have to consider how the National Labor Relations Act alleviates the large-number problem and in other ways fosters effective if incomplete cartelization of labor markets.

To begin with, through the concept of the employer unfair labor practice, the Act prevents the employer from engaging in the kind of rational predatory activity that, as I suggested earlier, could be used to defeat unionization in its incipient stage. Put differently (for those skeptical of the economic rationality of predatory behavior in any form), the Act prevents competition between two groups of workers: those willing to work for the competitive wage and those willing to devote time to (and take risks in the hope of) obtaining a higher wage through unionization. The employer is forbidden to substitute members of the former group for members of the latter; it is as if a consumer were forbidden to switch his patronage to price cutters.

Next, the Act increases the wealth of unions and thus helps them play their vital role as agents for organizing workers. The union's role corresponds to that of trade associations, exclusive sales agencies, the old railroad rate bureaus, and other institutions for organizing competitors in product markets, but the union is more essential because of the large number of competitors to be organized. The Act, as interpreted by the Board and the courts, helps unions in several ways. It forbids the employer during the union-organizing campaign to offer (or even promise) its workers the higher wages or better fringe benefits that the union has promised to press for. Such an offer, if accepted, would undermine the union by preventing it from recouping the expenses of organizing by collecting union dues. The Act protects unions from another form of free riding by forbidding workers, after the union has been certified as the exclusive bargaining representative, to negotiate separately with the employer and by empowering the union, without regard to the wishes of individual members, to negotiate a provision in the collective-bargaining contract requiring all members of the bargaining unit to pay union dues.[59] Such a provision prevents an individual worker from obtaining the benefits of unionization without paying his share of the costs. Without dues, unions could not function. Indeed, assuming that what unions seek to maximize is their dues income,[60] if there is competition between unions that income will be proportionate to the benefits that the union confers on the workers it represents. The union's income would in any case be much less if a worker could enjoy the benefits conferred by the union without paying any dues.

The devices for preventing free riding on a union's organizing and other activities are very far from being perfect. If an employer, in an effort to discourage a union from organizing his workers, pays a wage that is less than the union scale by a smaller margin than the union's dues—as he can do without violating the Act—both the workers and the employer will be better off than if the union or-

---

[59] The Taft-Hartley Act, however, allows the states to forbid "union security clauses," as they are called, *see* National Labor Relations Act (as amended by Taft-Hartley Act) § 14(b), 29 U.S.C. § 164(b) (1982), and a number of states, disproportionately southern, have taken up this option, *see, e.g.*, ALA. CODE §§ 25-7-30 to -36 (1975); GA. CODE ANN. § 34-6-21 to -28 (1982); MISS. CODE ANN. § 71-1-47 (1972).

[60] There is great debate over just what it is that unions maximize. For a discussion of contending positions, see DONALD L. MARTIN, AN OWNERSHIP THEORY OF THE TRADE UNION 6-30 (1980). Dues maximization seems the natural assumption but is not essential to my analysis.

ganizes the workers. Yet it is only the threat of unionization that enables this benefit to be obtained, and the union receives no compensation for creating it. Furthermore, although every worker must pay union dues once the union has become the collective-bargaining agent for his unit and has negotiated a union security clause with the employer, the union cannot force the workers to honor a strike call[61] (unless they are union members—not just dues-payers—and have not quit the union before crossing the picket line[62]). Much like the fringe firm in a cartelized market, the individual worker may seek the best of both worlds by continuing to work during the strike while hoping that the union will succeed in wresting concessions from the employer so that after the strike the worker's wages will be higher as a result of it. If enough workers think this way, the strike will fail and all the workers may be worse off than if they had joined it. But this is the same phenomenon as occurs when a cartel of product sellers fails because of defections by members of the cartel who think they can have the best of all worlds by free riding. Such failures are common.

What limits the form of free riding that consists of refusing to honor a strike call is a practical sanction that has no counterpart in nonlabor markets. The worker who continues to work during the strike knows that once it is over he will be working side-by-side with the workers who struck (unless all of their places are filled by permanent replacements), and he may fear retaliation in forms difficult to detect and prevent. Even if the strikers have been permanently replaced, the workers who refused to honor the strike will know that the strikers may eventually come back to work because, as noted earlier, the Act puts the strikers at the head of the queue to be hired (technically, reinstated) when vacancies occur. The prospect of eventually finding oneself working side-by-side with the former strikers will not only increase the likelihood that a strike call will be honored by all; it will also, as I mentioned earlier, discourage some new workers from signing on as permanent replacements in the first place, especially since they cannot be paid a higher wage for doing so.

Genuinely peaceful picketing is thus the counterpart in the la-

---

[61] *See* NLRB v. Textile Workers Local 1029, 409 U.S. 213, 215-18 (1972).

[62] There is divided authority on a union's right to prevent an employee from resigning from the union during a strike. *Compare* Pattern Makers' League v. NLRB, 724 F.2d 57 (7th Cir. 1983) (allowing resignation), *cert. granted*, 53 U.S.L.W. 3235 (U.S. Oct. 1, 1984), *and* International Assoc. of Machinists, Local 1414, 270 N.L.R.B. Dec. No. 209 (June 22, 1984) (same), *with* Local 1327, Int'l Ass'n of Machinists v. NLRB, 725 F.2d 1212 (9th Cir. 1984) (prohibiting resignation).

bor setting of the practice (required, for example, in the rail and trucking industries by the Interstate Commerce Act) of pricing in accordance with published tariffs. The published tariff shores up a cartel by enabling competitors to detect cheating on the cartel price immediately. Picketing serves a similar function by enabling the striking workers, corresponding to the members of a cartel who observe the cartel price, to identify any member of the cartel (i.e., any fellow worker) who is cheating by continuing to work during the strike. In this analysis, picketing is not really an informative activity (setting aside the information that is implicit in any threat); it is an information-gathering activity.[63]

The cartel analogy may help explain why unions invariably insist that the collective-bargaining contract provide some form of job security. No doubt, part of the reason is merely to back up the law's prohibition of discrimination against union supporters,[64] but the theory of cartels suggests a further point. An important object of job-security provisions is to obtain preferential treatment for senior workers. Some workers laid off during a business downturn will find other jobs during the period of layoff and not return to their original employer, who will therefore be hiring replacements for them. And just by the workings of chance, these replacements may be less well disposed to the union than those who were laid off and later quit. So the union will want some criterion for the order of layoffs that will ensure so far as possible that those workers who are least likely to favor the union will be laid off first. These are the younger workers.

Much casual observation supports this proposition, but it also has a theoretical basis. Younger workers are more mobile than older ones. The older ones are more likely to have family obligations that make it difficult to relocate geographically, and their

---

[63] This has possible implications for the analysis of the first amendment rights of pickets, but I shall not attempt to develop those implications here.

[64] Besides overt discrimination, employers might find subtle ways of discouraging unionization. For example, workers must differ in their propensity to vote for unions, to go out on strike, and otherwise to engage in cartel-promoting behavior. Therefore, in the absence of contractual job protection, the employer, after discovering that a majority of his workers wanted a union, might discharge some of the workers at random. (I am now assuming that he would not try to discharge solely, or disproportionately, those whom he knew to be union adherents, because that would be clearly unlawful conduct.) His hope would be that the replacement workers might, simply by chance, contain a lower proportion of union supporters, so that he might eventually be able to get the union decertified. Of course this would be a sensible strategy only if the employer thought that union support among his existing work force was above average for his industry, location, etc. The strategy would violate the law, but would be more difficult to detect than the firing of just (or mainly) union supporters.

human capital may have become specialized to the particular job they are doing for their employer (assuming that the older worker, on average, has worked longer for this employer than has the younger worker). Many younger workers are temporary employees, trying out one job after another; some are teenagers working part-time and bound for very different careers. Being less mobile, the older workers are more at the mercy of the employer (like share-holders whose shares are not freely tradable) and therefore have more to gain even in the short run from unionization. They also are more likely to be around to enjoy the benefits that the union generates for the workers in exchange for dues (the collection of dues begins before any of those benefits are realized). True, the younger workers, if they do stick around, will enjoy those benefits longer. But the discount rate applied to benefits from unionization other than those that can be realized in the immediate future must be high, not because workers are short-sighted, but because the union may be decertified or the plant closed before the benefits are realized. An additional point is that, at least in jobs that require strength or stamina, older workers may be less productive than younger workers, with whom—but for union-negotiated seniority protection—the older workers would be competing.

If this analysis is right, then by requiring the younger workers to be laid off first, the union is less likely to lose union adherents than if layoffs were random with respect to age. Moreover, they would never be random. The employer not confined by a collective-bargaining agreement would want to lay off the least productive workers first. They are likely to be disproportionately older and in any event disproportionately pro-union, for it is the least productive employees (whatever the reason why they are least productive) who fare the worst if wages are determined on a competitive basis.

This analysis also explains why unions want employers to use seniority to determine the order of layoffs even though productivity might be maximized, to the mutual benefit of employer and employees, if the union allowed the employer to choose whom to lay off in return for the generous compensation of any older worker laid off. Even if senior workers were made whole, there would still be a disadvantage from the union's standpoint: some of those laid off would find other jobs and therefore not return to their original employer when the layoff ended, and they would be replaced by younger workers less likely to support the union. Finally, we should note that a seniority rule, by making the employer's work force less mobile (senior workers have more to lose from quitting), generates additional support for the union.

Another important factor facilitating or retarding the organization of a plant or other facility is the determination of the bargaining unit (the electoral unit for the representation election). In general, the larger the unit the better off the employer is, and the smaller the unit the better off the union is.[65] The larger the unit is—that is, the more employees it has—the more difficult it will be for the union to obtain the majority vote that it needs in order to be designated the exclusive bargaining representative for the unit. This is not only because it takes more resources in absolute terms to get more votes (a national political election is more costly than a local one), but also because the members of the unit are more likely to have divergent interests with respect to tradeoffs among wages, fringe benefits, job security, and workplace safety. This will make it difficult for the union to appeal to a majority and, even if it gets a majority, will make it difficult for the union to formulate a coherent set of demands and enforce those demands by an effective strike threat. This is much like the problem of fixing prices in a producers' cartel when the producers have dissimilar cost functions.

A potentially offsetting factor is that a strike by a small unit may not impose substantial costs on the employer, in which event the union and the workers will gain little (in dues and in wages, respectively) from a successful organizing campaign, even if it is cheap to conduct. But if the unit is small precisely because the workers who comprise it do a different type of work from the other workers in the plant (so that making them a part of a larger unit would result in a heterogeneous unit), it is quite possible that if they go out on strike the plant will have to close down; the work they do, not being duplicated elsewhere in the plant, may well be essential. In addition, a small unit may be large relative to the size of the plant or facility in question. Both points are illustrated by health-care facilities (mainly hospitals and nursing homes), where unions have made great strides since the NLRB's authority was extended to nonprofit health-care facilities in 1974.[66] A hospital may have a small number of employees overall, divided as I noted earlier into several units (doctors, registered nurses, etc.), and a strike by any unit might close the facility down. Since the employer cannot produce for inventory, it will incur very substantial costs from even a short strike. This is why the law requires that

---

[65] *See* R. GORMAN, *supra* note 22, at 67-68.
[66] *See* Health Care Institutions Amendments Act, Pub. L. No. 93-360, 88 Stat. 395 (1974) (codified at 29 U.S.C. §§ 152, 158, 169, 183 (1982)).

unions give ten days' notice of a strike in a health-care facility;[67] it is another example of how current law tempers the pro-union policy introduced by the Wagner Act.

Professor Douglas Leslie has suggested that unions would often be better off with larger units because this would facilitate the mediation of conflicts among subgroups of employees.[68] If you have three local unions in a plant, however, their presidents should be able to negotiate some arrangement for mutual support; it is a negotiation among just three people, which the Coase Theorem suggests should be feasible, though there are possible "trilateral monopoly" problems and additional complications stemming from the fact that they will be negotiating in a representative capacity. But if the negotiation is within a unit, no faction has a representative who can negotiate on its behalf; the costs of negotiation will therefore be (I should think) higher; and if so the probability of unresolved conflict will also be higher. I am therefore led to predict that in periods when the NLRB is dominated by Democrats (whom most union leaders support), the Board will tend to certify smaller bargaining units than in periods when Republicans dominate. This would be a fruitful subject for empirical research.

If I am right in my contention that the National Labor Relations Act is best understood as a means of federal governmental support for the cartelization of the labor supply, this may also illuminate another feature of the Act: the vesting of primary responsibility for enforcing it in an administrative agency, the NLRB, rather than in the courts. Since the Act turned labor policy on its head, transforming a public policy of fostering competitive determination of wages and working conditions into one of fostering cartelization, it was quite sensible for Congress to be concerned that state and federal judges—who after all had largely fashioned the former policy—might resist its inversion. It would have made less sense if all the Act were doing was enhancing labor productivity—though Congress might have feared that the judges would misunderstand that this is what the Act was doing.

All that was years ago, and now there are very few judges, state or federal, who have any emotional or intellectual commitment to competitive labor markets. Although the word "cartelization" has negative overtones (more so, indeed, than in the 1930's, when the Depression was attributed in some quarters to excessive

---

[67] *See* National Labor Relations Act (as amended by Health Care Institutions Amendments Act) § 8(g), 29 U.S.C. § 158(g) (1982).

[68] Leslie, *supra* note 9, at 50.

competition), I am sure that most judges today would agree that if federal labor policy is one of facilitating the cartelization of labor, they should, and without much pain can, use this policy to guide them in reviewing the decisions of the NLRB. The only real difficulty is that with the Taft-Hartley amendments, the National Labor Relations Act no longer evinces a univocal policy of promoting cartelization. Even in its pristine Wagner Act form, the NLRA did not totally embrace such a policy. For example, the Act has since the early days been interpreted to allow employers to replace strikers, and has also been interpreted not to protect concerted activity that involves a danger of physical destruction (e.g., damaging the employer's machinery) or personal injury.[69] The rationale of this exception is not quite so obvious to an economist as it might appear to be. Strikes that destroy much more valuable intangible assets are protected. But there is a difference, and the exception for destruction of tangible assets does limit the power of unions. Destroying intangible assets (business goodwill, customers' time, etc.) usually requires a lengthy strike, which is costly to the workers as well as to the employer, his customers, and his suppliers; equally costly destruction of tangible assets might be accomplished in minutes.

A more ambiguous example of a limitation on the union-promoting policy of the Act (as it has been interpreted) is the requirement that the union get at least thirty percent of the workers in the bargaining unit to sign union authorization cards before a representation election will be ordered. It is not obvious that lowering the threshold would promote unionization. A weak union might get enough signatures to compel an election, then lose it resoundingly and by doing so make it harder for a stronger union to organize the plant subsequently.

But the Taft-Hartley Act did make a difference. Notably, by withholding the protection of federal law from supervisor unions (and as a result there are few such unions and most are powerless), the Act strengthened the hand of employers by enabling them to substitute for strikers other workers less likely than permanent replacements to be intimidated by returning strikers. It also outlawed the closed shop,[70] which is a device that minimizes free rid-

---

[69] *See* NLRB v. Fansteel Metallurgical Corp., 306 U.S. 240, 255 (1939) ("We are unable to conclude that Congress intended to . . . invest those who go on strike with an immunity from discharge for acts of trespass or violence against the employer's property . . . .").

[70] *See* National Labor Relations Act (as amended by Taft-Hartley Act) § 8(b)(2), 29 U.S.C. § 158(b)(2) (1982).

ing on union efforts by requiring the employer to hire from the ranks of those who already belong to the union, thus excluding those who join after the plant has been organized.

But the impact of the Taft-Hartley Act is easily exaggerated, as another example will show. Although the Act made no-strike clauses enforceable by damage suits against unions, it is very hard to see this provision as anti-union. A union doesn't have to agree to such a clause; and if it does, presumably it has been compensated for it. Expanding freedom of contract ought to benefit all parties to a potential transaction. It would be different if the Act allowed "yellow dog" contracts. Those are not contracts between unions and employers but between individual workers and employers and are a device by which employers can exploit the large-numbers problem that complicates unions' organizing efforts. Each worker knows that his signing an agreement with his employer not to strike while he is employed will have little effect on the success of any union organizing efforts in his plant because he is one of many; knowing this, he will sign such an agreement for only a modest consideration. If all or at least most workers think the same way (and why shouldn't they?), the employer will have succeeded in preventing union organizing at his plant for a total cost that may be much less than he would have to pay in higher wages if the plant were organized (provided there is not already in being a strong union that can pay the workers more than the company can pay to induce them not to sign "yellow dog" contracts). The banning of "yellow dog" contracts (accomplished in the Norris-La-Guardia Act a few years before the Wagner Act) not only is a rational component of a labor policy dedicated to facilitating labor cartels but is perfectly consistent with the provision in the Taft-Hartley Act allowing no-strike clauses to be enforced. Indeed, the federal labor laws as a whole appear to have a remarkable consistency and intelligibility when viewed as a legal regime for fostering (though not to the maximum possible extent) the cartelization of labor markets.

[3]

A BARGAINING ANALYSIS OF AMERICAN LABOR LAW AND THE SEARCH FOR BARGAINING EQUITY AND INDUSTRIAL PEACE

*Kenneth G. Dau-Schmidt**

* Professor of Law, Indiana University. B.A. 1978, University of Wisconsin; M.A. 1981, J.D. 1981, Ph.D. (Economics) 1984, University of Michigan. — Ed. I would like to thank Terry Bethel, Chris Bruce, George Cohen, Jerome Culp, Richard Epstein, Don Gjerdingen, Bob Heidt, Lynne Henderson, Barry Hirsch, Perry Hodges, Jason Johnston, Judith Lachman, Julia Lamber, Marc Linder, Bruce Markell, Beverly Moran, Eric Rasmusen, Bob Rasmussen, Stu Schwab, Jeff Stake, Ted St. Antoine, Randall Thomas, Lea Vander Velde, and the members of the Indiana, Iowa, and Vanderbilt Law School faculty colloquia for useful comments on prior drafts of this article. I would also like to thank Stephan Carol and Carl Greci for valuable research assistance. This paper was presented June 29, 1991 at the Annual Meeting of the Law and Society Association, Amsterdam, Netherlands; May 15, 1992 at the Annual Meeting of the American Law and Economics Association, Yale Law School, New Haven, Connecticut; and June 6, 1992 at the Annual Meeting of the Canadian Industrial Relations Association, Charlottetown, Prince Edward Island, Canada. The research for this paper was made possible by a generous grant from the Fund for Labor Relations Studies.

420   *Michigan Law Review*   [Vol. 91:419

INTRODUCTION

Since the 1930s, the fundamental tenet of American labor law has been that the government should foster employee organization and regulate industrial relations to promote equity in bargaining between employers and employees and to promote industrial peace.[1] Those

---

1. The findings and policies set forth in § 1 of the original Wagner Act stated in part:
  The denial by employers of the right of employees to organize and the refusal by employers to accept the procedure of collective bargaining lead to strikes and other forms of industrial strife or unrest, which have the intent or the necessary effect of burdening or obstructing commerce . . . .
  The inequality of bargaining power between employees who do not possess full freedom

who enacted our basic labor laws, as well as the majority of legal scholars who have since commented on those laws, believed unions necessary for workers to achieve the benefits of industrial democracy and a larger share of industry's profits.[2] Thus, they believed, the government should remove barriers to employee organization such as injunctions,[3] yellow-dog contracts,[4] and employer discrimination against

---

of association or actual liberty of contract, and employers who are organized in the corporate or other forms of ownership association substantially burdens and affects the flow of commerce, and tends to aggravate recurrent business depressions, by depressing wage rates and the purchasing power of wage earners in industry and by preventing the stabilization of competitive wage rates and working conditions within and between industries.

Experience has proved that protection by law of the right of employees to organize and bargain collectively safeguards commerce from injury, impairment, or interruption, and promotes the flow of commerce by removing certain recognized sources of industrial strife and unrest, by encouraging practices fundamental to the friendly adjustment of industrial disputes arising out of differences as to wages, hours, or other working conditions, and by restoring equality of bargaining power between employers and employees.

It is hereby declared to be the policy of the United States to eliminate the causes of certain substantial obstructions to the free flow of commerce and to mitigate and eliminate these obstructions when they have occurred by encouraging the practice and procedure of collective bargaining and by protecting the exercise by workers of full freedom of association, self-organization, and designation of representatives of their own choosing, for the purpose of negotiating the terms and conditions of their employment or other mutual aid or protection.

Wagner Act, ch. 372, § 1, 49 Stat. 449 (1935) (current version, the National Labor Relations Act, at 29 U.S.C. § 151 (1988)); see also the preamble to the Norris-LaGuardia Act, ch. 90, § 3, 47 Stat. 70 (1932) (current version at 29 U.S.C. § 102 (1988)).

2. *See* SENATE COMM. ON EDUC. AND LABOR, 74TH CONG., 1ST SESS., COMPARISON OF S. 2926 (73D CONGRESS) AND S. 1958 (74TH CONGRESS) 15 (Comm. Print 1935), *reprinted in* 1 NATIONAL LABOR RELATIONS BD., LEGISLATIVE HISTORY OF THE NATIONAL LABOR RELATIONS ACT, 1935, at 1338 (1985) [hereinafter NLRB, LEGISLATIVE HISTORY] (arguing that, "[i]n the absence of equality of bargaining power, the rate of wages fails to keep pace with the rate of industrial expansion, profits, etc., thus aggravating depressions and impairing economic stability, with consequent detriment to the free flow of interstate commerce"); 79 CONG. REC. 6183, 6184 (1935); ARCHIBALD COX ET AL., CASES AND MATERIALS ON LABOR LAW 87 (11th ed. 1991) ("[C]ollective bargaining replaces the weakness of the individual in bargaining and . . . substitutes . . . industrial democracy . . . for the unilateral and sometimes arbitrary power of the employer."); 1 THE DEVELOPING LABOR LAW 3 (Charles J. Morris et al. eds., 2d ed. 1983); JULIUS G. GETMAN & BERTRAND B. POGREBIN, LABOR RELATIONS 1 (1988); 1 JAMES A. GROSS, THE MAKING OF THE NATIONAL LABOR RELATIONS BOARD 16 (1974) (quoting letter from Sen. Robert F. Wagner to the Honorable Marion Smith dated Oct. 22, 1933, where Sen. Wagner wrote that program was designed to "make America safe for industrial democracy"); LEROY S. MERRIFIELD ET AL., LABOR RELATIONS LAW 20 (8th ed. 1989) ("Sooner or later it was inevitable not only that worker organizations should be tolerated under the law, but that they should be regarded as necessary and desirable institutions in promoting an effective democracy . . . ."); James A. Gross, *Conflicting Statutory Purposes: Another Look at Fifty Years of NLRB Law Making,* 39 INDUS. & LAB. REL. REV. 7, 10 (1985) (noting that Senator Wagner "considered the advancement of economic and social justice, rather than the reduction of industrial strife, to be the primary objective of the Wagner Act"); Leon H. Keyserling, *The Wagner Act: Its Origin and Current Significance,* 29 GEO. WASH. L. REV. 199, 218 (1960) (noting that Senator Wagner "valued the measure . . . as an affirmative vehicle for the economic and related social progress to which his life-long efforts were devoted"). For a contemporary call for industrial democracy, see Alan Hyde, *Democracy in Collective Bargaining,* 93 YALE L.J. 793 (1984).

3. 29 U.S.C. § 104 (1988). This section withdraws from the jurisdiction of federal courts the authority to issue injunctions in nonviolent labor disputes.

4. 29 U.S.C. § 103 (1988). A *yellow-dog contract* is an agreement between an employer and

422   *Michigan Law Review*   [Vol. 91:419

employees on the basis of union affiliation.[5] Moreover, these same legislators and scholars believed that the government stewardship of labor relations should go beyond the mere removal of barriers to
organization, to the active regulation of industrial relations conflicts
with respect to organizing, collective bargaining, and enforcing collective agreements. Elections, the requirement of bargaining in good
faith, and arbitration were advanced to replace the parties' cruder
methods of resolving such conflicts.[6] Without this extensive tutelage
of labor-management relations, the legislators and legal scholars believed that conflicts in labor relations would escalate into strife and
economic warfare and that many workers would be denied the benefits
of dealing with their employers on equal terms.[7]

The traditional economic analysis of unions and collective bargaining calls into question this fundamental tenet and thus the basis for
much of American labor law. Proponents of this analysis argue that
individual bargaining will secure for each worker all of the benefits to
which she is entitled in accordance with her productivity.[8] Unions
achieve higher wages and benefits for employees by establishing a labor cartel, to which the employer responds by raising prices, cutting
output, substituting capital for labor, and laying off workers.[9]
Although the union may gain benefits for some workers, these benefits
come only at the expense of consumers, other workers, and economic
efficiency.[10] Thus, the traditional economic analysis suggests that,

---

employee that the employee will not join a union during the employee's tenure of employment.
Section 103 declares all such agreements to be contrary to public policy and unenforceable.

    5. 29 U.S.C. § 158(a)(3) (1988). This section makes it an unfair labor practice for employers
to discriminate in hiring or other conditions of employment on the basis of union membership.

    6. 29 U.S.C. § 159(c) (1988) (elections); 29 U.S.C. § 158(a)(5), (b)(3) (1988) (bargaining in
good faith); Labor Management Relations (Taft-Hartley) Act, § 301, 29 U.S.C. § 185 (1988)
(arbitration). The Supreme Court has interpreted § 301 as providing federal substantive law for
the enforcement of agreements to arbitrate. *See* Textile Workers Union v. Lincoln Mills, 353
U.S. 448 (1957). The Supreme Court strengthened and elaborated its support for arbitration in
the *Steelworkers Trilogy* cases. *See* United Steelworkers v. American Mfg. Co., 363 U.S. 564
(1960); United Steelworkers v. Warrior & Gulf Navigation Co., 363 U.S. 574 (1960); United
Steelworkers v. Enterprise Wheel & Car Corp., 363 U.S. 593 (1960); *infra* notes 198-200.

    7. *See* H.R. REP. No. 972, 74th Cong., 1st Sess. 6-9 (1935), *reprinted in* 2 NLRB, LEGISLA-
TIVE HISTORY, *supra* note 2, at 2956, 2962-63; SENATE COMM. ON EDUC. AND LABOR, *supra*
note 2; 79 CONG. REC. 7565, 7565-67 (1935); S. REP. No. 573, 74th Cong., 1st Sess. 1-2 (1935),
reprinted in 2 NLRB, LEGISLATIVE HISTORY, *supra* note 2, at 2300, 2300-01; COX ET AL., *supra*
note 2, at 86-87; MERRIFIELD ET AL., *supra* note 2, at 20-21, 25; *see also* JAMES B. ATLESON,
VALUES AND ASSUMPTIONS IN AMERICAN LABOR LAW 111 (1983).

    8. *See* MILTON FRIEDMAN & ROSE D. FRIEDMAN, FREE TO CHOOSE 228-47 (1980); Rich-
ard A. Epstein, *A Common Law for Labor Relations: A Critique of the New Deal Labor Legislation,* 92 YALE L.J. 1357, 1365-67, 1382 (1983); Henry C. Simons, *Some Reflections on
Syndicalism,* 52 J. POL. ECON. 1, 12 (1944).

    9. *See* RONALD G. EHRENBERG & ROBERT S. SMITH, MODERN LABOR ECONOMICS: THE-
ORY AND PUBLIC POLICY 350-60 (1982).

    10. *Id.*

rather than fostering unions and collective bargaining, the government should undertake measures to extirpate them.[11] Far from promoting equity in bargaining between employers and employees, unions promote workers to a superior bargaining position — that of a labor cartel — and cause inefficiency and inequitable redistributions of income among similarly situated workers. Moreover, under this analysis, no sound basis exists for the government's efforts to regulate industrial relations to promote industrial peace.[12]

This traditional economic analysis of unions and collective bargaining is deficient for several reasons. First, it focuses on only one of several possible sources of union wage increases. Logical arguments and recent empirical evidence suggest that, as sources of union wage increases, employer rents, quasi-rents, and productivity increases associated with unionization are at least as important as labor cartelization.[13] Second, the analysis assumes that the employer responds to a union wage demand by moving up her labor demand curve to substitute capital for labor.[14] However, it can be shown that such a response is not Pareto optimal[15] for the union and employer and that both can make themselves better off by bargaining in a Coasean fashion[16] to achieve a contract off the demand curve with a lower wage and more employment. Again, recent empirical evidence suggests that the bargaining solution is the better model and that unionization causes only small capital and labor misallocations.[17] Finally, despite the fact that collective bargaining is commonly cited as an activity involving strategic behavior,[18] the traditional economic analysis of the union as a cartel and the employer as a price taker in collective bargaining precludes any rigorous consideration of employer and union strategic behavior. As a result, the monopoly model implicitly assumes that all of the costs of collective bargaining are ordinary time and information trans-

11. *See* Simons, *supra* note 8, at 25.

12. Epstein, *supra* note 8, at 1358; Stewart J. Schwab, *Collective Bargaining and the Coase Theorem*, 72 CORNELL L. REV. 245, 245-47 (1987).

13. BARRY T. HIRSCH & JOHN T. ADDISON, THE ECONOMIC ANALYSIS OF UNIONS 211-14 (1986); *see also infra* notes 202-25 and accompanying text.

14. *See infra* notes 226-37 and accompanying text.

15. Under the Pareto criterion, a resolution of a conflict or problem is said to be "Pareto optimal" if under that resolution no one can be made better off without making someone else worse off. HAL R. VARIAN, MICROECONOMIC ANALYSIS 269 (2d ed. 1984).

16. To assume that two parties bargain in a Coasean fashion is to assume that they effectively negotiate to exhaust all benefits of trade. *See generally* R.H. Coase, *The Problem of Social Cost*, 3 J.L. & ECON. 1 (1960).

17. *See infra* notes 232-37 and accompanying text.

18. *See, e.g.,* ROBERT M. AXELROD, THE EVOLUTION OF COOPERATION 221 n.5 (1984); HENRY HAMBURGER, GAMES AS MODELS OF SOCIAL PHENOMENA 107-08 (1979); Robert Cooter, *The Cost of Coase*, 11 J. LEGAL STUD. 1, 19 (1982).

action costs, with no tendency to escalate as each side seeks to gain the upper hand. Thus, it is not very surprising that the traditional economic analysis admits no comprehension of the purpose in American labor law of promoting industrial peace.

In this article, I present an alternative economic analysis of unions and collective bargaining that utilizes recent advances in labor economics and some simple applications of game theory to address the deficiencies of the traditional monopoly model. First, I assume that the primary sources of union benefits are employer rents, quasi-rents, and productivity increases associated with unionism. These rents and productivity increases constitute the cooperative surplus that the parties divide through collective bargaining. Individual bargaining will not secure for employees a share of this surplus. The workers must organize and bargain collectively to raise themselves to a position of rough equality relative to the employer and gain a share of the surplus.

Second, in examining the problem of dividing the cooperative surplus, I assume that the parties bargain in a Coasean fashion to achieve a Pareto optimal solution that maximizes the value of the cooperative surplus to the parties. If one assumes such optimal bargaining, then one can show that the parties will agree to a contract that specifies a level of employment exceeding that given by the employer's labor demand curve. Indeed, if one assumes that the parties bargain to maximize the monetary value of the cooperative surplus and that the surplus consists of employer rents, one can demonstrate that the employer will set the same product market price and that the parties will agree to the same level of employment that would have prevailed in the absence of a union.[19] This follows because, assuming the employer was optimally pricing and mixing capital and labor to maximize his rent before the advent of the union, any adjustment of these parameters will only decrease that rent. Combining this assumption of optimal bargaining with my previous assumption concerning the primary sources of union wage increases, I argue that employees' gains from organization come largely at the expense of their employers, rather than other employees or consumers, and that the productivity gains associated with unionism may outweigh any attendant inefficiencies. It is therefore equitable, and perhaps wealth maximizing, for the government to encourage employee organization.

Finally, I argue that in conflicts over the division of the cooperative surplus, including organizing, collective negotiations, and enforcement of the collective agreement, both sides have incentives to act

---

19. *See infra* notes 65-67 and accompanying text.

strategically, wasting a portion of the cooperative surplus in hopes of capturing a larger share of the surplus for themselves. Such strategic activities include discriminatory discharges, recognition strikes, intransigence in bargaining, and strikes or lockouts to enforce a given interpretation of the collective agreement. Moreover, because parties are often rewarded in these activities based on their recalcitrance relative to the other party, the costs of these conflicts are positional externalities that tend to escalate in the absence of government regulation. To illustrate these arguments, I present a simple game representing collective negotiations, which demonstrates that strategic behavior may be individually rational for each party to undertake, but collectively irrational, because it results in strikes that waste the cooperative surplus. Thus, it makes sense for the government to structure the conduct of organizing, collective negotiations, and enforcement of the collective agreement to prohibit or discourage strategic behavior and minimize waste of the cooperative surplus.

The article proceeds in four parts. In Part I, I provide a brief primer on the economic analysis of unions and collective bargaining. I discuss the various possible sources of union wage increases, possible employer responses to union wage demands, and alternative models of the costs of collective bargaining. In Part II, I outline the traditional monopoly theory of unions by combining the appropriate elements of the model discussed in the primer on economic analysis. I present both the theoretical implications of the traditional economic analysis for American labor law and a critique of this analysis from an economic perspective. In Part III, I describe my alternative bargaining analysis by combining the alternate elements of a model of unions and collective bargaining presented in the primer on economic analysis. Once again I examine the implications of economic analysis for American labor law, although this time with very different results. Finally, I present my conclusions about American labor law based on my analysis.

I. A PRIMER ON THE ECONOMIC ANALYSIS OF UNIONS AND COLLECTIVE BARGAINING

In this Part, I present alternate economic assumptions with respect to three issues that must be addressed to construct an economic model of unions and collective bargaining. First, I examine the source of union wage and benefit increases and present three possible alternatives. Next, I examine the employer's response to union wage and benefit demands and present both a demand curve and a bargaining analysis. Finally, I examine the costs of collective bargaining and present alternative treatments of these costs, first as simple transaction costs, then as positional externalities. As I show in Parts II and III, which of the alternate economic assumptions one uses to construct a model of unions and collective bargaining greatly affects the model's implications for public policy.

A. *Sources of Union Wage and Benefit Increases*

The primary objective of unions is to negotiate the employment of workers at wages and benefits superior to those that the employees would have received individually. Indeed, workers will desire to organize into unions only if such organization provides benefits in excess of the costs of organization. Empirical studies estimate that organized employees receive wages that are generally about ten to fifteen percent higher than similarly situated unorganized employees.[20] Organized employees also enjoy other benefits from collective bargaining, such as pensions, medical benefits, protection from discharge without just cause, and a grievance and arbitration system to enforce the collective agreement.[21] The value that these benefits confer on organized employees can also be represented as a wage increase in simple models of unions and collective bargaining.

However, if unions simply raised the wages of their members in a perfectly competitive economy, all they would achieve would be the unemployment of their members, through either their replacement with lower-paid unorganized workers or the bankruptcy of their employers.[22] Such a wage increase would raise the production costs of organized firms, putting them at a competitive disadvantage. If the organized firms failed to replace the organized workers with lower-paid unorganized workers, they would either have to raise their prices or accept lower profits to cover the wage increase. If the organized employers raised their prices to cover the increase in production costs, unorganized firms would sell their products at lower prices, expanding

---

20. *See* RICHARD B. FREEMAN & JAMES L. MEDOFF, WHAT DO UNIONS DO? 46-47 (1984); H. GREGG LEWIS, UNIONISM AND RELATIVE WAGES IN THE UNITED STATES (1963); Orley Ashenfelter, *Union Relative Wage Effects: New Evidence and a Survey of Their Implications for Wage Inflation, in* ECONOMETRIC CONTRIBUTIONS TO PUBLIC POLICY 31, 32-38 (Richard Stone & William Peterson eds., 1978); H. Gregg Lewis, *Union Relative Wage Effects, in* 2 HANDBOOK OF LABOR ECONOMICS 1139, 1163-76 (Orley Ashenfelter & Richard Layard eds., 1986).

21. *See* FREEMAN & MEDOFF, *supra* note 20, at 68; Greg J. Duncan, *Earnings Functions and Nonpecuniary Benefits,* 11 J. HUM. RESOURCES 462 (1976); Richard B. Freeman, *The Effect of Unionism on Fringe Benefits,* 34 INDUS. & LAB. REL. REV. 489 (1981).

22. For previous presentations of this argument, *see* FREEMAN & MEDOFF, *supra* note 20, at 6-7; HIRSCH & ADDISON, *supra* note 13, at 21-22, 208-10; compare PAUL C. WEILER, GOVERNING THE WORKPLACE: THE FUTURE OF LABOR AND EMPLOYMENT LAW 132 (1990) ("[A] union is not and cannot be a cartel that exercises true monopoly power in an otherwise competitive market.").

their production in the affected markets and driving the organized firms out of the market. Similarly, if the organized employers accepted lower profits, the organized employers would not be able to pay a competitive rate of return to borrow capital and would go out of business. In time, only unorganized workers and firms would exist. To survive for any appreciable period of time in an economy, unions must derive their members' benefits from a source that is insulated from the machinations of the competitive market. At least three such sources exist.

1. *Labor Cartel Rents*

The first possible source of union wage increases, although by no means the most likely, is the formation of an effective labor cartel by the employees.[23] In order for this source to bear fruit, both the organized employees' labor market and the organized employers' product market must have *barriers to entry* — cost advantages enjoyed by the incumbents of a market but not by new entrants.[24] Examples of barriers to entry in the labor market include licensure, location, firm-specific training, and expensive general training;[25] examples of barriers to entry in the product market include patents, tariffs, transportation costs, and large start-up investments in capital, advertising, or learning how to produce the product.[26] If the employees can establish a labor cartel in a market with the requisite barriers to entry, they can raise their wages without fear that their employers will replace them, and their employers can raise prices to cover the increased production costs without fear that unorganized firms will drive them out of the market. The size of the barriers to entry in the relevant labor and product markets will limit the size of the union wage increase.[27]

---

23. *See* HIRSCH & ADDISON, *supra* note 13, at 21-22.

24. F.M. SCHERER, INDUSTRIAL MARKET STRUCTURE AND ECONOMIC PERFORMANCE 236 (2d ed. 1980).

25. *See* GARY S. BECKER, HUMAN CAPITAL (2d ed. 1975). *Firm-specific training* is training that has value only to one firm; *general training* is training valuable to more than one firm. *See id.* at 26.

26. RICHARD A. POSNER & FRANK H. EASTERBROOK, ANTITRUST: CASES, ECONOMIC NOTES, AND OTHER MATERIALS 513-16 (2d ed. 1981). There is some disagreement over whether large initial investments such as expensive general training for employees or start-up costs for firms are really a barrier to entry, because the incumbents in the market also once had to undertake those costs. *See id.* at 514. However, at least in an economy with imperfect capital markets that make borrowing large sums of money impossible or costly, the necessity of such borrowing for start-up costs may effectively limit the number of potential entrants.

27. The employees cannot raise their wages above the value of the barriers to entry to the labor market; if they do, the employer will replace them. Similarly, if they raise their wages so high that their employer must price above her product market barriers to entry, unorganized employers and employees will enter the market and replace them.

To establish an effective cartel, the employees probably need not organize all of the members of an occupation of a given employer, or all of the employers in the product market. Unions may be able to establish effective bargaining power with an employer by organizing only a significant subset of the firm's employees. Moreover, although the short-run individual interests of unorganized employers will be to cut prices and expand their market share,[28] a small number of unorganized employers may be able to see their long-run collective interest in declining to cut prices, earning excess profits, and using part of those profits to raise their workers' wages to stave off employee organization.[29] To the extent the employees' cartel is imperfect, however, its wage-setting ability will be undermined, and organized employers will have greater ability and incentive to replace organized with unorganized workers.

2. *Employer Rents*

The second possible source of union wage increases is employer rents on capital.[30] In economics a *rent* is any payment for a resource in excess of what would be necessary to entice the owner of the resource to bring it into employment in a perfectly competitive market.[31] In other words, a rent is any payment for a resource that exceeds the competitive price for that resource. At least two forms of such rents may serve as sources for union wage increases for an indefinite period of time, and an additional form of "quasi-rent" could serve as a source of union wage increases in the short run.[32]

The first form of employer rent that can serve as a source of union wage increases is employer market power rents from the product market.[33] *Market power rents* are those profits earned by the employer in

---

28. POSNER & EASTERBROOK, *supra* note 26, at 334.

29. The strategy of offering wage and benefit increases to stave off unionization seems fairly benign, because by redistributing wealth from the employer to the employees it achieves one of the objectives of allowing unions. However, if society wants to encourage employee organization, such "bribes" are undesirable because they encourage free riding on union efforts and result in too little union organizing activity. *See infra* note 317 and accompanying text.

30. *See* HIRSCH & ADDISON, *supra* note 13, at 21.

31. *See* THE MIT DICTIONARY OF MODERN ECONOMICS 120 (David W. Pearce ed., 3d ed. 1986); RICHARD A. POSNER, ECONOMIC ANALYSIS OF LAW 9-10 (4th ed. 1992).

32. *See* HIRSCH & ADDISON, *supra* note 13, at 21; BARRY T. HIRSCH, LABOR UNIONS AND THE ECONOMIC PERFORMANCE OF FIRMS 3 (1991). An additional employer "rent" that may serve as a source of union wage increases is employer profits due to monopsony power in the labor market. However, although employer monopsony power may be an important source of union wage increases in certain industries and professions, labor economists generally do not believe it to be a pervasive source of union wage increases in the economy as a whole. *See* EHRENBERG & SMITH, *supra* note 9, at 65-66. For further treatment of the monopsony employer case, see *infra* notes 112-17 and accompanying text.

33. *See* HIRSCH & ADDISON, *supra* note 13, at 21.

excess of the competitive rate of return because the employer is a monopoly or participates in an oligopoly or cartel in the product market.[34] As in the case of the labor cartel, there must be barriers to entry in the labor and product markets for employer market power rents to yield union wage increases. If the employees in an occupation with barriers to entry can organize an employer who enjoys market power rents in a product market protected by barriers to entry, then the employees can raise their wages without fear of replacement, and the employer can raise her prices or cut her profits without fear of replacement or fear that she will not be able to borrow capital. As before, the relevant barriers to entry limit the size of the union wage increase. If the employer has already increased her product price to the full extent of the product market barriers to entry, then the wage increase will have to be paid entirely out of profits without any increase in price. Again, the employees need not organize all of the members of a given occupation employed by an employer or all of the employers in a given product market to succeed in obtaining union wages. In fact, if employer market power rents represent the source of the union wage increase, the workers can achieve a wage increase even if they organize only one employer.

The second form of employer rent that can serve as a source of union wage increases is Ricardian rents.[35] *Ricardian rents* are profits earned on a resource that exceed the competitive rate of return because the resource is not generally available in the market and has some characteristic that makes it unusually productive.[36] Examples of such resources include particularly fertile soil and a particularly rich vein of ore.[37] There must be some limit on the availability of the resource in the market; otherwise, competing producers who owned the resource would have incentives to cut prices and vitiate the rent. If the employees in an occupation with barriers to entry can organize an employer who enjoys Ricardian rents, the employees can raise their wages without fear of replacement, and the employer can pay these higher wages out of his rent without raising prices or going out of business. Indeed, if the only source of the union benefits is Ricardian rents, then the competitive market will set the product price, and the

---

34. *See* SCHERER, *supra* note 24, at 11.

35. *See* HIRSCH & ADDISON, *supra* note 13, at 21.

36. DAVID RICARDO, ON THE PRINCIPLES OF POLITICAL ECONOMY, AND TAXATION 91-108 (R.M. Hartwell ed., Penguin Books 1971) (1817).

37. Although both of these examples are capital resources, human or labor resources can also earn Ricardian rents. For example, a person may have an unusual talent that makes him very productive at a given activity. However, as long as there is more than one employer for this unusual talent, the employee will theoretically be compensated for this superior productivity.

employer will not be able to raise the product price without being driven out of business. The size of the possible union wage increase is limited to the size of the labor market barriers to entry or the Ricardian rent, whichever is smaller. As in the case of monopoly rents, the employees can gain a share of Ricardian rents even if they organize fewer than all the employees of only one employer in the relevant product market.

The final form of employer "rent" that merits discussion here is quasi-rents on capital investments. *Quasi-rents* are those profits earned on a resource in excess of what could be earned on that resource by transferring it to its next best use.[38] As the name implies, quasi-rents are not true rents, because they are not payments in excess of the competitive rate of return. For resources that are readily transferrable to other uses through transport or sale, such as common machinery like an adding machine, quasi-rents will be very small or zero. However, for resources that are highly specialized and hard to transport, such as a unique steel smelter, quasi-rents may constitute nearly the entire competitive return on the resource. If the employees in an occupation with barriers to entry can organize an employer who earns significant quasi-rents on a specialized machine, then the employees can raise their wages to the limits of their barriers to entry, and the employer will be forced to pay the higher wages out of the competitive return she would have earned on the machine. The employer will not be able to recapture the value of the machine through resale or transfer and, assuming the employer is operating in a competitive market, will not be able to raise her product price. Moreover, as long as the employer earns some positive return on the machine that will minimize her losses, the employer will not shut down the machine. However, such a strategy for gaining wage increases can only be a short-run strategy because, if the employer earns less than the competitive rate of return on her investment, the employer will probably avoid future investments in the same plant or perhaps even the same industry.[39] Accordingly, as soon as the useful life of the specialized machine is exhausted, the employer will close the plant, and the organized workers will find themselves unemployed. As with true employer rents, the employees can obtain a share of quasi-rents even if

---

38. HIRSCH, *supra* note 32, at 7; *see also* Armen A. Alchian, *Decision Sharing and Expropriable Specific Quasi-Rents: A Theory of* First National Maintenance Corporation v. NLRB, 1 SUP. CT. ECON. REV. 235 (1982); Carliss Y. Baldwin, *Productivity and Labor Unions: An Application of the Theory of Self-Enforcing Contracts,* 56 J. BUS. 155 (1983).

39. HIRSCH, *supra* note 32, at 10.

they organize fewer than all of the employees of only one employer in a product market.

3. *Productivity Increases Associated with Employee Organization*

The final possible source of union wage increases is productivity increases associated with employee organization.[40] Labor economists have advanced several theories explaining how unions may increase productivity.

The first theory is the *union shock effect.*[41] Proponents of this theory argue that, as a result of lax management, some inefficiency exists in every firm, particularly firms insulated from competition by barriers to entry. Such laxity may occur because managers enjoy an easygoing management style and the owners of the firm cannot adequately monitor the managers to prevent waste.[42] An increase in wages brought on by employee organization, the argument goes, "shocks" the management into curing the existing inefficiencies to preserve profitability.[43] Others argue that, because employees have an interest in the profitability of their firm and are present in the workplace, they may sometimes be superior to absent owners as monitors of management efficiency.[44] Of course, to play this monitoring role without fear of discharge, the employees must be organized in a union. Thus, unions may raise productivity by prompting greater effort on the part of management.

The second theory asserts that unions allow for the enforcement of efficient, long-term implicit labor contracts.[45] To prevent shirking and

---

40. *See* FREEMAN & MEDOFF, *supra* note 20, at 7-11, 14-16; HIRSCH & ADDISON, *supra* note 13, at 22.

41. *See* HIRSCH & ADDISON, *supra* note 13, at 188.

42. Even where the owner runs the firm, unproductive practices can continue if the owner enjoys the practice. For example, it has been argued that discrimination persists in the economy, despite the fact that discriminatory firms are at a competitive disadvantage, because owners of businesses enjoy the practice and are willing to accept a lower rate of return on capital to indulge in it. *See* Matthew S. Goldberg, *Discrimination, Nepotism, and Long-Run Wage Differentials,* 97 Q.J. ECON. 307 (1982).

43. *See id.* at 308-14.

44. *See* PETER KUHN, MALFEASANCE IN LONG TERM EMPLOYMENT CONTRACTS: A NEW GENERAL MODEL WITH AN APPLICATION TO UNIONISM 28-29 (National Bureau of Economic Research Working Paper No. 1045, 1982); *see also* Peter Kuhn, *Union Productivity Effects and Economic Efficiency,* 6 J. LAB. RES. 229 (1985).

45. For excellent expositions of this argument, along with some interesting applications of the argument to legal problems, see Keith N. Hylton & Maria O. Hylton, *Rent Appropriation and the Labor Law Doctrine of Successorship,* 70 B.U. L. REV. 821 (1990); Douglas L. Leslie, *Labor Bargaining Units,* 70 VA. L. REV. 353, 364-71 (1984); Michael L. Wachter & George M. Cohen, *The Law and Economics of Collective Bargaining: An Introduction and Application to the Problems of Subcontracting, Partial Closure, and Relocation,* 136 U. PA. L. REV. 1349, 1356-67 (1988). There is an extensive economic literature on implicit labor market contracts. Recent surveys can be found in Donald O. Parsons, *The Employment Relationship: Job Attachment, Work Effort, and the Nature of Contracts, in* 2 HANDBOOK OF LABOR ECONOMICS, *supra* note

to compensate workers for investments in firm-specific training, it is efficient for employees and employers to enter into long-term contracts in which some of the employees' compensation is deferred until later in their careers.[46] These contracts remain implicit because of the costs of negotiation and enforcement.[47] Unfortunately, such deferred compensation creates incentives for employers to act opportunistically and fire employees before they receive their deferred wages.[48] Unions facilitate the enforcement of such long-term implicit contracts by protecting employees from employers' opportunistic behavior with collective action, seniority rules, just-cause provisions, and arbitration provisions. Accordingly, unions promote efficient measures to prevent shirking and encourage efficient investment in firm-specific training.[49]

The third theory contends that unions raise productivity by promoting the efficient consumption of public goods in the workplace.[50] Many conditions of employment, including the level of safety, lighting, heating, and speed of the production line, are uniform and shared among all workers in a given workplace. Such uniform and shared conditions of employment are public goods, in that other workers cannot be excluded from improvements negotiated by one worker. As a result, in individual bargaining, workers tend to let others negotiate improvements in such conditions and enjoy the benefits at no cost.

20, at 789, 799-802; Sherwin Rosen, *Implicit Contracts: A Survey,* 23 J. ECON. LITERATURE 1144 (1985).

46. The employer can defer a portion of an employee's compensation by paying the employee less than her marginal product early in the employee's career and more than her marginal product later in the employee's career. This creates disincentives for shirking because, if the employee is caught shirking and fired, the employee loses the deferred wages. Wachter & Cohen, *supra* note 45, at 1360-61. Deferred wages can also represent employee investments in, and payments for, firm-specific training. When the employee is young, she invests in firm-specific training by taking a wage below her marginal product; when the employee is older, she is paid returns on that investment in the form of wages in excess of her marginal product. *Id.*

47. To be complete, such contracts would have to specify appropriate conduct by the parties in a wide variety of situations, such as how much diligence the employee was required to undertake in all circumstances and the required severity of economic hardship before the employer could lay off the employee. Completely specifying such a contract would be very costly. Leslie, *supra* note 45, at 368. Also, such a complete explicit contract would probably be of little use because proving in court whether one side had failed to comply with the complex terms of the agreement would be very costly. For example, it would be difficult to determine whether the employer laid off employees due to a legitimate reason, such as a decrease in demand for the employer's product, or to avoid paying deferred wages.

48. *See* Wachter & Cohen, *supra* note 45, at 1359, 1364.

49. KUHN, *supra* note 44; James M. Malcomson, *Trade Unions and Economic Efficiency,* 93 ECON. J. 51 (1983); M.W. Reder, *Unionism, Wages, and Contract Enforcement, in* RESEARCH IN LABOR ECONOMICS: NEW APPROACHES TO LABOR UNIONS 27 (Joseph D. Reid, Jr. ed., Supp. II 1983).

50. FREEMAN & MEDOFF, *supra* note 20, at 7-11, 14-16; Richard B. Freeman & James L. Medoff, *The Two Faces of Unionism,* 57 PUB. INTEREST 69 (1979). For some interesting applications of this argument to labor law, see Keith N. Hylton & Maria O. Hylton, *Rational Decisions and Regulation of Union Entry,* 34 VILL. L. REV. 145 (1989); Leslie, *supra* note 45, at 377.

Such "free riding" results in an inefficiently low level of consumption of these public goods. Unions help to solve this problem by giving the workers a collective voice through which they can more accurately represent their preferences on such matters.

Finally, some argue that unions raise productivity by promoting the adjustment of working conditions through the efficient expression of a collective voice rather than costly exit.[51] In a competitive labor market, a worker's primary mechanism for expressing dissatisfaction with working conditions is to take another job or *exit*. Individual bargaining over conditions of employment is difficult due to the free-rider effect previously discussed and because workers do not want to be identified by their employer as "troublemakers." However, exit is an inefficient mechanism by which to encourage changes in working conditions. The mere fact that an employee leaves a job does not communicate much about what that worker felt was wrong with the conditions of employment. Exit also imposes search and retraining costs on both the employee who leaves and the employer who must replace the employee. Unions help solve this problem by giving workers a collective voice through which they can express dissatisfaction with working conditions without the problems of free riding or employer retaliation. Besides being a more effective method of expressing dissatisfaction with working conditions, the collective voice also saves money by reducing the number of workers who leave jobs and thus the amount of search and retraining costs.

If unions increase productivity, then, to the extent of the productivity increase, unionized employees can raise their wages without forcing their employer to raise output prices or putting their employer at a competitive disadvantage in obtaining capital. Indeed, to the extent that the unionized employer shares in the benefits of the productivity increase, the employer will be at a competitive advantage in the industry and will be able to lower product price and increase output.[52]

---

51. FREEMAN & MEDOFF, *supra* note 20, at 7-11, 14-16; Freeman & Medoff, *supra* note 50, at 70-78.

52. This point has led some to argue that unions cannot yield productivity increases because, if they did, employers would voluntarily organize and split the benefits with their employees. *See, e.g.,* Thomas J. Campbell, *Labor Law and Economics,* 38 STAN. L. REV. 991, 996-97 (1986); Richard A. Posner, *Some Economics of Labor Law,* 51 U. CHI. L. REV. 988, 1000-01 (1984). I deal with this argument at length *infra* notes 209-12 and accompanying text. For now, suffice it to say that this argument misses the point that, in fact, employers in industries where employee organization yields productivity increases *are* anxious to organize employees in captive organizations or mimic union contracts in order to achieve a portion of the productivity increases that are possible through unionism. These employers just are not interested in *independent* employee organizations that may gain a share of employer rents or impinge on management prerogatives. As I will argue later, union wage increases generally exceed associated productivity increases, taking a share of employer rents and decreasing company profits. In addition, most American managers simply do not enjoy having their discretion compromised by negotiations with a union.

434   *Michigan Law Review*   [Vol. 91:419]

The nature of the problem of dividing productivity increases associated with employee organization between the employees and the employer depends on how widely such productivity increases are shared across the product market either through widespread unionization, growth of union firms, or free riding by unorganized employers who mimic union contracts. If such productivity increases are widely shared, then the benefits of the productivity increase will be divided according to the dictates of the market, with both the employees and the employer being paid according to their marginal product and consumers enjoying a somewhat lower product price. If such productivity increases are not widely enjoyed across the market, then, at least in the short run,[53] they become Ricardian rents that the employees and employer split in an indeterminate bargaining problem. To the extent that employers do not like unions despite productivity increases, either due to union wages exceeding productivity increases associated with employee organization or because employers prefer to remain unorganized, employees will need barriers to entry in the labor market to protect them. As with employer rents, wage increases based on productivity increases associated with employee organization can probably be obtained by organizing only a substantial number of the employees of only one employer.

B. *Employer Responses to Union Wage Demands*

Even if the union wage increase is sheltered from the competitive market so that the employer will neither replace the organized employees nor go out of business, how the employer responds to a union wage demand may affect the analysis of unions and collective bargaining. Labor economists employ two basic models of the employer's response to union wage demands in their analyses.

1. *The Employer Demand Curve Response*

Under the first model, one simply assumes that, in response to a union wage demand, the employer moves up his labor demand curve

---

Thus, employers generally resist independent employee organization even where such organization yields significant productivity increases.

53. Absent barriers to growth, if only a few firms in an industry enjoy productivity increases associated with employee organization and the employers in those firms share in the benefits of the productivity increases, then those firms will enjoy a competitive advantage and could expand to dominate the market. The empirical significance of this scenario, however, is mitigated by the ability of unorganized employers to free ride on at least a portion of the productivity increases associated with unionism by mimicking union contracts and by the fact that employers rarely share in the productivity increases associated with unionism because union wage premiums generally exceed estimated productivity increases. *See infra* note 225 and accompanying text.

and employs less labor.[54] This response is depicted in Figure 1, where the vertical axis measures the employees' wage, the horizontal axis measures the number of full-time employees, and the line marked D represents the number of full-time employees demanded by the employer at each possible wage. The employer's labor demand curve slopes downward because of the declining marginal product of labor.[55] As the union raises the employees' wage from the competitive wage, W_c to the union wage, W_u, the employer decreases the number of employees he employs from N_c to N_u. The employer reduces the number of employees he uses in the plant by producing less and by substituting capital, such as labor saving machines, for the now more expensive workers.[56]

However, unless one wants to assume that unions are entirely indifferent to the unemployment of their members, or that transaction costs prevent the parties from bargaining in a Coasean fashion[57] over the terms of employment, such a simple labor demand response by the employer will not be Pareto optimal[58] for the parties. The employer's labor demand curve may give the appropriate employer response to a market increase in the wage. If, however, the wage increase results from the formation of a union that can bargain over wages and employment, the employer and union can negotiate a wage and employment agreement that specifies a higher level of employment and a lower wage that both the employer and union will prefer to the employer's labor demand response.[59] Indeed, if one assumes that the parties bargain to maximize the monetary value of rents and productivity

---

54. *See* HIRSCH & ADDISON, *supra* note 13, at 10-14; James N. Brown & Orley Ashenfelter, *Testing the Efficiency of Employment Contracts,* 94 J. POL. ECON. S40, S41 (1986); Kim B. Clark, *Unionization and Firm Performance: The Impact on Profits, Growth, and Productivity,* 74 AM. ECON. REV. 893, 894-97 (1984); Thomas E. MaCurdy & John H. Pencavel, *Testing Between Competing Models of Wage and Employment Determination in Unionized Markets,* 94 J. POL. ECON. S3, S4, S8-S9 (1986).

55. EHRENBERG & SMITH, *supra* note 9, at 21-25. The marginal product of an input is the change in total output that results from the addition of the last unit of that input employed. To say that labor has a declining marginal product means that, as the employer adds additional workers to his plant, total production may go up, but production goes up by a smaller amount with each additional worker. Because the addition to total output is less with each additional worker, the employer will be willing to hire additional workers only if the wage of the workers is reduced. Accordingly, the employer is willing to employ more workers as the workers' wage declines, and the employer's labor demand curve slopes downward.

56. *Id.*

57. See *supra* note 16 for a definition of *Coasean bargaining.*

58. See *supra* note 15 for a definition of *Pareto optimality.*

59. *See* HIRSCH & ADDISON, *supra* note 13, at 14-18; Brown & Ashenfelter, *supra* note 54; Clark, *supra* note 54; Robert E. Hall & David M. Lilien, *Efficient Wage Bargains Under Uncertain Supply and Demand,* 69 AM. ECON. REV. 868 (1979); MaCurdy & Pencavel, *supra* note 54, at S10-13; Ian M. McDonald & Robert M. Solow, *Wage Bargaining and Employment,* 71 AM. ECON. REV. 896 (1981).

FIGURE 1

The Employer's Labor Demand Curve

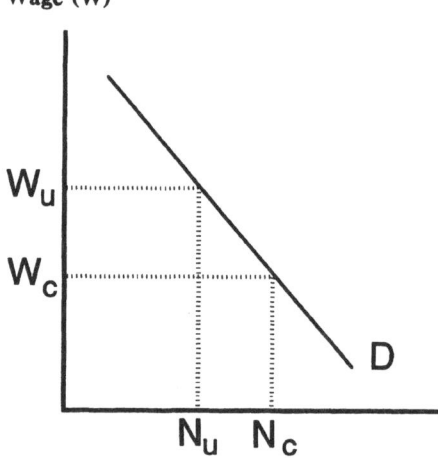

increases due to unionization, one can demonstrate that the parties will seek to minimize the impact of the union on product price and firm employment levels. For example, if the union and employer seek to divide employer rents, then the parties will agree to the same level of employment that would have existed in the absence of the union, and no substitution of capital for labor will result from the union wage increase.[60]

2.   *The Employer Bargaining Response*

To demonstrate the superior bargaining solution, in Figure 2 I have redrawn the labor demand analysis of Figure 1 and added some graphical representations concerning the employer's profitmaking opportunities and the union's preferences among different wage and employment contracts.[61]   Just as in Figure 1, the vertical axis measures

---

60. *See* HIRSCH & ADDISON, *supra* note 13, at 14-18; John M. Abowd, *The Effect of Wage Bargains on the Stock Market Value of the Firm,* 79 AM. ECON. REV. 774, 777, 793 (1989); Clark, *supra* note 54, at 897-98. As I discuss below, productivity increases associated with employee organization may even increase the optimal level of employment over what prevailed in the absence of a union. *See infra* note 256 and accompanying text.

61. The labor economics literature reaches no consensus on the best model to represent the preferences or objectives of unions. Some have developed models assuming that unions seek to maximize the wage bill; others have employed public choice analysis and modeled union objectives according to the preferences of the median voter in union elections; still others have modeled union preferences in a manner analogous to an individual's utility function with a trade-off between wages and employment for union members. *See, e.g.,* HIRSCH & ADDISON, *supra*

FIGURE 2

The Employer and Union's Wage-Employment Contract Curve

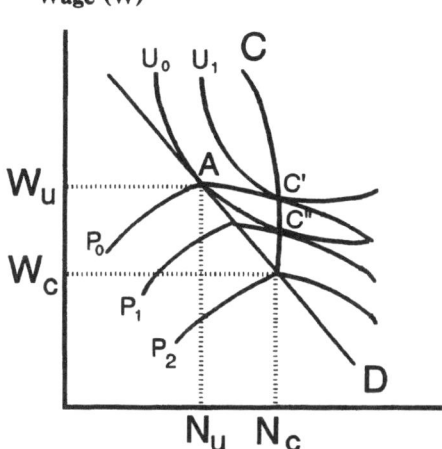

Employment (N)

the employees' wage, the horizontal axis measures the number of full-time employees employed, and the solid downward sloping curve labeled *D* represents the employer's labor demand curve. However, this time I have added the employer's isoprofit curves P_0, P_1, and P_2, which descend on each side of the labor demand curve. Each isoprofit curve graphs wage and employment mixes that yield equivalent levels of profit. Isoprofit curves that are lower in the graph *(P_2)* specify a higher level of profits than those that are higher in the graph *(P_0)*. For any given wage, profit is maximized on the labor demand curve; however, identical profits can be made with either more or less labor at a lower wage rate. Accordingly, the isoprofit curves slope down on either side of the labor demand curve. Also shown in Figure 2 are the union's indifference curves, U_0 and U_1. Each indifference curve graphs wage and employment mixes that yield equal utility to the union as a collective entity. Indifference curves that are further from the origin *(U_1)* yield higher utility than those that are closer to the origin *(U_0)*. Assuming that the union's utility is an increasing function of both wages and employment, the union's indifference curves will be concave

note 13, at 9-10; Henry S. Farber, *The Analysis of Union Behavior, in* 2 HANDBOOK OF LABOR ECONOMICS, *supra* note 20, at 1039. I have chosen the third option because it is perhaps the most general and lends itself well to exposition of the arguments based on bargaining analysis that I want to make.

toward the origin as depicted in Figure 2.[62]

Figure 2 allows easy demonstration of the superior bargaining solution. When the employees organize and demand a union wage, W_u, the employer's labor demand response will be to move to point A and decrease the number of workers employed to N_u. However, by moving to the right along the firm's isoprofit curve P_0, which descends out of A, one sees that by agreeing to any point on P_0 between A and C' the firm achieves the same level of profits while allowing the union to achieve a higher level of utility. Similarly, by moving to the right from A along the union's indifference curve U_0, which comes out of A, one sees that by agreeing to any point on U_0 between A and C'' the union achieves the same level of utility while allowing the firm to achieve a higher level of profits. Thus, the employer's labor demand response is not Pareto optimal from the perspective of the employer and the union, and one or both of the parties can be made better off by moving off the demand curve to a point in the triangle $AC'C''$. The tangencies between the firm's isoprofit curves and the union's indifference curves describe the set of Pareto optimal solutions to the bargaining problem between the employer and the union.[63] To the right or left of these tangencies, including points on the employer's labor demand curve, benefits remain to be gained from bargaining in that one or both parties can be made better off without making the other worse off. The graph of these tangencies is called the *contract curve* between the two parties and is labeled C in Figure 2.[64] Depending on the technology of

---

62. I also assume that the union's utility function is twice continuously differentiable and strictly concave.

63. To be precise, such solutions are Pareto optimal taking the firm and the union as the relevant parties for application of the Pareto criterion. The "optimal" solution applying the Pareto criterion to the firm and the union may differ from the "optimal" solution applying the Pareto criterion to the firm and the individual workers, because the aggregate representation of workers' preferences through union democracy may differ from their representation through the marketplace. In particular, average workers' preferences probably receive greater weight under union representation while marginal workers' preferences probably receive greater representation in the marketplace. *See* FREEMAN & MEDOFF, *supra* note 20, at 9-10. As a result, one might expect organized employees to negotiate contract terms more favorable to average workers than those negotiated by unorganized workers; examples might include pension provisions and just-cause clauses. Moreover, the invariance hypothesis of the Coase Theorem would probably not hold with respect to the entitlement to organize because the workers would probably value the entitlement differently collectively, when the entitlement was to organize, than they would individually, when the entitlement was not to organize.

This possible variance between the workers' collective and individual preferences creates some ambiguity in the meaning of *efficiency* in labor law because it is not immediately clear whether the Pareto criterion should be applied to the union or the workers in defining efficiency. A strong tendency certainly exists in economics to choose the individual as the baseline for all arguments; however, the Pareto criterion is commonly applied to collections of entrepreneurs in the form of firms or corporations. For purposes of this article, I will define *efficiency* based on application of the Pareto criterion to individual workers.

64. *See* HIRSCH & ADDISON, *supra* note 13, at 16.

the firm and the preferences of the union, the contract curve can slope to the left, be vertical, or slope to the right.[65] However, barring complete union indifference to the employment of its members, the contract curve will lie to the right of the employer's labor demand curve. Assuming the parties bargain in a Coasean fashion to exhaust all benefits of trade, they will arrive at a wage and employment mix that is to the right of the demand curve on the portion of the contract curve between C' and C''. Exactly where on this portion of the contract curve the parties will end up is an indeterminate bargaining problem. Under any of these possible solutions, however, the employer will continue to employ more labor after the union wage increase than the amount specified by the employer's labor demand curve.

The argument can be made in a more simple and compelling manner if one assumes that the employer and the union bargain to maximize the monetary value of the rents and productivity increases to be divided between them. In such a case, beyond any initial disruption of the competitive market necessary to generate the rent to be divided, the parties have incentives to minimize any deviations in the allocation of resources from what would have occurred under the competitive market. Additional deviations, such as a mix of capital and labor that varies from what would have occurred in a competitive market, only increase the costs of production and decrease the total value of the rent and productivity increase to be divided between the parties.[66] For example, if the parties negotiated to divide employer rents, one would expect the parties to agree to the employment of the same amount of labor that would have been used in the absence of a union and the employer to set the same product price that she would have set in the absence of a union. Assuming that, prior to the union, the employer mixed capital and labor and set the product price so as to maximize the value of her rent, adjustment of any of these parameters after the formation of the union only decreases the total value of the rent. In terms of Figure 2, assuming that the parties bargain to maximize the value of rents is analogous to assuming that union indifference curves

---

65. MaCurdy & Pencavel, *supra* note 54, at S10-S12. For example, given a well-behaved technology for the firm, if the union is willing to trade employment for wages, perhaps because it is dominated by senior workers who do not care about the job prospects of younger workers who will be laid off, then the contract curve will lean to the left. On the other hand, if the union desires to trade wages for employment, effectively spending a portion of its share of the rents on employing unneeded workers, then the contract curve will lean to the right. *See id.* This second case is commonly referred to as *featherbedding* and seems most likely to occur in industries that have recently suffered a massive contraction in the number of available jobs. *See id.* at S17-18, S34 (studying the wage and employment bargains of the International Typographical Union and finding employment above the rent-maximizing level); *see also* Brown & Ashenfelter, *supra* note 54, at S43.

66. *See* HIRSCH & ADDISON, *supra* note 13, at 14-18; Clark, *supra* note 54, at 898.

and firm isoprofit curves sketch out a contract curve that is vertical at the competitive level of employment (N_c).[67]

C. *The Costs of Collective Bargaining*

Any economic analysis of collective bargaining should consider the costs associated with the phenomenon. First, organizing campaigns impose costs in the form of the resources expended on publicity, litigation, discriminatory discharges, and, prior to the National Labor Relations Act, organizational strikes. Second, negotiation of the collective agreement imposes costs, the most dramatic of which is the lost production due to a strike or lockout. Finally, enforcing the collective agreement imposes costs, including the resources expended on arbitration, litigation, and possibly strikes or lockouts. Irrespective of the source of the union benefit increase or the model of employer response, these costs are relevant to any consideration of the efficiency or equity of unions and collective bargaining. Under any model, these costs must be subtracted from any benefits derived from collective bargaining, and under the bargaining model of the employer's response to a union wage increase, the costs of collective negotiations may prevent the realization of benefits of trade.[68]

1. *The Costs of Collective Bargaining as Ordinary Transaction Costs*

Traditionally economists have modeled these costs without explicitly taking into account the strategic nature of the underlying activities.[69] Organizational activities are modeled in a market setting with a demand and supply for union services.[70] It is assumed that the amount employees spend on organizational activities increases with

---

67. HIRSCH & ADDISON, *supra* note 13, at 14-18; Clark, *supra* note 54, at 898.

68. A model of the costs of collective bargaining may complete the basic economic analysis for purposes of the principal features of the National Labor Relations Act and the Norris-La-Guardia Act. However, to examine the equity and efficiency of the duty of fair representation and the Labor-Management Reporting and Disclosure Act of 1959, 29 U.S.C. §§ 401-483 (1988), one would have to add a model of how unions divide the employees' share of the rents and productivity increases among their members. On models of the internal workings of unions, see Farber, *supra* note 61.

69. Many authors have acknowledged the strategic nature of collective bargaining. *See, e.g.,* Epstein, *supra* note 8, at 1384-85; Posner, *supra* note 52, at 997. However, few have explicitly taken account of it in their models.

70. *See, e.g.,* HIRSCH & ADDISON, *supra* note 13, at 29-38; Orley Ashenfelter & George E. Johnson, *Unionism, Relative Wages, and Labor Quality in U.S. Manufacturing Industries,* 13 INTL. ECON. REV. 488 (1972); Orley Ashenfelter & John H. Pencavel, *American Trade Union Growth: 1900-1960,* 83 Q.J. ECON. 434 (1969); Monroe Berkowitz, *The Economics of Trade Union Organization and Administration,* 7 INDUS. & LAB. REL. REV. 575 (1954); John H. Pencavel, *The Demand for Union Services: An Exercise,* 24 INDUS. & LAB. REL. REV. 180 (1971).

the expected rents available in a given industry,[71] while employers concede these high-rent industries, spending more to prevent unionism in competitive industries where organization would threaten the life of the firm.[72] Similarly, economists commonly assume that parties undertake collective negotiations in a cooperative fashion.[73] Under this assumption, strikes and lockouts become a very curious phenomenon. Why would two rational parties engage in such costly activity to arrive at a bargain that is necessarily inferior to the one they could have negotiated before the strike or lockout dissipated some of the mutual benefits of production?[74] At the very least, one would expect two cooperative parties to forgo the strike or lockout, adopt the contract they would have obtained after the work stoppage, and split the benefits of production gained by continuing production. Traditionally, economists explain strikes as the result of imperfect information.[75] Unions undertake strikes either to adjust unrealistic expectations among rank-and-file workers as to the wage increase that is possible[76] or to allow the union to sort out low-wage from high-wage employers when less

---

71. HIRSCH & ADDISON, *supra* note 13, at 31. The amount the employees spend on organizing also depends on their taste for unionism. *Id.* at 30.

72. *Id.* at 34. The amount employers spend resisting organization also depends on the taste of the employer for an unorganized workplace. *Id.*

73. *See* John Kennan, *The Economics of Strikes, in* 2 HANDBOOK OF LABOR ECONOMICS, *supra* note 20, at 1091, 1104-12; Schwab, *supra* note 12, at 246.

74. This puzzle has given rise to some consideration among economists. Indeed, under the famous "Hicks paradox" it is "impossible" to derive an accurate theory on the incidence, duration and results of strikes because, if the parties had access to such a theory, they would merely agree to the predicted post-strike bargain and forgo the strike, thus obviating the predictive ability of the model. SIR JOHN RICHARD HICKS, THE THEORY OF WAGES 144-47 (2d ed. 1963); *see also* Kennan, *supra* note 73, at 1091.

75. DAVID CARD, STRIKES AND WAGES: A TEST OF A SIGNALLING MODEL 1 (National Bureau of Economic Research Working Paper No. 2550, 1988); Raquel Fernandez & Jacob Glazer, *Striking for a Bargain Between Two Completely Informed Agents,* 81 AM. ECON. REV. 240 (1991) (observing that most economists explain strikes as the result of imperfect information, but offering an explanation for strikes consistent with perfect information). Although Hicks subscribed to the idea that imperfect information was the primary cause of strikes, he also proposed in his famous "rusty weapon" passage the idea that unions may strike occasionally to maintain their ability to strike and to exert bargaining power:

Weapons grow rusty if unused, and a Union which never strikes may lose the ability to organise a formidable strike, so that its threats become less effective. The most able Trade Union leadership will embark on strikes occasionally, . . . in order to keep their weapon burnished for future use . . . .

Under a system of collective bargaining, some strikes are more or less inevitable for this reason; but nevertheless the majority of actual strikes are doubtless the result of faulty negotiation. . . . Any means which enables either side to appreciate better the position of the other will make settlement easier; adequate knowledge will always make a settlement possible.

HICKS, *supra* note 74, at 146-47. To my knowledge no rigorous model of this theory of strikes has ever been constructed.

76. Orley Ashenfelter & George E. Johnson, *Bargaining Theory, Trade Unions and Industrial Strike Activity,* 59 AM. ECON. REV. 35, 36-37 (1969).

expensive methods are not available.[77] Thus, strikes are merely the cheapest way to educate the workers as to the optimal wage that can be extracted from the employer. Labor economists have paid much less attention to the problem of enforcement of the collective agreement. When they consider it, economists typically treat enforcement in a neutral fashion, as simply one of the services unions provide their members and as a cost of union administration.[78] Under this analysis, the costs of collective bargaining are merely simple transaction costs to be subtracted from any benefits of collective bargaining.

2. *The Costs of Collective Bargaining as Positional Externalities*

Alternatively, one could explicitly account for the strategic nature of collective bargaining in modeling its costs. I define *strategic behavior* as any activity undertaken by one party to an agreement to increase its benefit from the agreement at the expense of the other party to the agreement.[79] Examples of such activity include firing productive prounion employees, lying in negotiations, and intransigence or "hard bargaining" in negotiations or enforcement of the agreement. This type of activity results in costs, such as search and retraining to replace productive employees and strikes due to lying or intransigence in bargaining or enforcement. Thus, although these activities may increase one side's expected benefit from the agreement, they decrease the total expected value of the agreement to both parties. Moreover, to the extent that the division of the benefits from the agreement depends on the relative performance of the parties in collective bargaining, both sides may have incentives to act strategically. If one party decides to act strategically, the other side must either respond in like manner or forfeit the contest over the benefits of the agreement. In such a case, the costs incurred in attempting to gain the upper hand in the agreement are known as a *positional externality*.[80] This is because the parties are competing for a relative position in undertaking the strategic behavior, for example who can be the most intransigent in bargaining, and the costs of responding to strategic behavior are external to the original decision to undertake such behavior. Due to this

---

77. Beth Hayes, *Unions and Strikes with Asymmetric Information,* 2 J. LAB. ECON. 57, 58 (1984); *see* Oliver Hart, *Bargaining and Strikes,* 104 Q.J. ECON. 25 (1989) (critiquing models used to explain the occurrence of strikes in the bargaining process); *cf.* Peter C. Cramton, *Bargaining with Incomplete Information: An Infinite-Horizon Model with Two-Sided Uncertainty,* 51 REV. ECON. STUD. 579 (1984).

78. *See* Ashenfelter & Pencavel, *supra* note 70, at 430; Pencavel, *supra* note 70, at 181.

79. *See* Wachter & Cohen, *supra* note 45, at 1359 n.42. *See generally* Jason S. Johnston, *Strategic Bargaining and the Economic Theory of Contract Default Rules,* 100 YALE L.J. 615 (1990).

80. ROBERT H. FRANK, MICROECONOMICS AND BEHAVIOR 629-38 (1991).

externality, the individual interests of the parties in pursuing strategic behavior diverge from their collective interest in avoiding it, and the conflict tends to escalate in cost even though the parties succeed only in wasting a portion of the benefit of the agreement.

The costs of collective bargaining can be modeled as positional externalities using game theory. In game theory, positional externalities arise in *mixed motive* or *dilemma games* that involve a divergence of individual and collective interests.[81] The most famous such game is the "prisoner's dilemma," in which two accomplices in crime face certain conviction on a lesser offense and probable exoneration on a greater offense. The prosecuting attorney gives each the following choice: turn state's evidence against your accomplice and receive a suspended sentence for the lesser offense while your accomplice is convicted of the greater offense; or remain silent and hope your accomplice does not rat on you. In this game, the strategic behavior is turning state's evidence while the positional externality is the additional jail time a criminal serves when his accomplice rats on him. Due to this externality, each criminal's individual interest in turning state's evidence diverges from their collective interest in remaining silent. Each has individual incentive to turn state's evidence to reduce his jail time, but if each follows this individually rational choice they will both do time for the more serious offense.

A similar simple dilemma game can represent the problem of strategic behavior and positional externalities in collective negotiations. Consider the problem of a union and an employer in deciding how to divide the benefits of their agreement to produce some product. For purposes of simplicity, assume that the union and the employer have already maximized the potential benefit of their agreement by including all terms or conditions for which the benefits to the parties exceed their costs and are now bargaining over how to divide the total benefit of their agreement.[82] Each party must receive at least the benefit its

---

81. *See* HAMBURGER, *supra* note 18, at 69; MARTIN SHUBIK, GAME THEORY IN THE SOCIAL SCIENCES 240 (1989).

82. In reality, strategic behavior may sometimes prevent the negotiation of efficient contract terms. For example, in negotiating over the inclusion of an employee benefit such as a pension in the collective agreement, the union will have incentive to underrepresent the value of a pension while the employer will have incentive to overrepresent the cost of a pension in order to influence the ultimate division of the benefits of the agreement in their favor. *See* HAMBURGER, *supra* note 18, at 117-22. If both are too successful in this misrepresentation strategy, the parties may fail to assess accurately whether a pension is worth more to the employees than it costs the employer and thus fail to include an efficient term regarding pensions in the contract. *Id.* at 122. For purposes of simplicity I exclude such possibilities from my negotiations game. I discuss below the realism of this assumption by examining whether transaction costs will prevent the negotiation of efficient contract terms in collective negotiations. *See infra* note 228 and accompanying text.

members or investors could receive for their invested time and resources by changing to other employers or employees; otherwise, they will pursue those options. In collective negotiations this minimum payment, known as the *threat value* of the agreement,[83] would be equal to the competitive wage for the employees and a competitive return on capital for the employer. The benefit of the agreement in excess of these minimum values is the real subject of dispute and is known as the *cooperative surplus.*[84] As previously discussed, in labor relations, this cooperative surplus will be made up of rents and productivity increases that are protected by barriers to entry. For the purposes of this negotiating game, assume that the total cooperative surplus to be divided by the parties over the term of the agreement is $10.

In this simple negotiating game, each side must decide whether to adopt a bargaining strategy of cooperation or intransigence in its efforts to divide the cooperative surplus.[85] As previously discussed, intransigence constitutes a positional externality in collective negotiations.[86] This can be seen by examining the common sense assumptions about the division of the cooperative surplus between the employees and the employer in Figure 3. The outermost diagonal line in Figure 3 shows all possible divisions of the cooperative surplus of $10 between the employees and the employer, from $10 for the employees and none for the employer, to $5 for each, to none for the employees and $10 for the employer. Assume that, if both parties bargain cooperatively over the division of the surplus, they will decide to divide it in half with $5 each for the employees and the employer. This "split the difference" assumption concerning the results of cooperative collective bargaining is simple, but it comports with other much more sophisticated models of divisional bargaining.[87] If one side is intransigent in bargaining while the other is cooperative, the intransigent side will presumably achieve a larger share of the cooperative surplus. Thus, assume that, if the union is intransigent while the

---

83. ROBERT COOTER & THOMAS ULEN, LAW AND ECONOMICS 93-94 (1988).

84. *Id.*

85. This assumption may seem somewhat unrealistic because parties to collective negotiations could adopt one strategy, for example cooperation, and then later change that strategy if the other side's actions warranted change. However, even if one were to take account of the potential dynamic nature of strategies in collective negotiations, one would obtain results similar to those of my simple model due to a similar dilemma in the incentives to change strategies.

86. *See supra* notes 79-80 and accompanying text.

87. *See* Jules L. Coleman et al., *A Bargaining Theory Approach to Default Provisions and Disclosure Rules in Contract Law,* 12 HARV. J.L. & PUB. POL'Y. 639, 660 (1989); Douglas Heckathorn, *A Unified Model for Bargaining Conflict,* 25 BEHAV. SCI. 261 (1980); John F. Nash, Jr., *The Bargaining Problem,* 18 ECONOMETRICA 155 (1950).

FIGURE 3

Possible Divisions of the Cooperative Surplus Between the Employer and
the Employees

Employees' Share

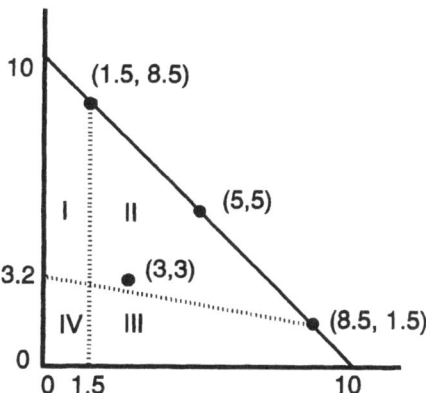

Employer's Share

employer is cooperative, the division of the cooperative surplus will be
$8.50 for the employees and $1.50 for the employer, while if the union
is cooperative while the employer is intransigent, the division is $1.50
for the union and $8.50 for the employer. However, if both sides are
intransigent, a strike ensues, which consumes $4 of the cooperative
surplus in the form of $2 in lost profits and $2 in lost net benefits from
employment. The parties ultimately settle by agreeing to share equally
the remaining cooperative surplus, with $3 each for the employees and
the employer.

To complete the negotiations game, all that is needed are assumptions about the time and information costs of collective negotiations
and the distribution of bargaining benefits and costs among union and
nonunion employees. Intransigence in bargaining will presumably
also increase the time and information costs of negotiations. Thus, if
both sides cooperate, then bargaining goes quickly, information is relatively cheap to obtain, and the time and information costs of negotiations are $0.25 for each party. However, if one or both sides are
intransigent, then negotiations take longer, information is harder to
obtain, and the time and information costs of negotiations are $0.50
for each party. Regarding the distribution of the benefits and costs of
bargaining among employees, assume that two thirds of the employees

are union members and that, although the benefits of negotiations are spread equally among all employees, the employees' share of the costs of bargaining, including strikes, is borne only by union members.[88] Finally, assume that in playing the negotiations game the union is concerned only with the benefits and costs to union members.

The union and employer payoffs for each possible combination of bargaining strategies that can be selected by the parties are given in Matrix 1. The employer payoff for each combination of choices is given in the upper right-hand corner of the cell representing that combination of choices, while the union's payoff for the same combination is given in the lower left-hand corner of the cell. These payoffs are computed by taking the relevant division of the cooperative surplus from Figure 3 and subtracting the relevant bargaining costs outlined in the above assumptions. For example, the employer's payoff when both parties are uncooperative in bargaining ($2.50) is computed by taking the employer's share of the cooperative surplus given in Figure 3 ($3) and subtracting the employer's time and information costs of bargaining ($0.50). Similarly, the union's payoff when both parties are uncooperative ($0.83) is computed by taking the union members' share of the cooperative surplus given in Figure 3 (2/3 x $3) minus the union's time and information costs in bargaining ($0.50) and the nonmembers' share of the costs of the strike, because all strike costs are borne by union members (1/3 x $2). Following game theory convention, I will refer to the cells of Matrix 1 from left to right, top to bottom, respectively, as cells 1, 2, 3, and 4.

Examining the payoffs of this game, one can see the divergence between individual and collective interests that characterizes positional externalities and dilemma games. From the individual perspective of each party, the strategy of intransigence in bargaining dominates because it yields a higher payoff regardless of what the other side does. Looking at the employer's payoffs, one sees that, if the union decides to cooperate, the employer does better by being intransigent ($8) than by being cooperative ($4.75), and, if the union decides to be intransigent, the employer again does better by being intransigent ($2.50) than by being cooperative ($1). Similarly, examining the union's payoffs, one sees that, if the employer decides to cooperate, the union does better by being intransigent ($5.17) than by

---

88. The assumption that union members bear all the costs of strikes is roughly equivalent to the assumption that whenever there is a strike the employer maintains partial operations using the employees who are not union members. The assumption is somewhat unrealistic even on this account because it implicitly assumes that, during the strike, the strikebreakers always receive the wage for which the union ultimately settles. This unrealistic assumption, however, does not affect the conclusions of my model.

MATRIX 1

Union and Employer Expected Payoffs for the Negotiations Game

		Employer	
		Cooperative Bargaining	Intransigent Bargaining
Union	Cooperative Bargaining	4.75 3.08	8.0 0.5
	Intransigent Bargaining	1.0 5.17	2.5 0.83

Including the values of union benefits received by employees who are not union members, the total wealth of each cell 1 through 4 is, respectively, 9.5, 9, 9, and 5.

being cooperative ($3.08), and, if the employer decides to be intransigent, the union still does better by being intransigent ($0.83) than by being cooperative ($0.50). Thus, if each party acts according to its own individual interests, one would expect both to be intransigent and cell 4 to be the expected outcome or equilibrium for the game. However, from the collective perspective of both parties this outcome is clearly suboptimal. Both of the parties can do better if they cooperate and confine their conflict to cell 1 ($3.08 for the union and $4.75 for the employer) rather than escalating the conflict to a strike that wastes a portion of the cooperative surplus as represented in cell 4 ($0.83 for the union and $2.50 for the employer). Thus, to the extent the parties act individually rather than collectively, the conflict will tend to escalate despite the best interests of both parties.

Although the results of a particular game can be changed by changing assumptions about the costs and benefits of intransigent behavior, the basic nature of collective negotiations as a dilemma game remains. Examining Figure 3 again, one can divide the triangle representing all possible divisions of the cooperative surplus after a strike into sectors I through IV according to the diagonal line from (0, 3.2) to (8.5, 1.5)[89] and the vertical line at (1.5, 0).[90] If the expected settlement after a strike is in sector I, the employer will give in and not take a strike because he will earn more ($1.50) by capitulating. Similarly, if the expected settlement after a strike is in sector III, the union will give in and not strike because it will gain more benefits for its members by capitulating. The upper border of this sector slopes down, rather than being horizontal at (0, 1.5), due to the free riding of nonmembers on the benefits of undertaking a strike. However, if the expected settlement after a strike is in sector II or IV, both sides will have individual incentives to undertake a strike. This is true in sector II because each side will do better by striking than by capitulating to the other's hard bargaining. A strike is also possible in sector IV because, although each does better by capitulating, each will act recalcitrantly and hope that the other capitulates first.[91] One can change the results of a particular game by changing the assumptions that determine the division of the surplus after a strike or the boundaries of the four sectors in Figure 3. For example, one could move the expected payoffs after a strike by assuming the union gains a larger share through a strike, or one could shift the boundaries of the four sectors by assuming each side gets a higher payoff for capitulating. However, if in a negotiations game between two parties the expected payoffs for a strike are consistently in sectors I or III so that one side is always capitulating, the other side will have incentive to lessen the share it gives for capitulation, expanding sectors II and IV and increasing the chances that the other side's expected payoffs recommend intransigence and a strike. History demonstrates that, in industrial relations, the parties

---

89. This line is determined by comparing the union's net benefit after a strike with the union's net benefit from capitulating without a strike for a generalized division of the surplus after the strike. Assume that the employees' share of the surplus after a strike is Y while the employer's share is X. Accordingly, the union's net benefit after a strike is its portion of the employees' share $((2/3) \cdot Y)$ minus the costs of negotiations ($0.50) minus the free riders' share of the costs of the strike $((1/3) \cdot (1/2) \cdot (\$10 - (X + Y)))$. The union's net benefit if it capitulates without a strike is merely its portion of the employees' share $(2/3 \cdot \$1.50)$ minus the costs of negotiations ($0.50). Setting the union's net benefits with and without a strike equal to each other and simplifying, one obtains the equation $Y = 3.2 - 0.2X$, which is the diagonal line from (0, 3.2) to (8.5, 1.5). If the expected division between the employer and the employees after a strike is above this line, the union does better by striking; if it is below, the union does better by capitulating.

90. If the expected division between the employer and employees after a strike is to the right of this line, the employer does better by taking a strike. If the expected division between the employer and the employees after a strike is to the left of this line, the employer does better by capitulating.

91. In game theory, as on the playground, games with such payoff structures are known as games of "Chicken." HAMBURGER, *supra* note 18, at 83-87; SHUBIK, *supra* note 81, at 394. Games of chicken have an unstable "solution" where, as in dilemma games, individual incentives diverge from collective incentives and collectively irrational outcomes can result. HAMBURGER, *supra* note 18, at 86-87.

commonly feel that it pays to contest strikes — in other words, that both sides' expected payoffs from a strike are in either sector II or IV.[92] Putting aside my many simplifying assumptions, if one accepts that the nature of intransigence in bargaining is that of a positional externality, then one must accept the dilemma nature of collective negotiations.

By proposing this simple game as an illustration of the problems of strategic behavior and positional externalities in collective negotiations, I do not argue that unregulated collective negotiations inevitably degenerate into a strike. Both the employer and the union should recognize their dilemma and, to their mutual benefit, often be able to curb the temptation to bargain in an intransigent manner. The parties will be aided in this effort by the fact that, unlike some other dilemma games, employer-union negotiations often involve an established relationship and communication.[93] Particularly in mature collective bargaining relationships where the parties have a history of cooperative bargaining and can foresee future negotiations that could be jeopardized by present strategic behavior, the parties usually will be able to avoid the costs of intransigent bargaining. My point is that, despite the parties' common incentive and frequent success at solving the dilemma game of collective negotiations to their mutual benefit, at the heart of the game lie individual incentives that tend to escalate the game and sometimes produce suboptimal solutions that waste a portion of the cooperative surplus.

Similar dilemma games can be constructed for organizing campaigns and enforcement of the collective agreement. With respect to organizing, the cooperative or low-cost strategy might correspond to the mere publicity of pro- or antiunion views in an employee election on union representation, while the recalcitrant or high-cost strategies might correspond to organizational strikes and discriminatory discharges. It seems reasonable to assume that a party's payoff in organizing depends on its relative performance, because resort to the recalcitrant or high-cost strategy by only one party will increase that party's chances of prevailing, while if both parties resort to the recalcitrant or high-cost strategy their efforts will tend to cancel each other

---

92. *See, e.g.,* FOSTER R. DULLES, LABOR IN AMERICA: A HISTORY 166-83 (3d ed. 1966) (recounting the violent Homestead and Pullman strikes).

93. The prisoner's dilemma game previously discussed is commonly characterized as a dilemma in which the parties cannot communicate. *See supra* notes 81-82 and accompanying text. However, even when the parties to a dilemma game cannot communicate and have no relationship, empirical evidence suggests that many people can solve the dilemma to their collective benefit. *See, e.g.,* Lester B. Lave, *An Empirical Approach to the Prisoners' Dilemma Game,* 76 Q.J. ECON. 424 (1962).

out with respect to resolving the conflict. Thus, one would expect that organizational campaigns would have a tendency to escalate into costly affairs, wasting a portion of the cooperative surplus, in much the same way that negotiation conflicts can escalate. The parties are probably less likely to arrive at the mutually beneficial armistice of confining themselves to the cooperative or low-cost strategy in the case of the organizing game than in the case of the negotiations game, because in an organizing campaign the parties have not yet established a constructive relationship or steady communication and are probably quite hostile to one another.

With respect to enforcement of the collective agreement, the cooperative or low-cost strategy is to resolve disputes over interpretation of the agreement through arbitration, while the recalcitrant or high-cost strategy is to resort to more costly litigation or strikes to resolve contract disputes. Again, it seems reasonable to assume that a party's payoff in enforcement depends on its relative performance, because resort to the recalcitrant or high-cost strategy by only one party will increase that party's chances of prevailing, while if both parties resort to the recalcitrant or high-cost strategy their efforts will tend to cancel each other out with respect to resolving the conflict. Thus, one would expect that enforcement conflicts have a tendency to escalate, wasting a portion of the cooperative surplus, in much the same way that negotiation conflicts tend to escalate. In the enforcement game, it would seem very likely that the parties would achieve a mutually beneficial armistice by agreeing to confine their contract disputes to the cooperative or low-cost strategies because they have an established relationship and communication, and indeed have already successfully negotiated a collective agreement. It is thus not surprising that the vast majority of collective bargaining agreements provide arbitration as the means of resolving contract disputes.[94]

II. THE TRADITIONAL MONOPOLY MODEL OF UNIONS AND AMERICAN LABOR LAW

Having established a sound basis in the economic analysis of unions and collective bargaining, we can now examine the traditional monopoly model of unions and its implications for American labor law. In this Part, I present the traditional analysis, apply it to American labor law, and critique it from an economic perspective.[95]

---

94. Approximately 99% of collective bargaining agreements sampled contain provisions to arbitrate contract disputes. 51 Collective Bargaining Negot. & Cont. (BNA) 5 (Jan. 23, 1992).

95. Several valuable critiques of monopoly model applications to American labor law have already been made from a historical and legal perspective. *See* WEILER, *supra* note 22; Julius G.

A. *The Model and Its Implications for Public Policy*

The traditional monopoly model of unions and collective bargaining combines the first assumption discussed in each of the three sections of the primer on economic analysis.[96] First, practitioners of the monopoly model commonly assume that union wage increases come from labor cartels.[97] Although economists have long acknowledged employer product market power rents and Ricardian rents as possible sources of union wage increases,[98] the traditional analysis has consistently focused on the labor cartel as the source of union benefits.[99] Second, proponents of the traditional monopoly model of unions and collective bargaining assume that the employer responds to a union wage demand by moving up her labor demand curve.[100] Many expositions of the monopoly analysis never consider the possibility of optimal bargaining,[101] although some more sophisticated presentations assume that transaction costs prevent such bargaining.[102] Finally, adherents of the traditional monopoly model of unions and collective bargaining implicitly assume that the costs of collective bargaining are simple transaction costs without any strategic nature. If one assumes that unions unilaterally set wages while employers unilaterally set levels of employment, there is little room to consider strategic behavior in collective negotiations.[103] As previously discussed, the traditional model holds that strikes occur due to imperfect information. The traditional analysis also generally treats the costs of organizing the employees and enforcing the contract without explicitly taking account of the strategic nature of the underlying behavior.[104]

Getman & Thomas C. Kohler, *The Common Law, Labor Law, and Reality: A Response to Professor Epstein,* 92 YALE L.J. 1415 (1983); Paul R. Verkuil, *Whose Common Law for Labor Relations?,* 92 YALE L.J. 1409 (1983).

96. For other expositions of the monopoly theory of unions, see EHRENBERG & SMITH, *supra* note 9, at 328-65; HIRSCH & ADDISON, *supra* note 13, at 21-22.

97. See sources cited *supra* note 96.

98. *See* HICKS, *supra* note 74, at 140; HIRSCH & ADDISON, *supra* note 13, at 21; ALBERT REES, THE ECONOMICS OF WORK AND PAY 157-58 (1973).

99. This also holds true for the applications of this theory to law. For example, although Epstein briefly discusses Ricardian rents as a source of union benefits, *see* Epstein, *supra* note 8, at 1384-85, he fails to deal consistently with this possibility throughout his analysis. For a similar treatment, see Campbell, *supra* note 52, at 1017.

100. HIRSCH & ADDISON, *supra* note 13, at 21-22.

101. *See* Epstein, *supra* note 8; Posner, *supra* note 52.

102. *See, e.g.,* HIRSCH & ADDISON, *supra* note 13, at 16.

103. The only instance for strategic behavior under the monopoly model occurs when the monopoly union faces a monopsonist employer. However, as discussed below, this possibility has been traditionally dismissed in the labor economics literature due to the supposed rarity of employer monopsony power. *See infra* notes 112-17 and accompanying text.

104. *See supra* note 69 and accompanying text.

452   *Michigan Law Review*   [Vol. 91:419]

FIGURE 4

The Organized Labor Market

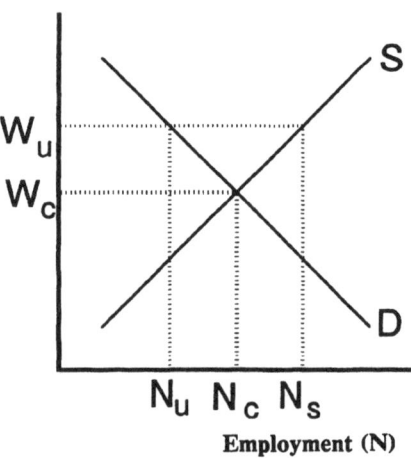

The traditional monopoly analysis of unions and collective bargaining is presented in Figures 4, 5, and 6. Respectively, these figures depict the organized labor market, the unorganized labor market, and the product market of the organized employers. In constructing these figures, I have assumed that both the organized occupation and the product market of the organized employers enjoy barriers to entry. Under the traditional analysis, when the union organizes a sufficient number of employees in an occupation in the relevant product market, it imposes an increase in their wage from W_c to W_u as shown in Figure 4.[105] The occupational barriers to entry prevent the organized employers from replacing the employees, and the employers respond by moving up their demand curve, reducing employment from N_c to N_u. The employers accomplish this decrease in employment by reducing production and substituting capital for labor in the production process. This substitution of capital for labor results in "production inefficiency"[106] because the organized firms now employ too much capital relative to labor, given the marginal productivity of capital and labor

---

105. The size of the wage increase the union imposes depends on the union's estimate of the decline in employment that will accompany the wage increase and the union's priorities in choosing between higher wages or more employment. However, in no case can the union wage exceed the occupational barriers to entry or cause the employer's price to exceed the barriers to entry to the product market. *See supra* notes 24-27 and accompanying text.

106. *See* EHRENBERG & SMITH, *supra* note 9, at 360; HIRSCH & ADDISON, *supra* note 13, at 21-22, 181.

FIGURE 5

The Unorganized Labor Market

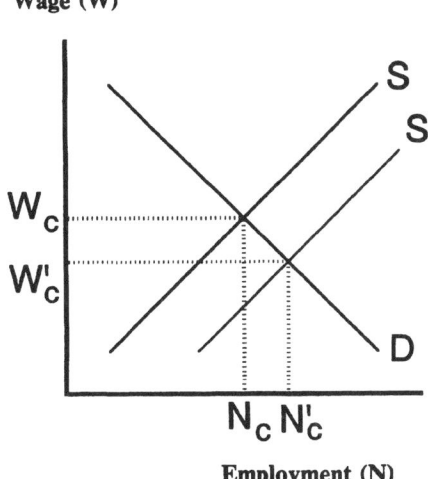

Employment (N)

and their respective opportunity costs in terms of the competitive interest rate and wage.[107] The higher union wage also results in unemployment because more workers (N_s) would like to work at the union wage than employers are willing to employ (N_u). As shown in Figure 5, some of these workers $(N_c - N_u)$ will seek employment in the unorganized labor market,[108] pushing out the labor supply curve in that market from S to S' and depressing wages from W_c to W_c'. This movement of workers from the organized to the unorganized labor market

107. A profit-maximizing firm will employ additional units of an input only as long as the value of the marginal product those units of input produce exceeds the cost of those additional units of input to the firm. HAL R. VARIAN, INTERMEDIATE MICROECONOMICS: A MODERN APPROACH 325-29 (1987). In a competitive market, the price of an input will be set equal to its opportunity cost in terms of the value of its marginal product in the best alternative use. *Id.* at 326. Thus, when input prices are set competitively, the firm's profit-maximizing activity will result in efficient production, and the firm will employ an additional unit of input only if its value to the firm exceeds its value in its next best use. *Id.* at 515-16. Under the traditional monopoly theory of unions, firms respond to a union wage increase by employing only those units of labor the value of whose marginal product exceeds the higher union wage and substituting units of capital that are now relatively cheap in the firm's production process. This results in inefficient production because the firm now employs too little labor, given its opportunity cost, sending workers to be employed in less productive uses, and too much capital, given its opportunity cost, employing capital that could be better employed in other uses. Total wealth could be increased by doing away with the artificially high union wage so that inputs could once again be employed in their most valuable uses.

108. Assuming that prior to organization the equilibrium wages in the organized and unorganized labor markets were comparable (both W_c), the number of workers who will leave the organized labor market to seek work in the unorganized labor market equals the number who were previously employed in the organized labor market (N_c) minus those who are still employed there (N_u).

FIGURE 6

The Organized Product Market

Price (P)

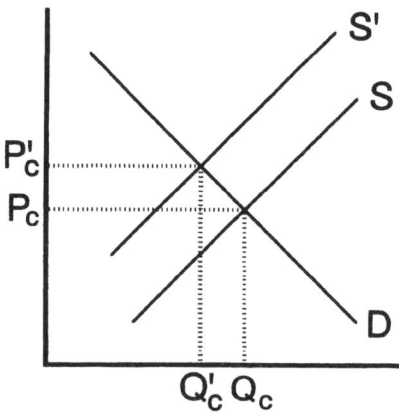

Quantity (Q)

is commonly referred to as the "displacement effect."[109] Finally, as represented in Figure 6, the decrease in production by the organized firms that accompanies the higher union wage results in a backward shift of the relevant product supply curve from S to S', an increase in the product price from P_c to P_c' and a decrease in consumption of the good from Q_c to Q_c'. This decrease in consumption results in "consumption inefficiency"[110] because consumers now enjoy too little of the product relative to other goods, given the opportunity costs of employing resources in the production of the organized good relative to other goods.[111] The barriers to entry in the product market prevent

---

109. HAROLD W. DAVEY ET AL., CONTEMPORARY COLLECTIVE BARGAINING 306 (4th ed. 1982); EHRENBERG & SMITH, *supra* note 9, at 350; *see* REES, *supra* note 98, at 160.

110. *See* EHRENBERG & SMITH, *supra* note 9, at 360; HIRSCH & ADDISON, *supra* note 13, at 22, 181.

111. In a competitive economy, firms will price their product at the marginal cost of producing that product, which in turn equals the opportunity cost of employing the resources used to produce the product in their next best use. VARIAN, *supra* note 107, at 322, 371. Efficient consumption ensues because consumers will purchase the good only if the benefit they derive from it exceeds the value that could be obtained by employing the resources used to produce the good in their next most valuable use. Under the monopoly analysis of unions, when the union raises the price of labor the employer must raise the price of the good above its opportunity cost, resulting in decreased consumer demand for the good and a shifting of that demand to less valued goods. Total wealth could be increased by doing away with the high union wages and correspondingly high union product price and allowing consumers once again to purchase goods for their opportunity cost.

FIGURE 7

The Profit Maximization Problem of a Monopsonistic Employer

Wage (W)

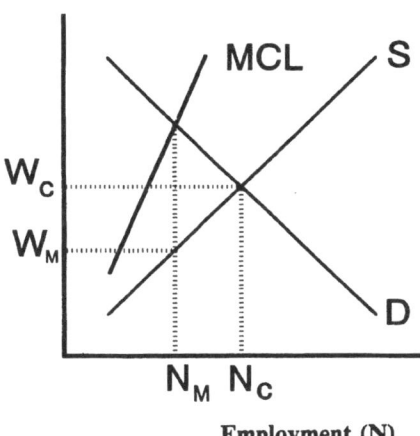

Employment (N)

other firms from entering and driving the product price back down to the competitive level.

The only exception to the above analysis that is traditionally considered in the monopoly model occurs when the employers exercise monopsony power in the labor market.[112] Monopsony power exists when there is only one employer, or so few employers that they can explicitly or implicitly collude in offering wages.[113] When an effective monopsony exists in the labor market, the employers no longer accept the market wage as given, but instead realize that they can drive down the market wage by employing fewer employees. As characterized in Figure 7, the monopsony maximizes profits by employing fewer employees (N_m) and driving the wage down from W_c to W_m.[114] The oper-

---

112. *See* DAVEY ET AL., *supra* note 109, at 307-08; HIRSCH & ADDISON, *supra* note 13, at 22; Posner, *supra* note 52, at 991-92.

113. *See* DAVEY ET AL., *supra* note 109, at 307.

114. The marginal cost of labor curve for the monopsony *(MCL)* lies above the labor supply curve. This is because the monopsony realizes that purchasing additional labor drives up the wage; the marginal cost of additional labor for the monopsonist equals the increased wage it must pay for the additional labor plus the increase in wages that must be paid to each previously purchased unit of labor. Because the height of the labor supply curve is equal to the wage at every level of employment, the marginal cost of the labor curve must lie above this curve. As depicted in Figure 6, the monopsony maximizes profits by employing labor until the point where the marginal cost of labor equals the marginal benefit of labor as represented by the labor demand curve (i.e., the monopsony will employ the quantity of labor (N_m) given by the intersection of the marginal cost of labor curve *(MCL)* and the labor demand curve *(D)*). This follows because, at levels of employment below this amount, the marginal benefit of additional employees exceeds their marginal cost, and the total net benefit of employing labor is increasing, while at

ation of the monopsony results in production inefficiency because the monopsony employs less than the efficient amount of labor in the production process. A union solves this problem because, by fixing the wage for labor at a given rate, it prevents the monopsony from driving down wages by employing fewer workers. Because the monopsony can no longer drive down the wage by cutting employment, the monopsony no longer has incentive to employ fewer than the efficient number of employees.[115] The problem of the negotiation of a wage between a monopsony employer and a monopoly union represents an indeterminate bargaining problem, but if one assumes the employer and the union seek to maximize the monetary value of the rents from their endeavors, they will bargain to the competitive wage (W_c) and the competitive level of employment (N_c).[116] Thus, when facing employer monopsony power, monopoly unions can increase employment and economic efficiency. Traditionally, however, economists limit the importance of this exception by arguing that employer monopsony power is rare in the economy.[117]

The costs of collective bargaining merely make employee organization even less attractive from a societal perspective. Under the monopoly model, employee organization will lower the short-run profits of organized firms because, at higher union wages and prices, the organized product market experiences excess capacity until the requisite number of producers leave the market to achieve the new organized

---

levels of employment above this amount, the marginal benefit of additional employees is less than their marginal cost, and the total net benefit of employing labor is decreasing. Thus, at the point where the marginal cost of labor and the labor demand curve cross, the total net benefit of employing labor is maximized. The wage the monopsonist will seek to pay to employ this amount of labor (W_m) is given by the labor supply curve, because this is the minimum amount the monopsony can pay to elicit the profit-maximizing amount of labor (N_m).

115. When confronted by a union, the monopsony faces a marginal cost of labor curve that is horizontal at the union wage from the origin until the labor supply curve and then rises above the labor supply curve.

116. DAVEY ET AL., *supra* note 109, at 308-09; *see also* W. Kip Viscusi, *Unions, Labor Market Structure, and the Welfare Implications of the Quality of Work*, 1 J. LAB. RES. 175 (1980).

117. *See* DAVEY ET AL., *supra* note 109, at 309; BELTON M. FLEISCHER & THOMAS J. KNIESNER, LABOR ECONOMICS: THEORY, EVIDENCE, AND POLICY 210-12, 219 (3d ed. 1984); HIRSCH & ADDISON, *supra* note 13, at 22; WEILER, *supra* note 22, at 126 ("Rarely does a firm enjoy a monopsonistic position vis-a-vis workers."); Daniel R. Fischel, *Labor Markets and Labor Law Compared with Capital Markets and Corporate Law*, 51 U. CHI. L. REV. 1061, 1068 (1984); Posner, *supra* note 52, at 991-92. *But see* LLOYD G. REYNOLDS ET AL., LABOR ECONOMICS AND LABOR RELATIONS 51 (9th ed. 1986) (arguing that employer monopsony power is not uncommon). Despite the widespread belief among labor economists that employer monopsony power is not in general an important factor in the dynamics of the American labor market, some recent empirical work suggests that employer monopsony power can be important in some professions, including nursing and teaching. *See* B.G. Dahlby, *Monopsony and the Shortage of School Teachers in England and Wales, 1948-73*, 13 APPLIED ECON. 303 (1981); Richard W. Stratton, *Monopoly, Monopsony and Union Strength and Local Market Wage Differentials*, 44 AM. J. ECON. & SOC. 305 (1985); Daniel Sullivan, *Monopsony Power in the Market for Nurses*, 32 J.L. & ECON. S135 (1989).

market equilibrium.[118] It also seems safe to assume that employee organization conflicts with the preferences of most managers. Thus, firms will have incentives to expend resources publicizing their views or firing productive prounion employees to resist employee organization.[119] Organization will gain some employees a monopoly rent. However, because all workers commonly share the same wages and benefits whether they are union members or not,[120] employees have individual incentives to "free ride" on the efforts of others by not actively participating in the union even though they enjoy its benefits.[121] Unions will thus have incentive to expend resources publicizing their views, absorbing discriminatory discharges, and undertaking other organizational activities, such as rallies or strikes, in order to overcome employer resistance and individual defection.[122] Additionally, both the union and the employer incur time and information costs in undertaking collective negotiations. Indeed, under the monopoly model, the fact that the employees have imperfect information regarding the optimal wage that can be extracted from the employer can lead to a strike to adjust employee expectations or sort out employers who can afford to pay a high wage from those who can only afford a low wage.[123] Such a strike imposes costs on the employer and employees in the forms of lost profits and lost wages. If the strike is so widespread in a given product market that adequate substitute goods are not available, such a strike will also impose costs on consumers in the form of forgone consumption.

Finally, given the imprecision of language, disagreements over the interpretation of the contract are inevitable. Because the value of an agreement is only as good as its enforcement, both the union and the employer will have incentives to expend resources to resolve disputes

---

118. *See* HIRSCH & ADDISON, *supra* note 13, at 12-14, 21-22.

119. Given the incentives of employers and unions, respectively, to resist and undertake employee organization under the monopoly model, it makes sense to call these activities "strategic behaviors" within the model because they are undertaken to benefit one party at the expense of the other. However, neither this characteristic of the activity nor the nature of these costs as a positional externality is ever explicitly taken account of in the model.

120. Indeed, similar treatment of union and nonunion employees is required by law. 29 U.S.C. § 158(a)(3) (1988).

121. Within the context of the monopoly model of unions such "free riding" is part of the ordinary defection from a cartel one would expect in a competitive economy.

122. Employers and unions might also expend resources to lower or raise barriers to entry or to shift demand and supply curves to gain an advantage in organizing or negotiation of the union wage. Campbell, *supra* note 52, at 1007-09. For now, I will take barriers to entry and demand and supply curves as given and concentrate on the costs of collective bargaining discussed in the text. I consider these costs more central to the analysis of American labor law.

123. Recall my discussion of imperfect information theories of strikes, *supra* notes 74-77 and accompanying text.

that arise under the agreement. These costs of collective bargaining are generally assumed to exceed the corresponding negotiation and enforcement costs that would be incurred under a competitive market.[124] Under the monopoly model of unions and collective bargaining, the excess costs of undertaking collective bargaining are waste, because they further no productive purpose but only the cartelization of the labor market.

The traditional monopoly analysis concludes that unions and collective bargaining are inefficient and inequitable. Unions and their associated higher wages impose inefficiency in both the production and consumption of union goods. In addition, the collective bargaining process imposes costs on society in the form of discriminatory discharges, strikes, and possibly foregone consumption. These costs exceed the negotiation and enforcement costs of a competitive labor market and represent a deadweight loss to society.[125] Unions are inequitable in that they achieve higher wages at the expense of other employees, who are displaced to now-depressed labor markets, and consumers, who have to pay higher prices for fewer goods. Given that these workers and consumers are likely to be similarly situated with respect to the initial distribution of wealth, it is hard to justify this redistribution of wealth on the basis of egalitarian or other common normative principles. In short, under the monopoly analysis, unions are bad and should be discouraged or outlawed. Moreover, any limitations on union power, such as employer resistance or employee free riding, are beneficial and should be encouraged.

B. *Application of the Model to American Labor Law*

Various authors have analyzed American labor law from the perspective of the monopoly model of unions and collective bargaining.[126]

---

124. This assumption is implicit in many analyses. *See* Epstein, *supra* note 8, at 1396-97; Posner, *supra* note 52, at 997-98. Arguably there would be economies of scale in collective bargaining with respect to the ordinary time and information costs of negotiation and enforcement of labor agreements. However, proponents of the monopoly model of unions and collective bargaining typically assume that these economies of scale are outweighed by the organizing and strike costs of collective bargaining that are not incurred in a competitive market. *See, e.g.,* Epstein, *supra* note 8, at 1396-97. To my knowledge no rigorous empirical test of either of these assumptions exists.

125. In economics a *deadweight loss* is a cost that does not yield productive service or is not merely a transfer of wealth from one party to another. THE MIT DICTIONARY OF MODERN ECONOMICS, *supra* note 31, at 97.

126. *See* Campbell, *supra* note 52, at 998-1003; Epstein, *supra* note 8; Fischel, *supra* note 117; H. Gregg Lewis, *The Labor-Monopoly Problem: A Positive Program,* 59 J. POL. ECON. 277 (1951); Bernard D. Meltzer, *Labor Unions, Collective Bargaining, and the Antitrust Laws,* 32 U. CHI. L. REV. 659 (1965); Posner, *supra* note 52; Simons, *supra* note 8; Ralph K. Winter, Jr., *Collective Bargaining and Competition: The Application of Antitrust Standards to Union Activities,* 73 YALE L.J. 14, 21-23 (1963).

Perhaps the most comprehensive of these studies was undertaken by Richard Epstein.[127] In characterizing Epstein's work as a traditional monopoly analysis, I do not mean to oversimplify his arguments. Epstein notes exceptions to the simple monopoly analysis, acknowledging possible sources of union wage increases besides labor cartel rents[128] and acknowledging the strategic nature of collective bargaining.[129] Moreover, Epstein expressly rejects one of the key conclusions of the monopoly model, that unions ought to be outlawed.[130] However, although Epstein notes exceptions to the monopoly model, he does not consistently take account of these deviations throughout his analysis,[131] the dominant thrust of which is unmistakably that of the traditional monopoly model.[132] Epstein's conclusions have proved very controversial among traditional labor law theorists.[133] Accordingly, I believe it is useful to examine Epstein's arguments within the context

---

127. Although his analysis is couched in terms of "libertarian values" and "utilitarianism," Epstein acknowledges the strong relationship between his analysis and the traditional economic analysis of unions. Epstein attributes the insights of his article to "recent advances" in legal theory and law and economics. Epstein, *supra* note 8, at 1358. He explicitly equates his brand of utilitarianism with wealth maximization. *See id.* at 1379 n.70, 1380. He further states that the key difference between his utilitarian and libertarian analyses is that the former takes account of third-party effects, *id.* at 1380-81, a distinction which seems to make little difference to the conclusions of his analysis.

128. *See id.* 1384-85 & n.85 (Ricardian rents), 1402 (product market rents).

129. *See id.* at 1384, 1396-97.

130. Epstein would allow voluntary contracts among workers to form unions, *see id.* at 1366, but would not afford union members any protection from employer discrimination. *See id.* at 1394-95.

131. For example, Epstein acknowledges the possibility of employer rents as a source of union wage increases, *see id.* at 1384-85 & n.85, 1402, but never takes this possibility into account in his discussion of the legality of yellow-dog contracts. *See id.* at 1370-75. Following the traditional monopoly union analysis, Epstein argues that yellow-dog contracts should be legal because, in a competitive market, workers will be compensated with higher wages for any losses they suffer in making such agreements. *Id.* However, if employer rents are available for employees to share, the employees' share of such rents is a public good among the employees that, due to free-rider problems, they will individually sign away for much less than their share is worth. Similarly, Epstein argues that employers cannot dictate wages to individual workers, because if they could they would reduce their wages to zero. *See id.* at 1372. He concludes that workers who individually bargain will not be taken advantage of in negotiations with their employer. However, if there are employer rents, then the employees can gain a share of those rents only by bargaining collectively. If the workers individually bargain, the employer will indeed reduce their share of any cooperative surplus to zero.

132. In his analysis, Epstein also generally assumes that competitive markets will prevail in the absence of unions, *see id.* at 1359, 1372, 1382; *but see id.* at 1384-85, 1402 (acknowledging employer rents as a possible source of union wage increases); that unions are labor monopolies, *see id.* at 1380-81, 1384; and that employers will respond to union wage demands by moving up their demand curve. *See id.* at 1362, 1380-81. Epstein's analysis is inconsistent on the nature of negotiations between employers and unions because he adopts all of the other assumptions of the monopoly model and several times assumes employers have no monopsony power, *see id.* at 1372, 1405, thereby logically precluding strategic behavior in collective negotiations, *see supra* note 117 and accompanying text, but he assumes that a union's formation creates a case of bilateral monopoly that will result in wasteful strategic behavior.

133. *See* Getman & Kohler, *supra* note 95; Verkuil, *supra* note 95.

of the monopoly model and to comment on them in light of my alternative bargaining model.

1. *The Public Policy of Fostering Unions and Collective Bargaining*

The public policy of fostering unions and collective bargaining that has served as the foundation of American labor law since the 1930s does not make sense from the perspective of the monopoly model of unions. The drafters of the New Deal labor statutes[134] believed that individual bargaining often failed the interests of workers and that collective organization was a positive good that would allow workers to "exercise actual liberty of contract" and "obtain acceptable terms and conditions of employment."[135] However, under the monopoly model of unions, individual bargaining will obtain for workers all the wages and benefits to which their productivity entitles them.[136] Moreover, unions are both inequitable[137] and inefficient,[138] decreasing total wealth. Thus, the monopoly theory of unions, far from providing any logical basis for a law promoting employee organization, suggests unions should be prohibited.

Despite this fairly straightforward implication of the model, it is hard to find proponents of the monopoly model who actually advocate the prohibition of employee organization.[139] Adherents of the model will sometimes acknowledge this deviation of existing law from the recommendations of the model but accept the basic determination to allow the cartelization of the labor market as a normative legislative decision.[140] Even Epstein, who is among the most devoted to the model, would allow private voluntary agreements among workers to negotiate collectively and withhold labor as part of the realization of his libertarian ideals.[141] However, Epstein would allow employers to discharge and discriminate against union members,[142] and almost everywhere, the logic of his analysis leads to the solution of no un-

---

134. Like Epstein, I include in my definition of the New Deal labor statutes the Norris-LaGuardia Act, 29 U.S.C. §§ 101-115 (1988), and the Wagner Act, 29 U.S.C. §§ 151-169 (1988). *See* Epstein, *supra* note 8, at 1357.

135. Norris-LaGuardia Act, ch. 90, § 2, 47 Stat. 70 (1932) (current version at 29 U.S.C. § 102 (1988)).

136. *See supra* notes 8, 107 and accompanying text.

137. *See supra* notes 9-10, 105-11 and accompanying text.

138. *See supra* notes 105-11, 118-25 and accompanying text.

139. The only monopoly theorist I can find who has actually advocated prohibiting employee organization is Henry Simons. *See* Simons, *supra* note 8, at 1.

140. *See, e.g.,* Campbell, *supra* note 52, at 995, 999; Posner, *supra* note 52, at 990.

141. *See* Epstein, *supra* note 8, at 1365-66.

142. *See id.* at 1389, 1391, 1394.

ions.[143] Epstein believes that individual bargaining is adequate to secure for workers all the wages and benefits to which they are entitled[144] and that collective bargaining is a needless complication, largely the creation of statute, that only wastes resources.[145] Epstein also views individual defections from a union as part of the natural workings of the marketplace that serve to undermine the labor cartel's monopoly profits.[146]

2. *The Purposes of Promoting Bargaining Equity and Industrial Peace*

The monopoly theory of unions and collective bargaining provides no logical basis for the twin purposes of American labor law: promoting equality of bargaining power between employers and employees and promoting industrial peace. As previously discussed,[147] the drafters of the New Deal labor legislation sought to foster unionism as a means of promoting "industrial democracy" and greater equality of bargaining power between employers and employees.[148] The monopoly theory recognizes no need for workers to combine to negotiate with their employers. The discipline of the market ensures that the employer will pay the employees all that their productivity entitles them to and no more. By encouraging employee organization, the law actually promotes employees to a bargaining position superior to that of their employer, allowing them to form a cartel that can then dictate the market wage.

The proponents of the Wagner Act and the Taft-Hartley amendments also believed that encouraging collective bargaining and regulating the conduct of industrial relations could decrease the strife and conflict that had too often characterized American industrial relations, thereby promoting industrial peace.[149] The traditional monopoly model of unions recognizes little opportunity for conflict in bargaining. Absent a strike that is undertaken as the low-cost method of lowering unrealistic rank-and-file workers' expectations or of sorting out low-wage employers from high-wage employers, the union merely tells the employer what the wage will be, and the employer responds by

---

143. *See id.* at 1384-85, 1393-94, 1397, 1405-06.

144. *See id.* at 1366, 1371-72.

145. *See id.* at 1397-98, 1405.

146. *See id.* at 1384.

147. *See supra* note 2 and accompanying text.

148. *See* Norris-LaGuardia Act, ch. 90, § 3, 47 Stat. 70 (1932) (current version at 29 U.S.C. § 102 (1988)); Wagner Act, ch. 372, § 1, 49 Stat. 449 (1935) (current version, the NLRA, at 29 U.S.C. § 151 (1988)); *supra* note 2 and accompanying text.

149. *See* 29 U.S.C. § 151 (1988); *supra* note 2 and accompanying text.

telling the employees how many of them should show up for work the next day.[150] Any law that sought to promote industrial peace and minimize the number of such informational strikes would focus merely on the reliable transmission to the employees of information about the employer's profitability rather than undertaking the wide-ranging regulation of collective bargaining contained in the current law.[151] Moreover, there would seem to be little the law could do to minimize the number of such strikes because, if there were a cheaper means of conveying the information necessary to lower worker expectations or signal that the employer was a low-wage employer, the parties would voluntarily undertake it to avoid the costs of a strike.[152]

Epstein's arguments concerning the twin purposes of American labor law only partially track those of the monopoly model.[153] True to the theory of the monopoly model of unions, Epstein views collective bargaining as a needless and detrimental alternative to individual bargaining.[154] The power of the individual worker to leave his employer for work elsewhere will protect the worker from exploitation by his employer.[155] Allowing workers to organize across a product market allows them to dictate that market's wages and prices.[156] However, with respect to the purpose of promoting industrial peace, Epstein deviates from the analysis of the traditional monopoly model of unions. Epstein argues that the current law creates a situation of bilateral monopoly between unions and employers in which these parties play noncooperative games of bluff and bluster that lead to costly strikes.[157] In Epstein's view, the purpose of promoting industrial peace would be better served by leaving labor negotiations to individual bargaining that avoids such costly games.[158] This deviation from the monopoly model is problematic because Epstein fails to identify the source of the employer's power to resist a labor monopoly in a

---

150. *See supra* note 22 and accompanying text.

151. *See supra* notes 3-5 and accompanying text.

152. This statement is only strictly true if the third-party costs of the strike are insignificant. If such costs are significant, a reliable method of communicating such information may exist that the parties would not voluntarily undertake because it is more costly to them than a strike, but that nonetheless costs society as a whole less than a strike. However, ignoring third-party effects, if, for example, completely opening the company books to the union would sufficiently lower worker expectations or sufficiently clearly indicate that the employer was a low-wage employer to avoid a strike, one would predict that the employer would do so voluntarily.

153. *See* Epstein, *supra* note 8, at 1403-08.

154. *See id.* at 1405-06.

155. *See id.* at 1370-72.

156. *See id.* at 1381-82, 1384.

157. *Id.* at 1396-97.

158. *See id.* at 1404.

bilateral relationship and survive in the economy.[159] Furthermore, Epstein fails to examine the implications of such sources of employer power and the results of bilateral bargaining solutions consistently throughout his analysis.[160] Thus, although Epstein abandons the monopoly model of unions on the subject of strikes where its logic and explanatory power seems weakest, he fails to treat consistently the implications of this desertion throughout his analysis.[161]

3. *The Law on Organizing*

The law on organizing also does not make sense from the perspective of the monopoly model of unions. Under the National Labor Relations Act,[162] the question of employee organization is determined by majority rule of the affected employees.[163] The primary means of determining employee majority sentiment is through an election supervised by the National Labor Relations Board.[164] Current law prohibits certain employer strategies in resisting unions, including yellow-dog contracts,[165] company unions,[166] discrimination on the basis of union affiliation,[167] and the making of threats or promises of benefits on the basis of union support.[168] By providing this system of elections and restricting employer strategies, American labor law lowers employees' costs of organizing.[169] From the perspective of the monopoly theory of unions, the government should not facilitate the cartelization of labor markets by lowering the cost of organizing.

---

159. Although elsewhere in his article Epstein acknowledges both Ricardian rents and product market rents as possible bones of contention between the employees and employer, his arguments on industrial peace do not disclose the surplus that is the source of the bilateral negotiations. *See id.* at 1404-08.

160. *See supra* note 131.

161. Posner also abandons the pure form of the monopoly model of unions in discussing strikes and fails to take account of the implications of this abandonment for the rest of his analysis. *See* Posner, *supra* note 52, at 997.

162. 29 U.S.C. § 151 (1988).

163. 29 U.S.C. § 159(a) (1988); *see* MERRIFIELD ET AL., *supra* note 2, at 27.

164. 29 U.S.C. § 159(c) (1988). Unions can also demonstrate majority status through voluntary recognition by their employer, *see* 1 THE DEVELOPING LABOR LAW, *supra* note 2, at 341, or merely by a show of authorization cards signed by a majority of the affected employees where violations of the law by the employer preclude holding a meaningful election. NLRB v. Gissel Packing Co., 395 U.S. 575 (1969).

165. 29 U.S.C. § 103 (1988); *see supra* note 4.

166. 29 U.S.C. § 158(a)(2) (1988). A *company union* is an association of employees organized and controlled by the employer. COX ET AL., *supra* note 2, at 41. Such organizations can be used as a bulwark against independent unions because they give the employees a portion of the benefits of organization and give some of the employees a vested interest in the employer's organization.

167. 29 U.S.C. § 158(a)(3) (1988).

168. 29 U.S.C. § 158(c) (1988).

169. Posner, *supra* note 52, at 994.

Epstein's analysis of the laws on organizing directly tracks the monopoly union analysis. Epstein advocates abolishing the doctrine of exclusive representation[170] that underlies the current system of elections, on the basis that individual employees have the right not to be represented by a union and individual defections will serve to undermine labor cartel rents.[171] Moreover, Epstein argues that employers should be able to resort to any strategy in resisting unions, short of fraud or violence.[172] Epstein denigrates arguments that employees are effectively compelled to accept yellow-dog contracts as a condition of employment due to an inequality in bargaining power between employers and employees, arguing that if employers could compel employees to accept unfavorable contract terms they could logically reduce wages to zero.[173] Through the machinations of the competitive market, employees will be compensated for any loss they suffer in accepting yellow-dog contracts; otherwise, they would not agree to employment under such terms.[174] Similarly, Epstein argues that there may be value in the adjustment of grievances by a company union, and, if such a union is in fact a sham or even a burden to the employees, the employer will have to compensate them accordingly to retain them.[175] Epstein views the prohibition of discriminatory hiring and discharge as a similar, but more intrusive, restriction to that of the prohibition of yellow-dog contracts.[176] He argues that employers should not be prohibited from retaining only loyal employees who are the most valuable to the firm for the sake of encouraging employee organization.[177] Finally, Epstein argues that employers should be able to prohibit all employee organizing activities from their property and to make any antiunion statements they desire, short of fraud or threats of violence, including threats of reprisals or promises of benefits on the basis of union support.[178] The basis of his argument is that the employer cannot reasonably be expected to provide an in-kind subsidy to a union it considers antithetical to its prosperity, or to remain neutral on a question of such enormous self-interest to the firm.[179]

170. Epstein, *supra* note 8, at 1398-99.
171. *Id.* at 1384, 1398-99.
172. *See id.* at 1365-66.
173. *Id.* at 1371-72.
174. *Id.* at 1382.
175. *Id.* at 1391-92.
176. *Id.* at 1392-93.
177. *Id.*
178. *Id.* at 1388-91.
179. *Id.*

4. *The Law on Collective Negotiations*

Similarly, the law on collective negotiations makes no sense under the monopoly theory of unions. Current law designates the union selected by the majority of the employees as the exclusive representative of all the employees in the unit[180] and requires the employer to bargain with the union in good faith.[181] In Epstein's view, the designation of the union as the exclusive representative combined with the obligation that the employer bargain in good faith merely places the force of law behind the union's labor cartel.[182] Returning to a competitive market, by allowing employers to partake in or even insist on negotiations with individual employees, would be more equitable and more efficient. Except where prohibited by state law,[183] unions are allowed to negotiate and enforce "union security" agreements with their employers that require, as a condition of employment, that all employees contribute to the costs of collective bargaining.[184] In addition, current law prohibits the employer from discharging striking employees,[185] although it does allow the employer to permanently replace them.[186] As Epstein points out, allowing the negotiation and enforcement of union security agreements and prohibiting the discharge of striking employees merely provides additional barriers to the market forces that would naturally tend to erode and limit union monopoly power.[187]

Moreover, the monopoly model yields no coherent basis on which to distinguish "good faith" from "bad faith" bargaining. To determine if a party is bargaining in good faith, the Board and courts examine whether the party has a bona fide intent to reach agreement.[188] The presence or absence of such intent is judged from the totality of

---

180. 29 U.S.C. § 159(a) (1988). The employer is prohibited from negotiating with individual employees concerning terms and conditions of employment, GETMAN & POGREBIN, *supra* note 2, at 97, and even preexisting individual employment contracts are superseded by any collective agreement. J.I. Case Co. v. NLRB, 321 U.S. 332, 339 (1944). Similarly, bargaining efforts or "wildcat" strikes by individual employees or groups of employees do not enjoy the protections of the National Labor Relations Act. Emporium Capwell Co. v. Western Addition Community Org., 420 U.S. 50, 65-70 (1974).

181. 29 U.S.C. § 158(d) (1988).

182. Epstein, *supra* note 8, at 1395-98.

183. 29 U.S.C. § 164(b) (1988).

184. 29 U.S.C. § 158(a)(3) (1988); *see* Communication Workers v. Beck, 487 U.S. 735, 738 (1988).

185. *See* 29 U.S.C. § 157 (1988); 2 THE DEVELOPING LABOR LAW, *supra* note 2, at 1003.

186. NLRB v. Mackay Radio & Tel. Co., 304 U.S. 333, 345 (1938).

187. Epstein, *supra* note 8, at 1384 (discussing union security agreements), 1392-94 (discussing discriminatory discharges).

188. *See* NLRB v. General Elec. Co. 418 F.2d 736, 756-61 (2d Cir. 1969), *cert. denied*, 397 U.S. 965 (1970); NLRB v. Montgomery Ward & Co., 133 F.2d 676, 683-84 (9th Cir. 1943). Alternatively, *bad faith* has sometimes been defined as the desire not to reach an agreement. NLRB v. Reed & Prince Mfg. Co., 205 F.2d 131, 134 (1st Cir.), *cert. denied*, 346 U.S. 887 (1953).

466   *Michigan Law Review*   [Vol. 91:419]

circumstances surrounding the negotiations.[189] Although such a determination is very subjective, the Board and courts have determined that certain strategies and conduct are presumptively bad faith bargaining.[190] In one such strategy, known as *Boulwareism,*[191] the employer determines a bargaining position and presents it to the union on a "take it or leave it" basis combined with an extensive publicity campaign proclaiming that the offer will not be changed.[192] Another such strategy, of particular interest to the discussion at hand, is the failure of the employer to provide requested information reasonably necessary for the union to perform its function as exclusive representative.[193]

As previously discussed, the traditional monopoly model employs only a very simple model of collective negotiations in which the union sets the wage and the employer sets the level of employment.[194] Such a primitive model provides no basis for defining "good faith" or for evaluating various bargaining tactics such as Boulwareism. Epstein realizes this, but he blames his inability to rationalize the problem on the intractability of the concept of "good faith" rather than on the inadequacy of his model.[195] Because under the monopoly model strikes are the result of imperfect information, one might hope that the model could explain why the law requires employers to provide unions with certain information. However, under the monopoly model one would expect that employers will provide such information to unions voluntarily if doing so is the lowest-cost method of avoiding strikes.[196]

---

189. NLRB v. Truitt Mfg. Co., 351 U.S. 149, 153-54 (1956); *General Electric Co.,* 418 F.2d at 756.

190. "Hard bargaining" is not in and of itself a violation of the duty to bargain in good faith. Dierks Forests, Inc., 148 N.L.R.B. 923, 930 (1964). Both sides are allowed to make a firm final offer at some juncture in the negotiations. *See, e.g.,* Philip Carey Mfg. Co., Miami Cabinet Div. v. NLRB, 331 F.2d 720, 725 (6th Cir. 1964), *cert. denied,* 379 U.S. 888 (1964). Moreover, the Act specifically states that the obligation to bargain in good faith "does not compel either party to agree to a proposal or require the making of a concession." 29 U.S.C. § 158(d) (1988). However, where a party's pattern of conduct in failing to meet sufficiently with the other side, respond to proposals, make and explain counterproposals, supply information, and supply a representative who can effectively negotiate on its behalf evidences a lack of a genuine desire to reach agreement, the Board will find a failure to bargain in good faith. *See* GETMAN & POGREBIN, *supra* note 2, at 126.

191. The tactic is named after the man who developed it in the late 1940s, former General Electric Vice-President Lemuel Boulware. MERRIFIELD ET AL., *supra* note 2, at 512.

192. *General Electric Co.,* 418 F.2d at 756.

193. J.I. Case Co. v. NLRB, 253 F.2d 149, 154-55 (7th Cir. 1958). Unions have a similar obligation to supply relevant information. Local 13, Detroit Newspaper Printing & Graphic Communications Union, 233 N.L.R.B. 994, 996 (1977), *affd.,* 598 F.2d 267 (D.C. Cir. 1979). But from a practical perspective it is much less important.

194. *See supra* note 22 and accompanying text.

195. *See* Epstein, *supra* note 8, at 1395-96.

196. As previously discussed, this statement is only strictly true if the third-party effects of strikes are insignificant. *See supra* note 152. If there are significant third-party effects, then

Even if one attempts to append a more realistic model of bargaining to the monopoly model of unions to account for the possibility of strategic behavior, these efforts to regulate collective bargaining make no sense. As Epstein notes, requiring disclosure of information to labor unions is merely another method of lowering the costs of organization, thereby encouraging labor cartelization with all its attendant problems.[197]

5. *The Law on Enforcement of the Collective Agreement*

Finally, the law on the enforcement of collective agreements seems somewhat inconsistent with the monopoly model of unions. Collective bargaining agreements are enforceable as a matter of federal substantive law under section 301 of the Labor Management Relations Act.[198] The Supreme Court has interpreted this federal substantive law to include federal authority to enforce agreements to arbitrate[199] and several other features that encourage the resolution of disputes under collective bargaining agreements through arbitration.[200] Given the existence of a collective agreement, one could logically argue that, even under the monopoly theory of unions, the law should encourage arbitration as the low-cost method of resolving disputes over the contract. Within the context of the monopoly model of unions, encouraging arbitration would minimize the costs of collective bargaining to society, given the alternative solutions of resolving such disputes through economic warfare or through protracted and costly litigation. However, this argument still seems at odds with the monopoly model's general conclusion that collective bargaining is inequitable and inefficient. Why encourage the cartelization of the labor market by providing an inexpensive means of enforcing cartel contracts? Perhaps if the enforcement of cartel contracts were expensive enough, the cost would

---

requiring the disclosure of information may minimize total societal costs even through it does not minimize the union's and employer's costs.

197. *See* Epstein, *supra* note 8, at 1397.

198. 29 U.S.C. § 185 (1988); *see* Textile Workers Union v. Lincoln Mills, 353 U.S. 448, 449-52 (1957).

199. *Textile Workers Union,* 353 U.S. at 449-56.

200. In Local 174, Teamsters v. Lucas Flour Co., 369 U.S. 95, 104-06 (1962), the Court found that agreements to arbitrate include implied agreements not to strike or lock out over arbitrable issues. Moreover, in Boys Mkts., Inc. v. Retail Clerks' Union, 398 U.S. 235, 253 (1970), the Court found federal authority to enjoin strikes in contravention of an arbitration agreement despite clear language in the Norris-LaGuardia Act to the contrary. Finally, in the *Steelworkers Trilogy,* the Supreme Court announced a federal policy of deferring to arbitration in determining which issues are arbitrable and in resolving those disputes. United Steelworkers v. American Mfg. Co., 363 U.S. 564, 568-69 (1960); United Steelworkers v. Warrior & Gulf Navigation Co., 363 U.S. 574, 582-83 (1960); United Steelworkers v. Enterprise Wheel & Car Corp., 363 U.S. 593, 596 (1960).

discourage cartelization. Moreover, one might argue that, even if society encourages the low-cost method of enforcing cartel contracts, consumers and unorganized workers who are injured by the cartel should have a right of action against the cartel similar to private suits for damages under the Clayton Act.[201]

C. *A Critique of the Monopoly Model from an Economic Perspective*

As previously discussed, in resolving the three issues presented in the primer on labor economics, the traditional monopoly model of unions and collective bargaining combines the first of the various possible assumptions presented with respect to each issue. The monopoly analysis assumes that the source of union benefits is a labor cartel, that employers respond to union wage increases by moving up their labor demand curve, and that the costs of collective bargaining should be treated as ordinary transaction costs. The choice of each of these three assumptions is questionable on grounds of both logical arguments and empirical evidence.

1. *The Assumption of a Labor Cartel as the Source of Union Wage Increases*

It seems very doubtful that cartelization of the labor market is the sole, or even the primary, source of union wage increases in the American economy.[202] The establishment of a labor cartel in any market without licensure would seem very difficult.[203] Workers are the consummate atomistic competitors. Moreover, if labor cartel power were the only source of union wage increases, an organizing campaign that proceeded to organize one competitive employer at a time would get nowhere because there would be only costs of unionization, but no benefits, to show employees until the requisite number of employers was organized. A labor cartel in a competitive product market without employer rents or productivity increases associated with unionism would have to be simultaneously organized across many employers in order to survive — like Athena springing full-grown from Zeus' head.

Employer product market power rents, Ricardian rents, and quasirents constitute much more likely sources of union wage increases. If the requisite barriers to entry to a product market exist, the employers

---

201. 15 U.S.C. § 15 (1988).

202. WEILER, *supra* note 22, at 124-33; Fischel, *supra* note 117, at 1072-73.

203. The members of an occupation can use licensure to generate labor cartel rents by lobbying to raise the requirements of licensure above what is needed to successfully perform in the occupation, thereby restricting the supply of labor in the occupation. In such a case the force of the licensure law enforces the labor cartel.

would be more likely to exploit them than would a labor cartel. The employers are much more concentrated than individual employees; moreover, normal economic profits sustain employers while they organize their cartel or increase their grasp on market share through expansion or merger. Indeed, when significant economies of scale exist in an industry, the employers, as producers, will naturally gravitate toward oligopoly or monopoly.[204] No such anticompetitive gravity compels the workers to combination.[205] Finally, it seems much more plausible that unions could organize employers who enjoy monopoly rents, Ricardian rents, or quasi-rents, because such organization could be undertaken on a more manageable basis, one employer at a time.[206]

The arguments for the existence of at least some productivity increases associated with unionism also seem compelling. The argument that long-term implicit contracts yield benefits in monitoring and firm-specific human capital investment is intuitively appealing and well established in the economics literature.[207] Without unions, workers are left with only the uncertain and inefficient discipline of reputation to

---

204. *See* SCHERER, *supra* note 24, at 81-118; WILLIAM G. SHEPHERD & CLAIR WILCOX, PUBLIC POLICIES TOWARD BUSINESS 45-48 (6th ed. 1979).

205. The fact that antitrust laws prohibit employers from explicit cartelization and some means of achieving monopoly, *see* Sherman Act, 15 U.S.C. §§ 1-2 (1988), while not prohibiting labor cartelization, *see* Clayton Act, 15 U.S.C. § 17 (1988); Apex Hosiery Co. v. Leader, 310 U.S. 469 (1940), does not seem a very convincing basis for arguing that employer product market power rents are a less likely source of union wage increases than labor cartel rents. The laws still allow tacit collusion, *see* Theatre Enters. Inc. v. Paramount Film Distrib. Corp., 346 U.S. 537 (1954), and monopolization through legitimate means of competition. *See* United States v. Griffith, 334 U.S. 100, 107 (1948) (citing United States v. Aluminum Co. of Am., 148 F.2d 416 (2d Cir. 1945)); *see also* Berkey Photo, Inc. v. Eastman Kodak Co., 603 F.2d 263, 276 (2d Cir. 1979), *cert. denied,* 444 U.S. 1093 (1980); United States v. United Shoe Mach. Corp., 110 F. Supp. 295, 342-45 (D. Mass. 1953), *affd.,* 347 U.S. 521 (1954). Moreover, historically the antitrust laws have been notoriously ineffective, *see* Kenneth G. Elzinga, *The Antimerger Law: Pyrrhic Victories?,* 12 J.L. & ECON. 43 (1969); Malcolm R. Pfunder et al., *Compliance with Divestiture Orders Under Section 7 of the Clayton Act: An Analysis of the Relief Obtained,* 17 ANTITRUST BULL. 19 (1972), with slack enforcement and minuscule penalties. *See* 2 JAMES M. CLABAULT & MICHAEL K. BLOCK, SHERMAN ACT INDICTMENTS 1955-1980, at 732-33 (1981) (showing that average antitrust fines range approximately from 0.1% to 4% of the volume of commerce involved in the cases); POSNER & EASTERBROOK, *supra* note 26, at 320-22 (showing that incarceration of antitrust offenders is rare and almost never exceeds three months). *See generally* Walter Adams et al., *Pareto Optimality and Antitrust Policy: The Old Chicago and the New Learning,* 58 S. ECON. J. 1 (1991); Walter Adams & James W. Brock, *1980s Gigantomania Follies,* CHALLENGE, Mar.-Apr. 1992, at 4; Walter Adams & James W. Brock, *Corporate Size and the Bailout Factor,* 21 J. ECON. ISSUES 61 (1987); Walter Adams & James W. Brock, *Corporate Power and Economic Sabotage,* 20 J. ECON. ISSUES 919, 936 (1986).

206. In fact, unions have historically organized one employer at a time. *See, e.g.,* VICTOR G. REUTHER, THE BROTHERS REUTHER AND THE STORY OF THE UAW 146-47 (1976) (discussing UAW attempts to organize General Motors); *cf.* COX ET AL., *supra* note 2, at 281-82, 288 (noting that unions may prefer to organize divisions of a single employer separately). *See generally* DULLES, *supra* note 92, at 88-90 (describing early attempts to form national unions); HENRY PELLING, AMERICAN LABOR 70 (1960).

207. *See* Parsons, *supra* note 45, at 789; Rosen, *supra* note 45; *supra* notes 45-49 and accompanying text.

prevent employers from breaching such contracts. Similarly, public goods dominate the conditions of employment in most employment contracts and pose a serious problem for the negotiation of efficient individual contracts.[208] It seems quite plausible that collective bargaining could help rectify this problem, as well as lower worker turnover, by giving employees a superior means of expressing their concerns.

Several authors have argued that union productivity increases cannot be real or substantial because, if they were, employers would encourage unionism and split the proceeds from these productivity increases with employees.[209] This argument ignores the fact that many employers *are* anxious to organize employees in committees or associations for the purposes of communication. Perhaps not coincidentally, the decline of unions in the United States has been accompanied by a rash of cases testing the legal bounds of employer efforts to organize employees despite the National Labor Relations Act's prohibition against company unions.[210] What employers are *not* interested in is organizing independent unions that could vie for a share of employer rents and interfere with management prerogatives. Even though such independent organization would yield greater productivity increases due to effective enforcement of long-term implicit contracts, greater accuracy in the assessment of employee preferences with respect to collective goods, and more effective monitoring of management efficiency,[211] employers do not want independent organi-

---

208. *See supra* note 50 and accompanying text. Addressing this public good problem is one of the primary goals of the new field of study called Human Resources Management. *See, e.g.,* ROBERT E. SIBSON, STRATEGIC PLANNING FOR HUMAN RESOURCES MANAGEMENT 142-55 (1991); GEORGE E. STEVENS, CASES AND EXERCISES IN HUMAN RESOURCES MANAGEMENT (5th ed. 1991).

209. *See* Campbell, *supra* note 52, at 996-97; Epstein, *supra* note 8, at 1402-03; Posner, *supra* note 52, at 1000-01.

210. *See* NLRB v. Streamway Div. of Scott & Fetzer Co., 691 F.2d 288 (6th Cir. 1982); Hertzka & Knowles v. NLRB, 503 F.2d 625 (9th Cir. 1974), *cert. denied,* 423 U.S. 875 (1975); *Member Raudabaugh Forecasts NLRB Ruling in* Electromation *Case Before December 1992,* Daily Lab. Rep. (BNA) No. 141, at A-4 (July 22, 1992) (predicting that the *Electromation, Inc.* opinion on "employee involvement programs and quality circles" will be released before Christmas, 1992). Prior to the enactment of the Wagner Act, three out of five union members belonged to unions organized by their employers. COX ET AL., *supra* note 2, at 201. Although some of these company unions were undoubtedly organized merely as a bulwark against independent organization, some were honest attempts at increasing communication between the employer and employees that incidentally discouraged true organization. *Id.*

211. Although employer organization of employee committees holds the promise of some productivity increases due to greater communication between employers and employees, it seems unlikely that employer-organized committees could achieve the full productivity increases that are possible with independent unions. Captive committees could not be as effective as independent unions in enforcing long-term implicit contracts against the employer, solving the free-rider problem of collective goods in the workplace, or monitoring management, because the committee would be merely an extension of the employer. *See* JOHN F. WITTE, DEMOCRACY, AUTHORITY,

zation because sharing rents with employees decreases profits, and managers prefer not to be effectively monitored.[212] Furthermore, employers can realize some of the productivity increases associated with independent employee organization by free riding on the information obtained by observing the production and employment practices of their organized competitors.

Empirical evidence also suggests that labor cartel power is less important than other sources of union wage increases. Based on available statistics, there seem to be few product markets in the United States that contain a percentage of organized workers that might even be imagined a labor cartel. Nationally, the proportion of private sector employees represented by a union is currently about 14%.[213] Among industry groups and occupations for which such statistics are collected by the Bureau of Labor Statistics, the highest representation in any industry group on a national basis is 39%, while the highest representation in any particular occupation on a national basis is 42%.[214] Although the percent organized in particular industries, such as automobiles or steel, is undoubtedly higher, typically such industries suffered from product market concentration prior to organization.[215] Similarly, the highest percentage organized in any state is 36%, although variations undoubtedly exist among local product markets.[216]

AND ALIENATION IN WORK: WORKERS' PARTICIPATION IN AN AMERICAN CORPORATION 90-91 (1980); *cf.* FREEMAN & MEDOFF, *supra* note 20, at 8-9 (noting the difficulties faced by a worker without an independent union to back her up in addressing these problems). Of course captive employee committees would presumably also not tend to create the inefficiencies of consumption and production that independent unions sometimes create. *See supra* notes 10, 20 and accompanying text. However, because empirical studies show that these inefficiencies are relatively small, *see supra* notes 50-53 and accompanying text, it seems safe to assume that the greater productivity effects of independent unions usually outweigh the inefficiencies.

212. Empirical studies suggest that, despite possible productivity effects associated with employee organization, unions typically decrease company profits. FREEMAN & MEDOFF, *supra* note 20, at 181-90; HIRSCH & ADDISON, *supra* note 13, at 211-14. This is because the wage increase associated with unionism generally exceeds the productivity increase employee organization yields. FREEMAN & MEDOFF, *supra* note 20, at 22.

213. There were approximately 82,462,000 private sector employees in the United States in 1987, of whom 10,859,000 were union members and 11,887,000 were represented by unions. BUREAU OF LABOR STATISTICS, U.S. DEPT. OF LABOR, CURRENT WAGE DEVELOPMENTS 7 (Feb. 1988); *see also* LEO TROY & NEIL SHEFLIN, UNION SOURCEBOOK (1985); U.S. DEPT. OF LABOR, NEWS: UNION MEMBERS IN 1989, at 2 (1990).

214. BUREAU OF LABOR STATISTICS, *supra* note 213, at 7. The most highly represented industries are communications and public utilities while the most highly represented occupation is protective services. *Id.; see also* Michael A. Curme et al., *Union Membership and Contract Coverage in the United States, 1983-1988*, 44 INDUS. & LAB. REL. REV. 5 (1990).

215. *See, e.g.,* United States v. United States Steel Corp., 251 U.S. 417, 437-38 (1920) (noting the concentration of the steel industry in 1920). Price negotiation was also a factor in generating employer rents prior to organization in industries such as trucking and the airlines.

216. STATISTICAL ABSTRACT OF THE UNITED STATES Table No. 666 (1988) (using 1982 data); TROY & SHEFLIN, *supra* note 213, at 7-4 (using 1982 data). Unlike the previous figures,

Direct empirical evidence of the source of union wage increases is difficult to produce due to the strategic incentives of employers in labor negotiations. Product price increases may be associated with the negotiation of a union contract even if the union wage increase will be paid out of employer monopoly rents, because the employer has incentive to underprice and plead poverty during negotiations and then adjust prices up after negotiation of the contract.[217] However, the best available evidence suggests that union wage increases come largely at the expense of employers[218] and are strongly associated with the market power of the employing firm.[219] Most empirical models,[220] and even many modern presentations of the monopoly theory of unions, depend on employer product market power, Ricardian rents, or quasi-rents as the source of union wage increases.[221]

Finally, studies have found convincing evidence that some industries enjoy significant productivity increases from unionism.[222] Perhaps the best of these studies was conducted by Kim Clark, who compared the physical output of cement plants before and after organization and between different organized and unorganized plants, finding statistically significant productivity increases with organization

cited *supra* notes 213-14 and accompanying text, this figure includes the more highly organized public sector. As of 1982, the most highly organized state was New York, followed closely by Michigan. TROY & SHEFLIN, *supra* note 213, at 7-4.

217. ALBERT REES, THE ECONOMICS OF TRADE UNIONS 101 (rev. ed. 1977).

218. *See* RICHARD B. FREEMAN, UNIONISM, PRICE-COST MARGINS, AND THE RETURN TO CAPITAL (National Bureau of Economic Research Working Paper No. 1164, 1983); HIRSCH & ADDISON, *supra* note 13, at 211-14; Clark, *supra* note 54, at 918 (using accounting data on over 900 product-line businesses to conclude that unionization substantially decreased profits but had little effect on price, output, or capital-to-labor mix); Paula B. Voos & Lawrence R. Mishel, *The Union Impact on Profits: Evidence from Industry Price-Cost Margin Data*, 4 J. LAB. ECON. 105, 128-29 (1986) (using price-cost margin data on 139 industries over the years 1968-1970 to estimate that on average 80% of union wage and benefit increases was paid out of company profits and only 20% was paid out of price increases to consumers).

219. *See* HIRSCH & ADDISON, *supra* note 13, at 208-14; Thomas Karier, *Unions and Monopoly Profits*, 67 REV. ECON. & STAT. 34 (1985); Thomas A. Pugel, *Profitability, Concentration and the Interindustry Variation in Wages*, 62 REV. ECON. & STAT. 248 (1980); Nancy L. Rose, *Labor Rent Sharing and Regulation: Evidence from the Trucking Industry*, 95 J. POL. ECON. 1146, 1175 (1987); Michael A. Salinger, *Tobin's q, Unionization, and the Concentration-Profits Relationship*, 15 RAND J. ECON. 159 (1984). Rose and Salinger found that, where unions are successful in organizing, they can capture the lion's share of firm monopoly profits (about 75% according to Rose's study). For a similar empirical argument that unions primarily share in employer product market rents based on the deregulation of the airlines, see WEILER, *supra* note 22, at 131-32.

220. *See, e.g.,* HIRSCH, *supra* note 32; Clark, *supra* note 54.

221. HIRSCH & ADDISON, *supra* note 13, at 21.

222. *See* FREEMAN & MEDOFF, *supra* note 20, at 168-69; HIRSCH & ADDISON, *supra* note 13, at 195-208 (surveying and interpreting the relevant literature). *But see* John T. Addison & Barry T. Hirsch, *Union Effects on Productivity, Profits, and Growth: Has the Long Run Arrived?*, 7 J. LAB. ECON. 72 (1989) (concluding that productivity effect of unions has not yet been proved); Peter J. Turnbull, *Trade Unions and Productivity: Opening the Harvard "Black Boxes"*, 12 J. LAB. RES. 135 (1991).

that ranged from 6% to 10%.[223] However, other studies suggest that not all industries enjoy such productivity gains[224] and that productivity increases associated with employee organization can evaporate if labor relations turn sour.[225] Although further work needs to be done in identifying the sources of union wage increases in particular industries and over the American economy as a whole, it now appears to be a gross oversimplification and mischaracterization to assume that labor cartelization is the sole or even the dominant source of union wage increases in the American economy.

2. The Assumption That Employers Respond to Union Wage Demands by Moving Up Their Demand Curves

The assumption that employers will respond to union wage demands by moving up their labor demand curve rather than bargaining over wages and employment is also theoretically unsound. The logic of the employer's and employees' incentive to bargain to solutions off the employer's labor demand curve has already been demonstrated.[226] The only real question is to what extent transaction costs prevent the negotiation of optimal terms. The relevant transaction costs include time and information costs, failures to negotiate efficient contract terms due to strategic lying,[227] and enforcement costs.

Traditionally, economists have assumed that time and information costs are relatively low under collective bargaining compared with other bargaining situations because the process generally involves only two principal parties who can readily meet and who understand the subject of negotiations.[228] Accordingly, it seems unlikely such costs would prevent the negotiation of optimal contract terms in collective bargaining. The parties' knowledge will also make strategic lying difficult, particularly as to the optimal capital-labor mix. If nothing else,

---

223. *See* Kim B. Clark, *The Impact of Unionization on Productivity: A Case Study*, 33 IN-DUS. & LAB. REL. REV. 451 (1980); Kim B. Clark, *Unionization and Productivity: Micro-Economic Evidence*, 95 Q.J. ECON. 613 (1980) [hereinafter Clark, *Evidence*].

224. The available studies yield estimates of changes in productivity associated with employee organization from -18% to 32%. HIRSCH & ADDISON, *supra* note 13, at 196-97.

225. *See* HIRSCH & ADDISON, *supra* note 13, at 200.

226. *See supra* notes 54-60 and accompanying text.

227. Among the possible strategic behaviors in bargaining, strategic lying is the only one that poses a serious threat to the negotiation of optimal contract terms. The others, including hard bargaining, pose more of a threat to the peaceful division of the cooperative surplus. Accordingly, these strategic behaviors have a greater impact on whether a collective agreement can be reached without a strike than on the terms that will ultimately be negotiated in the collective agreement.

228. *See* Schwab, *supra* note 12, at 267-68.

474   *Michigan Law Review*   [Vol. 91:419

the union can check employer representations merely by observing what competing firms are doing.

Regarding enforcement costs, arguably it may be difficult to negotiate an optimal level of employment that can be effectively enforced. Employers need flexibility to respond to changes in demand by adjusting the level of output and employment, and it would seem difficult for the union to police changes in employment to determine whether the employer is laying off workers to respond to a drop in product demand or to return opportunistically to his labor demand curve.[229] However, the union could detect such opportunism on the part of the employer by monitoring the capital-labor mix. If such opportunism is a serious problem, the contract could specify the composition of work crews for each station with the requirement that if the workers are laid off their machines must be idled.[230] Alternatively, unions could lessen employers' incentives to act opportunistically by negotiating lump-sum payments to cover the employees' share of the expected cooperative surplus and a competitive hourly wage to cover the employees' opportunity costs in employment.[231] Moreover, given the parties' continuing relationship, the optimal level of employment could plausibly be set by implicit agreement with the union punishing perceived opportunistic behavior by the employer in later negotiations.

Recent empirical work strongly endorses the employer bargaining response over the employer labor demand curve response. Although transaction costs may prevent optimal bargaining in some individual cases, studies examining whether organized employers operate on their labor demand curve or at some higher negotiated level of employment consistently reject the labor demand curve response.[232] The shape of

---

229. Indeed, collective bargaining agreements that explicitly specify the level of employment are not common. HIRSCH & ADDISON, *supra* note 13, at 16; ANDREW J. OSWALD, EFFICIENT CONTRACTS ARE ON THE LABOR DEMAND CURVE: THEORY AND FACTS (Industrial Relations Section, Princeton University Working Paper No. 178, 1984).

230. Such *sunk cost loss provisions*, requiring that the employer suffer a demonstrated loss (idling the machine) when purportedly responding to decreases in demand, decrease the employer's incentive to act opportunistically and prevent her from moving to an inefficient capital-labor mix. Wachter & Cohen, *supra* note 45, at 1378-79. Examples of such provisions include specifying the minimum number of musicians in an orchestra, the minimum crew size, or the maximum number of students in a classroom. *See* Randall W. Eberts & Joe A. Stone, *On the Contract Curve: A Test of Alternative Models of Bargaining,* 4 J. LAB. ECON. 66 (1986); Frederick R. Warren-Boulton, *Vertical Control by Labor Unions,* 67 AM. ECON. REV. 309 (1977).

231. Campbell, *supra* note 52, at 1017-18. A variety of other devices can be used to achieve agreements off the employer's labor demand curve without explicit provisions governing the number of workers or hours. These devices include work reduction provisions, provisions covering changes in technology, profit sharing, tenure and seniority provisions, equipment differentials, and taxes on output. *See* Clark, *supra* note 54, at 897; Eberts & Stone, *supra* note 230; Warren-Boulton, *supra* note 230. Such provisions are fairly common in collective bargaining agreements.

232. *See* John M. Abowd, *The Effects of Wage Bargains on the Stock Market Value of the*

the contract curve between the parties will vary from case to case, and studies have found examples of both rightward- and leftward-leaning contract curves.[233] Although further work needs to be done, perhaps the best characterization of the impact of unions in this regard, based on the available empirical evidence, is that unions negotiate optimal contracts that have little impact on the capital-labor mix or the level of output by organized employers. This characterization is based primarily on two studies, one by Kim Clark, the other by John Abowd.[234] Clark examined a sample of over 900 union and nonunion businesses to gauge the impact of employee organization on various measures of firm performance, including return on capital, growth, and capital-labor mix. He found that, although organized firms tend to earn substantially lower returns on capital than nonunion firms operating in comparable technological and competitive environments, employee organization had little effect on firm growth and the capital-labor mix.[235] Abowd examined the effect of unexpected changes in collectively bargained labor costs on the value of common stock for a broadly representative sample of organized businesses. He found that, on average, unexpected increases in wealth to workers corresponded to decreases of similar size in the value of the common stock to shareholders.[236] This equal and opposite relationship in worker and shareholder wealth is consistent with the bargaining analysis[237] and the characterization of the contract curve between employers and unions as typically vertical over the economy as a whole.

3. *The Failure To Account for the Strategic Nature of Collective Bargaining*

Finally, the traditional monopoly model of unions is deficient because it fails to account explicitly for the strategic nature of collective bargaining and the fact that many of the costs of collective bargaining are positional externalities. Perhaps the most damning shortcoming of

---

Firm, 79 AM. ECON. REV. 774 (1989); Brown & Ashenfelter, *supra* note 54, at S40; David Card, *Efficient Contracts with Costly Adjustment: Short-Run Employment Determination for Airline Mechanics,* 76 AM. ECON. REV. 1045, 1066-67 (1986); Eberts & Stone, *supra* note 230; MaCurdy & Pencavel, *supra* note 54, at S3.

233. In his study, Card found a leftward-leaning contract curve, showing a willingness on the part of the examined unions to trade employment for wages. Card, *supra* note 232, at 1065-66. In the typographical industry, MaCurdy and Pencavel found a rightward-leaning contract curve, indicating a willingness on the part of the union to trade wages for jobs. MaCurdy & Pencavel, *supra* note 54.

234. *See* Abowd, *supra* note 232; Clark, *supra* note 54.

235. Clark, *supra* note 54, at 918.

236. Abowd, *supra* note 232, at 775.

237. *Id.*

476   *Michigan Law Review*   [Vol. 9 :419

the traditional monopoly model is that the adoption of the first wo assumptions of the model — that unions are labor cartels and hat employers respond to union wage demands by moving up their demand curve — logically precludes the consideration of strategic behavior in the conduct of collective negotiations.[238] To preclude consideration of this fundamental characteristic of collective barg;iining in an economic model would seem to be a very serious mistal:e.

Although some of the costs of collective bargaining are ordinary time and information costs,[239] it is quite evident that many activities in collective bargaining are strategic in nature and result in costs that are positional externalities. Organizing campaigns, discriminatory discharges, recalcitrant bargaining, and some enforcement activities are all undertaken for the purpose of gaining a larger share of the joint benefits of production for the active party.[240] Moreover, the reward of each party based on relative performance and the tendency for conflicts in collective bargaining to escalate into costly affairs are also evident. It seems reasonable that the more one side spends in an organizing campaign relative to the other, the better will be that side's chances of prevailing in the campaign. Because finishing second in an organizing campaign does neither the employer nor the union any good, both will have incentives to expend resources up to the amount the organized employees would be expected to benefit at the expense of the employer by successfully organizing, if they think it will allow them to prevail.[241] Far from conceding high-rent industries to unions, employers will thus presumably contest these industries all the more vigorously to preserve their claim on the high rents.[242]

Similarly, "hard bargaining" can have its rewards in collective negotiations. However, if both sides follow this individually rational strategy, the result may be the waste of resources in a strike or lockout that reduces the total value of the rents and productivity increases to be divided between the parties.[243] The answer to the question of why

---

238. *See supra* note 103 and accompanying text.

239. Some minimum level of expenditure to negotiate and enforce an agreement is inevitable due to the costs of acquiring information, meeting a minimum number of times to negotiate the agreement, and good-faith disagreements over the later interpretation of the agreement.

240. *See* HAMBURGER, *supra* note 18, at 107-08; Posner, *supra* note 52, at 993-94.

241. When a rent (here, the organized employees' expected benefit at the expense of the employer) is open to more than one-party competition, acquiring that rent can theoretically consume the entire rent as well as prompt similar wasted expenditures by the losing side. Posner has made a similar argument with respect to the waste of monopoly rents by firm competition for the monopoly position. *See* RICHARD A. POSNER, ANTITRUST LAW: AN ECONOMIC PERSPECTIVE 12-13 (1976).

242. Some economists have begun to take account of this strategic argument. *See, e.g.,* HIRSCH & ADDISON, *supra* note 13, at 31.

243. Many authors have realized the strategic nature of collective bargaining and strikes,

the parties sometimes engage in strikes and lockouts despite their dele-
terious effect on the ultimate bargain is that activities like intransigence in bargaining may be individually rational even though they do
not always produce collectively rational results.[244]

Finally, enforcement of the collective agreement creates incentives
for strategic behavior. If resort to economic weapons is allowed during the course of the agreement, the union has incentives to reinterpret
or renegotiate the contract whenever there is a backlog of orders and
the employer is vulnerable, while the employer has similar incentives
whenever demand for the product lags and the union is vulnerable.[245]
The result, of course, would be a dramatic increase in bargaining and
enforcement costs. Similarly, resort to costly litigation by a party
whenever it loses an arbitration might yield individual gains but would
significantly decrease the benefit of the agreement to both sides.

Although it is too early to judge the empirical success of models
that account for the strategic nature of collective bargaining, models of
strikes as merely the result of asymmetric information do not adequately explain the phenomenon. Models that explain strikes as necessary to lower unrealistic worker wage expectations do well
explaining aggregate macrodata of strike frequency, but these results
depend on intuitive guesses as to the determinants of workers' resistance and concessions in strikes, rather than any analysis of rational
economic behavior.[246] Moreover, these models are intuitively unap-
pealing because they implicitly assume that the union leadership un-

---

although few have incorporated it explicitly in their analysis of unions and collective bargaining
or labor law. *See, e.g.,* Epstein, *supra* note 8, at 1396-97; Posner, *supra* note 52, at 994. Probably
the most extensive consideration of this aspect of collective bargaining and strikes can be found
in Schwab, *supra* note 12, at 268-72. In his analysis Schwab intuits many of the results I derive
in my more formal game theory analysis.

244. Recently some sophisticated game theory models of strikes have taken advantage of the
strategic nature of strikes to explain strike activity in models with perfect information. *See, e.g.,*
Fernandez & Glazer, *supra* note 75. In addition, Professor Masahiko Aoki has written some
interesting articles describing firm production and growth as a cooperative game between share-
holders and employees. *See* Masahiko Aoki, *A Model of the Firm as a Stockholder-Employee
Cooperative Game,* 70 AM. ECON. REV. 600 (1980); Masahiko Aoki, *Equilibrium Growth of the
Hierarchical Firm: Shareholder-Employee Cooperative Game Approach,* 72 AM. ECON. REV.
1097 (1982). Another bargaining model that may prove useful in the analysis of labor law has
been developed in Robert Cooter et al., *Bargaining in the Shadow of the Law: A Testable Model
of Strategic Behavior,* 11 J. LEGAL STUD. 225 (1982). Finally, Professor Joel Rogers has recognized and discussed the implications of dilemma games among workers in organizing. *See* Joel
Rogers, *Divide and Conquer: Further "Reflections on the Distinctive Character of American Labor Laws,"* 1990 WIS. L. REV. 1, 10.

245. The strategic nature of contract enforcement has long been recognized with respect to
contracts in general. *See* RICHARD A. POSNER, ECONOMIC ANALYSIS OF LAW 42-43 (1st ed.
1972); Daniel A. Farber, *Contract Law and Modern Economic Theory,* 78 NW. U. L. REV. 303,
310-11 (1983). However, to my knowledge no one has yet applied these arguments to labor law.

246. Kennan, *supra* note 73, at 1102.

dertakes every strike knowing that the union will lose.[247] Similarly, models that explain strikes as the low-cost method for unions to sort out high- and low-wage employers do not fare well empirically. These models predict an increase in the incidence of strikes when the economy declines and such sorting of employers would be useful, when in fact strike incidence decreases during recessions.[248] Such models also predict that wage increases after long strikes that should successfully sort out low-wage employers should be lower, *ceteris paribus,* when again the opposite is true.[249]

III. A BARGAINING ANALYSIS OF UNIONS AND COLLECTIVE BARGAINING

The shortcomings of the traditional monopoly model of unions suggest a need for greater examination of the alternative elements of an economic model of unions and collective bargaining discussed in Part I of this article. In this Part, I present a model of unions and collective bargaining that employs these alternate assumptions and explore its implications for public policy. Previous authors have provided analyses combining alternative assumptions concerning the source of union wage increases with the assumption of the employer's bargaining response to a union wage increase.[250] I extend these analyses by adding arguments regarding the strategic nature of collective bargaining and the proper characterization of many costs of collective bargaining as positional externalities. As will be seen later, these arguments hold particular relevance for the economic analysis of labor law. I refer to this model as the *bargaining model* of unions and collective bargaining because it examines the possible bargaining solution between employers and employees to the problem of producing and dividing the benefits of their joint enterprise.[251]

---

247. EHRENBERG & SMITH, *supra* note 9, at 346.

248. *See* Kennan, *supra* note 73, at 1112. *But see* Peter C. Cramton & Joseph Tracy, *Strikes and Holdouts in Wage Bargaining: Theory and Data,* 82 AM. ECON. REV. 100 (1992) (arguing that if one takes account of "holdouts" in which workers work without a contract, as well as strikes, asymmetric information models do better at explaining observed data).

249. *See* Kennan, *supra* note 73, at 1114.

250. *See* HIRSCH & ADDISON, *supra* note 13, at 14-18; Clark, *supra* note 54, at 894; MaCurdy & Pencavel, *supra* note 54, at S3.

251. In the labor economics literature the term *bargaining model* or *bargaining analysis* is generally associated only with the assumption that the employer responds to a union wage increase by bargaining over wages and employment, not necessarily with assumptions concerning the source of union wage increases or the proper characterization of the costs of collective bargaining. *See, e.g.,* HIRSCH & ADDISON, *supra* note 13, at 14-18. Thus, I use this term in a somewhat more restrictive manner than is common in the literature.

A. *The Model and Its Implications for Public Policy*

In the bargaining model of unions and collective bargaining I combine all of the assumptions concerning unions and collective bargaining discussed in Part I of this article that were not adopted in the
traditional monopoly model of unions. First, I assume that product
market power rents, Ricardian rents, quasi-rents, and productivity increases associated with worker organization together constitute the
dominant source of union wage increases that the model should consider, although the implications of labor cartel rents are also considered. To the extent that organizational productivity increases are not
generally enjoyed throughout the product market, these productivity
increases and the employer product market rents constitute the cooperative surplus to be produced and divided by the parties in my bargaining analysis.[252] Second, I assume that employers and unions seek
to negotiate optimal contracts with respect to both wages and employment. To ease exposition, I assume that the employer and the union
negotiate to maximize the monetary value of the cooperative surplus
and thus have a vertical contract curve. However, the implications of
a leftward- or rightward-leaning contract curve are also considered.
Finally, I explore the implications for public policy of explicitly accounting for the strategic nature of collective bargaining and the fact
that many of the costs associated with collective bargaining are positional externalities. Based on my criticisms of the monopoly model of
unions, I argue that this bargaining model of unions more accurately
describes the typical operation of unions and collective bargaining in
the American economy. However, at the very least it allows me to
clarify the debate about the equity and efficiency of unions and to explore the implications of relaxing some of the assumptions of the traditional monopoly model.

The conclusions about the equity and efficiency of unions derived
from the bargaining model differ markedly from those derived from
the traditional monopoly model. As shown in Figure 8, when confronted with a union wage demand, rather than retreating along his
labor demand curve, the employer bargains with the union to reach a
joint welfare maximizing solution on the contract curve *(C)*. To maximize the monetary value of employer rents, the employer and the
union will agree to the employment of the same amount of labor *(N_c)*
that would have been employed in a competitive market. Where the
union is more willing to trade employment for wages the contract

---

252. See *supra* notes 40-53 and accompanying text for a discussion of the "cooperative
surplus."

FIGURE 8

The Employer and Union's Wage-Employment Contract Curve with
Possible Productivity Increases

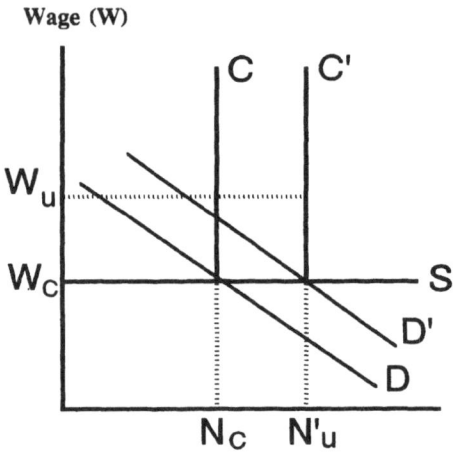

Wage (W)

Employment (N)

curve will lean to the left, and there will be some decrease in the level
of employment associated with employee organization. Moreover,
where the union delves into employer quasi-rents to raise wages, the
long-run contract curve will lie to the left of the short-run contract
curve, because in the long run the employer will cut back on his union
workforce with the exhaustion of the firm's capital investments.[253] In
addition, if the rents that the union gains are from an effective labor
cartel, then in the long run the employment of workers in the industry
will fall as employers leave the industry to gain more competitive rates
of return on their investment.[254] However, this decrease in employment will be less than predicted by the traditional monopoly model
because it will be mitigated by the bargaining response.[255]

Any productivity increases associated with employee organization

---

253. HIRSCH, *supra* note 32, at 10-11, 16-17.

254. If the union can establish an effective labor cartel then it can dictate where on the
contract curve the parties operate. Assuming the union selects a wage higher than the competitive wage, the employers in the organized industry will earn less than the competitive rate of
return they had previously earned, and there will be incentive for employers to leave the industry
to gain greater returns elsewhere. This exodus of employers will continue until the supply of the
good produced by the industry has fallen to the point where the now-higher price of the good
yields a competitive rate of return on the remaining employers' investment.

255. Because the contract curve lies to the right of the demand curve, the bargaining model
predicts less decrease in employment and less increase in product price from the establishment of
an effective labor cartel than does the traditional monopoly model.

will shift the employer's labor demand curve and the contract curve to the right (D' and C' respectively) because the employer will want to employ more labor at any given wage.[256] Such a productivity shift will increase the optimal level of employment negotiated by the employer and will tend to counteract any willingness on the part of the union to trade employment for wages in negotiations or any decrease in employment due to the formation of an effective labor cartel. Where the union is more willing to trade wages for employment so that the contract curve leans to the right, the union in essence spends a portion of the employees' share of the cooperative surplus to increase the number of job openings above the competitive level.[257] Because in each of these cases the union wage exceeds the competitive wage, there should presumably be an excess supply of workers willing to take union jobs. However, under the bargaining model where employer rents and productivity increases are the dominant source of union wage increases, little if any production inefficiency or displacement of workers from one labor market to another occurs. On the contrary, worker organization may lead to production efficiencies and an increase in employment in organized firms.

Similarly, under the bargaining model the employer has little incentive or opportunity to pass on any of the union wage increase to consumers. Assuming that the employer was optimally pricing to maximize the value of his rents before the employees organized, any adjustment away from this optimal price will only reduce the rents that are divided between the employer and the employees. Where the union is willing to trade employment for wages so that the contract curve leans to the left, an employer who enjoys product market power rents may profit by decreasing supply and increasing price.[258] However, no such price increase is possible where the employer has already fully exploited the extent of his product market barriers to entry before the advent of the union.[259] Where the union establishes an ef-

---

256. Productivity increases associated with employee organization are like any technological innovation in that they shift the employer's labor demand curve and may change the optimal labor-capital mix. HIRSCH & ADDISON, *supra* note 13, at 202-04; Clark, *supra* note 54, at 896-97.

257. As previously stated, this most likely occurs in industries in which the level of employment is severely contracting so that even with attrition and productivity increases associated with organization, the employer's desired level of employment is well below the level desired by union members. Indeed, such a rightward-leaning contract curve has been found in the typographical industry, which has recently suffered a severe contraction in jobs due to technological innovations. MaCurdy & Pencavel, *supra* note 54.

258. If the employer enjoyed only Ricardian rents, quasi-rents, and productivity increases associated with employee organization, she would not be able to raise the product price, because the employer is a price taker in the product market.

259. Empirical evidence suggests that most cartels and monopolists price at the limit of their

fective labor cartel, the price of the good will rise as output is decreased, but once again the bargaining response will mitigate this effect.[260]

Also, as before, productivity increases associated with employee organization will offset in part or in whole any tendency to increase price due to the willingness of the union to trade employment for wages or the establishment of an effective labor cartel. Indeed, to the extent that such productivity increases spread throughout the product market through organization, firm expansion, or free riding, they will tend to drive down the optimal price, and consumers may even enjoy lower prices due to employee organization.[261] Where the union is willing to trade wages for employment so that the contract curve leans to the right, the resulting contract can only increase output and reduce price relative to what would have existed in a competitive market, assuming the additional workers add anything to production. Under the bargaining model there is thus little, if any, consumption inefficiency or product price increase associated with employee organization, and, to the extent productivity increases associated with employee organization spread throughout the product market, consumers may enjoy a price decrease due to organization.

Thus, one can argue under the bargaining analysis that unions serve the goal of equity and perhaps even the goal of efficiency. The absence of any appreciable displacement of workers or product price increase associated with employee organization means that union benefits come largely at the expense of employers and from productivity increases associated with employee organization rather than from other workers or consumers. Assuming that the average stockholder

---

barriers to entry rather than at the theoretically optimal price given by the product market demand curve at the output level where marginal revenue equals marginal costs. Measured elasticities of demand for various industries range from 1.98 to 0.03 with 0.56 as the unscientific "mean." HENDRIK S. HOUTHAKKER & LESTER D. TAYLOR, CONSUMER DEMAND IN THE UNITED STATES: ANALYSES AND PROJECTIONS 61-144 (2d ed. 1970); A. Koutsoyiannis, *Goals of Oligopolistic Firms: An Empirical Test of Competing Hypotheses,* 51 S. ECON. J. 540 (1984); Ahsan Mansur & John Whalley, *Numerical Specification of Applied General Equilibrium Models: Estimation, Calibration and Data, in* APPLIED GENERAL EQUILIBRIUM ANALYSIS 69-127 (Herbert E. Searf & John B. Shoven eds., 1984). Assuming a linear demand curve and a moderate increase in the marginal costs of production so that the ratio of the optimal monopoly price to the competitive price is equal to the elasticity of demand plus 0.25 divided by the elasticity of demand, POSNER, *supra* note 241, at 245-48, these elasticities suggest optimal price markups for cartels and monopolies of from 13% to 833% with an unscientific "mean" of about 45%. However, typical markups from real cartels and monopolies range from 12% to 35%. Mark A. Cohen & David T. Scheffman, *The Antitrust Sentencing Guidelines: Is the Punishment Worth the Costs?,* 27 AM. CRIM. L. REV. 331, 347 (1989). Given the historically low penalties and slack enforcement of our antitrust laws, this disparity suggests that cartels and monopolists typically raise their prices to the full extent of available barriers to entry.

260. *See supra* note 255 and accompanying text.

261. Clark, *supra* note 54, at 896-97.

is wealthier than the average worker and society generally favors re-distributing wealth from rich to poor, or that society believes workers should share in the rents generated by their joint enterprise with employers regardless of the parties' relative wealth, unions serve society's redistributive goals.[262] Moreover, if the productivity increases associated with employee organization exceed associated inefficiencies due to unions' willingness to trade employment for wages, unions' ability to establish effective labor cartels, possible increases in transaction costs due to collective bargaining, and any external costs on the public from strikes, then employee organization is also wealth maximizing.[263] It follows that, at the very least, unions should be lawful and collective bargaining agreements should be enforceable. But are these two simple policies enough to ensure an optimal social policy with respect to industrial relations, or does society need more extensive regulation of the conduct of collective bargaining?

The third assumption of the bargaining model, that collective bargaining is a strategic endeavor and that many of its associated costs are positional externalities, suggests the need for extensive regulation

---

262. There is no efficiency reason why some of the employer product market power or Ricardian rents should not be redistributed to the workers who help produce them, because these rents are payments in excess of that necessary to call forth the employment of the employer's capital resources. Indeed, to the extent that unions force employers to share product market power rents, they discourage employer cartelization of the product market and increase economic efficiency.

263. It seems plausible that employee organization is wealth maximizing in some industries. As previously discussed, in what are perhaps the most careful studies of productivity increases associated with employee organization, Clark found an increase in production of 8% to 10% in the cement industry. Clark, *Evidence, supra* note 223, at 635. One study found that the efficiency gain from removing the union relative wage effect (using the monopoly model of unions) never exceeds 0.2% of GNP. Robert H. DeFina, *Unions, Relative Wages, and Economic Efficiency,* 1 J. LAB. ECON. 408, 428 (1983); *see also* REES, *supra* note 217, at 96-97; Albert Rees, *The Effects of Unions on Resource Allocation,* 6 J.L. & ECON. 69, 69-78 (1963). Taking this estimate as an outside estimate of any production or consumption inefficiency under the bargaining model, and assuming that 20% of employees are organized in the economy as a whole, one obtains an estimate of the average production and consumption inefficiency associated with an organized employer of about 1%. There are probably economies of scale from collective bargaining with respect to time, information, and enforcement costs. Assuming that these costs are the same for collective and individual bargaining, the only potential excess costs from collective bargaining are the costs of organization and strikes. The average worker covered by a collective bargaining agreement spends fewer than three days a year on strike. Kennan, *supra* note 73, at 1125. Tripling this, to include a crude accounting of organizational costs and external costs on the public from strikes, and assuming that the decrease in productivity associated with strikes is proportional to the number of days missed, one gets a rough estimate of about 3.6% as the decrease in productivity due to the excess costs of collective bargaining. Thus, a generous estimate of the total average loss of efficiency in a shop due to collective bargaining is under 5%.

Even if unions are not wealth maximizing, some authors have argued that there are sociopolitical benefits from allowing workers to organize and act as a voice for workers and a counterbalance to organized capital in social and political fora. *See* FREEMAN & MEDOFF, *supra* note 20, at 191-206; Getman & Kohler, *supra* note 95, at 1433. If that is the case, even putting aside redistributive objectives, unions may be social welfare maximizing even if they are not wealth maximizing.

of the conduct of labor relations. Recall that, as demonstrated in the negotiations game, because uncooperative or recalcitrant bargaining is a positional externality, conflicts in collective negotiations tend to escalate into costly strikes despite the parties' mutual interest in avoiding such strikes. Similarly, because many of the more costly strategies in organizing and contract enforcement, such as discriminatory discharges, strikes, lockouts, and resort to litigation, are also positional externalities, conflicts in these areas tend to escalate into costly affairs despite the mutual interest of the parties to avoid such escalation. Escalation of conflicts between employers and employees is not desirable from a societal perspective because it wastes the cooperative surplus produced by the parties.[264] Therefore, it makes sense for the government to undertake reasonable measures to regulate labor relations to avoid such waste and promote the efficient resolution of such disputes.

There are two basic methods by which the government can seek to avoid such escalation and promote more efficient solutions to conflicts involving positional externalities.[265] First, the government can change the expected payoffs of the game by penalizing or prohibiting the wasteful high-cost strategies so that it becomes individually rational for each party to confine itself to the efficient low-cost strategies.[266] For example, in the bargaining game presented earlier, if the government prohibited intransigent bargaining and enforced this prohibition with an expected penalty of $4, both the employer and the union would decide to bargain cooperatively.[267] Second, the government can

---

264. Returning to the bargaining game represented in Matrix 1, by combining all the benefits to the parties associated with the game and subtracting all costs, we see that the mutually cooperative solution of cell 1 is wealth maximizing while the mutually uncooperative solution of cell 4 is wealth minimizing. See Matrix 1, *supra* text accompanying notes 86-87. In addition, there may be some external costs to consumers from the strike not accounted for in the game if adequate substitutes do not exist and the consumers have to forgo consumption during the strike. These costs further undermine the mutually uncooperative solution of cell 4 from a wealth maximization perspective.

265. HAMBURGER, *supra* note 18, at 177-81. The government or society can also attempt to solve dilemmas by a third method: shaping people's preferences to promote cooperative behavior. Families teach taking turns or sharing to solve dilemmas that arise out of conflicting desires as to which activities to undertake together or who will use common resources that only one person can use at a time. HAMBURGER, *supra* note 18, at 128-30. The government also uses preference shaping to attempt to solve dilemmas. For example, the government uses criminal punishment to promote preferences for respecting our common interest in respect for bodily and property integrity over individual interests in assault and theft. *See* DENNIS C. MUELLER, PUBLIC CHOICE II 9-15 (1989) (positing a model of crime as a dilemma game); Kenneth G. Dau-Schmidt, *An Economic Analysis of the Criminal Law as a Preference-Shaping Policy,* 1990 DUKE L.J. 1. To date, however, preference shaping has not been used as an important solution to dilemmas in labor relations.

266. HAMBURGER, *supra* note 18, at 188-89; Peter Huber, *Competition, Conglomerates, and the Evolution of Cooperation,* 93 YALE L.J. 1147, 1164-68 (1984) (book review).

267. The expected employer payoffs for cells 1 through 4 would then be, respectively, 4.75, 4, 1 and -1.5, with the cooperative strategy dominating. Similarly, the expected union payoffs for

enact measures that promote the parties' ability to recognize and follow their collective interest in not escalating the conflict and to observe an explicit or implicit private armistice that confines the resolution of their conflicts to the efficient low-cost strategies. Through logical arguments and empirical studies, social scientists have identified the following measures as promoting cooperative or low-cost solutions to dilemma games like those found in industrial relations: promoting homogeneity among the constituencies of the players of the game; limiting the number of players; requiring exchanges of information among the players; prohibiting certain bargaining strategies, including lying, committing to third parties, or cutting off negotiations; promoting repeated play of the dilemma game; and enforcing explicit private agreements to refrain from undertaking the high-cost strategies.[268] Promoting homogeneity and reducing the number of players simplifies the game so that the players are more likely to see their collective interest in cooperation.[269] Reducing the number of players also prevents a few uncooperative players from free riding on the cooperative efforts of the rest.[270] Requiring exchanges of information on the game allows the parties to see their collective interest in avoiding escalation and promotes trust.[271] Bargaining strategies such

---

cells 1 through 4 would be, respectively, 3.08, 0.5, 1.17 and -3.17, with the cooperative strategy dominating. This example assumes that the recalcitrant party pays the entire penalty. Under different bargaining models, the incidence of a penalty for strategic behavior may not be so straightforward. For example, a penalty for employer recalcitrance in organizing will reduce the cooperative surplus and perhaps the union's share of that surplus. Although this subject deserves serious scholarly attention in the future, for the purposes of this article I will assume that penalties on either party do not affect the other's ability to gain a share of the cooperative surplus and that the incidence of a penalty therefore falls entirely on the offending party.

268. HAMBURGER, *supra* note 18, at 114-16, 121-22, 126-27, 173, 190, 241-42; HOWARD RAIFFA, THE ART AND SCIENCE OF NEGOTIATION 12-19 (1982); Coleman et al., *supra* note 87, at 671-89; Jules L. Coleman, *Afterword: The Rational Approach to Legal Rules,* 65 CHI.-KENT L. REV. 177, 187 (1989); Huber, *supra* note 266, at 1164-67 (1984).

269. MUELLER, *supra* note 265, at 13; *see* HAMBURGER, *supra* note 18, at 173, 190, 242-43; Coleman et al., *supra* note 87, at 676; John Fox & Melvin Guyer, *Group Size and Others' Strategy in an N-Person Game,* 21 J. CONFLICT RESOL. 323 (1977); Henry Hamburger, *Dynamics of Cooperation in Take-Some Games, in* MATHEMATICAL MODELS FOR SOCIAL PSYCHOLOGY (Wilhelm F. Kempf & Bruno H. Repp eds., 1977). The Coase Theorem, which is dependent on cooperative bargaining, can break down with as few as three bargainers due to potential complexities in negotiations. MUELLER, *supra* note 265, at 31.

270. HAMBURGER, *supra* note 18, at 242-43; *see* MANCUR OLSON, THE LOGIC OF COLLECTIVE ACTION 9-15 (1971); Coleman et al., *supra* note 87, at 676. For example, if an employer has to negotiate with three separate groups of employees of approximately equal size, all of which are necessary to production, and two groups are cooperative, the third may hold out, free riding on the cooperative surplus produced by the other employees. In such a case, the per capita benefits to the holdout group would be greater than if the employees all bargained in one group, and the chances of employer retaliation against one holdout would be smaller because the employer would not want to waste the cooperative surplus produced with the other employees. Hamburger provides a means to analyze such situations using relatively simple graphs. *See* HAMBURGER, *supra* note 18, at 161.

271. *See* HAMBURGER, *supra* note 18, at 116, 126, 173, 241; ANATOL RAPOPORT & ALBERT

as lying, committing to third parties, and cutting off negotiations are themselves strategic acts that can jeopardize the larger game.[272] Repeated play increases the costs of strategic behavior by making such behavior a threat not only to current negotiations but also to future negotiations.[273] Finally, making explicit private armistices enforceable encourages the parties to negotiate such armistices and changes the payoffs of the game to make cooperation individually rational.[274]

Which of the two solutions the government should employ in a particular situation depends on their relative costs and benefits in that situation. For example, in conflicts over employee organization, the high-cost strategies of discriminatory discharges and strikes are relatively easy to identify and monitor, and the chance of a voluntary armistice between the two unfamiliar, hostile parties seems remote. In

M. CHAMMAH, PRISONER'S DILEMMA 87-102 (1965); John Fox & Melvin Guyer, *"Public" Choice and Cooperation in N-Person Prisoner's Dilemma,* 22 J. CONFLICT RESOL. 469 (1978); Schwab, *supra* note 12, at 279.

272. Although a party might capture a larger share of the cooperative surplus by misrepresenting the value or cost of a contract term, if both parties successfully undertake this strategy they may miss opportunities for efficient exchange. *See supra* text accompanying note 86. Similarly, although one party might gain a larger share of the cooperative surplus by committing to a third party for a favorable division of the surplus, both parties' following this strategy can prevent efficient contracts. For example, if during collective negotiations an employer commits to a creditor that he will obtain 80% of the cooperative surplus, the employer gains a great bargaining advantage. However, if the union follows a similar strategy by committing to the membership or public, in language too strong to retract, that it will obtain 80% of the cooperative surplus, clearly no contract can be reached that meets both of these commitments. In like fashion, each party might individually gain a strategic advantage by giving a final take-it-or-leave-it offer and cutting off negotiations, but if both parties follow this strategy negotiations break down. HAMBURGER, *supra* note 18, at 117-22; Schwab, *supra* note 12, at 271-72. However, some bargaining strategies, such as the use of contingent offers, can help to promote cooperative solutions. HAMBURGER, *supra* note 18, at 186. The common practice in collective negotiations of using tentative agreements on specific terms, subject to the understanding that "nothing is agreed to until everything is agreed to," may be as such a contingent bargaining device.

273. *See* AXELROD, *supra* note 18, at 12; HAMBURGER, *supra* note 18, at 114-15, 126, 233; ROBERT D. COOTER, THE STRUCTURAL APPROACH TO ADJUDICATING SOCIAL NORMS 17 (Univ. Cal. Berkeley Working Paper No. 90-5, 1990); Coleman et al., *supra* note 87, at 672. Actually, by the logic of backward induction, if each party acts only according to its individual rationality, finite repeat play should not help solve dilemma games because it pays to be uncooperative in the last play of the game when there are no future games for revenge, and accordingly it pays to be uncooperative in the next-to-last game, and so forth; any incentives to be cooperative based on future plays of the game "unravel." *See* SHUBIK, *supra* note 81, at 259-60; MICHAEL TAYLOR, ANARCHY AND COOPERATION 29 (1976); Alexander J. Field, *Microeconomics, Norms, and Rationality,* 32 ECON. REV. & CULTURAL CHANGE 684, 698 (1984). This argument breaks down, however, if the end of the relationship is uncertain or if the parties are willing to settle for a strategy that is only slightly short of the self-interested maximum. Drew Fudenberg & Eric Maskin, *The Folk Theorem in Repeated Games With Discounting or with Incomplete Information,* 54 ECONOMETRICA 533 (1986); Roy Radner, *Monitoring Cooperative Agreements in a Repeated Principal-Agent Relationship,* 49 ECONOMETRICA 1127-28 (1981). Moreover, empirical studies of dilemma games show higher levels of cooperation in finite repeated games than nonrepeated games, although cooperation rates are lower in the beginning of play while people are learning to cooperate and also lower toward the end of play when they begin to act opportunistically. *See* Lave, *supra* note 93.

274. AXELROD, *supra* note 18, at 11; Cooter, *supra* note 273, at 14-16.

such a situation, the efficient government policy to promote cooperative or low-cost solutions in industrial relations would be to rely primarily on penalties and prohibitions to regulate organizing conflicts.
As a counterexample, in conflicts over collective negotiations, the
high-cost strategy of intransigence may be harder to identify and monitor, while the probability of a voluntary armistice between two parties
with an established relationship is significant. In this circumstance,
the efficient government policy to regulate labor relations would be to
rely more heavily on measures that promote voluntary armistices in
regulating collective negotiations. Finally, in conflicts over enforcement of the collective agreement, the parties have a working relationship, having successfully negotiated a contract, and they have had the
opportunity to agree explicitly to a voluntary armistice. Because so
many employers and unions seem willing to include the armistice of
final binding arbitration in their collective agreements voluntarily,[275] it
seems adequate to confine government efforts in regulating enforcement conflicts to the strategy of promoting such agreements and making them enforceable, even though the high-cost strategies of strikes
and litigation are easy to identify and monitor.

The optimal labor policy that seems to emerge from the bargaining
analysis is one that makes unions lawful and regulates labor relations
to promote low-cost resolution of conflicts in collective bargaining.[276]
Such a solution affords society the benefits of unions in redistributing
and perhaps maximizing wealth while avoiding needless waste in industrial relations disputes. However, based on the analysis to this
point, one could advocate some alternative policies as optimal. First,
if employer strategic behavior is merely wasteful rent seeking, why allow it at all? The government could heavily fine employers for any
resistance to employees in organizing or negotiations, and the employees could run the firm as a cooperative, taking all available rents. This
proposal would seem to have the benefits of saving the strategic costs
of even the low-cost strategies of resolving industrial conflicts and
would redistribute even more wealth from employers to employees.
Second, even if we are going to allow some employer resistance to unions, why limit union strategic behavior? Although employer strategic
behavior is a waste, union strategic behavior serves the beneficial purpose of redistributing wealth from the employer to the employees.
One could argue that if a little redistribution is good, the larger

---

275. *See supra* text accompanying note 94.

276. Within the context of the negotiating game presented in Matrix 1, this position amounts
to promoting cell 1 as the optimal solution the government should encourage in its labor relations policy.

amounts that would occur if unions had the upper hand in industrial conflicts would be even better.[277] Finally, assuming that the primary benefit of unions is their redistribution of rents from employers to employees, why undertake such a complex labor policy as outlined above? It would seem preferable simply to enact a stricter antitrust policy or a tax on employer rents that would redistribute this wealth more broadly among the population. By examining the limitations of these alternate proposals, one can see additional arguments and assumptions that are necessary to support the adoption of a policy encouraging unions and limiting both sides to balanced, low-cost strategies for the resolution of labor relations conflicts.

Each of the first two proposals entails significant costs. Prohibiting all employer resistance to unions would undermine the efficient operation of organized businesses. Independent management must offer some efficiency in the operation of a business, most probably in the monitoring of work effort, or else they would have been displaced by cooperatives in our economy a long time ago.[278] Some minimum amount of employer resistance is part of the cost of maintaining independent employers. Besides, despite their obviously self-interested motive, employer communications regarding the desirability of employee organization or union demands undoubtedly carry some information of value to the employees in deciding whether to organize and what negotiating demands to make.[279] Similarly, allowing unlimited union strategic behavior would entail an expenditure of resources. Even in a one-sided contest, recognitional strikes, union recalcitrance in bargaining, and strikes to interpret the contract would waste a portion of the cooperative surplus.[280] Thus, it seems unlikely that either

---

277. Within the context of the negotiating game presented in Matrix 1, this position would amount to advocating cell 3 as the solution the government should promote rather than cell 1.

278. Indeed, to date worker cooperatives have had little success in American economy. It seems that whatever savings they realize in avoiding fights between the employer and the employees over shares of the cooperative surplus are more than made up for by problems of shirking and inability to make decisions. *But see* WHEN WORKERS DECIDE: WORKPLACE DEMOCRACY TAKES OVER NORTH AMERICA (Len Krimerman & Frank Lindenfelf eds., 1992); C. GEORGE BENELLO, *The Challenge of Mondragon, in* FROM THE GROUND UP: ESSAYS ON GRASSROOTS AND WORKPLACE DEMOCRACY 89 (1992) (discussing the success of the Mondragon cooperative).

279. The elimination of all employer resistance would also impinge on other concerns. Employers have a limited First Amendment right to speak out against employee organization and union demands. *See* NLRB v. Virginia Elec. & Power Co., 314 U.S. 469, 477 (1941) (suggesting that First Amendment concerns would be implicated if an employer were prevented from "expressing its views on labor policies or problems"); NLRB v. Golub Corp., 388 F.2d 921, 928-29 (2d Cir. 1967) (finding that the First Amendment protects an employer's prediction that unionization would harm the company and its workers).

280. This waste can be seen by comparing the total wealth of cell 3, which represents a one-sided contest in favor of the union, and cell 1, which represents the low-cost balanced solution, in the negotiating game represented in Matrix 1.

of the first two proposals would be wealth maximizing.[281]

Moreover, although some might favor the additional redistribution of wealth these policies would entail, society as a whole may not share this view. A policy that involved only a limited redistribution of wealth could be supported by a widespread subjective belief that the additional benefits of redistribution to be gained by prohibiting employer resistance or allowing unlimited union strategic behavior are not worth the losses in efficiency those policies entail. Alternatively, a widespread belief may exist among the members of society that there should be some "equity" or balance in the contest between labor and management to divide the fruits of their joint efforts. Thus, in weighing the tradeoff between efficiency and redistribution inherent in the selection among alternate possible labor policies, or in determining what rules lead to a fair and equitable distribution of the cooperative surplus, society might decide to restrict both sides in labor relations conflicts to the cooperative or low-cost solutions for normative reasons, believing that this leads to the optimal distribution of the cooperative surplus. Such a normative decision on a distributional matter is, of course, largely a matter of taste on which reasonable minds can differ.[282]

On the possibility of preventing or taxing employer rents through our antitrust and tax policies, although some adjustment of these policies might be desirable, it would be very costly and probably impossible to eliminate all employer rents through such measures. The government is at a substantial disadvantage, relative to the employer and the union, in identifying and pursuing employer rents. Information on market demand, competitiveness, barriers to entry, and methods of production that is necessary to estimate employer rents is available to the parties as part of their production process but would be very costly for the government to obtain. Moreover, economies of scale ensure that, under an efficient antitrust policy, some markets will inevitably become concentrated enough for firms to earn market power rents. Such rents could be eliminated only by pursuing divestitures that would result in inefficient production and raise prices to

---

281. However, a proposal to encourage employee stock ownership as a means of reducing incentives to strike would work along these same lines and may have some merit. If employees owned a significant share of the company, their interests in dividing the cooperative surplus would more closely coincide with those of the employer, decreasing the incentive for either side to act strategically. Under such an arrangement, effective monitoring by management and the employees would probably still be possible.

282. Indeed, on a normative basis, one could even argue for the complete prohibition of unions if one believed employers should receive all of the cooperative surplus and that the social benefits of such an antiredistributive answer to the distributional question outweighed any possible wealth-increasing effects of unions.

consumers.[283] There may also be normative objections to taxing away all Ricardian rents from those who jointly produce them. Thus, it seems that under any antitrust or tax policy that could be pursued at reasonable cost, employer market power and Ricardian rents would exist that would be available for redistribution through employee organization.

In summary, the bargaining analysis concludes that unions and collective bargaining are equitable and perhaps even efficient. Unions increase employees' wages by gaining for employees a share of employer rents and by increasing productivity. Unions and employers have incentives to lessen the impact of the union wage increase on the level of employment and product price in order to maximize the value of the rents and productivity increases they divide. Employers are further limited in their ability to pass on union wage increases to consumers in the form of price increases to the extent of the product market barriers to entry they enjoy but have not yet exploited. Thus, union wage increases come largely at the expense of employers and not other workers or consumers. If the productivity increases associated with employee organization exceed any inefficiencies unions cause and any increase in bargaining costs associated with collective bargaining, unions and collective bargaining will also be efficient. Therefore, it makes sense for the government to permit and encourage employee organization.

Moreover, under the bargaining analysis, conflicts in collective bargaining are strategic endeavors, the costs of which tend to escalate in the absence of government regulation. In conflicts concerning organizing, negotiations, or enforcement of the collective agreement, the parties are commonly rewarded based on their relative performance with respect to various costly strategic behaviors. As a result, the costs of such conflicts are positional externalities that tend to escalate even though such escalation serves only to waste the joint benefits of production. Such waste is socially undesirable because it is inefficient. Thus, it makes sense for the government to regulate the conduct of labor relations to prohibit or discourage such waste. The government can accomplish this either by prohibiting costly strategic behaviors or by enacting measures to promote the parties' ability to perceive and act in their collective interest to avoid escalation. Which of these two strategies the government should adopt to govern a particular conflict will depend on the relative costs and benefits of each strategy as applied to the conflict. Finally, there are efficiency losses associated with

---

283. ROBERT H. BORK, THE ANTITRUST PARADOX: A POLICY AT WAR WITH ITSELF 223-24 (1978).

either prohibiting all employer resistance to unions or in allowing unions to undertake unlimited strategic behavior. Assuming that society values these losses in efficiency more than the additional redistribution of wealth that would accompany such policies, or assuming society desires some balance or "equity" between unions and employers in industrial relations conflicts, society should attempt to limit both unions and employers to cooperative or low-cost strategies in the resolution of industrial relations conflicts.

B. *Application of the Model to American Labor Law*

1. *The Public Policy of Fostering Unions and Collective Bargaining*

The pervasive policy in American labor law of fostering unions and collective bargaining[284] makes sense under the bargaining model of unions. The bargaining model holds that unions redistribute employer product market and Ricardian rents from employers to employees.[285] Thus, unions serve societal goals by redistributing wealth progressively and allowing workers to gain a more equitable share of the proceeds from their labor. There is no productive reason why employers should not share these rents, which are payments in excess of what is necessary to call forth the employer's resources into employment. In addition, fostering unions may maximize wealth. Under the bargaining solution, employers and unions who seek to maximize the monetary value of the employer rents they divide will employ the same amount of labor and set the same product price as they would in the absence of a union. Inefficiency in production and consumption will occur only to the extent that the union is willing to trade employment for wages at the expense of maximizing the monetary value of the cooperative surplus and to the extent that the union derives its wage increases from an effective labor cartel. Assuming that the union values the employment of its members, such inefficiency will be less than that predicted by the monopoly model of unions. Furthermore, unions promote efficiency by spurring management to undertake greater efforts, enforcing long-term implicit contracts, negotiating efficient levels of public goods, and decreasing turnover costs as workers exercise their collective voice to address dissatisfaction with working conditions. In many cases, the increases in efficiency associated with employee organization will outweigh the decreases in efficiency associated with such organization.

---

284. *See supra* note 2 and accompanying text.
285. *See supra* notes 253-63 and accompanying text.

492   *Michigan Law Review*   [Vol. 91:419

2. *The Purposes of Promoting Bargaining Equity and Industrial Peace*

American labor law's twin purposes of promoting greater equity in bargaining power between employers and employees[286] and promoting industrial peace find ready recognition within the context of the bargaining model.[287] Employees can gain a share of the cooperative surplus only by binding together to negotiate. Each individually will receive at most only the competitive wage for his services.[288] In addition, only by binding together can the workers achieve all of the productivity increases associated with employee organization, such as the monitoring of management efforts, the enforcement of long-term implicit contracts, and the efficient negotiation of public goods.[289] Thus, by fostering unions and collective bargaining, the law allows workers to elevate their bargaining power to a position of rough parity with their employer's and affords them the opportunity to make a productive contribution to the governance of the workplace. Similarly, the bargaining model suggests that the government should attempt to minimize the extent to which the parties engage in strategic behavior. Such behavior is costly and, although it may be individually rational, from a larger societal perspective it serves only to waste the cooperative surplus. Thus, the purpose of promoting industrial peace finds direct translation into the bargaining model as society's desire to minimize wasteful strategic behavior on the part of unions and employers.

This interpretation of the purpose of promoting equity in bargaining power also provides a rationale for several of the provisions of

---

286. *See supra* note 1 and accompanying text.

287. *See supra* notes 1, 6 and accompanying text.

288. Various Board and court decisions discussing the Act's purpose of promoting equality in bargaining power seem consistent with this view. *See, e.g.,* NLRB v. E.C. Atkins & Co., 331 U.S. 398, 404 (1947); NLRB v. Jones & Laughlin Steel Corp., 301 U.S. 1, 23 n.2, 33-34 (1937); Lewis v. Quality Coal Corp., 270 F.2d 140, 143 (7th Cir. 1959), *cert. denied,* 361 U.S. 929 (1960) (holding that union's threat to strike does not create unfair bargaining power in favor of employees sufficient to render employment contract illegal); Beckwith v. United Parcel Serv., 703 F. Supp. 138, 141 (D. Me. 1988) (noting that the NLRA is concerned with equating bargaining power between employer and employees), *affd.,* 889 F.2d 344 (1st Cir. 1989); United States v. International Union, United Mine Workers, 77 F. Supp. 563, 567 (D.D.C. 1948) (stating that organization is the *only* means by which employees can achieve a measure of equality of bargaining power with employers); National Maritime Union v. Herzog, 78 F. Supp. 146, 155-56 (D.D.C.) (holding that Congress sought to promote equality of bargaining power not only by guaranteeing employees the right to act collectively but also by protecting an elected union's exclusivity as a bargaining agent and imposing on employers the duty to bargain in good faith), *affd.,* 334 U.S. 854 (1948); Kinder-Care Learning Centers, Inc., 299 N.L.R.B. 1171, 1172 (1990) (finding that employees are at a disadvantage in bargaining with their employer unless they are able to organize and bargain collectively); Meyers Indus., 281 N.L.R.B. 882 (1986) (holding that NLRA contemplates collective action as a means of achieving equality of bargaining power), *affd. sub nom.* Prill v. NLRB, 835 F.2d 1481, 1484 (D.C. Cir. 1987).

289. *See supra* notes 40-53 and accompanying text.

American labor law previously discussed in relation to the monopoly model of unions.[290] The bilateral relationship between the employer and the union created by the grant of authority of exclusive representation and the employer's obligation to bargain in good faith is no longer the prelude to labor cartel exploitation envisioned by Epstein.[291] Instead, this bilateral relationship and the employees' right to strike are the necessary prerequisites to the employees' fully sharing in the proceeds of the enterprise and fully contributing to its total product. Similarly, the prohibition of yellow-dog contracts and the allowance of union security agreements do not needlessly interfere with the individual's right to contract, as maintained by Epstein,[292] but instead rightly permit the employees to solve the free-rider problem that otherwise might undermine their ability to secure collectively a share of the cooperative surplus and to express their views on consumption and production. Because the benefits of collective bargaining constitute a public good, individual bargaining will not adequately protect the employees' interest in collective bargaining, and the employees will individually bargain away their right to the benefits of collective bargaining by signing yellow-dog contracts for much less than those benefits are collectively worth.[293] In the same fashion, without union security agreements, it is individually rational for the employees to free ride on the efforts of the union, thereby undermining the chance that the union will actually succeed in gaining a share of the cooperative surplus and a voice in the running of the business. The allowance of state right-to-work laws under section 14(b) of the National Labor Relations Act[294] undermines the employees' ability to solve the free-rider problem and thus seems contrary to the fundamental purposes of the Act.

Similarly, the bargaining model's interpretation of the purpose of promoting industrial peace as an effort to discourage wasteful strategic behavior provides a rationale for the general strategy for regulating industrial relations found in American labor law. As discussed earlier, the government can seek to promote cooperative solutions to the dilemma games that arise in collective bargaining in two basic ways:

---

290. *See supra* notes 126-201 and accompanying text.

291. *See supra* note 182 and accompanying text.

292. *See supra* note 145 and accompanying text.

293. This analysis is consistent with the historical view, denigrated by Epstein, that employees would too easily surrender their right to organize to employers. *See* Epstein, *supra* note 8, at 1371-72. A similar argument can be made within the context of the monopoly model, but there we do not want employees to solve the free-rider problem because doing so results in a labor cartel.

294. 29 U.S.C. § 164(b) (1988).

prohibit or fine costly strategic behavior, and enact measures that promote the parties' ability to recognize and follow their collective interest in avoiding strategic behavior.[295] American labor law contains both types of provisions. Moreover, the relative reliance on each of these methods to discourage strategic behavior and promote cooperative solutions varies under the law in a way that seems efficient under the bargaining model. In regulating organizing, where the lack of an established relationship, beyond antagonism, between the parties dims the prospect that the parties will realize and follow their collective interest in avoiding strategic behavior, the law relies almost exclusively on prohibiting strategic behavior to promote cooperative solutions. In regulating collective negotiations, where the established relationship between the parties improves the prospect that they will realize and follow a cooperative solution, the law relies both on prohibitions of strategic behavior and on measures designed to encourage the parties to achieve the cooperative solution themselves.[296] In the area of enforcing collective agreements, where the parties have an established relationship and where the vast majority of parties achieve agreement on the cooperative method of resolving disputes through arbitration, the law merely endeavors to make such agreements enforceable.

3. *The Law on Organizing*

American labor law's basic approach to organizing makes sense under the bargaining theory of unions and collective bargaining. The law severely restricts or prohibits the most costly strategic behaviors on both sides in favor of the cheaper method of determining representation questions through a Board-supervised election. The National Labor Relations Act severely limits both the circumstances under which unions may lawfully engage in recognitional picketing and strikes and the length of time that such activities may persist.[297] These

---

295. *See supra* notes 93-94 and accompanying text.

296. As a remedy to the problem that many a union never achieves a contract after being elected as the bargaining representative, Weiler has proposed that unions and employers have recourse to interest arbitration for impasses in the negotiation of first contracts. *See* WEILER, *supra* note 22, at 249-51. This proposal seems consistent with the bargaining model of unions and collective bargaining because in such cases, even though the parties are through the organizing stage, they still have no established relationship and thus would seem relatively unlikely to realize the cooperative solution on their own. *See supra* notes 93, 275 and accompanying text.

297. The Act prohibits employees from engaging in recognitional picketing for more than a "reasonable" period, not to exceed 30 days, without seeking an election and entirely prohibits them from engaging in recognitional picketing if the employer has lawfully recognized another union or a valid election has occurred within the past 12 months. 29 U.S.C. § 158(b)(7) (1988). The employer may cut short even this limited period of lawful recognitional picketing by petitioning for an election as soon as any picketing begins. 29 U.S.C. § 159(c)(1)(B) (1988).

limitations, combined with the availability of the relatively inexpensive alternative of conducting an election campaign, have led unions to rely on the election procedure as the primary method of resolving representation disputes. Similarly, the Act prohibits employers from undertaking discriminatory discharges, blacklisting employees,[298] locking out employees,[299] or relocating the plant in order to avoid union organization.[300] In contrast to the monopoly model, where such activities are useful because they undermine labor cartel power,[301] these activities are merely wasteful rent-seeking on the part of the employer that should be prevented in the context of the bargaining model. One may wonder how effective these prohibitions are, because the remedies under the Act are merely reparative, and employer incentives to commit the offenses may greatly exceed the expected costs of the remedies.[302] However, the effort to discourage costly strategic behavior in favor of the less expensive resolution of organizing disputes through elections seems well founded under the bargaining theory of unions.

Even the *Darlington* doctrine, which states that the employer is allowed to close his plant completely to avoid unionism as long as this act is not intended to intimidate employees in other plants operated by the employer,[303] finds support within the context of the bargaining model. Under the model, a complete closure without intimidating intent is distinguishable from a case in which the employer moves his plant to avoid unionism or locks out his employees to discourage unionism. When the employer closes his plant, the employer cannot hope to recoup any of the costs of this behavior from future rents that the firm might earn.[304] Because there is no hope of recouping the costs of closing from the future rents of the firm, the complete closing of a plant without intimidating intent cannot be a strategic activity.[305] Instead, the decision to close must be based on either the employer's conclusion that the employees have miscalculated in selecting a union and that insufficient rents or productivity increases exist to support

---

298. *See supra* note 5 and accompanying text.

299. Flora Constr. Co., 132 N.L.R.B. 776 (1961), *enforced*, 311 F.2d 310 (10th Cir. 1962).

300. Local 57, Intl. Ladies Garment Workers' Union v. NLRB, 374 F.2d 295 (D.C. Cir 1967).

301. *See supra* notes 165-79 and accompanying text.

302. *See infra* notes 370-76 and accompanying text.

303. Textile Workers v. Darlington Mfg. Co., 380 U.S. 263, 273-74 (1965).

304. The absence of future benefits is precisely the basis on which the Court in *Darlington* distinguished these cases. *See* 380 U.S. at 272-73.

305. Wachter and Cohen have made similar arguments with respect to the Supreme Court's decisions on subcontracting and partial closing in Fibreboard Paper Prods. Corp. v. NLRB, 379 U.S. 203 (1964), and First Natl. Maintenance Corp. v. NLRB, 452 U.S. 666 (1981). *See* Wachter & Cohen, *supra* note 45, at 1386-405.

employee organization, or on the employer's strong personal distaste for dealing with organized employees. Thus, complete closure without intent to intimidate other employees is not a strategic behavior that the law should attempt to minimize under the bargaining theory of unions.

Contrary to Epstein's analysis,[306] the redistributive and wealth-maximization arguments of the bargaining model support the complete prohibition of company unions. Although company-sponsored employee organizations may be able to achieve some of the productivity-enhancing effects associated with employee organization, they probably never could achieve all of the productivity increases associated with independent unionism.[307] Moreover, even if employer organizations are wealth maximizing,[308] the employer has incentive to structure such organizations so that they never constitute an independent bargaining power that would vie for a share of the cooperative surplus.[309] To the extent that such organizations act as a bulwark against independent organization, either by mitigating some employee concerns or by giving some employees a personal investment in the company employee organization, employers may promote them even in the absence of productivity increases to avoid sharing the cooperative surplus with the employees. By totally prohibiting company unions, the National Labor Relations Act encourages independent employee organization, the productivity increases such organization entails, and the sharing of the cooperative surplus between employers and employees.[310]

The bargaining model's analysis also supports the provisions that govern the conduct of representation elections. In contrast to the monopoly model,[311] the bargaining model affirms the proposition that the government should facilitate means by which the employees can make

---

306. *See supra* note 175 and accompanying text.

307. *See supra* notes 210-12 and accompanying text.

308. This would be the case if inefficiencies associated with independent unionism outweighed any increases in productivity that could be achieved only through independent unionism.

309. Thus, such organizations historically did not allow for employee meetings outside of the employer's supervision, procedures for voting to strike, or the accumulation of a strike fund. S. REP. No. 573, 74th Cong., 1st Sess. 9-11 (1935), *reprinted in* 2 NLRB, LEGISLATIVE HISTORY, *supra* note 2, at 2309-11.

310. Under this analysis, recent cases allowing employer-sponsored employee organizations based on the "newfound" benefits of employer-employee "cooperation" are misguided in that they ignore the purpose of the NLRA of promoting independent unions that can achieve not only the benefits of cooperation but also a share of the cooperative surplus. *See, e.g.,* NLRB v. Streamway Div. of Scott & Fetzer Co., 691 F.2d 288 (6th Cir. 1982); Hertzka & Knowles v. NLRB, 503 F.2d 625 (9th Cir. 1974).

311. *See supra* notes 162-69 and accompanying text.

a reasoned decision about whether organizing is in their economic interest.[312] A Board-supervised election is an inexpensive procedure by which just such a decision can be made. The only legitimate role for the employer in such a procedure is to provide accurate information on the relative costs and benefits of organization to the employees. Because of the employer's strong incentives to do much more and to act strategically in coercing the employees not to organize, the government must carefully regulate the employer's conduct in representation elections.

Several provisions of American labor law seem aimed at minimizing the costs of elections. Allowing unions access to the names and addresses of all eligible employees and allowing employees access to the employer's property for purposes of union solicitation on nonwork time[313] seems consistent with the objective of lowering election costs. However, the doctrine of allowing employers to exclude nonemployees from making union solicitations even in nonwork areas on nonwork time[314] seems to raise the costs of elections, with the principal effect of merely indulging employers' strategic interest in resisting employee organization. The legitimate employer interest that this rule ostensibly preserves is the integrity of the employer's private property interest in the plant.[315] However, the benefits of preserving such an interest in a public area such as a parking lot seem small compared with the costs the rule places on the process of organization.

Similarly, many of the decisions governing the conduct of elections seem designed to limit the employer's role to providing useful information and to prohibit employer strategic behavior or efforts to encourage the employees to free ride on others' collective efforts. For example, the doctrine that employer predictions about the consequences of unionization must be based on objective facts and convey the employer's genuine belief as to demonstrable consequences beyond his control further these purposes.[316] This doctrine limits the employer to conveying potentially useful information as to whether the rents earned by the firm merit employee organization. The doctrine

---

312. This conclusion seems consistent with the Board's description of its objective to provide "laboratory conditions" in representation elections. *See* Peerless Plywood Co., 107 N.L.R.B. 427, 429-30 (1953); General Shoe Corp., 77 N.L.R.B. 124, 126-27 (1948); GETMAN & POGREBIN, *supra* note 2, at 37.

313. Republic Aviation Corp. v. NLRB, 324 U.S. 793 (1945).

314. NLRB v. Babcock & Wilcox Co., 351 U.S. 105 (1956).

315. 351 U.S. at 112; GETMAN & POGREBIN, *supra* note 2, at 41.

316. NLRB v. Gissel Packing Co., 395 U.S. 575, 618-19 (1969); GETMAN & POGREBIN, *supra* note 2, at 47.

appropriately prohibits employer threats or promises of benefits[317] because these are merely efforts to coerce or bribe the employees into sacrificing their collective interest in organization. Such activities undermine collective bargaining by encouraging employees to act only on the basis of their individual interests and to free ride on others' collective action. Even benefit increases that the employer offers to all employees and does not condition on the rejection of employee organization but grants in an effort to prevent employee organization should be prohibited under the bargaining theory, because they encourage the employees to free ride on the collective action of employees outside the bargaining unit and will result in a less than optimal amount of union organizing.[318]

One possibly contrary doctrine currently in the law is that the Board will not review campaign statements by employers or unions as to their truth or falsity.[319] Intentional falsehoods would seem to have no place in a system designed to allow employees, at minimum cost, to decide what is in their own collective interest with respect to organization. However, the Board may be correct that regulating campaign speech as to truth or falsity is just too costly and that such regulation impinges on First Amendment interests.[320] Again, one should wonder whether the simple reparative remedies of the National Labor Relations Act offer sufficient incentive for the enforcement of the rules governing union organizing.[321]

4. *The Law on Collective Negotiations*

The law with respect to collective negotiations is designed to discourage strategic behavior and to promote industrial peace and thus is consistent with the arguments of the bargaining model. The law at-

---

317. 29 U.S.C. § 158(c) (1988).

318. Employers grant such benefits not out of the goodness of their hearts but because other employees have organized unions that pose a viable threat of organizing the employer's shop. If the employer is allowed to frustrate organizing merely by offering the employees a wage increase equal or close to the union wage whenever organization threatens, the employees will be tempted to act in their individual interests and take the benefits of organizing without contributing to its costs; the result will be that too few employees will support collective activities and there will be too few unions. Fewer unions will provide less reason for employers to offer benefits to prevent employee organization and less realization of the redistributive and productivity benefits of employee organization.

319. Although the Board has oscillated in its view on the subject, *see* GETMAN & POGREBIN, *supra* note 2, at 59-61, the Board will not currently set aside an election based on misrepresentation in election solicitations. Midland Natl. Life Ins. Co., 263 N.L.R.B. 127 (1982). The only exceptions to this rule are cases when one party invokes the Board and its processes in its solicitation, 263 N.L.R.B. at 133 n.25, or uses forged documents in a solicitation. 263 N.L.R.B. at 133.

320. 263 N.L.R.B. at 131-32.

321. *See infra* notes 370-76 and accompanying text.

tempts to prohibit intransigence in negotiations by requiring the parties to bargain "in good faith."[322] As depicted in the simple negotiations game, "bad faith" or intransigence in bargaining is precisely what leads to strikes.[323] Depending on one's model of bargaining, one could haggle over the best standard for good-faith bargaining; however, the existing standard of subjective intent to reach agreement seems aimed at precisely the problem of intransigence described in the game. One can raise legitimate questions about the Board's ability to determine intent[324] and about the adequacy of existing remedies to discourage intransigence in bargaining,[325] but the general concept of attempting to require cooperative bargaining in collective negotiations seems sound within the context of the bargaining model.

Moreover, unlike the monopoly model,[326] the bargaining model provides a basis on which to evaluate strategies or conduct in collective negotiations that have been found to be in "bad faith." The prohibition against Boulwareism that exists under current law seems sound under the bargaining model because Boulwareism is basically a strategy under which the employer makes a strong commitment to the employees and the public not to change his bargaining position.[327] If only one side commits to a given solution of the bargaining problem, it can help ensure a solution that favors that side, but if both sides make such commitments in their own favor, the result will be a deadlock that prevents a cooperative solution.[328] Moreover, the unilateral method by which the employer arrives at her offer under Boulwareism bypasses potential productivity increases associated with employee organization. Even if the employer honestly tries to poll the employees as to their preferences and ideas, she cannot hope to do as well in assessing those preferences and ideas as an independent union, due to the employees' incentives to free ride and their fear of employer retaliation.[329]

Similarly, the doctrine that employers are required to supply the

---

322. 29 U.S.C. § 158(d) (1988).

323. *See supra* notes 81-94 and accompanying text.

324. *See* LABOR STUDY GROUP, THE PUBLIC INTEREST IN NATIONAL LABOR POLICY 82 (1961); MERRIFIELD ET AL., *supra* note 2, at 505-06.

325. *See infra* notes 368-80 and accompanying text.

326. *See supra* notes 102-03 and accompanying text.

327. *See* NLRB v. General Elec. Co., 418 F.2d 736, 740, 762-63 (2d Cir. 1969), *cert. denied,* 397 U.S. 965 (1970).

328. *See supra* notes 79-80 and accompanying text. By the same token, other methods of "painting oneself into a corner" should be discouraged in collective bargaining. However, the law should not discourage making "final offers" where the intent is not to act strategically but instead to communicate the extent of the cooperative surplus.

329. FREEMAN & MEDOFF, *supra* note 20, at 8-9.

employees with all relevant information for the purposes of collective bargaining[330] finds support within the context of the bargaining model because such information allows the parties to see mutually beneficial cooperative solutions and engenders trust on both sides. However, the limitation on this doctrine that the employer is only required to give information on his ability to meet union demands when he claims inability to pay[331] seems inconsistent with the Act's purpose of limiting strategic behavior and promoting industrial peace. Although this rule requires the full sharing of information when the chances of resort to economic warfare are probably greatest, the law, by allowing the employer to keep such information to herself absent a plea of poverty, encourages strategic behavior on the part of the employer in representing her ability to pay and decreases the chances of a cooperative solution in negotiations. The only purpose served by allowing such strategic behavior is to allow the employer to trick the union into accepting a smaller share of the cooperative surplus. A rule on the sharing of information that sought to minimize the chances of strategic behavior and to maximize the parties' ability to realize cooperative solutions would require the full sharing of all relevant information.[332]

The distinction between mandatory and permissive subjects of bargaining is another doctrine that finds some support within the context of the bargaining model.[333] Under current law, employers and unions are only required to bargain over "mandatory subjects" that fall within the broad meaning of the statutory phrase "wages, hours . . . , or other conditions of employment"[334] and that "settle an aspect of the relationship between the employer and the employees."[335] Bar-

---

330. J.I. Case Co. v. NLRB, 253 F.2d 149 (7th Cir. 1958); *see* NLRB v. Truitt Mfg. Co., 351 U.S. 149 (1956).

331. MERRIFIELD ET AL., *supra* note 2, at 550.

332. *See* NEIL W. CHAMBERLAIN & JAMES W. KUHN, COLLECTIVE BARGAINING 78 (2d ed. 1965); ROGER FISHER & WILLIAM URY, GETTING TO YES: NEGOTIATING AGREEMENT WITHOUT GIVING IN (Bruce Patton ed., 1981); LAVANIA HALL, NEGOTIATION: STRATEGIES FOR MUTUAL GAIN (1993); *see also* Schwab, *supra* note 12, at 278-80. *But see* Wachter & Cohen, *supra* note 45, at 1373 (arguing that full disclosure of information is rarely efficient).

333. Contrast this with Epstein's analysis of the obligation to bargain in good faith. *See supra* note 182 and accompanying text.

334. 29 U.S.C. § 159(a) (1988).

335. Allied Chem. & Alkali Workers v. Pittsburgh Plate Glass Co., 404 U.S. 157, 178 (1971); *see also* First Natl. Maintenance Corp. v. NLRB, 452 U.S. 666, 678 (1981); Fibreboard Paper Prods. Corp. v. NLRB, 379 U.S. 203, 211 (1964); NLRB v. Wooster Div. of Borg-Warner Corp., 356 U.S. 342, 350 (1958). Industry practice concerning the accepted subjects of collective bargaining is "highly relevant" in determining which subjects are mandatory. THE DEVELOPING LABOR LAW, *supra* note 2, at 761; *see also* GETMAN & POGREBIN, *supra* note 2, at 121-23. Examples of mandatory subjects include wages, hours, pensions, health benefits, safety precautions, shift differentials, and union security agreements where they are not prohibited by state law. THE DEVELOPING LABOR LAW, *supra* note 2, at 772-844.

gaining over other subjects concerning the employer's relationship with third parties or the union's relationship with the employees is "permitted," but not required, and neither side may resort to a work stoppage to enforce demands over such permissive subjects.[336] By restricting the obligation to bargain to subjects that concern the employment relationship, the law simplifies the bargaining game. Negotiations over subjects that primarily concern the parties' relationship with other people would seem very likely to complicate the negotiations game in ways the parties cannot themselves resolve.[337] However, due to the benefits of collective bargaining under the bargaining model, the scope of mandatory subjects under the Act should be broadly construed. The Court's recent willingness to narrow the purview of mandatory bargaining and to find certain business decisions concerning the scope and direction of the enterprise to be peculiarly within the sole prerogative of management seems ill founded under the bargaining model.[338] The Court's argument that the employer will voluntarily undertake bargaining with the employees on

---

336. *Borg-Warner*, 356 U.S. at 342. Permissive subjects are those the Board or courts consider too remote from the employment relationship or deem a peculiar prerogative of either the employer or the union. MERRIFIELD ET AL., *supra* note 2, at 557. Examples of permissive subjects include benefits for nonemployees, provisions governing the internal operations of the union, and multiunit bargaining. *Allied Chem. & Alkali Workers*, 404 U.S. at 160 (discussing benefits for nonemployees); *Borg-Warner*, 356 U.S. at 350 (discussing internal operation of union); Oil, Chem. & Atomic Workers, Intl. Union v. NLRB, 486 F.2d 1266, 1268 (D.C. Cir. 1973) (discussing scope of the bargaining unit).

337. Moreover, the restriction of the obligation to bargain to subjects that concern the employment relationship helps ensure that collective bargaining and the possible resort to economic warfare are used only to further the purposes of employee organization of transferring wealth from employers to employees and achieving productivity increases in compensation and production. For example, negotiations of terms related to political objectives are not considered mandatory subjects of bargaining, and so strikes over such issues would not be protected activities under the National Labor Relations Act. However, the ban on injunctions of strikes contained in the Norris-LaGuardia Act has been interpreted to preclude injunction of such strikes. International Longshoremen's Assn. v. Allied Intl., 456 U.S. 212 (1982); Jacksonville Bulk Terminals, Inc. v. International Longshoremen's Assn., 457 U.S. 702 (1982).

338. In *First National Maintenance*, 452 U.S. at 666, the Court determined that the employer had no obligation to negotiate over a decision to close his business partially. Even though the subject was of paramount importance to the employees, the Court found other concerns of profitability and efficiency that justified a unilateral employer decision on the matter. 452 U.S. at 682-83, 686. According to the Court, "Congress had no expectation that the elected union representative would become an equal partner in the running of the business," 452 U.S. at 676, and "[m]anagement must be free from the constraints of the bargaining process to the extent essential for the running of a profitable business." 452 U.S. at 678-79 (footnote omitted). Following the Court's lead, a plurality of the Board announced in Otis Elevator Co., 269 N.L.R.B. 891 (1984), that henceforth all decisions affecting the direction, scope, or nature of a business would be treated as nonmandatory topics unless they turned upon labor costs and that the employer would be free to make such decisions without bargaining with the union. 269 N.L.R.B. at 893. However, in Dubuque Packing Co., 303 N.L.R.B. No. 66 (1991), the Board retreated from this position and employed an analysis that was more sensitive to the problem of employer strategic behavior and the benefits of collective bargaining to devise a rule covering decisions to relocate the business. This analysis expressly examined whether the employer's decision would result in the replacement of the employees, whether its scope was akin to a decision not to be in business

Michigan Law Review   [Vol. 91:419

such topics if bargaining will be profitable[339] misses the point that, due to the divergence of individual and collective interests in dilemma games such as collective negotiations, employers may decide not to bargain in good faith based on individual incentives when in fact such bargaining would be wealth maximizing from a collective perspective.[340] Moreover, within the context of the bargaining model, employees may have productivity-enhancing proposals to make through collective bargaining with regard to decisions concerning the scope and direction of the enterprise.

Other provisions of the law prevent strategic behavior and promote industrial peace by facilitating the parties' ability to realize their collective interest in reaching cooperative solutions in bargaining. The limitation that employees can organize only in "appropriate bargaining units"[341] seems designed to promote homogeneity in bargaining interests among the employees represented by the union. Under current doctrine, the Board includes in a unit only those employees who share a sufficient "community of interest" with respect to their terms and conditions of employment.[342] As previously discussed, such ho-

---

at all, and whether it turned on labor costs, to determine whether the decision was a mandatory subject of bargaining. *Id.* at 15.

339. 452 U.S. at 682.

340. *See supra* notes 93-94 and accompanying text. This argument does not apply to management decisions that cannot result in a strategic behavior, for example the closing of a plant, because if there is no strategic gain for the employer in such decisions then there will be no divergence of his individual interests from the collective interests. Wachter and Cohen have made a convincing argument that, at least to date, the Court's determinations as to which decisions concerning the scope or direction of the enterprise are not mandatory subjects of bargaining correspond to those decisions that cannot result in strategic behavior. Wachter & Cohen, *supra* note 45, at 1386-95. If this trend continues, the Supreme Court's doctrine on this subject will not pose a serious problem under the bargaining model. However, the rhetoric of the Court's opinion in *First National Maintenance* is broader than a rule that simply allowed unilateral employer decisions where no strategic behavior was possible, *see supra* note 338, and I am not sanguine that the current trend will continue.

341. Before conducting an election, the Board will determine if the employees the union has petitioned to represent constitute an appropriate unit for the purposes of collective bargaining. *See* 29 U.S.C. § 159(b) (1988). In the absence of agreement between the union and the employer on an appropriate unit, the Board will conduct a hearing to determine whether the unit proposed by the union is appropriate. To be approved, the unit sought by the union need not be the "only" or "most" appropriate unit, but instead merely "an" appropriate unit, possibly among several acceptable formulations. Continental Banking Co., 99 N.L.R.B. 777, 782-83 (1952).

342. Kalamazoo Paper Box Corp., 136 N.L.R.B. 134 (1962); JOHN E. ABODEELY, THE NLRB AND THE APPROPRIATE BARGAINING UNIT 7-14 (1971); GETMAN & POGREBIN, *supra* note 2, at 24-25. In deciding whether employees share the requisite community of interest, the Board will consider a wide variety of factors, including methods of compensation, hours of work, employment benefits, supervision, training and skills, job functions and situs, contact with other employees, integration of work, and bargaining history. JOHN D. FEERICK ET AL., NLRA REPRESENTATION ELECTIONS § 8.2, at 290-96 (2d ed. 1985); GETMAN & POGREBIN, *supra* note 2, at 25. With respect to situs, in most industries a single geographically distinct facility is presumptively appropriate. *See* A. Harris & Co., 116 N.L.R.B. 1628 (1956). Bargaining history is given weight largely because continuing an established unit is viewed as promoting stability in labor

mogeneity on the part of the employees simplifies the bargaining game and increases the likelihood that the parties will realize the cooperative solution.[343] Board and court precedent confirms that the driving purpose behind the doctrine of appropriate bargaining units is to minimize strategic behavior or "promote industrial peace."[344] The current doctrine that allows the parties mutually to agree to bargain on a multiunit basis[345] probably does not undermine this purpose and may promote it, because parties would probably not agree to such an arrangement if it afforded one side a strategic advantage or if it decreased the total expected outcome from bargaining by increasing the chances of strategic behavior.[346] The prohibition of unilaterally withdrawing from such multiunit bargaining once negotiations have begun[347] was designed to prevent one side from strategically withdrawing from negotiations that it perceives as going badly, thereby increasing negotiating costs and decreasing the chances of a cooperative solution.[348]

The doctrine of exclusive representation also facilitates cooperative solutions in bargaining. By prohibiting individual and subgroup bargaining, the National Labor Relations Act limits the number of parties to the negotiations game, thus simplifying it and increasing the chances of a cooperative solution.[349] The success of this strategy in

---

relations and thus industrial peace, one of the purposes of the NLRA. Buffalo Broadcasting Co., 242 N.L.R.B. 1105 (1979); Marion Power Shovel Co., 230 N.L.R.B. 576 (1977).

343. *See supra* notes 268-71 and accompanying text. Professor Leslie has previously argued that the legal doctrine on appropriate bargaining units is designed to group employees according to their preference with respect to public goods in order to facilitate the optimal provision of those goods in the workplace. Leslie, *supra* note 45, at 407-08. Although it may be true that the current rules fulfill this function, I would argue that the purpose of the rules goes beyond promoting the optimal consumption of public goods to simplifying the negotiations game and promoting cooperative solutions without economic warfare.

344. Mallinckrodt Chem. Works, 162 N.L.R.B. 387, 392 (1966) (holding that, in defining an appropriate unit, the Board will take into account the interest of employees and the public in stability of labor relations and accordingly uninterrupted operation of facilities); COX ET AL., *supra* note 2, at 286 (demonstrating that Board's rule on hospital units was drafted with intent of minimizing work stoppages); *see also* Charles D. Bonanno Linen Serv. v. NLRB, 454 U.S. 404, 412 (1982) (stating that rules on multiemployer bargaining were designed to promote industrial peace).

345. *See* Retail Assoc., 120 N.L.R.B. 388, 395 (1958).

346. However, society may want to prohibit such multiunit bargaining because it facilitates labor cartelization and horizontal price-fixing among employers. Epstein, *supra* note 8, at 1382; Leslie, *supra* note 45, at 418.

347. Western Pac. Roofing Corp., 244 N.L.R.B. 501 (1979), *affd.*, 669 F.2d 1332 (9th Cir. 1982). This prohibition allows unilateral withdrawal after negotiations have begun only under "unusual circumstances." 244 N.L.R.B. at 507.

348. *Bonanno Linen Serv.*, 454 U.S. at 412. For a more traditional economic analysis of the multiunit bargaining rules, see Douglas L. Leslie, *Multiemployer Bargaining Rules*, 75 VA. L. REV. 241 (1989).

349. *See supra* notes 267-70 and accompanying text.

simplifying the bargaining problem is limited by the fact that there may be more than one appropriate unit among an employer's employees. Thus, in facilitating cooperative solutions, there is a tradeoff between organizing the employees according to homogeneity of bargaining interests and minimizing the number players to the bargaining game. Case law recognizes this tradeoff.[350]

Finally, the presumption of the union's continuing majority facilitates cooperative solutions in bargaining by increasing the expectations of repeated play of the bargaining game. Under current legal doctrine, once a union has been recognized as the representative of the employees, it enjoys a strong presumption of continuing majority status.[351] This presumption is sometimes irrebuttable. For example, the Board will not entertain evidence of loss of majority status, or even petitions for an election on that status, within a "reasonable time" after voluntary recognition,[352] within one year after certifying the union pursuant to a valid election,[353] or within the first three years of the life of a collective bargaining agreement.[354] However, even outside these instances, the presumption remains strong. The Board has been very hesitant to accept employer evidence that a recognized union lacks majority status, preferring instead to see such issues resolved through decertification elections.[355] The presumption of continuing majority even extends to cases involving successor employers who purchase the assets of a business and hire a majority of employees from the old unit.[356] By increasing the expectations that the union will be around for a while and that the bargaining game will be repeated, the doctrine raises the expected costs of strategic behavior, because such behavior threatens the success not only of current negotiations but also of future negotiations in which the other side might seek revenge.[357] The

---

350. *See, e.g.,* Mallinckrodt Chem. Works, 162 N.L.R.B. 387, 392 (1966).

351. GETMAN & POGREBIN, *supra* note 2, at 29-34. This presumption exists whether the union was voluntarily recognized by the employer or certified by the Board pursuant to an election. *Id.*

352. *Id.* at 83 n.63.

353. 29 U.S.C. § 159(c)(3) (1988); Brooks v. NLRB, 348 U.S. 96 (1954). This rule is commonly known as the *election bar rule* because a valid election will bar reconsideration of the union's majority status for one year.

354. General Cable Corp., 139 N.L.R.B. 1123 (1962). This rule is commonly known as the *contract bar rule* because negotiation of a valid contract will bar reconsideration of the union's majority status for up to three years.

355. GETMAN & POGREBIN, *supra* note 2, at 31.

356. Fall River Dyeing & Finishing Corp. v. NLRB, 482 U.S. 27 (1987). In order to take advantage of the presumption in this circumstance, the union must request bargaining before or at a time when the new employer has hired a "representative complement" of employees that includes a majority of employees from the old unit. 482 U.S. at 46-54.

357. *See supra* note 273 and accompanying text.

Supreme Court's announced purpose behind the presumption of the union's continuing majority comports with this interpretation of its value in reducing strategic behavior and promoting industrial peace.[358]

5. *The Law on Enforcement of the Collective Agreement*

The law on the enforcement of collective bargaining agreements also seems prudent under the analysis of the bargaining model. As previously discussed, the Supreme Court has found that agreements to arbitrate disputes under collective bargaining agreements are enforceable as a matter of federal substantive law.[359] The courts can compel either side to comply with the agreement to arbitrate and can enjoin strikes or lockouts in contravention of that agreement.[360] Moreover, the courts must show great deference to arbitrators, as to both their jurisdiction under the agreement and their resolution of the dispute, forsaking the temptation to allow the parties to litigate such matters.[361] Agreements to arbitrate disputes under the collective bargaining agreement are the logical low-cost cooperative solution to the problem of contract enforcement. Resorting to economic warfare or costly litigation to resolve contract disputes is a positional externality that wastes the cooperative surplus. Thus, courts properly should enforce and encourage agreements to arbitrate while prohibiting or severely limiting the parties' recourse to economic or legal weapons. Moreover, the rationale for such provisions under the bargaining theory is that they will discourage wasteful strategic behavior and promote industrial peace, precisely the rationales given by the Court in developing this doctrine.[362]

---

358. *Fall River Dyeing & Finishing,* 482 U.S. at 38-39 ("The upshot of the presumptions [of a continuing majority] is to permit unions to develop stable bargaining relationships with employers, which will enable the unions to pursue the goals of their members, and this pursuit, in turn, will further industrial peace.").

359. Textile Workers Union v. Lincoln Mills, 353 U.S. 448, 449-56 (1957); *see supra* note 6 and accompanying text.

360. United Steel Workers v. American Mfg. Co., 363 U.S. 564, 564-69 (1960).

361. United Steel Workers v. Warrior & Gulf Navigation Co., 363 U.S. 574, 583-85 (1960).

362. *Textile Workers Union,* 353 U.S. at 455 ("It [the Labor Management Relations Act] expresses a federal policy that federal courts should enforce . . . agreements [to arbitrate] . . . and that industrial peace can be best obtained only in that way."); Teamsters Local 174 v. Lucas Flour Co. 369 U.S. 95, 105 (1962) ("We approve that doctrine [of finding implied no-strike clauses in agreements to arbitrate]. . . . [A] contrary view would be completely at odds with the basic policy of national labor legislation to promote the arbitral process as a substitute for economic warfare.") (footnote omitted); *see also American Mfg. Co.,* 363 U.S. at 567-68; *Warrior & Gulf Navigation Co.,* 363 U.S. at 578-85; United Steelworkers v. Enterprise Wheel & Car Corp., 363 U.S. 593 (1960).

6. *Recent Proposals for Labor Law Reform*

Up to this point in my application of the bargaining model to American labor law, my objective has been to demonstrate how the bargaining model confirms the logic of the core principles of American labor law and to contrast that confirmation with the condemnation those same principles receive under the monopoly model of unions. However, the bargaining model does not confirm the wisdom of every doctrine under current law. Some problems under the bargaining model with current law, including the allowance of state right-to-work laws under section 14(b) of the National Labor Relations Act,[363] the restrictions on union access to employees during organizing,[364] the limitations on the union's access to financial information,[365] and the recent trend in cases expanding the category of permissive subjects of bargaining to include management decisions over the scope of operation,[366] have already been mentioned in passing. These imperfections may pose substantial barriers to the effective operation of unions,[367] thus denying workers some of the benefits of unions that an interpretation of the National Labor Relations Act that was fully consistent with the bargaining model would allow. This section examines several of the recent proposals for reform of American labor law and evaluates them in light of the bargaining model. The analysis reveals several important ways in which current American labor law does not coincide with the optimal labor policy prescribed by the bargaining model.

One possible reform discussed by many legal theorists[368] is to increase the penalties for violations of the National Labor Relations Act. The Supreme Court has held that the Board's power to respond to violations of the Act is remedial, not punitive, in nature.[369] Accord-

---

363. *See supra* note 294 and accompanying text.

364. *See supra* note 314 and accompanying text.

365. *See supra* note 331 and accompanying text.

366. *See supra* note 338 and accompanying text.

367. Karl E. Klare, *Judicial Deradicalization of the Wagner Act and the Origins of Modern Legal Consciousness, 1937-1941,* 62 MINN. L. REV. 265, 307-10 (1978); Rogers, *supra* note 244, at 113-44.

368. *See* J. FREEDLEY HUNSICKER, JR. ET AL., NLRB REMEDIES FOR UNFAIR LABOR PRACTICES (rev. ed. 1986); MERRIFIELD ET AL., *supra* note 2, at 540; WEILER, *supra* note 22, at 247-49, 251-52; William B. Gould IV, *Some Reflections on Fifty Years of the National Labor Relations Act: The Need for Labor Board and Labor Law Reform,* 38 STAN. L. REV. 937, 939 (1986); Charles Morris, *The Role of the NLRB and the Courts in the Collective Bargaining Process: A Fresh Look at the Conventional Wisdom and Unconventional Remedies,* 30 VAND. L. REV. 661, 676-87 (1977); Theodore St. Antoine, *A Touchstone for Labor Board Remedies,* 14 WAYNE L. REV. 1039 (1968).

369. Phelps Dodge Corp. v. NLRB, 313 U.S. 177, 208 (1941) (Stone, J., concurring) (citing Consolidated Edison Co. v. NLRB, 305 U.S. 197 (1938)).

ingly, the Board can fashion a remedy that attempts to correct the harm done, but it cannot punish a union or an employer to deter future misconduct. In policing organizing campaigns, the Board most often uses its remedial authority to undo benefits or reprisals distributed on the basis of union support or to set aside elections that have been tainted by unfair labor practices or a lack of the requisite "laboratory conditions."[370] For employees who have been discharged for union affiliation, the Board can order reinstatement and backpay, with interest, net of any interim earnings.[371] Moreover, because the Board has decided that "make whole" remedies in which employees are compensated for lost wages and benefits due to employer failure to bargain in good faith are outside its power under the Act,[372] the Board lacks full remedial power to remedy bargaining offenses. For the most part, the Board's remedies for bargaining violations consist of cease-and-desist orders combined with affirmative orders to bargain in good faith.[373] When an employer or union has committed an unfair labor

---

370. GETMAN & POGREBIN, *supra* note 2, at 73. Under NLRB v. Gissel Packing Co., 395 U.S. 575 (1969), the Board can order an employer to bargain with a union on the basis of authorization cards signed by a majority of the employees where the employer has won the election but has committed such serious unfair labor practices that they effectively preclude the running of a fair rerun election. However, this remedial power is exercised sparingly. GETMAN & POGREBIN, *supra* note 2, at 74-77. In some cases of repeated and flagrant violations, the Board has awarded litigation and organizing expenses to a union. Autoprod, Inc., 265 N.L.R.B. 331, 332 (1982); GETMAN & POGREBIN, *supra* note 2, at 148. The Board also has authority, under § 10(j) of the NLRA, to seek immediate injunctions of such unfair labor practices as the discriminatory discharge of an employee during an election campaign. 29 U.S.C. § 160(j) (1988). However, the Board has been loath to exercise this power, perhaps fearing that such remedies would themselves unduly influence the outcome of the election. GETMAN & POGREBIN, *supra* note 2, at 73.

371. Isis Plumbing & Heating Co., 138 N.L.R.B. 716 (1962), *revd. on other grounds,* 322 F.2d 913 (9th Cir. 1963). Similarly, in the case of an employer who relocates to avoid unionization, the Board can order that the aggrieved employees be offered jobs in the new shop and receive backpay until they take the new jobs or find comparable employment in the old location. GETMAN & POGREBIN, *supra* note 2, at 78.

372. Ex-Cell-O Corp., 185 N.L.R.B. 107 (1970). The Board's rationale was that such a "make whole" remedy would be tantamount to requiring the employer to accept a contract term, a remedy that defies the statute's premise of freedom of contract. 185 N.L.R.B. at 110; *see also* 29 U.S.C. § 158(d) (1988); H.K. Porter Co. v. NLRB, 397 U.S. 99 (1970).

373. MERRIFIELD ET AL., *supra* note 2, at 540. Such *bargaining orders* are ultimately enforced through the contempt powers of the federal courts. 29 U.S.C. § 160(e) (1988). An additional remedy for a bargaining violation may be reinstatement after a strike or the loss of a troublesome employee. If an employer's unfair labor practice contributes in whole or in part to the employees' decision to strike, or if such a practice prolongs a strike, then the strike becomes what is known as an *unfair labor practice strike* and the strikers have a right to reinstatement even if they are permanently replaced. GETMAN & POGREBIN, *supra* note 2, at 148. Similarly, if the union commits an unfair labor practice by, for example, striking over a permissive subject, then striking employees can be discharged without right to reinstatement. Mastro Plastics Corp. v. NLRB, 350 U.S. 270, 284-89 (1956); NLRB v. Mackay Radio & Tel. Co., 304 U.S. 333, 345-46 (1938). If an individual employee commits misconduct during a strike, such as violence or vandalism, he can be discharged without right to reinstatement. NLRB v. Fansteel Metallurgical Corp., 306 U.S. 240, 256-57 (1939); NLRB v. Ohio Calcium Co., 133 F.2d 721, 726-27 (6th Cir. 1943); Clear Pine Mouldings, Inc., 1983-84 NLRB Dec. (CCH) ¶ 16,083, at 27,418 (1984).

508   *Michigan Law Review*   [Vol. 91:419

practice, the Board will also order the offending party to post notices stating that it will no longer violate employee rights under the National Labor Relations Act.[374] Many scholars believe these purely remedial penalties are inadequate to deter employers and unions from committing violations of the Act.[375] As a result, proposals have been made to increase penalties, including double backpay for workers discharged during organizing campaigns and monetary compensation for employer refusals to bargain in good faith.[376]

Analysis of the problem under the bargaining model confirms the need to increase penalties under the National Labor Relations Act. Even if society valued the benefits the parties received from violating the Act, economic theory would suggest that, to maximize social welfare, the penalties for such activities should be set so that the perpetrator's expected cost from engaging in the activity equaled the cost the activity imposed on other people.[377] Because not all violators are successfully caught and prosecuted, this would mean that the actual penalties for violations of the Act should be set higher than mere remedial damages so that the expected cost to the perpetrator equaled the costs imposed on the victim.[378] However, under the bargaining model, violations of the Act, such as firing prounion employees and refusing to bargain in good faith, merely constitute wasteful rent-seeking on the part of the perpetrator and do not yield social benefits. Ideally, to maximize social welfare, society should set penalties for such activities so high that potential perpetrators will always be deterred from undertaking the activities.[379] In the real world, however, arbitrarily high penalties for dismissing prounion employees may deter legitimate discharges based on job performance, and employers or unions may be mistakenly convicted of bargaining in bad faith when no violation has

---

374. GETMAN & POGREBIN, *supra* note 2, at 73.

375. *See supra* text accompanying note 368.

376. H.R. REP. No. 637, 95th Cong., 1st Sess. 1 (1977) [hereinafter Labor Reform Act]; WEILER, *supra* note 22, at 247-49, 251; George Meany, *Common Sense in Labor Law*, 27 LABOR L.J. 603, 607-08 (1978).

377. Gary S. Becker, *Crime and Punishment: An Economic Approach*, 76 J. POL. ECON. 169, 191-93 (1968). Setting the penalty at this level maximizes social welfare because the perpetrator will commit the offense only if the benefits he receives from it exceed the costs of the offense to others. *Id.*

378. The expected cost of a violation of the Act to a perpetrator equals the probability that she will be caught and successfully prosecuted times the actual penalty. If not all offenders are successfully caught and punished, the probability of being successfully caught and punished must be less than one. Therefore, in order for the expected costs of the offense to the perpetrator to equal the costs of the offense to the victim, the actual penalty for the offense must exceed the costs of the offense to the victim.

379. Steven Shavell, *Criminal Law and the Optimal Use of Non-monetary Sanctions as a Deterrent*, 85 COLUM. L. REV. 1232, 1242 (1985).

occurred. Accordingly, economic theory suggests that, to maximize social welfare, penalties for socially valueless activities should be set so that the social benefits from increased deterrence equal the social costs of deterring marginally lawful activity and sometimes mistakenly imposing penalties on innocent defendants.[380] The current remedial penalties of the National Labor Relations Act, which often do not even fully compensate the victim, fail to meet this standard.

Another commonly suggested reform is to streamline and speed the union certification process.[381] The current system of elections, the argument goes, allows employers too many opportunities to delay and to coerce employees through threats or the discharge of union supporters.[382] Statistics on the filing of unfair labor practice charges against employers during organizing campaigns suggest that the problem has substantially worsened in the late 1970s and 1980s.[383] To remedy this problem, some have proposed relatively simple solutions, such as setting shorter deadlines for holding elections after filing certification petitions.[384] Paul Weiler has proposed the more extreme solution of adopting the Canadian system — certifying unions based on cards signed by a majority of employees stating that they want the union as their representative.[385] This system avoids the need for lengthy election proceedings and denies employers the opportunity to coerce employees.

Under the bargaining model, the purpose of certification elections is to provide an inexpensive means by which the workers can accurately weigh the benefits of organization against its cost.[386] Delays, and the opportunity for strategic behavior they create, are a cost of the certification process that should be kept to a minimum. Shorter deadlines for elections are desirable as long as they leave employees ade-

---

380. *Id.* at 1243-45. Theoretically, one should also take into account the marginal costs of destroying marginal incentives for good behavior. *Id.* I have omitted this point from the text for purposes of simplicity. The costs of deterring marginally lawful behavior, mistaken punishment, and destroying marginal incentives for good behavior all also enter the problem of setting the optimal penalty when society values the perpetrator's benefits from the offense. They are, however, generally omitted from simple analyses of that problem because they are commonly assumed to be swamped by the costs of deterring the beneficial but prohibited activity.

381. Labor Reform Act, *supra* note 376, at 5; Meany, *supra* note 376; Paul Weiler, *Promises to Keep: Securing Workers' Rights to Self-Organization Under the NLRA*, 96 HARV. L. REV. 1769, 1776-86 (1983).

382. Weiler, *supra* note 381, at 1776-86.

383. *Id.* at 1780. Weiler's statistics show that in 1970, 1975, and 1980 the numbers of employer discrimination charges filed in organizing campaigns were 9290, 13,426, and 18,315, respectively. During this time the number of petitions filed by unions for representation elections declined from 7773 and 8061 in 1970 and 1975, respectively, to 7296 in 1980. *Id.*

384. *See* Labor Reform Act, *supra* note 376, at 5.

385. Weiler, *supra* note 381, at 1806-19.

386. *See supra* notes 268-70 and accompanying text.

Economics of Labor and Employment Law I

quate time to consider the question and make a reasoned decision. As for Weiler's proposal, whether the current system of elections or the Canadian system based on cards is the cheaper means of determining union representation is an empirical question. Although his proposal would undoubtedly save costs over the present system by precluding employer opportunistic behavior, it would also impose some additional costs by preventing employers from providing useful information on the question of representation and by increasing the possibility of fraud and coercion on the part of unions. The benefit of Weiler's proposal in discouraging employer opportunistic behavior might be lessened if the National Labor Relations Act had penalties adequate to deter such behavior. However, Weiler can reasonably argue that the current system's costs in terms of employer opportunistic behavior outweigh any additional costs that would be incurred under his proposal.[387]

Another reform that has recently gained support is to limit or proscribe the employer's ability to permanently replace striking employees. Under the provisions of the National Labor Relations Act, employers are prohibited from firing or discriminating against striking employees.[388] However, in an opinion that baffles even my best students, the Supreme Court in *Mackay Radio* held that the Act did not prohibit employers from "permanently replacing" striking employees.[389] Initially, the problems posed by this case were largely theoretical because few employers permanently replaced employees. However, employers have recently resorted to this strategy with increasing frequency.[390] As a result, in the 1980s and early 1990s there has been a growing consensus that the loophole created by *Mackay* must be addressed,[391] and indeed a bill currently before Congress, which has passed the House, would limit employers' ability to perma-

---

387. This seems particularly true given the Board's current determination that it cannot effectively police the truth or falsity of campaign statements. *See supra* note 319 and accompanying text.

388. 29 U.S.C. § 158(a)(1) (1988); NLRB v. International Van Lines, 409 U.S. 48 (1972).

389. NLRB v. Mackay Radio & Tel. Co., 304 U.S. 333, 345 (1938). The primary distinctions between permanent replacement and discharge are that an employer must have a replacement employee in hand in order for the act to be a replacement, and permanently replaced strikers enjoy a preference in filling positions as they become open with the employer, while discharged employees do not. Laidlaw Corp., 171 N.L.R.B. 1366 (1968).

390. WEILER, *supra* note 22, at 111; *see also* 137 CONG. REC. H5454 (daily ed. July 16, 1991) (statement of Rep. Fazio) ("[Employers in the 1980s have] discovered a forgotten loophole that [allows] them to permanently replace striking workers, [and] they used it every chance they got."). According to Rep. Owens, the threat of permanent replacements, while held over workers' heads, was not used until recently. *Id.* at H5455. Rep. Levin noted that the purpose of H.R. 5 is to restore the NLRA to its historic purpose of promoting democracy, equity, and stability, and not to permit the 1990s to be a repeat of the 1980s. *Id.*

391. Weiler was among the first to make this argument. Paul Weiler, *Striking a New Bal-*

nently replace striking employees.[392]

The bargaining model offers qualified support for this proposal. Allowing employers to permanently replace striking employees creates a tremendous opportunity for costly strategic behavior whereby the employer escapes the bargaining game by permanently replacing prounion employees with justifiably intimidated employees. Allowing permanent replacements provides some impetus toward cooperation in bargaining on the part of the union by raising its expected costs from a strike; however, the one-sided nature of this impetus frustrates the redistributive purposes of encouraging unions. Allowing employers to permanently replace strikers merely leads to union capitulation, not bargaining equity and industrial peace.[393] However, even from the perspective of the bargaining model, if one were concerned about the potential growth of labor cartel power, one might want to adopt some intermediate policy discouraging employer strategic behavior without completely prohibiting the permanent replacement of striking employees. In addition to preventing employer strategic behavior, the complete prohibition of permanent replacements also raises significant barriers to entry in the labor market that could facilitate cartelization.[394]

A final proposal on which the bargaining model allows useful comment is Weiler's proposal to include interest arbitration as a remedy for employers' failure to bargain in good faith in first-time contract negotiations.[395] Citing the recent rise in the failure rate of unions to obtain first contracts after organizing an employer,[396] Weiler has argued that such a bargaining remedy would put some teeth in the Act's directive to bargain in good faith and help ensure that employees real-

---

ance: Freedom of Contract and the Prospects for Union Representation, 98 HARV. L. REV. 351, 387-94 (1984).

392. H.R. 5, 102d Cong., 1st Sess. (1991). The bill's stated purpose is "[t]o amend the National Labor Relations Act and the Railway Labor Act to prevent discrimination based on participation in labor disputes." The bill would prevent employers from hiring permanent replacement workers for employees engaged in a lawful strike.

393. If employers need the alternative of continuing operations during a strike to achieve an "equitable" balance of bargaining power, this problem can be met with temporary replacements. The National Labor Relations Act allows the temporary replacement of strikers. 2 THE DEVELOPING LABOR LAW, *supra* note 2, at 1012-13. Any additional benefit the employer could achieve by obtaining more or better replacements with the promise of permanent positions would be outweighed by the tremendous opportunity for strategic behavior that allowing permanent replacements creates.

394. Of course, if one is really concerned about the existence or growth of labor cartel power, probably none of these proposals for labor law reform makes sense.

395. *See* Weiler, *supra* note 391, at 405-12.

396. *Id.* at 354-55. Between 1950 and 1980, the rate at which unions achieved first contracts after organizing an employer decreased from 86% to 63%. *Id.*

ize their right to bargain collectively after choosing to organize.[397] Although increasing monetary penalties for failure to bargain in good faith may also solve the problem, Weiler's proposal has some appeal under the bargaining model because it recognizes that the parties' awareness of their collective interest in cooperation will be weakest when their relationship has just begun. Accordingly, the proposal reserves the most extreme and intrusive remedy, having a neutral party specify the terms of the collective agreement, for the cases in which the parties' ability to see their collective interest in agreement is probably lowest.

CONCLUSION

The traditional monopoly model of unions and collective bargaining is deficient for three reasons. First, the model focuses on only one among several possible sources of union wage increases, the cartelization of the labor market. Logical arguments and empirical evidence suggest that this exclusive focus on labor cartelization is misplaced and that employer rents, quasi-rents, and productivity increases associated with unionism are also important in the American economy as sources of union wage increases. Second, the model assumes that employers respond to union wage demands by moving up their demand curves when such a response is not Pareto optimal and both the employees and employers could be made better off by negotiating agreements that call for lower wages and higher levels of employment. Empirical evidence rejects the employer demand curve response and supports the proposition that employers and unions negotiate optimal contract terms. Finally, the model implicitly assumes that the costs of collective bargaining are ordinary time and information transaction costs, ignoring the strategic nature of collective bargaining. These deficiencies suggest the need for a new economic model of unions and collective bargaining that recognizes alternative sources of union wage increases, assumes that the parties optimally bargain over contract terms, and explicitly recognizes the strategic nature of collective bargaining. In this article, I have developed such a model, which I call the *bargaining model* of unions and collective bargaining.

The bargaining model confirms the basic logic of the fundamental tenet of American labor law that the government should foster unions and regulate the conduct of industrial relations in order to promote bargaining equity and industrial peace. Under this analysis, unions allow workers to gain a greater share of the proceeds of the business

---

397. *Id.* at 405-12.

and to make valuable contributions in the running of that business through the expression of their collective voice. Thus, by promoting workers to a more equitable bargaining position relative to their employer, unions can serve societal goals of redistributing wealth from employers to employees and perhaps even maximizing total wealth. Despite these beneficial attributes of collective bargaining, both employers and unions often have individual incentives for strategic behavior in the conflicts that occur in organizing, negotiations and enforcement of the collective agreement. Because of these incentives, the conflicts of collective bargaining have a tendency to escalate into costly affairs, wasting a portion of the potential proceeds of the business, despite the parties' — and society's — collective interest in avoiding such waste. The government can minimize such waste by regulating the conduct of collective bargaining to prohibit or discourage strategic behavior and to promote industrial peace.

Many specific provisions of American labor law make sense within the context of the bargaining model. To resolve conflicts in organizing, the National Labor Relations Act promotes elections as a relatively low-cost method for employees to make a reasoned decision about whether the benefits of organization outweigh its costs. The employer is prohibited from using yellow-dog contracts or promises of benefits or reprisals to encourage employee free riding on efforts to organize. Costly strategic behavior by either side, such as discriminatory discharges or recognitional picketing, is prohibited or severely limited. To resolve conflicts in collective negotiations, the law enforces a bilateral relationship in which the employer is required to bargain with the union, as the exclusive representative of the employees, over wages, hours, and working conditions. This bilateral relationship promotes equity in bargaining between employers and employees with its attendant benefits of wealth redistribution and increased productivity. Strategies or behaviors in collective negotiations that are likely to result in costly strikes, such as intransigence in bargaining and Boulwareism, are prohibited or discouraged. Moreover, the law promotes the parties' ability to recognize their collective interests in cooperative bargaining by organizing the employees in relatively homogeneous units, encouraging repeat negotiations through the presumption of a continuing majority, and requiring exchanges of relevant information. Finally, to resolve conflicts in the enforcement of collective agreements, the law enforces and encourages agreements to arbitrate as the low-cost method of resolving such disputes while discouraging resort to costly litigation or strikes.

The bargaining model also suggests several ways in which current

American labor law could be improved. Perhaps chief among these improvements would be a substantial increase in penalties for violations of current law. The current remedial penalties of the National Labor Relations Act do not adequately deter costly strategic behavior. Additional benefits from collective bargaining can be gained by further facilitating employee organizing and promoting cooperative solutions in collective bargaining. This might be achieved by giving unions greater access to employees on employer property during organizing campaigns; streamlining employee organizational campaigns; giving the union greater access to employer financial information; repealing section 14(b) of the National Labor Relations Act, which allows state right-to-work laws; and requiring good-faith bargaining on all subjects of direct relevance to the employees' and employer's relationship. Finally, the bargaining model provides qualified support for recent legislative efforts to restrict employers' ability to permanently replace striking employees. The possibility of permanently replacing striking employees creates tremendous potential for costly strategic behavior on the part of employers and encourages union capitulation to employer demands, frustrating the redistributive purposes of allowing employee organization. Although the bargaining model demonstrates the consistent logic behind the core principles of American labor law, some further substantial changes would allow workers to enjoy more fully the benefits of collective bargaining.

[4]

VIRGINIA LAW REVIEW

VOLUME 87	APRIL 2001	NUMBER 2

ARTICLE

HUMAN BEHAVIOR AND THE LAW OF WORK

*Cass R. Sunstein**

INTRODUCTION

A. A Problem and a Proposal

IN allocating rights in the workplace, the law has many options. It might, for example, confer certain rights on employers, but allow employees to purchase those rights (to, say, parental leave, health insurance, or vacation time) through a voluntary trade. It might make certain employers' rights nonwaivable; it might say, for example, that an employee, or a group of employees, cannot buy an employer's right to donate money to political campaigns. It might give employees certain waivable rights, saying, for example, that an employee is presumed to have a right to at least four weeks of vacation each year, but that employers can buy that right through a suitable deal. Or it might give employees rights that cannot be waived, saying, for example, that no worker may be asked to trade

* Karl N. Llewellyn Distinguished Service Professor of Jurisprudence, University of Chicago Law School and Department of Political Science. This Article is the foundation for the McCorkle Lecture, delivered at the University of Virginia on September 25, 2000. Because it is the foundation for a lecture, it avoids the usual extensive footnoting; the reader is asked to make allowances for an Article originally prepared for oral presentation. I am grateful to comments from many people, including Alan Hyde, Russell Korobkin, David Laibson, Eric Posner, and Richard Posner. Participants in the Summer Institute on Behavioral Economics, held in July 2000, provided valuable comments. Special thanks to Daniel Kahneman, for specific and general help, and also to Richard Thaler for overall guidance on behavioral economics. None of these people should be held responsible for errors here.

the right to four weeks of vacation each year. There are many possible variations.

The basic purpose of this Article is to bring a better understanding of human behavior, with the assistance of cognitive psychology and behavioral economics,[1] to bear on the most basic questions in employment law.[2] I offer two general claims. The first is that waivable workers' rights represent a promising approach for the future, partly because waivable rights lack the rigidity of nonwaivable ones, and partly because they ensure that employers will provide key information to workers. The second claim is that traditional understandings of employee behavior and employment law make many blunders, because they are based on an inadequate sense of workers' actual values and behavior. Contrary to the conventional wisdom:

- Workers are especially averse to losses, and not as much concerned with obtaining gains;

- Workers often do not know about legal rules, including key rules denying them rights;

- Workers may well suffer from excessive optimism;

- Workers care a great deal about being treated fairly, and are willing to punish employers who have treated them unfairly, even at the workers' own expense;[3]

- Workers often prefer increasing wage profiles;

- Many workers greatly discount the future, sometimes treating it as irrelevant; and

---

[1] See Behavioral Law and Economics (Cass R. Sunstein ed., 2000); Richard H. Thaler, Quasi Rational Economics (1991); Christine Jolls et al., A Behavioral Approach to Law and Economics, 50 Stan. L. Rev. 1471 (1998).

[2] I use this term to refer to both "labor law," traditionally taken to refer to the law relating to unions and unionization, and "employment law," traditionally taken to refer to the law relating to statutory protections of workers.

[3] This is the basic theme of Truman F. Bewley, Why Wages Don't Fall During A Recession (1999). Id. at 173–80 (discussing this point in particular). In a series of important papers, Ernst Fehr and his colleagues have explored this point in many settings. See, e.g., Ernst Fehr et al., Reciprocal Fairness and Non-Compensating Wage Differentials, 152 J. Institutional & Theoretical Econ. 608 (1996); Ernst Kirchler et al., Social exchange in the labor market: Reciprocity and trust versus egoistic maximization, 17 J. Econ. Psych. 313 (1996).

- Workers often care more about their relative economic position, or how their income compares with others, than about their absolute economic position, or how many dollars they are making in the abstract.

In short, workers are like most people. They behave like *homo sapiens*, not like *homo economicus*.[4] Hence one of my principal purposes here is to bring an understanding of behavioral economics to bear on some of the central issues in the law of work—and to show how such an understanding helps correct the prevailing wisdom insofar as it is grounded in neoclassical economics.[5] We shall also find, in incipient form, what might be called the implicit behavioral rationality of certain aspects of contemporary law, as courts and legislatures show an understanding of the points listed above.

More specifically, I will attempt to show how a more realistic understanding of workers' thoughts and actions helps sort out the relevant inquiries in the choice among the four principal approaches to the law of labor-management relations: (1) waivable employers' rights, (2) waivable workers' rights, (3) nonwaivable workers' rights, and (4) waivable workers' rights with constraints on permissible waiver. I suggest that in many situations, the law should confer certain entitlements on employees rather than employers, but allow those entitlements to be waived, either at a market price (an "unconstrained waiver") or subject to governmentally determined floors, whether procedural or substantive (a "constrained waiver"). The principal purpose of this approach is to ensure that employers fully disclose contractual terms to employees and allow employees to waive only when waiver is thought to be worthwhile, without producing the rigidity, inefficiency, and potential harm to workers and consumers alike that are created by systems of nonwaivable, "one-size-fits-all" terms.[6]

---

[4] See Richard H. Thaler, From Homo Economicus to Homo Sapiens, 14 J. Econ. Persp. 133 (2000).

[5] See infra pp. 165–68 for an overview.

[6] A system of nonwaivable terms is urged in Charles Fried, Individual and Collective Rights in Work Relations: Reflections on the Current State of Labor Law and Its Prospects, 51 U. Chi. L. Rev. 1012 (1984); my criticisms of the more ad hoc system of modern statutory law apply to Fried's general proposal as well.

This basic idea could be applied to both unionized and non-unionized workplaces. It could even be applied to the question of whether workers are collectively organized at all: A default rule might specify collective organization and allow workers to opt out rather than specifying the opposite and allowing them to opt in.[7] It is especially important to see that the default rule matters. What I will ultimately suggest is a two-tiered system of employment law, involving (a) nonwaivable statutory minima, below which no workplace may go, and (b) waivable workers' rights, involving an ample set of safeguards that employers may buy for a fee agreed upon by both workers and employers.[8] The real questions should involve the content of the two categories.

B. An Unduly Limited Debate

In the workplace, as elsewhere, the law cannot "do nothing."[9] For even the most enthusiastic believers in private property and freedom of contract, it is necessary to start somewhere—not with nature or voluntary arrangements but with an initial allocation of legal rights.

Most debates in American employment law have been framed narrowly and in terms of three alternatives: waivable employers' rights, collective bargaining, and nonwaivable workers' rights. Under a system of waivable employers' rights, the law confers an initial entitlement on employers but allows employees to buy the relevant right if they have both the desire and the leverage to do so. It is important to emphasize that the employer has these rights not by nature, and not as a result of anything consensual, but because of a distinctly legal decision to confer the relevant rights on the employer rather than the employee. The rights at issue often involve the most fundamental questions for workers: job security; workplace safety; pensions; health insurance; leave policy; vacation time; freedom from race, sex, and age discrimination; and so forth.

---

[7] See Paul C. Weiler, Governing the Workplace 228–30 (1990).

[8] For a brief suggestion along the same lines for worker safety, see Susan Rose-Ackerman, Progressive Law and Economics—And the New Administrative Law, 98 Yale L.J. 341, 358–60 (1988).

[9] See Guido Calabresi & A. Douglas Melamed, Property Rules, Liability Rules, and Inalienability: One View of the Cathedral, 85 Harv. L. Rev. 1089, 1090 (1972).

2001]   *Human Behavior and the Law of Work*   209

This simple idea—of waivable employers' rights—captures much of the common law of labor relations.[10] The common law confers a wide range of entitlements on employers, subject to individual bargaining. The single exception is the labor power of the employee.[11] Of course, the law grants employees, not employers, the right to the employee's time and labor.[12] This is a right that employees can and do trade for money and other benefits of employment.

The flexibility of the common law approach is its great advantage. Such flexibility in one sense promotes liberty, because it allows diverse employers and employees to select the approach that fits them best, and also efficiency, because it promises to protect mutually satisfactory deals. But it is not clear that most workers have the information that would equip them to engage in appropriate bargaining, and it is possible to think that many individual employees, bargaining with employers, will lack the knowledge or the power to produce efficient or fair deals without some form of collective organization. In any case, the initial allocation of rights to employers remains to be defended.

In the 1930s, the United States ventured a second approach to labor-management relations. This approach, embodied in the National Labor Relations Act[13] ("NLRA"), was a dramatic, even revolutionary step: a mechanism for solution of disagreements via collective bargaining. On this view, entitlements are generally given to employers, as with the common law, but workers are allowed or encouraged to organize as a group. Workplace

---

[10] This is described and defended in Richard A. Epstein, A Common Law for Labor Relations: A Critique of the New Deal Labor Legislation, 92 Yale L.J. 1357 (1983). What Epstein does not sufficiently acknowledge is the extent to which a number of rights are conferred on the employer by the common law; any suggestion that the common law reflects "laissez-faire," or promotes "voluntary interactions," should be prefaced with this point. In this vein, see Fried, supra note 6, at 1016: "Only by assuming that the preexisting common law system of property rights had some natural, preconventional status can the expropriationary thrust of the Wagner Act (to the extent that there is one) be criticized." A better way to put it would be to suggest that the very claim that there is an expropriationary thrust in the Wagner Act depends on the (implausible) claim that the common law system of property rights has some natural, preconventional status.

[11] Note the contrast with a system of slavery, in which the law confers on employers a right to the employee's labor. The employers' right is waivable in the sense that the employer can pay the slave a salary or even grant the slave freedom.

[12] Slavery is an obvious exception.

[13] 29 U.S.C. §§ 151–169 (1994).

management is decided via a process of employer-employee bargaining, thus organized. In some ways, the NLRA's arrangement is more complicated and more interesting than this account suggests. With respect to mandatory subjects of bargaining—wages, hours, and working conditions—the NLRA removes common law rights from employers and creates bargaining entitlements, that is, entitlements that are not owned by anyone in particular but that will be a product of bargaining, having been deliberately placed, as an initial step, in the hands of neither side.[14]

This system of worker organization and collective rather than individual bargaining has been justified on many diverse grounds.[15] Most obviously, collective bargaining allows information to be shared and pooled among workers, and hence it should permit them to overcome the many evident barriers to informed bargaining (an issue to which I will return). A point especially congenial to the perspective here is that union representation might also respond to short-sightedness, or bounded rationality, on the part of individual workers, producing outcomes that would best serve their long-term interests.[16] Perhaps collective organization is simply necessary to produce industrial peace. At the same time, union representation resolves a collective action problem faced by individual workers who would compete, perhaps to their collective detriment, in the process of seeking employment.[17] Self-organization could create a kind of workers' cartel, justified on the ground that the result would be to extract better deals from em-

---

[14] See Michael L. Wachter & George M. Cohen, The Law and Economics of Collective Bargaining: An Introduction and Application to the Problems of Subcontracting, Partial Closure, and Relocation, 136 U. Pa. L. Rev. 1349, 1371–74 (1988).

[15] The literature is immense. For summaries, see Richard B. Freeman & James L. Medoff, What Do Unions Do? 3–25 (1984); Michael C. Harper & Samuel Estreicher, Labor Law 2–4 (4th ed. 1996).

[16] For relevant evidence, see Freeman & Medoff, supra note 15, at 20 (emphasizing distinct features of compensation packages favored by unions, including an emphasis on long-term problems).

[17] For an early statement, see John Stuart Mill, Principles of Political Economy, *in* Principles of Political Economy and Chapters on Socialism 1, 349–51 (Jonathan Riley ed., Oxford Univ. Press 1994) (1848). For more contemporary statements, see Freeman & Medoff, supra note 15, at 7–11; Richard A. Posner, Some Economics of Labor Law, 51 U. Chi. L. Rev. 988 (1984).

ployers (possibly at the expense of nonunionized workers).[18] In any case, many of the goods provided by employers—safety, decent lighting, heat, pension benefits, formal procedures in the event of arbitrary discharge—are "local public goods" in the sense that they cannot be provided to one without being simultaneously provided to all or most. In these circumstances a collective voice might ensure against the underproduction of such goods.[19] Whatever its goals, the collective bargaining approach has fallen on hard times with the decline of union representation since the 1950s, a decline related to workers' uncertainty about whether unionization would help or hurt them.[20]

The third approach involves nonwaivable employees' rights. Under this system, the law confers the relevant right on employees, and employers and employees are forbidden from contracting around the legal guaranty. The relevant right might be a right to protection from occupational risks; it might be a right to be free from discharge on grounds of race, sex, or age; it might be a right not to be discharged for engaging in collective bargaining or for refusing to violate the law on the employers' behalf. As a matter of history, the third approach seems largely a reaction to the first, fueled by complaints about employers' bargaining power and about the perceived injustice of the common law approach.[21] This approach dominates the current system of statutory protections for workers in America;[22] it also dominates the more aggressively

---

[18] The "union wage premium" is generally estimated at 10% to 30%. See Freeman & Medoff, supra note 15, at 43–60; Harper & Estreicher, supra note 15, at 14. Unions also produce a mix in the compensation package, with particularly favorable effects on fringe benefits. See Freeman & Medoff, supra note 15, at 61–77. Thus unionized "establishments are especially likely to allot funds to deferred forms of compensation favoring senior workers, such as pensions, insurance, and vacation pay, and to have a large impact on smaller establishments." Id. at 77.

[19] See Freeman & Medoff, supra note 15, at 8–9.

[20] See Samuel Estreicher, Labor Law Reform in a World of Competitive Product Markets, 69 Chi.-Kent L. Rev. 3, 4–20 (1993).

[21] See, e.g., Lawrence E. Blades, Employment at Will vs. Individual Freedom: On Limiting the Abusive Exercise of Employer Power, 67 Colum. L. Rev. 1404 (1967).

[22] See, e.g., 29 U.S.C. §§ 201–219 (1994) (Fair Labor Standards Act of 1938, with minimum wage and maximum hour provisions); id. §§ 651–678 (1994) (Occupational Safety and Health Act); id. §§ 2601–2654 (1994) (Family and Medical Leave Act); 42 U.S.C. §§ 2000e–2000e-17 (1994) (Civil Rights Act of 1964, Title VII).

worker-protective systems of employment and labor law in Europe.

The rise of nonwaivable employees' rights can be seen as a surrogate for a more robust system of collective bargaining.[23] But at the same time, it can be seen as a way of relieving any pressure to create that very system. If statutory protections are in place, a union might seem quite unnecessary, as the law is already giving employees what the union might have provided. A robust system of statutory guarantees would make union representation far less desirable. At the same time, an approach based on nonwaivable workers' rights might be criticized on grounds of its rigidity. Perhaps many workers would be better off with the flexibility to trade some goods for others, and perhaps consumers would benefit as well.[24]

C. Workers' Rights, With Bargaining

This, then, is a basic picture of contemporary issues and debates in employment law. But several things are missing from the picture. Most important: What if the law allocates the relevant entitlement to employees, but also makes the right waivable, in the sense that the employer could buy it, and the employee could sell it, for a fee? In principle, there is nothing at all strange about this idea. With respect to the employee's time, for example, the common law allocates rights in exactly this fashion; before employment, the individual has a property right over the course of his day that the employer can purchase for whatever amount the employee is willing to accept.[25] We could easily imagine a system in which rights of this sort were a far larger part of the picture than they currently are. For example, employees might have and be permitted to waive rights not to be discharged without good cause;

---

[23] Cf. Fried, supra note 6, at 1020–37 (arguing for a statement of nonwaivable entitlements as a replacement for collective bargaining). Fried's argument is criticized in Cass R. Sunstein, Rights, Minimal Terms, and Solidarity: A Comment, 51 U. Chi. L. Rev. 1041 (1984).

[24] This is a generalization of the argument in Richard A. Epstein, Forbidden Grounds (1995).

[25] This is meant not in the sense that workers can "sell themselves into slavery," but in the sense that workers can make binding contracts to do certain things, on pain of sanctions.

rights not to be fired on grounds of race, sex, religion, or age; rights to health insurance or occupational safety; rights to parental leave; or rights to vacation time. All of these rights would operate as default rules for employers to purchase if a mutually agreeable deal could be arranged. Waiver might operate individually or collectively; the law might or might not impose constraints on waivers.

What is absent from the traditional account is not only a full sense of the legal possibilities, but also an adequate picture of workers' judgments and motivations. To the extent that analysis of labor law has worked from any such picture, it is the one found in traditional economics.[26] But we know enough to know that this picture is inaccurate. Indeed, we know a great deal about how it is inaccurate, and about what must be done to make it more nearly correct.[27] I attempt here to bring a better understanding of human behavior to bear on the various alternatives.

This Article comes in six parts. Part I will discuss the debate over at-will employment, with reference to emerging developments that suggest a possible waivable right to be discharged for cause. The at-will debate is well-trodden ground, but a behavioral approach offers some new perspectives, and in many ways the particular issue is representative of many other problems in employment law. Part II will discuss some arguments for a nonwaivable background rule, the standard approach in modern statutory law. Part III will generalize the idea of waivable workers' rights by briefly exploring a number of contemporary questions in employment law. Part IV will discuss problems with allowing waiver, with particular reference to third-party effects, information-processing, and collective efforts to change norms and values. My goal will be to provide a refined sense of when and why waiver might be disallowed, in a way that goes beyond the conventional search for externalities. Part V will discuss the difference between individual waivers and union waivers. Part VI will address workers' concern with relative economic position, not just absolute economic position—a fact that supports the idea of nonwaivable terms by suggesting that such terms can maintain workers' relative position while giving them a

---

[26] See, e.g., Epstein, supra note 10, at 1358 (using the traditional economic mold).

[27] For an overview, see Thaler, supra note 1; see also Jolls et al, supra note 1, at 13–58 (providing a theory of economic analysis "that reflects a better understanding of human behavior and its wellsprings").

benefit such as more leisure time, better health, or more time with their families.

II. AN ILLUSTRATION: THE AT-WILL DEBATE

The debate over the contract at will has recently become one of the liveliest in all of private law.[28] This debate is in some ways unique, for reasons that I will discuss in some detail, but it also has features in common with related debates involving, for example, parental leave, vacation time, health care, and age discrimination. With the decline in private-sector unions,[29] the common law is now a principal arena for new contests about the nature of management-labor relations; the permissible grounds for discharge under the evolving common law have thus received a great deal of judicial as well as academic attention.[30] My particular goal is to show how a better understanding of human behavior casts new light on the issue,[31] in a way that unequivocally suggests the hazards of relying on a system of waivable employers' rights, and that also suggests, though more equivocally, the value of creating waivable employees' rights instead.

A. Background and Movement

In America, the general rule is that employment is at will: An employer can fire an employee for any reason or for no reason at

---

[28] See, e.g., Weiler, supra note 7, at 48–104 (challenging the at-will rule); Richard A. Epstein, In Defense of the Contract at Will, 51 U. Chi. L. Rev. 947 (1984) (arguing for the at-will rule); Pauline T. Kim, Bargaining with Imperfect Information: A Study of Worker Perceptions of Legal Protection in an At-Will World, 83 Cornell L. Rev. 105 (1997) [hereinafter Kim, Bargaining] (finding that workers lack information about the rule); Pauline T. Kim, Norms, Learning, and Law: Exploring the Influences on Workers' Legal Knowledge, 1999 U. Ill. L. Rev. 447 [hereinafter Kim, Norms] (reporting that workers view their legal rights in the context of at-will employment contracts); Stewart J. Schwab, Life-Cycle Justice: Accommodating Just Cause and Employment at Will, 92 Mich. L. Rev. 8 (1993) (discussing risk of opportunistic behavior).

[29] See Estreicher, supra note 20, at 4–20. The percentage of the private nonagricultural workforce belonging to unions fell from about 35.7% in 1953 to about 11.5% in 1992. Id. at 3 & n.1.

[30] See sources cited supra note 28; Samuel Issacharoff, Contracting for Employment: The Limited Return of the Common Law, 74 Tex. L. Rev. 1783, 1783–86 (1996).

[31] As far as I am aware, the only existing discussion of the contract at will, from this point of view, can be found in the illuminating discussion in Issacharoff, supra note 30.

all. In recent decades, however, courts have made three inroads on this rule, involving third-party effects, opportunistic behavior, and promises inferred from ambiguous statements.

1. Third-Party Effects

There is now a set of public policy exceptions to the at-will rule:[32] For example, an employer may not discharge an employee for refusing to commit a crime on his behalf. The key organizing idea behind the public policy exceptions is that when a third-party interest is at stake, the at-will principle does not apply.[33] Insofar as such interests are at stake, the decisions make a great deal of sense. The analysis is straightforward, and the decisions do not present difficult issues about workers and their motivations.

2. Opportunistic Discharges and the Implicit Behavioral Rationality of the Modern Common Law

In a separate and more complex line of cases, courts have found an implied "covenant of good faith and fair dealing."[34] This idea seems to forbid "opportunistic discharges"—as, for example, when an employer discharges an employee immediately before the employee is to receive a commission, a pension, or some other benefit that he seems to have earned.[35] The best rationale for these decisions is that they violate implicit contractual understandings.[36] To understand this point, some brief background is in order, for this is the first place where we shall see how a behavioral understanding unsettles the conventional view and better explains both the data and the case law.

---

[32] See, e.g., Belline v. K-Mart Corp., 940 F.2d 184, 186 (7th Cir. 1991); Petermann v. International Brotherhood of Teamsters, Local 396, 344 P.2d 25, 27 (Cal. Dist. Ct. App. 1959); Remington Freight Lines v. Larkey, 644 N.E.2d 931, 940 (Ind. Ct. App. 1994); Brigham v. Dillon Cos., 935 P.2d 1054, 1059 (Kan. 1997).

[33] See Stewart J. Schwab, Wrongful Discharge Law and the Search for Third-Party Effects, 74 Tex. L. Rev. 1943 (1996).

[34] Mark A. Rothstein et al., Employment Law 690–94 (2d ed. 1999).

[35] See Hoffman-La Roche v. Campbell, 512 So. 2d 725, 738–39 (Ala. 1987); Merrill v. Crothall-American 606 A.2d 96, 101 (Del. 1992); Fortune v. Nat'l Cash Register Co., 364 N.E.2d 1251, 1257 (Mass. 1977); K-Mart Corp. v. Ponsock, 732 P.2d 1364, 1370 (Nev. 1987); Rothstein et al., supra note 34, at 690–94.

[36] See Schwab, supra note 28, at 33.

In the conventional view,[37] the interests of workers and employers ensure against opportunistic discharges, understood as discharges in violation of the parties' implicit agreements. As the standard account of life-cycle justice goes, employers subsidize workers during an initial training period in which wages exceed productivity. Here the employer is making an investment in workers, hoping to recoup that investment after the training period is finished, as workers build up firm-specific human capital. After training, the worker's productivity inside the firm increases over time, as do workers' wages. But wages increase less rapidly than does productivity for the remainder of the worker's career. In effect, the worker was subsidized in the training period; after that time, he subsidizes the employer, because productivity is higher than wages even though both continue to increase.

For purposes of law, the distinctive feature of this account is that the law need not intervene to bind the employer to the employee, or the reverse. The worker wants to stay, because his inside wage is higher than his wage in other workplaces where he lacks firm-specific human capital. At the same time, the employer wants the worker to stay, because the worker's wage continues to be lower than his productivity inside the firm. The elegance of the account lies in its purported demonstration that the self-interest of both parties will prevent behavior that might be opportunistic, inefficient, or unfair.

As Stewart Schwab has shown in an important essay, there are serious problems with this conventional account.[38] An obvious difficulty is posed by the widespread existence of mandatory retirement rules, now unlawful under the Age Discrimination in Employment Act[39] ("ADEA"). If productivity continues to be higher than wages, why on earth would employers seek to get rid of older workers? The question suggests that productivity will not, at a certain stage, be higher than wages after all—or at least that an employer can do better with replacements. A further problem stems from evidence that workers' wages are, toward the end of ca-

---

[37] This account is outlined in detail in Schwab, supra note 28, at 13–15. I draw on Schwab's superb account throughout this discussion, adding only a fuller sense of the behavioral foundations of the view he defends.

[38] See id. at 15–19.

[39] 29 U.S.C. § 623(a) (1994).

reers, higher than productivity, so that late-career workers are, in effect, being subsidized by employers, in a way that apparently provides compensation for workers' subsidy of employers in mid-career.[40] An additional problem—or perhaps it is an explanation of the problem just noted—comes from detailed evidence of the "efficiency wage," by which employers pay employees a bit more than they must, in order to prevent shirking.[41] An examination of the relationship between productivity and wages suggests that promises of payment in late career, including pensions and wages above productivity, are part of a bargain by which employers induced good work from people who might otherwise choose merely adequate work.

On this account of the situation, the deal between employers and employees is not self-enforcing.[42] Employers have an incentive to behave opportunistically, by discharging late-career employees, in violation of the implicit deal. There is a potential role for law to prevent this opportunistic behavior, thus promoting efficiency and fairness alike. More specifically, law might forbid discharges in violation of the bargain revealed by an understanding of the life-cycle model of employment. In fact, a number of cases involving violations of an implied covenant of good faith and fair dealing seem to reflect a judgment of exactly this sort.[43] Thus it is possible to see, in the modern developments, an implicit behavioral foundation to the innovation away from the simplest form of the contract at will.[44]

I have yet to provide an understanding of *why* the relationship between productivity and wages takes the form that it does. Here behavioral economics provides some clues. The first point has to do with fairness and its relationship to morale. Behavioral econo-

---

[40] See James L. Medoff & Katherine G. Abraham, Are Those Paid More Really More Productive? The Case of Experience, 16 J. Hum. Resources 186 (1981); James L. Medoff & Katherine G. Abraham, Experience, Performance, and Earnings, 95 Q.J. Econ. 703 (1980); Schwab, supra note 28, at 16.

[41] See Schwab, supra note 28, at 16; see also George A. Akerlof, An Economic Theorist's Book of Tales 151–54 (1984) (describing the phenomenon as a partial gift).

[42] See Schwab, supra note 28, at 19.

[43] See sources cited supra note 35; see also Schwab, supra note 28, at 38–51 (describing cases best explained by the life-cycle model).

[44] See Schwab, supra note 28, at 19–28; see also Christine Jolls, Hands-Tying and the Age Discrimination in Employment Act, 74 Tex. L. Rev. 1813 (1996) [hereinafter Jolls, Hands-Tying] (supporting the ADEA as a potentially efficient response to the life-cycle model).

mists emphasize that people care about fairness—about being fair and perhaps even more about being treated fairly.[45] Hence they are likely to sacrifice economic self-interest, especially to punish those who have been unfair to them.[46] Evidence shows that workers care a great deal about being treated fairly, that judgments about fairness do not depend only on the absolute level of wages, and that employees are entirely willing to punish employers who violate employees' perception of fairness.[47] Employers are aware of this fact and behave accordingly, so as to maintain morale and thus prevent shirking or worse.[48] The existence of the efficiency wage is best explained in these terms. Employers give employees somewhat more than they need to give; in return, employees do the same for employers. At the same time, the promise of benefits down the line—pensions, increasing wages—encourages the employee to bind himself to the employer, both by staying there and by doing good work.

The second explanation for the revised understanding of the relationship between productivity and wages is that, like everyone else, employees are loss averse, in the sense that they do not like losses from the status quo. This preference imposes severe pressures on employers' ability to set wage structures.[49] Employees would predictably rebel against an employer's decision to set wages below productivity if the consequence was that late-career employees would find their wages gradually shrinking. Employers' failure to reduce the wages of older workers fits with the understanding that any reduction in wages would cause severe morale problems—a point that helps explain employers' general reluctance to reduce wages, even in recessions.[50]

A third and closely-related point is that employees appear to prefer rising wage profiles.[51] Many people would rather see wages

---

[45] See Jolls et al., supra note 1, at 1489–96.

[46] See id.; Bewley, supra note 3, at 175–76; Gary Charness & Matthew Rabin, Social Preferences: Some Simple Tests and a New Model 1 (Jan. 2000) (unpublished manuscript, on file with the Virginia Law Review Association).

[47] See Bewley, supra note 3, at 175–76.

[48] See id.

[49] See id.

[50] See id.

[51] See George Loewenstein & Nachum Sicherman, Do Workers Prefer Increasing Wage Profiles?, 9 J. Lab. Econ. 67 (1991).

for the next four years take the form $50,000, $55,000, $60,000, $70,000, rather than $70,000, $60,000, $55,000, $50,000—even though the latter is worth more. The observed steady increase in wages, even in the face of not-increasing or even decreasing productivity, undoubtedly has something to do with this motivation.

3. Inferences From Ambiguous Statements

Equally important for current purposes, courts have made some movement toward inferring a contractual term of job security. The inferences have been drawn on the basis of highly ambiguous commitments from employers, such as a vague promise (referring to permanent employment) and employee manuals (even those that contain express disclaimers).[52] Here, too, we can find an implicit behavioral rationality in the law, rooted in an understanding of what workers actually think.

As a consequence of these changes, the law is in flux in many states. For example, Montana has enacted a statutory program designed to replace the at-will rule with a nonwaivable for-cause regime,[53] and in 1991 the National Conference of Commissions on State Laws adopted a similar rule as the Uniform Employment Termination Act.[54]

B. Of Waiver and Default Rules: Does It Matter Who Has the Entitlement?

Under the at-will rule, the common law confers the relevant entitlement on the employer. But entirely within a system of freedom of contract, it would be equally possible to confer the entitlement on workers, protecting them against discharge without cause, but allowing them to waive that protection for an agreed-upon price. The initial question is whether, in a regime of freedom of contract, the default rule matters at all.

Under the conventional view, the default rule does not matter. Here is a second place where, as we shall see, the conventional view is wrong, and a behavioral approach does much better. The

---

[52] See infra Section II.E.
[53] See Mont. Code Ann. § 39-2-901 et. seq. (1999).
[54] See Model Employment Termination Act, *reprinted in* Mark A. Rothstein & Lance Liebman, Employment Law 208–19 (3d ed. Statutory Supp. 1997).

issue is complex, and lest the forest be lost for the trees, here is the simple conclusion: The default rule may well matter a great deal, because the party who is allocated the initial entitlement, in employment law or elsewhere, is likely to value it far more than he would if the initial entitlement were given to the other side. In other words, the default rule is highly likely to affect valuations, including workers' valuations.

1. The Endowment Effect and "Sticky" Default Rules

The Coase theorem states that if transaction costs are zero, the initial allocation of the entitlement does not matter.[55] The Coase theorem actually suggests two different points. First, whatever the content of the legal rule, the parties will bargain their way to the *efficient* solution. Second, whatever the content of the legal rule, the parties will bargain their way to the *same* solution. If these points are right, it does not matter, assuming no transaction costs, whether an employer or an employee is given the relevant entitlement. The question is how the Coase theorem bears on the selection of default rules in the context of employment law.

Let us begin by supposing that with respect to contracting around the job security term, transaction costs are zero. Is the Coase theorem correct? It is clear that the theorem is on firm ground insofar as it suggests that the parties will bargain their way to an efficient result, whatever the content of the legal rule. This is very close to a definition of efficiency. If the employer very much wants an at-will rule, and if the employee does not care much about job security, the contract will provide for at-will employment, regardless of the content of the legal rule. If the background rule is at will, there will be no contractual shift; if the background rule is for-cause, the parties will bargain their way to an at-will situation. Efficiency will follow no matter what the legal rule is.[56]

---

[55] See Ronald H. Coase, The Problem of Social Cost, 3 J.L. & Econ. 1, 8 (1960).

[56] Of course the legal rule may have distributional consequences. If the employment right at issue is a large part of the wealth of either side, its allocation to one or another side will contribute to relative wealth. But in this context, it is difficult to see how the choice of one or another waivable rule will have significant distributive effects. So long as the parties can bargain, workers are not going to be significantly poorer or richer if the default rule is one way rather than the other.

Will the legal rule be not merely efficient but also the same? Notwithstanding the Coase theorem, there is good reason to think that it will not be.[57] The principal reason is the *endowment effect*, a central behavioral finding in accordance with which people tend to place a far higher value on an object if it is initially allocated to them than if it is initially allocated to someone else.[58] Default rules have a tendency to stick, in labor contracts as elsewhere. If people are initially given a right to a certain good, they are likely to ask more to give it up than they would be willing to pay for it in the first instance.[59] We do not have direct evidence for the particular case of job security, but if for-cause protection is initially given to the employee, it is reasonable to predict that the employee will demand more to relinquish job security than he would be willing to pay to obtain the right in the first instance. It is less clear that the endowment effect holds for large commercial actors. But if a right to discharge at will is given to employers, it follows that some or many employers will demand more to give it up than they would pay to purchase it in the first instance. Thus the allocation of the legal entitlement, to workers or to employers, will likely matter in the sense that the ultimate outcome will be affected by the increased value placed upon the right simply by virtue of the initial allocation.[60]

So long as the right is initially allocated to one or another side, an endowment effect cannot be avoided. The only way to avoid such an effect would be for the law to refuse to allocate any initial right at all. At first glance this seems to be an incoherent and impossible idea: Any system, to get off the ground, requires an initial allocation of rights, from which bargaining will take place. But the idea is not as impossible as it seems.[61] The law might say, for example, that a contract cannot be enforced unless express provision has

---

[57] See Thaler, supra note 1, at 7–10.

[58] For evidence of the endowment effect in the area of default rules, see Russell Korobkin, Behavioral Economics, Contract Formation, and Contract Law, *in* Behavioral Law and Economics, supra note 1, at 116.

[59] See id.

[60] Compare the suggestion in Richard A. Posner, Economic Analysis of Law 359 (5th ed. 1998): "If the requirement were optimal it would be negotiated voluntarily." The suggestion is not wrong, but it neglects the possibility that the initial allocation of the right will determine what it is optimal.

[61] I am grateful to David Laibson for this suggestion.

been made for or against job security; without such a provision, the contract is void. Sometimes contract law does take this approach, by refusing to specify terms for the parties. To get a bit ahead of the story, this approach is a draconian form of *information-forcing*: It requires the parties to be clear, and refuses to create terms for them, even default terms.

But no one is now urging that the law should refuse to enforce contracts lacking an express term for job security. The real question, here and elsewhere, is how to select a default rule in the presence of endowment effects. This remains a largely unexplored question.[62] What I am emphasizing here is that the endowment effect confounds ordinary understandings of the problem, and I do not intend to solve the large question of how to choose a default rule when an endowment effect is inevitable. But the following considerations are relevant to understanding the problem.

- Whether one or another endowment effect is to be preferred cannot easily be decided on standard efficiency grounds. So long as transaction costs are zero, either allocation would produce efficiency. But a less standard analysis, also aimed at efficiency, might point in fruitful directions. It would ask *whose welfare would increase most by virtue of having the initial allocation.* Suppose, for example, that workers, if they were initially allocated for-cause protection, would generally demand a great deal to give it up (say, $1000); suppose too that employers, if they were not initially given at-will protection, would be willing to buy it only for a small price (say, $100). Suppose at the same time that if employers were given the initial right, they would not value it highly (and would sell it for, say, $110), and also that if employees were not given the initial right, they would not value it highly either (and would buy it only for, say, $120). If this is so, we would have reason to believe that efficiency favors a for-cause default rule because welfare would be higher given that rule. One problem with

---

[62] A helpful discussion is Russell Korobkin, Note, Policymaking and the Offer/Asking Price Gap: Toward a Theory of Efficient Entitlement Allocation, 46 Stan. L. Rev. 663 (1994). I explore the issue in more detail in Cass R. Sunstein, Switching the Default Rule (Jan. 9, 2001) (unpublished manuscript, on file with the Virginia Law Review Association).

this analysis is that it must usually be conducted in the absence of data and therefore involves some speculation about what people would do or prefer.

- The easiest cases for choosing one or another default rule involve third-party effects. Indeed, if there are significant third-party effects, a nonwaivable rule would probably be best. With job security, however, no such third-party effects are obvious. Compare this with the question of how to handle rights to parental leave. Suppose that children benefit from parental leave requirements (a proposition that is not obviously true; if such requirements reduce wages and employment, children might be hurt as well). If so, the best approach is probably to create a nonwaivable right to parental leave.

- It is important to ask whether there is a distributional reason to favor one or another rule. If the allocation of the initial entitlement to workers would have good distributional consequences, there is reason to favor that allocation. I will take up this issue in more detail below, but for the moment note that significant distributive effects should not be expected in this context, because the resource gain from the initial allocation is not a large part of workers' wealth. In any case the market is likely to adjust to any switch, by, for example, producing a reduction in workers' salaries, thus negating any distributive change.

- If we know *why* the endowment effect exists, we might be able to make some progress in deciding on the default rule. In asking about whether to use "willingness to pay" instead of "willingness to accept," some progress has been made on this question.[63] If the endowment effect stems from confusion, or from bargaining behavior, it would seem to make little sense to shift the entitlement.[64] Perhaps people, and workers in particular, believe that the initial allocation of the entitlement carries a certain moral weight, or presumptive validity, so much so as to drive a wedge

---

[63] As suggested in Korobkin, supra note 62.

[64] See id. at 689–97. See also Sunstein, supra note 62, for more detailed discussion of this point.

between willingness to pay and willingness to accept. In some circumstances, selling a good might appear to be illegitimate, an insult to dignity. Or perhaps some people simply ignore, much of the time, the existence of opportunity costs. For goods that are not simply money tokens, people appear to think that continued ownership is costless, or that the cost of not selling is far less than it is in actuality. This might well be simple confusion. If that is the source of the endowment effect, we should not use "willingness to accept,"and there is no good reason to switch the default rule.

- A final question is whether, aside from efficiency and distribution, desirable social effects would follow from creating a "sticky" default rule of a certain kind. An endowment effect of one or another sort might be supported if it could be shown to have valuable effects on social attitudes and norms. If, for example, it were thought important to inculcate an attitude, on the part of workers, of support for the right of job security, the case for a waivable workers' right would be strengthened. The point is perhaps easiest to see in the context of sexual harassment. If employers have a right to harass employees sexually, but employees can buy that entitlement through contractual protection, we might think that the situation would have harmful effects on norms and desires—and that a situation in which employees have the right, waivable or not, would be much better. As the example suggests, the line between a very sticky default rule and a nonwaivable right might be one of degree rather than one of kind; I take up this point below.

2. Nonzero Transaction Costs: Paper, Information, Signaling

Thus far we have been exploring the effect of the initial endowment on ultimate outcomes, assuming transaction costs are zero, and hence that workers and employers can costlessly contract around the default rule. Of course, transaction costs are not zero in the context of employment contracts. Some costs are present merely by virtue of the need to generate paper to contract around an undesired background rule. Some costs come from the phenomenon of signaling.[65]

a. Paper and Information

If courts select a rule that most parties dislike, the paper costs, while unlikely to be huge, may not be trivial. It would be necessary to produce formal documents where silence would otherwise be sufficient. Probably more important are information costs. Employers are repeat players, and many of them have sufficient information to know what they are doing when they ask for or sign a waiver. But employees are frequently imperfectly informed.[66] If the legal right is allocated to employers, employees may not ask for job security because they mistakenly believe that they have it, or because they are unable to think properly about the subject. The existence of information costs means that the initial allocation of the legal right might turn out to matter a great deal, both to efficiency and to the ultimate outcome. As stated, this point depends on no controversial claims from behavioral economics; I return to it shortly.

b. Signaling

Signaling creates special problems in the area of job security. An employer who is willing to offer job security might find that it is attracting marginal workers.[67] At the same time, an employee who presses hard for job security might be signaling that he will deserve to be discharged. Even if employers and employees would generally be better off with a system of job security, many individual employers and individual employees will rationally refuse to negotiate for it. Note that these points apply to many other contractual rights for which employees might bargain. An employee might fail to seek a right to parental leave, perhaps in the belief that such a right already exists, or, more likely, because he believes that the

---

[65] For a general discussion, see Eric A. Posner, Law and Social Norms (2000); in the context of employment law, see the discussion of severance pay in Bewley, supra note 3, at 270.

[66] See Kim, Bargaining, supra note 28, at 105–06.

[67] See Issacharoff, supra note 30, at 1794–1800; David I. Levine, Just-Cause Employment Policies in the Presence of Worker Adverse Selection, 9 J. Lab. Econ. 294 (1991).

very request would signal a lack of commitment to work. In these circumstances, a waivable employers' right is likely to stick even if it is undesirable. There is evidence that this happens with respect to severance pay; employees do not seek severance pay because doing so sends a bad signal.[68]

These points do not demonstrate that one waivable rule is better than another. But they are sufficient to show that the choice of the default rule is likely to matter a great deal—both to efficiency and to ultimate outcomes.

C. What Mimics the Market?

Suppose, then, that the legal rule will indeed matter. Under the conventional approach, one with obvious implications for labor-management relations in general, courts should seek the default rule that best "mimics the market," in the sense that it is the rule that employers and employees, armed with adequate information, would generally seek.[69] In the context of labor law, it is not clear that the legal system should choose the approach that would mimic the market, even if it can identify that approach. Perhaps a different approach will redistribute resources in a desired direction,[70] or will have a salutary effect on the formation of preferences. But let us begin by approaching the choice of the waivable term in the conventional terms.

1. The Simple Case for At-Will Employment

Those who argue for a waivable employers' right claim that this is what employees and employers would generally seek, and thus that the existing background rule mimics the market.[71] On this view, employers have a strong reason to resist a for-cause regime, to immunize themselves from illegitimate and even frivolous suits and to ensure against shirking. Certainly employment at will seems to be the general rule.[72] With an at-will rule, employers can prevent

---

[68] See Bewley, supra note 3, at 270.

[69] See, e.g., Epstein, supra note 28.

[70] See Christine Jolls, Accommodation Mandates, 53 Stan. L. Rev. 223 (2001) [hereinafter Jolls, Accommodation Mandates].

[71] This is the basic argument in Epstein, supra note 28.

[72] See J. Hoult Verkerke, An Empirical Perspective on Indefinite Term Employment Contracts, 1995 Wis. L. Rev. 837, 838–39.

2001]   *Human Behavior and the Law of Work*   227

costly litigation whenever someone is discharged. They can also counteract the risk of opportunistic behavior by employees; more particularly, the right to discharge at will operates as an obstacle to employee performance that falls well below what the employee is able to do—a special virtue in light of the fact that shirking is both hard to monitor and hard to prove to third parties.[73] Thus the employer's right to discharge the employee at will might be seen to complement the efficiency wage, with both operating to induce good, rather than adequate, performance. Because operating a for-cause system is likely to be expensive, and because its costs would be ultimately felt by employees as well as employers,[74] most employers, and most employees, are the beneficiaries of the at-will rule.[75]

For those who believe that at-will is the market-mimicking rule, it is also important to emphasize that most employees are generally unlikely to object to this rule. In a market economy, employers are quite unlikely to fire employees for no reason.[76] It is costly to get rid of good workers, and those who fire people for no reason will have some trouble replacing them, partly because arbitrary discharges will have harmful reputational consequences, thus leading prospective employees to seek work elsewhere. A separate point is that many employees develop at least some degree of firm-specific human capital: They are worth more to their own employer than they are worth to other employers, because they have experience with the firm and know something about its operations and expectations. Such firm-specific capital creates a safeguard against arbitrary discharges.[77]

If employers generally would lose a great deal from a for-cause system, and if employees generally would gain little, the at-will rule stands adequately defended as a background rule that replicates the likely result of bargaining. The only people who stand to gain

---

[73] See Schwab, supra note 28, at 21–22.

[74] See Price V. Fishback & Shawn Everett Kantor, A Prelude to the Welfare State 64–69 (2000) (showing wage reductions after enactment of workers' compensation programs).

[75] See James J. Heckman & Carmen Pagés, The Cost of Job Security Regulation: Evidence from Latin American Labor Markets (Nat'l Bureau of Econ. Research, Working Paper No. 7773, 2000).

[76] See Posner, supra note 60, at 358–59.

[77] See Schwab, supra note 28, at 21–25.

from a for-cause system are marginal workers—prominently including those who deserve to be discharged for poor job performance but who would be immunized, in practice though not in law, by an at-will system.

2. Problems

However plausible, this argument is not obviously correct. It depends on a number of contentious empirical assumptions.

Suppose, for example, that a for-cause regime would not much affect employer practices, because in any sensibly-designed system discharge could occur at low cost whenever cause really existed, and employers have little interest in discharging people for a reason other than cause.[78] If for-cause discharge is the ordinary practice and if arbitrary discharges are infrequent, employees should have little to lose from a legal rule that requires cause—unless (and perhaps this is the key point) the cost of administering a for-cause regime turns out to be high. But where cause exists, employees would of course lose their suits in any case, and hence they are unlikely to bring suit in the first place, especially in light of the cost of doing so. A mechanism that pushes contests toward low-cost resolution—such as arbitration—should ensure that employers have little to fear from a for-cause regime. For all these reasons, it is unclear that employers would greatly prefer an at-will system to a sensibly designed for-cause system.

At the same time, many employees might well care a great deal about obtaining for-cause protection, if only to obtain immunity from employer malice or mistake. We have seen that employee concern is likely to be greatest in late career, when opportunistic discharges become more probable; it is here that employers have special incentives to discharge employees in violation of the implicit deal.[79] But even earlier, employees are likely to be willing to pay something for job security, or to require employers to pay something to take it away. On this view, a for-cause regime might be the best market-mimicking approach. The crucial empirical is-

---

[78] This appears to be the aspiration of the Montana system, which encourages arbitration, and hence low-cost litigation. See Mont. Code Ann. § 39-2-901 et. seq. (1999).

[79] See Schwab, supra note 28, at 19.

sues here are, first, the cost of operating a for-cause system and, second, the extent to which employees would actually be at risk in an at-will system.

Because a final answer would depend on resolving those empirical issues, nothing said here demonstrates that a waivable workers' right would be the market-mimicking solution—that such an approach would actually reflect the outcome of informed bargaining by most employers and employees. But enough has been said to show that any judgment on that point depends on empirical questions that cannot be answered a priori.

3. Informational Problems and the Fairness Heuristic

An additional weakness of the argument that an at-will system is market-mimicking has to do with informational problems. The most important point is that employees appear unaware that in the face of contractual silence they are entering into an at-will arrangement. Even if they know the basic fact, they may not understand exactly what it means. Here, then, is a third problem with the conventional wisdom, illuminated by behavioral economics, though the mechanisms that account for employee ignorance remain unclear.

Recent evidence, compiled by Pauline Kim, strongly suggests that workers believe that employment is generally for cause, not at will, and that discharge is therefore unlawful unless there is a job-related reason for it.[80] In Missouri, for example, Kim found that extremely strong majorities of employees—80% or more—believe that the following grounds for discharge, entirely lawful in Missouri, are in fact unlawful: the employer wants to hire someone else to do the same job; the employer mistakenly believes that the employee stole money; and the employer personally dislikes the employee.[81] Similar results were found in California and New York, notwithstanding substantial variations in the law of the three states.[82] Overwhelming majorities falsely believe that discharges

---

[80] See Kim, Bargaining, supra note 28, at 105–06; see also Richard B. Freeman & Joel Rogers, What Workers Want 118–21 (1999) (finding pervasive employee ignorance about legal rights).

[81] See Kim, Bargaining, supra note 28, at 134 tbl.1.

[82] See Kim, Norms, supra note 28, at 451–52.

that fall short of good cause are prohibited by law.[83] Kim also found that worker ignorance cuts across distinctions that might be thought to make a difference—not only geography, but also age, work experience, and union experience. A more general survey found the same results, with worker ignorance and excessive optimism extending well beyond the setting of job security.[84]

Why do workers misstate the law so systematically? It is possible to provide both rational and quasi-rational explanations for worker ignorance. As Kim notes, workers' beliefs to this effect might be based on an understanding of workplace norms, rather than law.[85] Perhaps the informal law of the workplace bars arbitrary discharges, even when state law does not.[86] This is certainly possible, but is it obvious why workers would say that what employers *can* do, as a matter of law, is the same as what they actually do, as a matter of practice? People are usually capable of distinguishing practices from rights. In places where incivility is absent or rare, people know that incivility is absent or rare, but they do not believe that it is against the law. While workers' ignorance probably has something to do with the perceived norms of the workplace, this cannot be the whole explanation.[87]

Behavioral economics and cognitive psychology suggest alternative explanations. People tend to be optimists, and they often engage in wishful thinking;[88] they also like to reduce cognitive dissonance by drawing their beliefs about how things should be into

---

[83] The point casts doubt on Judge Posner's suggestion that in the context of job security, there "are not the sort of information problems that might defeat transactions over workplace safety, for discharges are not such rare events that workers can't be expected to evaluate the risk rationally." Posner, supra note 60, at 359 (citations omitted). If workers believe that the legal rule already protects them, they are unlikely to try to bargain for job security. As discussed below, there are other problems with the suggestion that risks will be evaluated rationally in this context. One of my principal points here is that claims like that of Judge Posner are empirical ones, to be assessed empirically, and cannot be asserted a priori.

[84] See Freeman & Rogers, supra note 80, at 118–21.

[85] Kim, Norms, supra note 28, at 452.

[86] See id. at 499–501.

[87] See Freeman & Rogers, supra note 80, at 118–21 (finding erroneous optimism in many contexts).

[88] See Shelley E. Taylor, Positive Illusions 10–11 (1989); Christine Jolls, Behavioral Economics Analysis of Redistributive Legal Rules, 51 Vand. L. Rev. 1653, 1658–62 (1998) [hereinafter Jolls, Behavioral Economics].

line with their views about how things are.[89] Sometimes people might believe that the law is as they wish it to be. People are also subject to self-serving bias; they care about fairness, but their judgments about what is fair are systematically skewed in their own direction.[90] Perhaps people believe that the law is generally fair, and their judgments about what is fair lead to (mistaken) judgments about what the law is. But I suggest a more particular hypothesis: *People's beliefs about what the law is tend to reflect their beliefs about what the law should be.* In the absence of solid evidence that the law is otherwise, people will say that the law is what they think it ought to be. The hypothesis remains to be tested.

For present purposes, the key point is simple. The fact that workers believe that they have legal protection against arbitrary discharge is devastating to the suggestion that an at-will default rule accurately captures the shared understanding of the parties. In fact the evidence is devastating to the at-will rule as conventionally defended.[91] Traditional understandings of workers' beliefs and motivations cannot easily account for workers' ignorance; behavioral economics provides some clues.

D. The Information-Eliciting Default Rule: A Waivable Workers' Right

If we are uncertain about what rule would mimic the market, we might seek a background rule that operates not to mimic the market but to elicit information—that imposes on one or another of the parties the obligation to provide the crucial information to the other side (and also to courts).[92] On which party should this burden be imposed? It makes obvious sense to say that employers can more cheaply propose a provision that will make matters clear. A simple conclusion follows: If employers really would like a system of at-will employment, then courts should say that the background

---

[89] See Taylor, supra note 88, at 25–28.

[90] Linda Babcock et al., Choosing the Wrong Pond: Social Comparisons in Negotiations That Reflect a Self-Serving Bias, 111 Q.J. Econ. 1, 4 (1996).

[91] This is not to say that the rule cannot be defended in other terms. See, e.g., Heckman & Pagés, supra note 75 (showing the harmful effect of job security requirements).

[92] See Ian Ayres & Robert Gertner, Filling Gaps in Incomplete Contracts: An Economic Theory of Default Rules, 99 Yale L.J. 87, 94 (1989).

rule is for-cause, simply to elicit a clear statement to this effect, so that both parties to the contract know its real content.[93] Here, then, is an effort to build employment law on a conventional efficiency analysis, informed by a better understanding of workers' beliefs and motivations.

In the abstract, this view might be defended simply on the ground that the choice of the market-mimicking rule depends on empirical issues that have not been resolved. Without evidence, and without reason to believe that evidence would strongly support one or another solution, an information-forcing rule seems best. Kim's findings provide further support for this view. They demonstrate that employees do not know that this is the rule and therefore do not enter into contracts with their eyes wide open. They strongly support the suggestion that the appropriate background rule is for-cause, not to mimic the market, but so as to ensure that employers furnish the relevant information to the employee, and obtain a waiver if they can.

The essential argument for a waivable workers' right to job security is now in place. We lack much ground for confidence about the content of a market-mimicking rule. Lacking that confidence, a for-cause regime seems best, as a way of forcing disclosure and overcoming what appears to be a lack of information on the part of workers. If the argument is sound, it applies in many areas of labor and employment law, as we shall shortly see.

E. Doctrinal Support

These suggestions are not entirely without doctrinal support. In the last two decades, courts have moved in the direction of creating an information-forcing default rule for job security. While mere silence does not create a waivable workers' right, ambiguous statements, plausibly interpreted as conferring job security, are often taken to prevent at-will discharge. If employers are to escape that result, they must do so via a disclaimer that is exceedingly clear. Here is another area in which we can find an implicit behavioral rationality in the emerging common law—a system of legal

---

[93] See id. at 95.

rules built on an accurate, rather than fanciful, sense of what work-, ers are likely to know and how they are likely to react.

1. Old Law

For many decades, an apparent but ambiguous promise by an employer would not create a contractual obligation to provide security.[94] Employment manuals, for example, would not count as part of any contractual relationship. In the same vein, a statement by an employer or a personnel manager to the effect that the employee could work "as long as he did a good job," or "permanently," would not provide a for-cause guaranty, at least if it was unaccompanied by a defined term for employment.[95]

These results seem odd. They treat a promise that apparently gives something to an employee as if it had no meaning at all. How might the pattern of decisions be explained? One possibility is that courts, in the relevant cases, are making a claim about the reasonable expectations of most workers who have heard statements of this sort. Perhaps an employee who has been told that he has "permanent" employment does not reasonably understand this as a promise, rather than a hope or expectation.[96] But a more interesting possibility is that courts are creating a kind of information-forcing default rule, to the effect that ambiguous statements will not create a for-cause situation, and employees must obtain greater clarity if this is in fact what they want. This seemingly harsh result prevents both parties and judges from guessing about the meaning of words that cannot really be taken at face value. An oral reference to permanent employment cannot mean that the employee

---

[94] See Clarke v. Atl. Stevedoring Co., 163 F. 423, 425 (C.C.E.D.N.Y. 1908); Comerford v. Int'l Harvester Co., 178 So. 894, 895–96 (Ala. 1938) ; see also Rothstein et al., supra note 34, at 674–88 (discussing the old law and modern changes).

[95] See Rothstein et al., supra note 34, at 674–88.

[96] A more conventional argument would be that employers cannot be bound because no contract exists unless both parties have manifested an intention to be bound. But here, as elsewhere, the argument is a fake. If there is any background rule, someone is going to be bound, whether or not an intention to be bound has been manifested. Under a system of at-will employment, employees are bound, in the sense that they can be fired for any reason, even though they have not manifested any intention to be bound in that way. The idea that people cannot be bound unless they have manifested an intention to be bound—the consent theory of contract—cannot be made intelligible without a background theory of "natural" entitlements, which in this context, is hard to generate.

will be allowed to work there forever; the statement must be qualified in various ways, and perhaps the court does not want to do the qualifying on its own. Treating the statement as a kind of goal, rather than a promise, prevents judicial guessing-games.

2. New Law

But the law has changed a great deal in the last two decades. Courts have read employment manuals to create enforceable obligations, even when the relevant terms have ambiguity, as in a statement that it is "the policy" of the company to fire people for cause. In *Toussaint v. Blue Cross & Blue Shield*,[97] for example, the personnel manual said in general terms that it "is the policy of the company to treat employees . . . in a fair and consistent manner and to release employees for just cause only."[98] It was clear that under long-standing law, this statement would not be sufficient to overcome the at-will presumption, in part because no term of years was identified. Nonetheless, the Michigan Supreme Court held that this was sufficient to create an obligation of continued employment, even without a specified term of years.[99] Other cases speak in similar terms,[100] and it is now clear that employment manuals can create obligations.[101]

Indeed, some cases have gone so far as to entrench the relevant provisions, in the sense that once something like a promise has been made, a disclaimer is unlikely to be effective unless it is exceptionally clear. Thus, for example, the Wyoming Supreme Court was confronted with an employee handbook containing the following language: "READ CAREFULLY BEFORE SIGNING. I agree that any offer of employment, and acceptance thereof, does not constitute a binding contract of any length, and that such employment is terminable at the will of either party, subject to appropriate state and/or federal laws."[102] The court held that the disclaimer was ineffective notwithstanding this express statement,

---

[97] 292 N.W.2d 880 (Mich. 1980).

[98] Id. at 903 (quotation marks and emphasis omitted).

[99] See id. at 885.

[100] See Kinoshita v. Canadian Pac. Airlines, 724 P.2d 110, 117 (Haw. 1986); Duldulao v. Saint Mary of Nazareth Hosp. Ctr., 505 N.E.2d 314, 318 (Ill. 1987).

[101] See Rothstein et al., supra note 34, at 674–84.

[102] McDonald v. Mobil Coal Producing, 820 P.2d 986, 988 (Wyo. 1991).

for it "was not set off by a border or larger print, was not capital-
ized, and was contained in a general welcoming section of the
handbook."[103] The court's decision is hardly unique. In a number of
cases, courts have said that disclaimers must be extremely clear.[104]

In addition, oral promises are frequently taken as binding, even
if they have a degree of ambiguity. Thus, for example, in *Toussaint*,[105] the court was confronted not only with personnel manuals
but also with allegations from the plaintiffs that they had been told
that they would be able to continue to work "as long as I did my
job," or "[I was] doing the job."[106] In an alternative holding, the
court held that these statements were sufficient to justify an action
for wrongful discharge, even if a specific term of years was not
identified.[107] Some cases find oral statements of this kind sufficient
to create a right not to be discharged without cause.[108]

These cases might reflect a new understanding of the reasonable
expectations of employees when presented with statements of this
kind. Perhaps the modern cases reflect a belief that reasonable
employees think that such statements give them job security. But
the decisions might also be understood as a modest step in the direction suggested here: toward a waivable workers' right to job
security, on information-forcing grounds and based on a realistic
sense of what workers are likely to think when presented with
statements containing apparent promises. The employer is in the
best position to control the statements made to employees, and if
ambiguous statements are made, the employer ought to correct the
ambiguity so as to negate any employee belief that a for-cause arrangement has been created. The disclaimer cases fit this rationale
particularly well. They create a kind of consumer protection meas-

---

[103] Id. at 989.

[104] See, e.g., Jimenez v. Colorado Interstate Gas Co., 690 F. Supp. 977, 980 (D. Wyo.
1988); Jones v. Cent. Peninsula Gen. Hosp., 779 P.2d 783, 788 (Alaska 1989); Brown
v. United Methodist Homes for the Aged, 815 P.2d 72, 84 (Kan. 1991). To be sure, the
law is quite unruly here. See Bouwens v. Centrilift, 974 P.2d 941, 947 (Wyo. 1999)
(finding a disclaimer effective).

[105] *Toussaint*, 292 N.W.2d at 890. *Toussaint* is read narrowly in Rowe v. Montgomery
Ward & Co., 473 N.W.2d 268 (Mich. 1991).

[106] *Toussaint*, 292 N.W.2d at 890.

[107] See id.

[108] See Rothstein et al., supra note 34, at 684–86. Generally, however, separate
consideration is required to make an oral statement binding.

ure, saying that if there is any chance that the employee will misunderstand what he has been promised, it is the employer's job to
make an unambiguous correction. If a for-cause agreement is not
in the parties' interest, the employer can be expected to make cor-
rections by notifying the employee of the situation in the clearest
possible terms.

It would not be a giant step from these cases to a waivable employees' right to job security. As we have seen, the evidence
suggests that ordinary employees, not told anything at all, are in
the same position as employees told that their employers' "policy"
is to retain them unless their performance is unsatisfactory.[109] Employees typically believe that this is both policy and law. And if this
is the understanding of most employees, employers should be required to make a correction.[110]

II. COUNTERARGUMENTS AND ANTI-WAIVER

Thus far I have suggested that in the context of job security, a
waivable employers' right might be preferred over a waivable
workers' right, on the ground that the former may be the market-
mimicking rule, but that without good evidence on that question, a
waivable workers' right seems better, because it is an information-
forcing rule, defensible in light of what we know about what workers think. I have also suggested that the default rule will indeed
matter. But I have not discussed whether a nonwaivable workers'
right would be best of all. It is now time to explore that possibility.

A. Unequal Bargaining Power and Redistribution

Many of those who challenge the at-will system stress the possible inequality of bargaining power between employers and (many)
employees. They suggest that a shift to a for-cause system would
produce a desirable form of redistribution to employees, particularly to the most vulnerable workers.[111] The reference to inequality
of bargaining power must mean that many of the deals between

---

[109] See Kim, Bargaining, supra note 28, at 110–11.

[110] See Issacharoff, supra note 30, at 1791–97; Peter Stone Partee, Note, Reversing
the Presumption of Employment At Will, 44 Vand. L. Rev. 689, 710 (1991).

[111] See Blades, supra note 21; Clyde W. Summers, Individual Protection Against
Unjust Dismissal: Time for a Statute, 62 Va. L. Rev. 481, 518–32 (1976).

Human Behavior and the Law of Work

employers and employees are harsh from the standpoint of the latter, and that the law should attempt to ensure a fairer arrangement. We should certainly accept the claim of harshness, at least with respect to many of the relevant deals. Some employees have few good options, and in these circumstances the best arrangement that they can get is often quite harsh, even unfair, in the sense that they are working very hard and receiving little in return. There is no reason whatsoever to think that the market wage has any special moral status.[112] It is important to find good ways to supplement employment packages that turn out to be harsh or disadvantageous.

But the redistributive argument nonetheless stands on fragile ground—not because the existing distribution of entitlements and resources is good, but because blocking the exchange, through a nonwaivable right to job security, is not the best way to produce the desired redistribution.[113] In fact, such a nonwaivable right might not produce the desired redistribution at all. A nonwaivable workers' right to job security—and here is a general lesson for employment law—is an unreliable method of redistributing resources to workers.[114] A for-cause provision does not directly redistribute resources from employers to employees; instead it creates restructured deals, which may or may not benefit employees as a class.

When mandatory for-cause provisions are imposed, someone must pay for them. The burden may well fall on consumers, or even workers themselves, in the form of lower wages, smaller retirement benefits, or lower employment on balance (through, for example, more extended screening of job candidates, or refusals to

---

[112] To some this will be a controversial claim. I will not defend it here.

[113] For an overview of the theoretical considerations, see Lawrence H. Summers, Some Simple Economics of Mandated Benefits, 79 Am. Econ. Rev. (Papers & Proceedings) 177 (1989). For a recent discussion with special reference to benefits limited to subgroups of workers, see Jolls, Accommodation Mandates, supra note 70. The Earned Income Tax Credit is a far more direct way of redistributing resources to poor workers. See, e.g., Anne L. Alstott, Work v. Freedom: A Liberal Challenge to Employment Subsidies, 108 Yale L.J. 967, 1048–56 (1999).

[114] In the context of accommodation mandates, this proposition is severely qualified, for as Jolls shows, there are conditions in which desired redistribution might well occur. See Jolls, Accommodation Mandates, supra note 70, at 30–33.

238   *Virginia Law Review*   [Vol. 87:205

take risks by employing people in the first instance).[115] There can be no assurance that any redistribution will make workers better off as a class.[116] Workers might lose in salary or other benefits most of, or as much as, they gain via the nonwaivable term[117] (with the qualification that unionized workers appear to suffer from lower, or no, wage offsets).[118]

The redistributive argument for nonwaivable terms might be fortified with the suggestion that in individual bargaining, workers face a collective-action problem that is best solved via law. John Stuart Mill outlined the argument long ago, suggesting that with respect to a reduction in hours worked, the limitation

> will not be adopted unless the body of operatives bind themselves to one another to abide by it . . . . For however beneficial the observance of the regulation might be to the class collectively, the immediate interest of every individual would lie in violating it: and the more numerous those were who adhered to the rule, the more would individuals gain by departing from it . . . . Assuming then that it really would be the interest of each to work only nine hours if he could be assured that all others would do the same, there might be no means of their attaining this object but by converting their supposed mutual agreement

---

[115] A good overview is Summers, supra note 113.

[116] See id.; Fishback & Kantor, supra note 74, at 64–69 (showing wage cuts after enactment of workers' compensation programs). Note the possibility that workers care not about absolute economic position but mostly or partly about relative economic position; if this is true, nonwaivable workers' rights might be justified on the ground that they provide a benefit, in the form of increased job security, while also keeping relative economic position constant. See Robert H. Frank, Choosing the Right Pond (1985); see also infra Part VI.

[117] For analyses finding substantial wage offsets, see Price V. Fishback & Shawn Everett Kantor, Did Workers Pay for the Passage of Workers' Compensation Laws, 110 Q.J. Econ. 713, 736 (1995) ("Analysis of the effect of the introduction of workers' compensation on wages shows that in the coal and lumber industries, workers experienced substantial wage offsets. In the coal industry the offsets were large enough to cover not only the expected monetary value of the benefits, but also the employers' costs of purchasing the insurance to provide those benefits."); Jonathan Gruber, The Incidence of Mandated Maternity Benefits, 84 Am. Econ. Rev. 622 (1994).

[118] See Fishback & Kantor, supra note 74, at 68–69 (showing no offsets in the unionized sector).

into an engagement under penalty, by consenting to have it en-forced by law.[119]

Mill's suggestion is sufficient to show that, with respect to any particular contract term, workers who are currently employed at a firm might do better with a nonwaivable legal constraint than without one. But it does not show that with respect to contracts as a whole, the nonwaivable right helps workers as a class. As an argument that nonwaivable terms promote redistribution, Mill's argument faces two problems. First, and as noted, the compensation package might be adjusted to the detriment of workers; it is even possible that workers will lose in wages what they gain in reduced hours and that the resulting package might be worse from their point of view.[120] Second, the result of the nonwaivable term might well be to decrease employment, even if—indeed precisely because—current workers are made better off.[121] The decrease in employment is a serious problem from the distributive point of view, especially because the people who are thrown into joblessness are likely to be among the least advantaged members of society.

These points do not demonstrate that nonwaivable terms are indefensible as a means of producing desirable redistribution.[122] Perhaps the wage offset will be less than 100%; in the building trades sector, for example, there appears to have been no wage offset as a result of workers' compensation legislation.[123] Perhaps the adverse effect on unemployment will be low and justified in light of the benefits of the nonwaivable term for larger classes of people; perhaps the problem of increased unemployment can be taken care of through other means. My conclusion is not that nonwaivable

---

[119] Mill, supra note 17, at 350–51.

[120] See the evidence of substantial wage offsets for workers' compensation and parental leave, sources cited supra note 117. But see the relative position problem, taken up infra Part VI.

[121] See Heckman & Pagés, supra note 75. On the ambiguous evidence that labor unions increase compensation packages while also decreasing employment, see Freeman & Medoff, supra note 15, at 21, 43–60.

[122] See Jolls, Accommodation Mandates, supra note 70, at 257 (discussing the circumstances in which desirable redistribution will occur from accommodation mandates).

[123] See Fishback & Kantor, supra note 117, at 734.

terms are always indefensible on redistributive grounds.[124] It is that the case for such terms, on those grounds, is fragile and depends on highly uncertain empirical issues.

B. The Problem of Information, With Notes from Behavioral Economics

One possible reason to create nonwaivable workers' rights is to respond to inadequate information on the part of workers—inadequate information that cannot, realistically speaking, be corrected with information alone. We have seen that shifting the entitlement to the worker, while maintaining freedom of contract, is a way of counteracting worker ignorance.[125] But this may not be sufficient. If workers are allocated the right, but asked to waive it, will they know what they are doing? This is an empirical question, and it lacks an obvious answer.

1. Intransigent Ignorance

With respect to job security, there is evidence that workers will not believe that a waiver is effective even if they are asked to sign it. The most striking evidence here comes from Kim's study.[126] Kim asked employees to evaluate the effects of a personnel manual providing that the employer "reserves the right to discharge employees at any time, for any reason, with or without cause." [127] In New York, California, and Missouri, this kind of provision eliminates any employer obligation. Nonetheless, in all three states

---

[124] It is generally agreed that regulation via a nonwaivable term is inferior to regulation via a redistributive income tax. See, e.g., A. Mitchell Polisnky, An Introduction to Law and Economics 105–13 (1983); Louis Kaplow & Steven Shavell, Why the Legal System Is Less Efficient than the Income Tax in Redistributing Income, 23 J. Legal Stud. 667 (1994). It is possible, though, that the choice is not between these two options, but between no redistribution at all and regulation via a nonwaivable term.

[125] It is also possible to think that job security, like safety, is a public good, in the sense that it cannot be provided to one employee without simultaneously being provided to many; job security requires procedures to test the legitimacy of termination, and these procedures are a public good. See Weiler, supra note 7, at 75. To keep the discussion from becoming unwieldy, I defer it until a treatment of the issue of safety.

[126] See supra notes 80–82 and accompanying text.

[127] Kim, Norms, supra note 28, at 465 (quotation marks omitted).

2001]   *Human Behavior and the Law of Work*   241

about three-quarters of respondents believed that a pure cost-saving discharge would be unlawful notwithstanding the disclaimer.[128]

It would be possible to respond to such evidence by endorsing a mandatory for-cause regime. Perhaps employees simply cannot be adequately informed of an employer's decision to purchase the relevant entitlement. The point may be right. But if the costs of a mandatory regime are very high for employers and workers alike, we have not defended it even if workers' ignorance is intractable. If the costs are high, and workers and employers will both lose, the at-will rule is likely to be best in any event. The best strategy might be to require extremely clear language so as to ensure that waivers are voluntary and knowing, as, for example, through strong verbs and specific language.[129] This approach would not ensure full information, but it would move things in the right direction, and do so without introducing the possibly substantial costs of a mandatory for-cause regime.

2. Excessive Optimism

I have noted that people tend to be risk optimists;[130] they believe that they are peculiarly immune from probabilistic harms faced by others. For example, 90% of drivers believe that they are safer than the average driver and less likely to be involved in a serious accident.[131] Perhaps workers who waive their rights will believe, wrongly, that they are peculiarly immune from the risk to which they are subjecting themselves. If so, waivers will be inadequately informed. But it is not clear how to respond to this possibility. Probably the best remedy is not to ban waiver, but to inform employees in the clearest possible terms, so as to ensure that they are made aware that the risks are ones that they themselves will face.

---

[128] Id.

[129] See id. at 465 n.63 (citing Deborah A. Schmedemann & Judi McLean Parks, Contract Formation and Employee Handbooks: Legal, Psychological, and Empirical Analyses, 29 Wake Forest L. Rev. 647, 674–77 (1994)).

[130] See Taylor, supra note 88, at 32–33; Jolls, Behavioral Economics, supra note 88, at 1659–63.

[131] See Taylor, supra note 88, at 10–11.

3. Inadequate Foresight

Signing contracts before the fact, workers may not have a good sense of what is in their long-term interest.[132] They might be myopic or short-sighted. Recent evidence so suggests.[133] This is another kind of information failure, one that might also argue against allowing waiver.

Consider an example. We have seen that the endowment effect means that those who have a benefit are likely to value it more than those who do not. Oddly, however, it appears that people do not anticipate the endowment effect. In simple studies, people did not see that they would value mundane goods, such as coffee mugs, far more if those goods were initially allocated to them.[134] Apparently people do not quite anticipate how bad it will be to lose something they once had. As Samuel Issacharoff has suggested, a possible conclusion is that workers will be in a poor position to decide whether or not to waive their rights, because they will not know, before the fact, how bad it would be to lose their jobs.[135] If this is so, waiver might be banned in workers' own interests.

This problem might be reduced within a system of waivable workers' rights. In such a system, the presumptive right is with employees, not employers, and hence the endowment effect need not be imagined. On the other hand, it may be quite hard for employees, at the time of signing the agreement, to have a full appreciation of what it is that they may be losing.[136] Workers may not sufficiently bargain to retain a legal right of some sort, simply

---

[132] Thus John Stuart Mill, no friend of government interference with freedom of contract, went so far as to suggest that an

> exception to the doctrine that individuals are the best judges of their own interest, is when an individual attempts to decide irrevocably now, what will be best for his interest at some future and distant time. The presumption in favour of individual judgment is only legitimate, where the judgment is grounded on actual, and especially on present, personal experience; not where it is formed antecedently to experience, and not suffered to be reversed even after experience has condemned it.

Mill, supra note 17, at 345.

[133] See Bewley, supra note 3, at 268–70 (discussing worker myopia).

[134] See id.; George Loewenstein & Daniel Adler, A Bias in the Prediction of Tastes, 105 Econ. J. 929, 934–36 (1995).

[135] See Issacharoff, supra note 30, at 1801.

[136] See id.

because they may not know how important, for example, continuation in a particular job will be to them.

4. *"Editing Out"*

People sometimes "edit out" events that have very low probability, even if the ultimate impact of the event is quite large, partly because of simplified "decisional paths" used for choices having multiple attributes.[137] The terms of employment contracts are numerous, and it is unlikely that most employees will be able to focus on more than a few of them. In fact protection against arbitrary discharge seems to be a low priority item for most employees, notwithstanding its potential importance.[138] There may be an analogy here with disaster insurance; people tend not to purchase disaster insurance (for floods and tornados, for example) even when the benefits of doing so clearly seem to exceed the costs.[139]

These various points hardly create a devastating argument on behalf of a system of nonwaivable employees' rights. They raise, first, a number of empirical questions about what is likely to produce waivers and, second, a number of normative questions about how to handle employee mistakes. Any judgment about whether to allow waivers will depend largely on comparing the likely costs of a nonwaivable rule against the likely costs of employee ignorance and mistake. If it is possible to design a nonwaivable rule with low costs of administration—as perhaps Montana has done[140]— speculations about employee ignorance may well be sufficient to carry the day. If, on the other hand, a nonwaivable rule will create serious problems, the speculations should require stronger empirical support before they can be made decisive.

C. Between Waivable and Nonwaivable: Constrained Waivers

Even if the various objections to waiver are taken to have substantial force, it does not follow that waiver should be banned. A more flexible approach would allow waiver, but only under certain

---

[137] Id.
[138] See id.
[139] See Howard Kunreuther, Disaster Insurance Protection: Public Policy Lessons 102–03 (1978).
[140] See supra note 78 and accompanying text.

constraints, perhaps in the form of floors on what employees may be allowed to trade in return for waiving their rights. On this approach, the relevant right would be "commodified" in the sense that it could be traded on the market, but to protect employees against an absence of information waivers, would be constrained. It is easy to imagine intermediate solutions.

1. Procedural Constraints

At one extreme, the law could provide that a waiver is acceptable, but not simply when an employee has signed an agreement to waive. The waiver must be shown to be fully informed, perhaps limited to instances where it is accompanied by clear language and a cooling-off period in which the employee is permitted to reconsider and, if he so desires, to consult a lawyer. Consider this a *procedural* constraint on waivers. A legal constraint of this kind could be designed to furnish information, directly and indirectly, by imposing requirements intended to signal the magnitude of the discussion. A procedural constraint on waiver could be minimal or much more than that.

The general idea has clear antecedents in current law. Under the common law as now understood, employer disclaimers must be extremely clear and conspicuous; explicit language is not enough. Under the ADEA, a similar approach is taken to waivers of anti-discrimination rights. For rights and claims arising before execution of the waiver, the statute permits waiver so long as it is "knowing and voluntary."[141] If it is, the waiver is an affirmative defense. To count as knowing and voluntary, the waiver must specifically refer "to rights or claims arising under" the ADEA;[142] the employee must be advised in writing to consult with an attorney before executing the agreement;[143] the employee must be given "at least 21 days within which to consider the agreement";[144] and the agreement must provide for a minimum of a seven day post-execution revocation period.[145] Most of these provisions also apply to waivers in

---

[141] 29 U.S.C. § 626(f)(1) (1994).
[142] Id. §626(f)(1)(B).
[143] Id. §626(f)(1)(E).
[144] Id. §626(f)(1)(F)(ii).
[145] Id. § 626(f)(1)(G).

settlement of charges filed with the EEOC.[146] These provisions of the ADEA are models of a procedurally constrained waiver.[147]

2. Substantive Constraints

At another extreme, waiver might be deemed acceptable, but only at a price determined by government, not at a price determined by the market. Here, there is a *substantive* constraint on waivers. Substantive constraints, like procedural ones, might be minimal or much more.

This approach also has a place in contemporary employment law. An example is the Fair Labor Standards Act, which allows employees to waive their right not to work more than forty hours a week, but only at a governmentally determined premium (time and a half),[148] Or consider the Model Employment Termination Act, which allows employers and employees to waive the right to for-cause discharge, but only on the basis of an agreement by the employer to provide a severance payment in the event of a discharge not based on poor job performance.[149] This severance payment consists of one month's salary for every year of employment and, interestingly, is therefore targeted to longevity of service in a way that maps onto the employees' likely growing stake in their jobs.

For those who are skeptical of both simple market waivers and government mandates, these various approaches supply a model in the form of a system of substantive constraints, designed to ensure that the employee is given something of definite value in return for waiver.

D. How To Handle Job Security

I have been attempting to work through issues of job security from a perspective informed by behavioral economics. The most important goal is to increase understanding of the underlying issues, not to recommend any particular reform. Nothing I have said suggests that courts should declare that contracts are presumed to

---

[146] Id. § 626(f)(2).

[147] Waivers may not apply to rights or claims that arise after the date the waiver is executed; here, waiver is entirely blocked. Id. § 626(f)(1)(C).

[148] See 29 U.S.C. § 207(f) (1994).

[149] See Model Employment Termination Act, supra note 54, § 4(c).

contain an implied term for job security. An obvious reason is that judicial activity of this kind would disrupt long-standing understandings on which many people have relied. To be sure, job security is an issue that has been resolved to a large degree by the common law. But when people have organized their relationships on the basis of one understanding, the presumption should be in favor of maintaining the status quo. Another problem is that courts cannot alone devise an important part of a sensible for-cause system: a simple, low-cost mechanism for resolving disputes about whether cause exists. By encouraging arbitration, as Montana has done,[150] a legislature can ensure that the consequence of any for-cause rule is not disastrous for either employers or employees. Even a waivable workers' right could produce serious problems if unaccompanied by a system that ensures that disputes are handled inexpensively. Because a shift in the default rule would have a disruptive effect on worker-employer relations, it probably should not be imposed by the judiciary alone.

There are substantive concerns as well. A waivable right of this kind would impose nontrivial transaction costs for those who seek waiver, and these costs will have to be borne by someone, perhaps consumers and workers themselves. If workers would generally waive, what is the point? The best answer is that we do not know if workers *would* generally waive, and without knowing whether they would, the point is to test the market by ensuring that waivers are informed. But under certain assumptions, it would make sense to favor an at-will background rule simply because of distrust of workers' refusal to waive, which might itself be inadequately informed—a product of some combination of confusion and alarmism. Perhaps workers would be unwilling to sell their right to job security, even at a fully reasonable price, and that unwillingness might not be in their best interests. On this view, the endowment effect, combined with employee ignorance, would lead employees to demand an exceedingly high premium for waiver, and the consequence would be adverse effects on workers themselves.[151] If

---

[150] See supra note 78.

[151] Compare the controversy over genetic engineering of food. Should genetically-engineered food be labeled as such? At first glance, the answer is yes; consumers should be informed of what they are eating. But what if genetically-engineered food is harmless, and consumers believe that it is dangerous? In these circumstances, labeling

workers would systematically overvalue job security, the at-will rule finds support—rather than a challenge—from an understanding of human cognition. This is a plausible speculation but no more than that; it too requires empirical testing.

I conclude with two proposals. First, courts should build on existing law so as to take ambiguous terms as an occasion to require employers to negate any possible worker inference of job security. Second, some state legislatures should experiment with a waivable workers' right. An approach of this sort would be more cautious and modest than the Montana solution, which appears not to have created serious problems.[152]

III. WORKERS' ENTITLEMENTS AND THE PROBLEM OF WAIVER

The analysis thus far might be applied to many areas of employment and labor law. I offer a large number of examples here, not to resolve any of them authoritatively, but to show the generality of the foregoing analysis of entitlements in employment, and also to explore the attractiveness of waivable workers' rights in various settings.

There are, however, potential differences between the contract at will situation and other contexts in which the legal system might choose among waivable employers' rights, waivable workers' rights, nonwaivable workers' rights, and constrained waivers. These include the existence of third-party effects as a result of some waivers; the possibility that the reform in question is attempting to change norms and preferences, rather than to take them as given; and the fact that some workplace benefits require employers to produce local public goods, for which individual bargaining is unreliable.

A. Occupational Safety and Health

Under federal law, workers are given certain safeguards against hazardous and unsafe conditions in the workplace.[153] But the rele-

---

could actually impair people's welfare, possibly even their health; in fact, accurate labels could even make people, in a sense, less informed.

[152] See Bruce Ellis Fein, Employment Effects of Montana's For-Cause Discharge Law (May 1999) (unpublished manuscript, on file with the Virginia Law Review Association).

[153] 29 U.S.C. § 651 (1994).

vant rights are not waivable. Should workers be allowed to make trades with their employers? Suppose that employees would willingly trade a certain level of safety in return for other benefits, such as cash, health care, or leisure time. Ought the law to authorize the trade? Recall that the redistributive objection to waiver rests on fragile grounds, because it is far from clear that if adequately informed workers are willing to waive their rights, workers as a whole would be better off if they were banned from doing so.

In an essay in very much the same spirit as this one, Susan Rose-Ackerman has suggested a mixed answer to this question, involving a two-tiered approach to protection of workers.[154] She proposes that the federal government should issue rules governing legal minima that would not be waivable, because they would reflect levels of safety that reasonable workers would not wish to relinquish.[155] At the same time, Rose-Ackerman suggests that OSHA should issue "benchmark standards," more protective than the legal minima, that workers could waive for compensation.[156] The waivers might be agreed upon individually or collectively, via unions or other representative structures.

The proposal has many virtues. By calling for certain nonwaivable minima for truly dangerous conditions, it responds to potential problems with inadequately informed waivers. At the same time, the proposal grants workers a presumptive right to extra protection; the endowment effect should ensure that workers do not relinquish that right for little or nothing. To those who fear that workers will waive their right to safety for too little, it might be responded that safety cannot be assessed through some "off-on" switch. The question is the appropriate degree of safety; informed people can sensibly resolve that question in different ways, trading degrees of safety in return for other goods. Moreover, expensive safety regulation can be harmful to both workers' incomes and to their health.[157] To the extent that such regulation decreases wages, increases unemployment, or otherwise reduces wealth, it can pro-

---

[154] See Rose-Ackerman, supra note 8, at 358–60.

[155] See id. at 359.

[156] Id.

[157] See Robert H. Hahn et al., Do Federal Regulations Reduce Mortality? 7–9, 15–22 (2000); Cass R. Sunstein, Free Markets and Social Justice 298–317 (1997); Symposium, Risk-Risk Analysis, 8 J. Risk & Uncertainty 5 (1994).

duce mortality and morbidity increases as well.[158] The central question is whether cognitive and motivational problems will lead workers to waive their rights for too little. If the set of nonwaivable minima is adequate, and if the initial grant of the right goes to workers, there is good reason to experiment with a two-tiered approach of this kind.

B. Age Discrimination

The ADEA forbids employers from discriminating against anyone who is over forty years of age; it also bans mandatory retirement practices.[159] Through these provisions, it creates an obvious incentive for employers to devise a retirement package by which older workers might be encouraged to leave the workforce. Although such packages might be deemed a form of age discrimination, it is easy to imagine circumstances in which such a package is in the mutual interest of employer and employee.

Suppose, for example, that the employee is generally interested in retiring but would not do so without some kind of financial cushion. Suppose too that the employer wants to replace the older worker with a younger one, believing that the younger worker will produce substantial productivity gains, at least in the long term. Incentives for early retirement seem a natural and mutually beneficial solution and were a widespread response to the ADEA.[160] To make the deal worthwhile, employers seek both retirement and a promise not to sue for violations of the ADEA. Congress eventually enacted the Older Workers Benefit Protection Act[161] ("OWBPA"), which authorizes knowing and voluntary waivers. Because OWBPA does not permit employees to waive rights that postdate the execution of the waiver, it does not amount to the kind of waivable workers' right that I have been discussing here. Instead it permits something like a settlement of a preexisting claim; the settlement operates as a waiver. The question therefore becomes why employers are not permitted to ask for waivers be-

---

[158] See Sunstein, supra note 157, at 302–05.

[159] 29 U.S.C. §§ 623–631(1994).

[160] See Linda Carleton Messinger, Voluntary Acceptance of Early Retirement Offers: Golden Handshake or Gilded Shove?, 20 Ariz. St. L.J. 797, 803–09 (1988).

[161] 29 U.S.C. § 626(f) (1994).

fore the unlawful activity occurs. Why shouldn't employers be allowed to obtain a waiver of a right to bring suit for alleged age discrimination, if employees are willing to agree?

Christine Jolls has suggested that prospective waivers should indeed be allowed.[162] On her view, the ADEA has, as one of its central purposes, the prevention of opportunistic discharges, which occur when employers discharge employees in late-career, in violation of an implicit promise to provide continued benefits. The statute therefore has a hands-tying rationale that ensures enforcement of these contracts in spite of employers' incentives to act opportunistically. This is an efficiency argument for the ADEA, but there is a parallel efficiency case for allowing the workers' right to be waivable. On Jolls' view,

> the basic efficiency argument in favor of prospective waivers is that they allow parties for whom age-based wages are not desirable—or at least not sufficiently desirable to warrant the costs of imposing legal liability for cost-based decisions about older workers—to avoid unnecessary and costly regulation of their private affairs.[163]

There is, however, a potential problem here: myopic behavior by workers. As Jolls acknowledges, young workers are in a poor position to assess the harms possibly to be incurred by their future selves several decades hence.[164] The possibility of myopia may be a sufficient ground to bar waiver. In principle, it does seem unlikely that waivers of the right to be free from age discrimination would be adequately informed. If waivers are nonetheless to be permitted—as I think they should be—it is because freedom from age discrimination is unlikely greatly to benefit workers, and hence the resulting deals are unlikely to hurt workers on balance.[165]

C. Vacation, Leave Time, and Health Care

A great deal of attention has recently been given to various proposals to improve workers' lives through longer vacations, extended leave time, and better health care benefits. The obvious

---

[162] See Jolls, Hands-Tying, supra note 44, at 1845.
[163] Id.
[164] See id.
[165] See Richard A. Posner, Aging and Old Age 319–63 (1995).

objection is that statutory mandates would impose a kind of rigid, one-size-fits-all approach on diverse workplaces, and that the best approach is to allow people to bargain. A system of mandatory health insurance, for example, might lead to reductions in wages and other benefits. It should now be clear that this criticism is quite reasonable.[166] If employees would like to sacrifice vacation and leave time, or health care benefits, in return for other elements of a compensation package, is it so clear that they should not be permitted to do so? Note here that good wages are both good for workers' health, and that good wages can be used to purchase education and health care for children. Does the analysis of job security strengthen or weaken the case for a waivable workers' right, or even a nonwaivable workers' right, for interests of this sort?

The contract at will situation has a special feature not present here: empirical evidence that workers believe that they already have the right in question. We lack evidence showing that workers believe that employers are obliged to provide them with vacation, or leave time, or health care. Perhaps they do; this is a worthy area for empirical study. But even if they do not, there are good reasons to ensure that if workers are not going to have these rights, they are made expressly aware of that fact. The natural proposal is that workers have waivable rights to a certain level of vacation and leave time and health care protection—and that employers are able to purchase these rights for a fee.

It is possible that workers will relinquish these rights too cheaply or that collective action problems will induce workers to act against their best interests. For reasons discussed above, this argument cannot be said to be wrong, but it rests on fragile grounds. It is possible that workers lack the information to give fully knowing waivers; it is also possible that a form of myopia will produce impulsive action. But these too are speculations. As in the context of occupational safety and health, the best response would be to produce nonwaivable minima along with procedural or substantive constraints on the waiver of rights that exceed those minima. What

---

[166] See sources cited supra note 117. In their book, however, Fishback & Kantor find that the workers' compensation program responded well to problems in the private insurance market, and benefits workers. See Fishback & Kantor, supra note 117, at 70–74.

I am generally envisioning, in short, is a two-tiered system in which workers are provided with a floor below which no workplace may go, together with a set of waivable rights that respond to the legitimate claim that one size does not fit all. Of course it would be necessary to say a great deal more in order to grapple with the details.

D. Parental Leave

In 1991 the United States adopted, for the first time, a statute requiring employers to provide parental leave.[167] The Family and Medical Leave Act ("FMLA") requires employers to allow employees up to twelve total weeks of leave during any twelve-month period, if the reason for the leave is to care for a newborn child, to care for a spouse, son, daughter, or parent with a serious health problem, or because of a serious health problem of the employee's own.[168] Employers are not required to allow employees to continue to work at a reduced rate, nor are they required to pay employees during the time off. The basic idea is that an employee will not lose her job if she takes leave for one of the stated reasons.

The most notable feature of this legislation is that in one bold stroke, it transforms a waivable employers' right into a nonwaivable workers' right. Is the legislation desirable? It is tempting to think that it is, because it gives employees an important right that they would otherwise be denied in many cases. Undoubtedly numerous employees are now spending time with their families under circumstances in which this would have been difficult or impossible prior to FMLA—a large gain. But—our now-familiar theme—this is no simple transfer of resources from employers to employees, and an obvious question is who really bears the costs of parental leave legislation. There is some evidence that those who bear the costs are likely to be the same as those who receive the benefits— that parental leave legislation results in a proportional wage reduction for its beneficiaries, mostly women.[169] If this is the case, is the statute undesirable for that reason? On one view, it certainly is. The government has simply forced workers to receive in leave time

---

[167] 29 U.S.C. § 2601 (1994).
[168] See id. § 2612.
[169] See Gruber, supra note 117, at 124–28.

what they would otherwise have received in income. Having been given the opportunity to contract for this right, workers chose not to do so, receiving higher salary and other benefits instead. If workers' choices reflect their best interests, the restructured deal, with parental leave but probably with a lower salary, is not going to benefit workers.

But by now it should be clear that this argument is not decisive.[170] Workers may be myopic in failing to seek parental leave protections, especially in light of the fact that before having a child, it is hard to have a full and vivid sense of the demands that arise once the child is born. For many workers, there may be no self-conscious thought about parental leave at all; this may be edited out at the time that employment is sought. As in the context of the contract at will, both employers and employees may face a signaling problem. Employers who offer parental leave may find themselves attracting a disproportionate number of workers who want to take such leave; employees who ask about leave policies in advance may be signaling that they are not entirely committed to the workforce. Indeed, workers may face a widespread norm against asking for or taking parental leave, and they may not even know that this norm is something that it is possible to challenge. In any case, parental leave policies can be defended, not principally as protecting workers, but as protecting children and others for whom workers would like to care. If there are third-party effects, the case for a nonwaivable right is greatly strengthened.

At first glance, these considerations would seem to be reasons for transferring the entitlement from employer to employee, and even for disallowing waivers. But they are not decisive. Children's interests are not entirely clear-cut: If parental wages fall as a result of parental leave legislation, children will be correspondingly hurt. In the general run of cases, there is probably little reason to think that parents will not consider the well-being of their children in deciding whether and how much leave time to demand at the time they are hired. Whether workers are in a poor position to make that balance in advance cannot be decided a priori. To be sure, a

---

[170] For an illuminating treatment of some of the complexities here, see generally Jolls, Accommodation Mandates, supra note 70 (discussing the effect of accommodation mandates on wage and employment levels).

real problem is that in initial bargaining, workers are unlikely to be thinking about parental leave.[171] But it would be possible to remedy this problem by giving employees the relevant right, and by allowing them to trade it if and only if the employers make the trade worth their while. It makes sense here to consider a two-tiered system, combining statutory minima with a more ample set of waivable rights.

E. Workers' Compensation

All states now provide workers' compensation programs. Moreover, the right to benefit from such programs is not waivable. Workers enter the employment relationship with assurance that in the event of accident, they will receive appropriate compensation. Workers' compensation programs do not merely have ex post consequences. They also have substantial incentive effects, leading employers to act to reduce accidents and injuries. Indeed, there is reason to think that workers' compensation programs are more effective—actually far more effective—than OSHA regulations in improving workplace safety.[172]

By themselves, however, these points do not justify making workers' compensation programs nonwaivable. As in the context of parental leave legislation, there is evidence that workers' wages are cut correspondingly; what they receive from the program, in the event that they need it, is what they lose in wages.[173] In these circumstances, why shouldn't workers be able to waive the relevant rights? If they did, they would be self-insurers, and self-insurance, so long as it is genuinely voluntary, is not an obviously implausible model for workplace injuries.[174]

The familiar answers might be given here. Workers may lack the information that would make a waiver sufficiently informed, perhaps because of myopia, excessive optimism, or dissonance reduction. But there is an independent issue: Workers who do not wish to waive their rights may face a special kind of collective ac-

---

[171] Compare the discussion of severance benefits in Bewley, supra note 3, at 268–69 (explaining why workers do not seek severance pay).

[172] See W. Kip Viscusi, Reforming Products Liability 178 (1991).

[173] See Fishback & Kantor, supra note 117, at 714.

[174] But see Fishback & Kantor, supra note 74, at 70–74 (describing problems in private insurance market).

tion problem, and this problem may well justify a nonwaivable workers' right.[175] More particularly, there is a distinctive free rider problem in this context. To see this, return to the fact that the consequence of workers' compensation programs is to lead employers to increase safety in the workplace. The increases often happen because employers introduce capital improvements designed to reduce deaths and injuries.[176] To the extent that these would have been made in any case, employees who waive their rights for a fee will receive many of the protections of the program without paying for it. It is here that there is a problem. If safety is a local private good—something that, when provided to some, will also be provided to all—rational individual choices by workers are likely to lead to a large number of waivers and hence fail to create incentives to increase safety. This, then, is an area where the argument for creating a nonwaivable workers' right is especially strong.[177]

F. Unionization: Company Unions, Ordinary Unions

What of the right to unionize itself? Should that right be waivable? By whom? These issues are best approached by dividing the inquiry into three issues: individual waivers of the right to unionize; appropriate default rules for union status; and collective waivers of the right not to be faced with company-dominated unions.

1. Nonwaivable Individual Employee Rights

The rights guaranteed by the Wagner Act,[178] the foundation of modern labor law, are not waivable by individual employees.[179] Employers may not buy the right to fire employees who join unions as through, for example, the "yellow dog" contract. The rights to join a union, to strike, and to engage in activity for mutual aid and protection are not subject to waiver. Why does the statute make this choice, rather than creating a system of waivable employees' rights?

---

[175] On related problems, see id.

[176] See Rose-Ackerman, supra note 8, at 359–60 (discussing safety as a local public good).

[177] See Fishback & Kantor, supra note 74, at 70–74 (describing problems in private insurance market for workers).

[178] 29 U.S.C. §§ 151–68 (1994).

[179] See id. §§ 158(a)(1), 158(a)(3).

There is no obvious answer.[180] One justification would rely on some combination of the behavioral grounds described above, involving informational, cognitive, and motivational problems. Perhaps many workers would not know what they were waiving, especially in light of the possibility that the potential benefits of unionization would not be readily apparent at the time the waiver was requested. Perhaps both employers and individual workers would face a signaling problem akin to that which could arise if, in an at-will regime, an employer emphasizes that it will provide job security, and thus attracts marginal workers, or an employee requests the same, and thus signals a realistic risk that the employer will want to fire him.

2. *Unions at All? The Current Presumption Against*

This system of nonwaivable workers' rights coexists with what is, from the standpoint of the real-world status of unions, probably even more important—the basic background set by a crucial waivable *employers'* right. No collective representative is in place until employees have affirmatively voted for it. The ordinary assumption of the workplace, and hence the default rule, is nonunion. The situation that workers face is one in which organization must be sought, through the processes of union election. Nothing is inevitable or natural about this situation. On the contrary, this "tilt has its roots in the common law background . . . the tacit legal assumption that the 'natural' status for a workplace is nonunion, with management exercising on behalf of the shareholder-owners the prerogatives of property and contract law to establish the firm's terms and conditions of employment."[181] It is easy to imagine an unusual regime, in which workers are presumed to favor collective organization, but in which they are permitted to vote otherwise. If union representation is thought to have significant advantages, a system of this sort might well be preferred.

Many variations are possible. On one approach, workers would start employment with a presumption in favor of collective organi-

---

[180] It is possible that the prohibition solves a collective action problem. For discussion, see Keith N. Hylton, A Theory of Minimum Contract Terms, with Implications for Labor Law, 74 Tex. L. Rev. 1741, 1749–51, 1756–65 (1996).

[181] Weiler, supra note 7, at 228.

zation. A vote would help to choose the particular form of that organization, including the particular union that would represent workers; at the same time, employees could be asked to reject the option of collective organization if they could be convinced that this is in their best interests. An advantage of this approach is that it could help overcome the effects of management tactics, many of them unlawful, to overcome unionization.[182] Another advantage is that this approach would work like an information-forcing default rule. If we are unsure whether failures of unionization stem from worker preferences or from employer pressure, a presumption in favor of collective organization would help untangle that issue. And to the extent that such organization confers benefits on workers without imposing correlative costs,[183] there is much to be said for enlisting the endowment effect on its behalf. In contrast, if collective organization is thought to produce few real benefits for organized workers, and at the same time to increase both prices and unemployment, the existing default rule would stand on firm ground. What is most important is to see that the default rule represents a choice among a range of options and that it is likely to have extremely important effects; any such rule has to be defended against reasonable alternatives.

3. Company Unions

Some of the most important and interesting issues in contemporary employment law arise as a result of the statutory ban on employer-sponsored workers' organizations.[184] Employers are not allowed to create labor organizations, even if employees would be satisfied with them—apparently on the theory that employer-sponsored labor organizations cannot be trusted to protect employee interests.[185] The theory seems to be that the employer should be on only one side of the negotiating table, not on both

---

[182] See id. at 230.

[183] This is the theme of Freeman & Medoff, supra note 15, at 246–51.

[184] See 29 U.S.C. § 158(a)(2) (1994).

[185] See Mark Barenberg, Democracy and Domination in the Law of Workplace Cooperation: From Bureaucratic to Flexible Production, 94 Colum. L. Rev. 753 (1994); Samuel Estreicher, Employee Involvement and the "Company Union" Prohibition: The Case for Partial Repeal of Section 8(a)(2) of the NLRA, 69 N.Y.U. L. Rev. 125 (1994).

sides. Thus Senator Wagner emphasized the coercion and decep-
tion involved in the use of company-dominated unions, with the
suggestion that such organizations actually served the employers'
interests, not those of workers. Hence the statutory prohibition was
(and is) defended with reference to a fear of employer coercion, a
belief that employees lack the information to make ex ante waivers, a risk of deceptive practice on the part of employers, and a
perception that workers' preferences, in this context, may be adap-
tive to an unjust status quo.

In theory, these objections may have made sense in the 1930s,
when company unions were primary tools in union avoidance, and
were commonly used as part of a package of union-busting tactics.
But in the last two decades, circumstances have changed in two
important ways.[186] First, private sector unions have dramatically declined, and hence the real choice is not between unions and
company-supported substitutes, but between no union and a company-supported substitute. It is hardly clear that no organization at
all is best for workers. Second, there has been a sharp decline in
Taylorist conceptions of the workplace, which posit a sharp split
between "brainwork" and the highly mechanical work of ordinary
laborers.[187] There is a great deal of new interest, on the part of employers themselves, in finding ways to increase the role of
employees in designing more efficient workplaces, partly because
this step increases worker satisfaction, and partly because it appears to have desirable effects on production. The consequence of
these two developments has been to impose sharp pressure on the
prohibition of employer-sponsored unions.

Suppose, for example, that an employer wants to create some
kind of employee organization to improve efficiency, safety, and
working conditions. Under current law, this step is likely forbidden.[188] The relevant right cannot be waived by workers acting
individually or even collectively. But suppose that workers have
thought long and hard about the issue, and have decided that they
would do better with a company union than without collective representation or with an ordinary union. The conventional response

---

[186] I borrow here from Estreicher, supra note 185, at 134–36.
[187] See sources cited supra note 185.
[188] See Electromation v. NLRB, 309 N.L.R.B. 990, 992, 995–97 (1992), enforced, 35
F.3d 1148 (7th Cir. 1994).

here is that the employees' judgment to this effect cannot be trusted because the result of a company union is to place the employer on both sides of the bargaining table. In this view, the ban on company unions is designed to ensure against a kind of deceptive packaging—the appearance without the reality of collective representation—and at the same time to counteract the risk that workers' preferences will adapt to an unjust status quo. If it were correct to say that without company unions, most workers would be faced with a choice between well-functioning unions and an absence of collective representation, this argument might be convincing. But the truth is that for a variety of reasons, unions are not a likely option for most workers—and also that for many workers, some kind of employee participation plan seems highly attractive as a source of genuine improvements in workers' well-being.[189]

The conclusion is that with procedural constraints designed to ensure real freedom of choice, workers should be allowed to waive the apparent protections of the ban on company unions, at least if they do so collectively. A constrained waiver, in short, would seem to be far better than the current nonwaivable one; this is the route that I suggest here.

IV. NONWAIVABLE WORKERS' RIGHTS

In this section, I generalize from the discussion to identify some grounds for disallowing waiver. The central cases involve third-party effects, inadequate information, and efforts to change norms and preferences, which involve third-party effects of a different kind. The discussion of third-party effects draws on conventional approaches; the treatment of inadequate information, and norm-change and preference-change, draws on behavioral economics.

A. Third-Party Effects

Most obviously, a nonwaivable background rule makes sense when there are third-party effects. There are many examples. As

---

[189] See Michael H. LeRoy, Employer Domination of Labor Organizations and the *Electromation* Case: An Empirical Public Policy Analysis, 61 Geo. Wash. L. Rev. 1812, 1822–26, 1837–41 (1990).

we will see, unions are not allowed to waive workers' rights to distribute work-related materials, partly because there is no identity of interests between the waiving union and the workers whose rights have been waived. The problem is that the waiver has effects on third parties—that is, workers with interests distinct from those of the union.

I have noted above that in a series of common law cases, courts have created public policy exceptions to the at-will rule. The core cases involve situations in which an employer discharges an employee for refusing to commit a crime (perjury, price fixing) on the employer's behalf.[190] In other cases, courts have disallowed discharges when the employer is punishing employees for cooperating with the authorities with respect to possible illegality at the company.[191] The defining theme is that employers may not discharge employees if the consequence is to impose harms on outsiders to the contractual relationship.[192] It should be obvious that waivers are unacceptable in these circumstances. The waiver is invalid not to protect workers, but to ensure that others are not adversely affected. For the most part this category of cases is reasonably straightforward, and hence it is not necessary to discuss it in detail here.

B. Inadequate Information

In some cases, waivers will be inadequately informed. As we will see, this is a key reason why the law is more hospitable to union waivers than to individual waivers: Unions are in a far better position to know what they are doing. Individual waivers may be inadequately informed for a large number of reasons, including excessive optimism, dissonance reduction, editing out, and myopia. A great deal of empirical research is necessary to establish the extent of the problem. For the moment, the best approach is to block exchanges of rights that most reasonable people would be unlikely to

---

[190] See, e.g., Tameny v. Atl. Richfield Co., 610 P.2d 1330 (Cal. 1980); Petermann v. International Brotherhood of Teamsters, Local 396, 344 P.2d 25, 27 (Cal. Dist. Ct. App. 1959); Sabine Pilot Serv. v. Hauck, 687 S.W.2d 733, 735 (Tex. 1985).

[191] See, e.g., Garibaldi v. Lucky Food Stores, 726 F.2d 1367 (9th Cir. 1984); Palmateer v. International Harvester Co., 421 N.E.2d 876, 879–80 (Ill. 1981); McQuary v. Bel Air Convalescent Homes, 684 P.2d 21 (Or. Ct. App. 1984).

[192] See Schwab, supra note 33, at 1945.

waive,[193] but otherwise to allow waiver unless there is a particular reason to believe that workers are giving up too much for too little. When there is a serious risk to this effect, it would be best not to block waiver entirely, but to impose procedural or substantive limits on acceptable waivers. Requirements of full disclosure, along with a cooling off period, might be a minimal way to proceed.

C. Norm and Preference Change

Now let us turn to some of the most difficult and interesting cases for waiver, involving what are perhaps best treated as subtle endowment effects and third-party effects.

1. Waiver: The Basic Case

Suppose that an employer is averse to the threat of race or sex discrimination suits. Seeking to produce a mutually advantageous solution, he asks his employees to sign an agreement waiving their rights to bring suit for race or sex discrimination. The employer adds that he believes that discrimination is wrong and that he does not plan to discriminate. He insists that he is not a discriminator. He asks everyone, not only African-Americans and women, to sign the waiver. He claims that he is willing to pay a premium for a waiver, not in order to discriminate, but to insulate himself from frivolous or trumped-up lawsuits. Suppose too that a small but non-trivial number of employees are willing to waive their rights, because they believe that this is otherwise a good place to work, because the premium is not tiny, and because they are willing to take their chances on race and sex discrimination.

Let us also assume, plausibly, that if employees are presumed to have the relevant entitlement, requests for waivers will be very rare, partly because of the kind of signal given by such requests. An employer who asks for these waivers will scare off a large number of employees and incur reputational sanctions. Nonetheless, it is highly likely that some waiver requests would be made if they were seen as valid. Note in this regard that there is evidence that some discrimination laws do have an adverse effect on hiring members of the protected class, precisely because of a fear of a

---

[193] See Rose-Ackerman, supra note 8, at 359.

lawsuit; an employee in that class represents a lawsuit waiting to happen.[194] Perhaps some of the disemployment effect could be removed with waivers. Should these waivers be upheld?

It might be tempting to see in the employer's proposal a coercive offer: An employee is asked to waive his rights in return for a job, and he may seem to have no choice but to waive. On this view, the law should provide protection, and enhance freedom, by banning the coercive deal. But this account is much too simple. In these cases, the employee is not in a position of having no choice; the question is whether the offer is worthwhile for the employee in light of the options, perhaps most of them bad, that are available. Unless there is an informational problem of some kind, the fact that the employee accepts the deal is strong evidence that it is worthwhile.

It is also possible to think that for some classes of workers, the sheer number of job applicants, and the relatively small number of jobs, will mean that employees will be forced to waive; those who do not waive will not end up with jobs. This is certainly imaginable. But in a market that is so unfavorable to workers, *all* employment terms will be pushed in unfavorable directions, including wages. Unless there is some kind of information problem, perhaps of the kind discussed here, employees who waive stand to gain if they can do so because those who waive will (by hypothesis) win more than they lose. The best solution, in a market with this degree of harshness for employees, is to improve the background conditions faced by those workers, not to block the best available deal, even though that deal may not be very good.

2. Third-Party Effects?

Thus far, at least, it seems that discrimination rights should be fully waivable. But might individual waivers have adverse effects on other workers? Begin with the context of sexual harassment, where it is easy to imagine that they would. If one woman waives her right and is thereafter subject to harassment, other women may well be harmed; the effect will not be easy to cabin. At least this is

---

[194] See Jolls, Accommodation Mandates, supra note 70, at 273–82 (discussing evidence of disemployment effect for disabled people); Posner, supra note 165, at 329–33 (discussing disemployment effect for older workers).

so if the waiver leads would-be harassers to believe that harassment is not entirely objectionable or unacceptable, or that reasonable women are willing to subject themselves to a risk of it for a wage premium. A man who believes that it is permissible to harass one woman might believe that it is permissible to harass more than one, even if few waivers have been signed.

The example is easily extended to sex and race discrimination in general. An African-American who is willing to waive the right to be free from racially-motivated adverse employment action might well be affecting other African-Americans, both by signaling the legitimacy of discrimination and by indicating that discrimination is not morally abhorrent but merely a cost, to be purchased and sold like other goods on the market. If discrimination is so regarded, there may well be more of it than if the signal is different—as, for example, where a flat ban suggests that discrimination is illicit, the sort of practice to be eliminated, rather than be brought to some optimal point.[195] Now this does not mean that discrimination should be eliminated at any price. It means only that the moral stigma that is sought to be imposed on discrimination, and properly so, might be weakened if waivers are permitted. If this is so, isolated waivers would have third-party effects.

3. Norm and Preference Change

This claim suggests several more concrete possibilities. Recall, from the earlier discussion of the endowment effect, that the allocation of the entitlement can have effects on values and preferences. In this light we can see that some antidiscrimination law is an attempt to produce *norm change*. The point of the law is to alter prevailing norms. If rights are waivable, that enterprise might be undermined. If workers are living in accordance with a norm that they abhor and wish to change, they are unlikely to be able to accomplish the change on their own. By its very nature, norm change requires collective action. The waiver is forbidden in

---

[195] Compare the area of pollution. Some people have objected to emissions trading—a kind of waivable nonpollution right—on the same ground. See Steven Kelman, What Price Incentives? 1 (1981). The best response is that there is an optimal level of pollution, and it is not zero, and polluting activity—so long as it is part of a legitimate business, and not an intentional tort—is not the kind of thing that it is appropriate to delegitimate as such.

order to ensure that certain norms are delegitimated. A closely related possibility is that the purpose of the relevant right is to produce *preference change*. If preferences are not being taken as given, but are being treated as endogenous and flexible, an argument for preventing waiver might be defended as a method for ensuring that preferences are in fact changed.

With respect to the validity of discrimination waivers, these arguments are not decisive in the abstract. In a period in which race and sex discrimination are widely stigmatized, it is reasonable to believe that permitting waivers would have few significant effects on workers not parties to the deal, or at the least that waivers would not have a material effect in entrenching objectionable norms and preferences. If an employer asks employees to waive the right to be free from race or sex discrimination, it is signaling that it is a possible discriminator—not the most attractive signal to send out to prospective employees. On the other hand, some employees—white and male—might welcome that signal, and in these circumstances the ban on waiver is understandable as an effort to prevent inevitable effects on third parties who are likely to be affected by the legitimation of the underlying practice. When the law is engaged in a self-conscious effort to change norms and preferences, allowing waivers is too likely to defeat the enterprise at hand.[196]

V. A BRIEF NOTE ON UNION WAIVERS

The discussion thus far has involved individual waivers, but a frequent issue in employment law is whether labor unions are themselves entitled to waive workers' rights. The general answer is that when there are no third-party effects, union waivers are legally acceptable,[197] though in some contexts there is a self-conscious ef-

---

[196] On the other hand, it is clear that victims of discrimination can settle, and at least if they do not "tender back" the money, a financial settlement appears to preclude a suit for reinstatement. See, e.g., Fleming v. United States Postal Serv. AMF O'Hare, 27 F.3d 259, 262 (7th Cir. 1994). But see Rangel v. El Paso Natural Gas Co., 996 F. Supp. 1093, 1096–99 (D.N.M. 1998) (allowing plaintiff's suit to continue without "tendering back" and requiring that severance pay offset any damages).

[197] See Metro. Edison Co. v. NLRB, 460 U.S. 693, 705 (1983); Mastro Plastics Corp. v. NLRB, 350 U.S. 270, 280 (1956); Lodges 743 & 1746, International Association of

fort to ensure that any waiver is knowing and voluntary, in a kind of procedural constraint on enforceable waivers.[198] Is it possible to explain the law's receptivity to union waivers?

There are two points here, sharply distinguishing union waivers from individual waivers. First, informational problems are highly likely to have been overcome in the union setting. When a union is waiving, it would be surprising, in the ordinary case, if it did so without really knowing what it is doing. In all probability the problem of myopia will also have been reduced. Note in this regard that unions are not solely concerned with wages, and that various fringe benefits, likely to be favored by those interested in the long term, are a special focus of union bargaining.[199] Second, unions overcome the collective action problem faced by individual workers, and this point lessens the danger that employers will be able to force individual workers to waive by ensuring that they compete to their collective detriment. It should be no wonder that serious concerns about union waivers seem to arise only when the union has a conflict of interest, and hence is not in a position to be a good representative of workers. Thus unions are permitted, in the most noteworthy case, to waive workers' right to strike.[200] With respect to the rights guaranteed by the NLRA, the situation is largely one of waivable workers' rights—with the rights being waivable collectively only, and emphatically *not* individually.

Compare in this regard cases in which the union cannot be trusted to be a fair representative of workers' interests, exemplified by *NLRB v. Magnovox Co.*[201] In that case, the union accepted a collective bargaining agreement that banned employees from distributing literature on any of the employer's property, including nonworking areas during nonworking time.[202] It is clear that this rule would violate the law if imposed unilaterally by the employer. Though the union had agreed to it, the Supreme Court held that the waiver was not binding, for a collective bargaining agreement could not eliminate these relevant rights. The Court said that

---

Machinists v. United Aircraft Corp., 534 F.2d 422 (2d Cir. 1975) (upholding waiver of reinstatement rights after settlement of a strike).

[198] See *Metro. Edison*, 460 U.S. at 709–10.

[199] See Freeman & Medoff, supra note 15, at 20.

[200] See *Mastro Plastics Corp.*, 350 U.S. at 280.

[201] 415 U.S. 322 (1974).

[202] See id. at 323.

waiver would not be permitted "where the rights of the employees to exercise their choice of a bargaining representative is involved—whether to have no bargaining representative, or to retain the present one, or to obtain a new one."[203] The key problem was one of agency—with respect to continuing debates about self-representation, the union could not be trusted to be the faithful agent of workers. This suggests a distinctive reason to disallow union waivers. *Magnavox* was followed by a series of cases that are generally receptive to waivers by unions, but not when the waiving union is likely to have divergent interests from those individuals whose rights are waived.[204]

One final wrinkle is important here. In many contexts, union waivers must be explicit and unambiguous. A general no-strike clause will not bar an unfair labor practice strike,[205] and it will not create an affirmative obligation on union leaders to avert strikes on pain of discipline or discharge.[206] If employers are going to obtain rights beyond those minimally contained in a no strike pledge, they must do so explicitly. Here is a procedural constraint on the waiver of workers' rights.

VI. THE PROBLEM OF RELATIVE POSITION

The discussion thus far has neglected an important and highly relevant point from behavioral economics. I do not discuss it in detail, because it raises many complexities and depends on empirical issues on which unambiguous evidence is lacking. But because the point has been almost universally neglected in the context of employment and labor law, it requires some discussion.

A. Relative Position and the Frame of Reference

Let us acknowledge that the cost of workers' rights, when they are not waived, might be borne in whole or in part by workers, in the sense that the legal grant of a right to workers will result in lower wages. Is the argument against the relevant right therefore

---

[203] Id. at 325.
[204] See Michael C. Harper, Union Waiver of Employee Rights Under the NLRA (pts. 1&2), 4 Indus. Rel. L.J. 335, 337 (1981).
[205] See *Mastro Plastics Corp.*, 350 U.S. at 280–84.
[206] See *Metro. Edison Co.*, 460 U.S. at 704–05.

2001]   *Human Behavior and the Law of Work*   267

established, on the ground that workers will be net losers? We have seen that one problem with an affirmative answer is that workers might not be net losers. But a more fundamental problem is that with respect to income, part of what workers seem to care about is *relative* economic position, rather than *absolute* economic position.[207] In other words, what matters to workers is partly how they compare to others, not how much money they are making in the abstract; and if all workers lose the same amount, each worker will lose very little, because relative position will not be affected. If what workers care about is relative position, nonwaivable rights might, in principle, make workers better off on the dimension along which they are helped, by giving them something important, while not making them worse off along the dimension along which they are apparently hurt, by decreasing their income while also decreasing that of everyone else.

Relative position is found by comparing the worker's income with that of other salient workers; absolute position is found by looking simply at the number of dollars that the worker makes. The question is whether workers are significantly worse off in a system in which all salient workers lose, for example, 0.5% of their salary, while receiving a benefit (such as increased leisure time, parental leave, safety, or job security). If the economic loss has no significant adverse effect, then any initiative that produces that loss will not, by virtue of that consequence, harm workers at all. If this is so, it is because income above a certain floor is a *positional good*—a good whose value depends on comparison with the holdings of others. The noteworthy possibility here is that legal initiatives might, in theory, produce real gains of one or another kind (again, leisure time, parental leave, safety, or job security, which are, by hypothesis, nonpositional or less positional goods), without producing real losses (because the only loss is to absolute position in terms of income, and because workers lose nothing if absolute position is slightly worse while relative position is held constant).

---

[207] See Frank, supra note 116, at 5; Robert H. Frank & Cass R. Sunstein, Cost Benefit Analysis and Relative Position, 68 U. Chi. L. Rev. (forthcoming 2001) (manuscript on file with the author).

There is considerable evidence that relative position is in fact what people care about, at least with respect to income.[208] Many people would prefer to work in a place where they earn $60,000 and the average worker earns $50,000, to working in a place where they earn $70,000 and the average worker earns $90,000.[209] This preference holds where everything else is equal—for example, where the cost of living is the same in the two places.[210] Why are people prepared to sacrifice income to ensure a certain place in the hierarchy? Undoubtedly envy and status-seeking play a large role. Some people would like to have a high status and are willing to lose money to ensure that they do. Perhaps more people would like not to have a low status and are willing to lose absolute income in order to ensure that they do not. But the more fundamental point is that the economic position of other people sets the *frame of reference* within which we evaluate various goods. If you now had the same computer that you used ten years ago, you would likely be dissatisfied and frustrated, simply because the frame of reference for evaluation of the computer has changed so dramatically. But if everyone had the same computers that they had ten years ago, your decade-old computer would not seem so bad; indeed it might not seem bad at all.

What is true for computers is no less true for a vast array of goods and services, including cars, radios, televisions, homes, and even artistic and literary work. People care about relative position not only because they care about their status, but also because they are aware that the frame of reference for evaluation is set not individually but socially.

B. Mandatory Terms and Relative Position

For the moment let us simply assume that relative rather than absolute economic position is what most workers care about—that worker well-being would not be decreased by (say) a decrease in annual wages of $25, $50, or $100, so long as all workers face the same decrease. In that event, some nonwaivable terms, such as a

---

[208] Frank, supra note 116, at 5; see also Frank & Sunstein, supra note 207, at 9–17 (presenting some of the evidence).

[209] See Frank & Sunstein, supra note 207, at 11.

[210] Id.

right to job security, might be justified on the following ground: The consequence of the new term is to decrease absolute income but to hold relative income constant. From this shift, there is little or no welfare loss to workers. At the same time, workers receive a substantial benefit, such as job security, vacation time, or health care. As far as the worker is concerned, the substantial benefit is given essentially for free, because relative position is held constant. If relative position is in fact what workers care about, this appears to be a powerful argument for a wide range of nonwaivable workers' rights.

C. Difficulties

I believe that this argument is largely correct, but as stated it is too abstract to be entirely convincing. It raises three questions in particular.

Perhaps relative position is also what workers care about with respect to the new, legally granted benefit; perhaps this too is a positional good. Many goods have a mixture of positional and nonpositional features. It does seem reasonable to say that such goods as job security, health care benefits, and leisure time have especially strong nonpositional features. It is important to have these things regardless of what other people have; an increase in any of them, far more than an increase in money, is an independent good. But job security, leisure time, and the like also have positional features; to lack, for example, job security when everyone else lacks job security is probably better than to lack job security when everyone else has it. For the argument on behalf of the nonwaivable term to be made convincing, it must be true that relative position is what matters with respect to income—or to whatever else is lost as a result of the nonwaivable term—but that what matters for the good in question, such as job security, is not relative but absolute position. Perhaps we can conclude that the nonpositional features of job security, health care benefits, and leisure time are enough to give the argument a kind of presumptive validity.

It is possible that a nonwaivable right to a certain largely nonpositional good, such as job security, will lead not only to reductions in income (by hypothesis a positional good) but also to reductions in nonpositional goods (such as vacation leave, sick leave, health care, or parental leave). If the grant of one nonpositional good leads to a decrease in others, there will be nothing to celebrate. There is an empirical question here: When government creates a mandatory benefit, to what extent does the result decrease not income, but other, less positional benefits associated with employment?

To what extent is income actually a positional good? There is considerable evidence that for most people, what matters to perceived well-being is their position in the relevant hierarchy, above a certain minimum level.[211] For very poor workers, of course, absolute income may be what matters. In poor nations, absolute increases in wealth affect self-reported happiness levels, and absolute increases affect self-reported happiness levels among the very poor. To the extent that mandatory terms reduce the income of people with little to live on, such terms are not likely to be justifiable on the ground that I have offered. Of course, few mandatory terms will have this effect.

The nonwaivable right might impose ancillary social costs. It might, for example, force prices to rise, and the resulting inefficiencies may bolster an argument against the nonwaivable term. Even when workers are benefited as a result, the term might not be justified on balance; an increase in prices is hardly good news for workers (especially poor ones), and if unemployment increases as well, the nonwaivable term may not be worthwhile.

In light of these points, an understanding of the importance of relative position does not create a decisive argument for nonwaivable terms in employment law. But it does raise a behavioral possibility, overlooked in conventional discussions of these problems: Even if such terms create a dollar-for-dollar reduction in wages, workers may still benefit as a result.

CONCLUSION

My basic goal in this Article has been to bring a better understanding of human behavior to bear on the three principal options for employment law: waivable employers' rights, waivable workers' rights, and nonwaivable workers' rights. Contrary to the Coase theorem, the default rule is likely to matter a great deal. Contrary

---

[211] See Robert H. Frank, Luxury Fever: Why Money Fails to Satisfy in an Era of Excess 107–21 (1999); Frank & Sunstein, supra note 207, at 9–17.

to the standard view in law and economics, workers are loss averse; they will be reluctant to give up rights and goods that have been initially allocated to them—a point confirmed by employers' reluctance to decrease wages, even during a recession.[212] Contrary to the conventional wisdom, workers do not understand that the current system is at will, even though the law to this effect is well-established. Contrary to the reflexive antipaternalism of many lawyers and economists, workers are likely to have difficulty in deciding whether to waive their rights, and hence the case for non-waivable terms, defended in behavioral terms, is far more plausible than it appears when defended in terms of simple redistribution. Contrary to the standard economic wisdom, workers often care about relative position, not absolute position. Contrary to standard legal practice, waivable workers' rights represent an attractive alternative in many contexts, responsive in particular to workers' lack of information. Contrary to a standard legal view, the difference between legal hostility to individual waivers and legal receptivity to union waivers is defensible on the ground that unions are less likely to suffer from myopia and other forms of bounded rationality.

We have seen more particularly that waivable workers' rights represent a distinctive, promising, and insufficiently explored approach to the law of labor relations. A system of this kind will often be preferable to the more standard alternatives of waivable employers' rights and nonwaivable workers' rights. To the extent that workers undervalue the rights initially allocated to them and sell them for a price that is too low, it is sensible to consider, as an alternative to a ban on waiver, a system of constrained waiver—ranging from requirements of disclosure, to a cooling-off period, to legal floors on what employees will receive through the relevant trades.

In the area of the contract at will, I have suggested that legislatures should experiment with waivable for-cause rules, and also that courts should move in this direction by penalizing employers who lead employees to believe that they have protection against at-will discharge (as, for example, through promises of permanent employment and through statements that company policy is to re-

---

[212] See Bewley, supra note 3.

tain all good employees). If progress is to be made in improving worker well-being without introducing excessive rigidity into the labor market, the best route for the future will consist of more creative experiments with waivable workers' rights.

For many problems, it would make sense to combine a system of nonwaivable statutory minima, consisting of safeguards that no worker should lack, with an ample set of waivable workers' rights that would be subject to bargaining. There is room for disagreement about what should count as the nonwaivable minima and what should count as the waivable workers' rights; it is in identifying the content of these categories, rather than in settling on the basic approach, that reasonable disputes will arise. An approach of this general kind is no blueprint, but it suggests an orientation that could provide the foundation for a new system of employment law in a wide range of areas. Equally important, an understanding of the nature of workers' judgments and motivations, and the possible grounds for choosing among the legal options, could provide the basis for orienting future inquiry and for making progress on the issues, many of them empirical in nature, that remain.

2001]   *Human Behavior and the Law of Work*   273

APPENDIX: ECONOMICS, BEHAVIORAL ECONOMICS,
AND THE WORKPLACE

In this Article I have discussed many issues in employment law and behavioral economics. The purpose of this Appendix is to outline the central parts of the conventional wisdom that are called into question by evidence and by' a better understanding of human behavior. Of special importance is the last column, emphasizing what we do not yet know. Much of my argument here has been for a degree of agnosticism with respect to positive issues (what people do) and normative issues (what the law should do). Much more work is necessary on both sorts of issues.

Conventional wisdom, grounded in once-standard or now-standard economic theory	Empirical difficulty	Behavioral mechanism(s)	Legal implications	Implicit behavioral rationality in current law	What we don't know
Continued employment is self-enforcing; opportunistic behavior will not occur	Mandatory retirement; wages increase faster than productivity	Loss aversion; fairness and reciprocity (labor markets as showing gift exchanges); workers' preference for rising wage profiles	Ban opportunistic discharges	Yes, through ban on opportunistic discharges	How much opportunistic behavior occurs? Does the market, via reputational sanctions, deter it?

Conventional wisdom	Empirical difficulty	Behavioral mechanism(s)	Legal implications	Implicit behavioral rationality in current law	What we don't know
Workers know about at-will and other default rules	Workers do not know about at-will and other default rules	Unclear. Perhaps excessive optimism; perhaps the "law-is-what-fairness-requires" heuristic	Take ambiguous promises as real promises; waivable for-cause rule	Yes, through aggressive reading of apparent promises	Is it possible to counteract worker ignorance? What is source of that ignorance? Would a waivable for-cause rule do any good? What other rights do workers believe, falsely, that they have?

Conventional wisdom	Empirical difficulty	Behavioral mechanism(s)	Legal implications	Implicit behavioral rationality in current law	What we don't know
Default rule is irrelevant without transaction costs	Default rule sticks in experimental and real-world settings	Endowment effect; loss aversion	Unclear	No, except perhaps through non-waivable rights	How should we choose a rule when there will be an endowment effect? Are there significant distributional effects here? How sticky are default rules, for employees and employers?
Informed workers will reach bargains that are in their interests	Workers appear not to bargain for some items that might be in their interest	Excessive optimism; signaling problems; myopia	Nonwaivable workers' rights	Maybe, through statutory bans on waiver	Are workers really excessively optimistic or myopic, in general or in specific cases?

Conventional wisdom	Empirical difficulty	Behavioral mechanism(s)	Legal implications	Implicit behavioral rationality in current law	What we don't know
Unions shouldn't be allowed to waive so much more easily than individuals	Law allows union waivers more readily than individual waivers	Bounded rationality, a problem reduced by unions	Allow union waivers more readily (implicit behavioral rationality in cases)	Yes, through legal distinction between union and individual waivers	Are unions really overcoming bounded rationality of individuals, or instead acting in a self-serving fashion?
Workers are paid their marginal product and hence nonwaivable terms can only help	Labor market appears to show wage compression; people appear willing to sacrifice income for good, or not bad, relative position	People care about relative position, not absolute position, with respect income	Nonwaivable workers' rights	Maybe, through nonwaivable rights to certain nonpositional goods	Which goods are positional goods? How much does relative position account for valuation?

Part III
The Impact on Economic Welfare of the Regulation of Labor in the US and the World

[5]

The Effect of State Policies on the Location of Manufacturing: Evidence from State Borders

Thomas J. Holmes

University of Minnesota and Federal Reserve Bank of Minneapolis

This paper provides new evidence that state policies play a role in the location of industry. The paper classifies a state as probusiness if it has a right-to-work law and antibusiness if it does not. The paper finds that, on average, there is a large, abrupt increase in manufacturing activity when one crosses a state border from an antibusiness state into a probusiness state.

I. Introduction

Do the probusiness policies pursued by some states attract manufacturing to these states? This is a controversial issue. In state capitals throughout the country, proponents of probusiness policies routinely claim that state policies are an important determinant of the location of manufacturing. But the results in the academic literature on this subject are mixed, and there is a lack of consensus as to whether or not differences in state policies have a large impact on manufacturing location (see Bartik [1991] and Wasylenko [1991] for surveys).

Progress in this literature has been hampered by the difficulty of

For helpful comments, I thank the referees, Shelby Gerking, Pete Klenow, Karl Scholz, Jim Schmitz, and seminar participants at the Federal Reserve Banks of Minneapolis and Chicago, the University of Chicago, the University of Rochester, Cornell University, the University of Houston, Southern Methodist University, the University of Arizona, the University of Wisconsin, and the 1997 meetings of the Regional Science Association International. The views expressed herein are those of the author and not necessarily those of the Federal Reserve Bank of Minneapolis or the Federal Reserve System.

[*Journal of Political Economy*, 1998, vol. 106, no. 4]

distinguishing the effects of state policies from the effects of other state characteristics that are unrelated to policy. This paper examines this issue with a fresh approach that circumvents this difficult identification problem. The approach considers what happens to manufacturing activity when one crosses state borders. Suppose that a state with a policy that is *probusiness* toward manufacturing is adjacent to a state with a policy that is *antibusiness* toward manufacturing. If state policies are an important determinant of the location of manufacturing, one should find an abrupt change in manufacturing activity when one crosses a border at which policy changes, because state characteristics unrelated to policy are the same on both sides of the border.

The paper finds that there is such an abrupt change. I estimate that manufacturing's share of total employment increases by about one-third when one crosses the border from an antibusiness state to a probusiness state. These results suggest that state policies matter.

II. Description of Method and Results

A. *The Measure of State Policy*

I classify a state as *probusiness* if it has a right-to-work law and *antibusiness* if it does not. A right-to-work law bans the union shop, that is, a workplace in which all employees are required to join the union. I focus on this crude, but easy to calculate, measure of state policy for two reasons. One is that a right-to-work law is a policy that has some appeal to manufacturers because a right-to-work law weakens unions.[1] The other is that the same forces in a state that lead to the passage of right-to-work laws also lead to the adoption of other policies favorable to manufacturing. This point is developed further below.

Florida and Arkansas passed the first right-to-work laws in 1944. Figure 1 shows which states have these laws today. With three exceptions, the map as it looks today was in place by 1958.[2] The geography of these laws is striking. No state in the traditional *manufacturing belt*

---

[1] A right-to-work law creates a free-rider problem among employees. Ellwood and Fine (1987) and Ichniowski and Zax (1991) present evidence that right-to-work laws have a small negative effect on unionization. There is great controversy in the literature as to how big these effects are. See Moore and Newman (1985) for a survey. Business and union interests have fought at great lengths about these laws, which suggests that the laws make some difference (see Gall 1988).

[2] The three exceptions are as follows: in 1965, Indiana repealed the right-to-work law it had passed in 1957; Louisiana passed its right-to-work law in 1976; and Idaho passed its law in 1986.

LOCATION OF MANUFACTURING   669

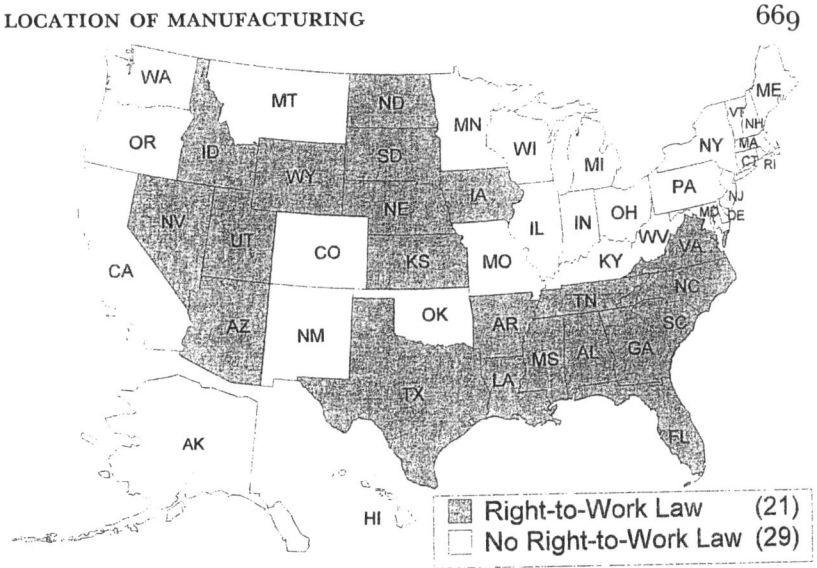

FIG. 1.—Geography of right-to-work laws

(the New England, mid-Atlantic, and Great Lakes states) has a right-to-work law. Every southern state that joined the Confederacy has one. Most of the Plains states west of the manufacturing belt (e.g., North and South Dakota) have these laws.

There are some remarkable facts about what has happened to manufacturing in the right-to-work states over the postwar period. Manufacturing employment in the states without right-to-work laws is virtually the same today as it was in 1947. In the right-to-work states, manufacturing employment has increased 150 percent. Eight of the 10 states with the highest manufacturing employment growth rates are right-to-work states. All 10 states with the lowest growth rates are not right-to-work states. A regression of state manufacturing growth on a dummy variable for a right-to-work law yields a large coefficient on the dummy variable with a huge t-statistic.

The National Right-to-Work Committee, an antiunion lobbying group, reports statistics such as these as supposed proof that right-to-work laws attract manufacturing. Newman (1983) and Plaut and Pluta (1983) run regressions like the one just mentioned and imply that they are learning something about the effects of state policies. These claims ignore a serious identification problem. The right-to-work states systematically differ in a number of geographic characteristics from the non-right-to-work states. The statistics reported above can say very little about the effects of state policy.

B.   The Identification Problem

In general, it is difficult to distinguish the effects of state policies from the effects of state characteristics that have nothing to do with state policies. This subsection explains why the problem is particularly severe in the case of concern here, that is, in identifying the effects of the policies pursued by the right-to-work states on the location of manufacturing. The subsection then explains how the border analysis resolves the identification problem.

The problem that must be confronted here is that even if state policies had no effect on the location of manufacturing, one would still expect to find a positive correlation between manufacturing growth and right-to-work laws because of the systematic way that right-to-work states differ from non-right-to-work states. This point can be made by considering the following four major forces of change over the postwar period in the location patterns of manufacturing.[3]

The productivity revolution in agriculture.—Because of this revolution, states that had high agricultural employment shares, like those in the South, experienced dramatic increases in manufacturing. But these same states also passed right-to-work laws because there were no strong industrial unions to block their passage.

Revolutions in transportation.—The substitution of trucking for rail transport may have diminished the forces that originally caused manufacturing to agglomerate in the manufacturing belt. As manufacturing has spread out, states that initially had low manufacturing employment shares have increased their manufacturing employment shares. But these were the same states to pass right-to-work laws, again because of the absence of powerful industrial unions.

Union avoidance.—It is widely believed that manufacturers left the North in part to escape unions (see, e.g., Olson 1982). Unions have been weak in the South and continue to be weak for various reasons, most of which probably have little to do with policy. Southerners as a group are perceived to have hostile attitudes toward unions. These attitudes made the South attractive to manufacturers. These attitudes also led to the passage of antiunion statutes such as right-to-work laws.

The advent of air conditioning.—This made the climate in the South relatively more attractive than the climate in the North. Air conditioning played a role in attracting people, and along with this migration of people came a migration of manufacturing activity. Since

---

[3] See Fuchs (1962) and Wheat (1973) for discussions of these major forces of change.

right-to-work states tend to be in the South, the advent of air conditioning alone would have induced a positive correlation between manufacturing growth and right-to-work status.

To estimate the effects of policy, I need some method that will enable me to control for differences across states in these various characteristics that are unrelated to policy. Traditional approaches to this problem would be difficult to implement. I would need a model of how manufacturing activity depends on geographic characteristics, such as the climate of a location; the fertility of the soil; access to an ocean, river, or lake; the proximity to raw materials; and the attitudes of people toward unions. A particularly difficult issue is how I might handle the possibility of agglomeration economies. Two locations might be identical in natural geographic factors. But because of agglomeration economies, manufacturing might concentrate in one of the locations and not the other.

This paper is able to draw inferences about the effects of state policies by examining what happens at state borders. At state borders, the geographic determinants of the distribution of manufacturing—for example, climate, soil fertility, access to transportation, and the level of agglomeration benefits—are approximately the same on both sides of the border. What differs at the border is policy. To the extent that the probusiness policies pursued by the right-to-work states have been a factor in the migration of industry, there should be an abrupt change in manufacturing activity at the border. In contrast, if the policies make no difference, there should be no abrupt change at the border.

Consider the case of climate. While the average temperature in the South is certainly much higher than in the North, in the border area, the temperature is approximately the same on both sides of the border. To the extent that the economic development of the South has been due to its favorable climate, there should be no abrupt change at the border.

C. The Results

I find evidence that manufacturing activity increases abruptly when one crosses the border from an antibusiness state to a probusiness state. To obtain my estimates, I use data on manufacturing employment levels for counties and classify each county by how far its population centroid is from the border. I find that manufacturing employment in a county as a percentage of total employment in the county increases, on average, by approximately one-third when one crosses the border into the probusiness side.

In addition to examining the levels of industrial activity, I look at growth rates in manufacturing employment over the postwar period 1947–92. As mentioned earlier, growth in the probusiness states is remarkably higher than in the antibusiness states. I find that there is a sharp difference in growth rates at the borders at which policy changes.

It is important to emphasize that my finding that the manufacturing employment share increases one-third at a state border does not imply that a probusiness policy increases the share by one-third throughout the state. As discussed in Section III, the effects of policy differences far from the border are smaller than the effects close to the border. Hence, the estimate of the effect at the border places an upper bound on the statewide effect of the policy.

It is also important to emphasize that the results reported here identify the overall effect at the border of adopting the set of probusiness policies that have been pursued by the right-to-work states. The results do not identify the contribution of any one policy to this overall effect. In particular, the results do not say what would happen if a state currently without a right-to-work law passed such a law but left all other policies fixed.

D. Right-to-Work States and Probusiness Policies

I use the term *probusiness policy* in a narrow sense in this paper compared with the common usage of the term. I mean it to include only those policies that have a disproportionate effect in attracting manufacturing to a state as opposed to those policies that equally benefit all sectors. In this subsection, I discuss various policies that are probusiness according to my definition, and I argue that states with right-to-work laws have tended to adopt other probusiness policies.

Any policy that weakens unions satisfies my definition of a probusiness policy. The manufacturing sector is more heavily unionized than the rest of the private sector, so laws that weaken unions make a bigger difference in the manufacturing sector. Weak environmental and safety regulations are also probusiness policies, since these regulations tend to be more relevant to the manufacturing sector than to other sectors. Subsidies for the construction of new manufacturing plants and grants of land for these projects obviously satisfy my definition of a probusiness policy.

A low overall tax rate is not a probusiness policy by my definition if all sectors benefit equally from the low tax. However, any low tax that disproportionately benefits manufacturing is probusiness. Low taxes on capital can be expected to favor manufacturing since the manufacturing sector tends to be more capital-intensive than other sectors.

As mentioned earlier, the same forces that led to the passage of right-to-work laws in right-to-work states have also led to the adoption of other probusiness policies in these states. For at least the past 50 years, the southern states have waged an aggressive campaign to attract manufacturing (see Cobb 1993). In addition to the passage of right-to-work laws, these states have been known for their subsidies for new factories, low taxes on capital, and lax regulations. Most of the states in the Plains region west of the manufacturing belt also passed right-to-work laws. This region is obviously different in many ways from the South. Nevertheless, like the southern states, the Plains states have a reputation for probusiness policies compared with the manufacturing belt states. For example, a study of border cities by the Minnesota Planning Division (1983) reports that a typical business could cut its taxes in half by crossing the border into North Dakota (a right-to-work state) from Minnesota (a non-right-to-work state).

Economists are generally suspicious of published rankings of state business climates. These rankings take crude measures of various state policies and aggregate them in an arbitrary way. Bearing in mind its limitations, in Section VI, I consider a well-known ranking of state business climates constructed by Fantus Consulting. The ranking is based on 15 characteristics of state policy. To a remarkable degree, the states that rank high on this overall index all have right-to-work laws, whereas states that rank low do not have these laws. This illustrates the close connection between adoption of right-to-work laws and adoption of other probusiness policies.

Section VI considers an extension of the analysis that uses the Fantus ranking instead of right-to-work status to classify state policies. I estimate that large differences in the Fantus ranking at state borders are associated with large differences in manufacturing activity at state borders. My finding that this is true at borders at which right-to-work status changes is to be expected from the earlier results since the Fantus ranking is highly correlated with right-to-work status. But there is also a big effect of the Fantus variable at borders at which right-to-work status does not change. The results of this preliminary analysis suggest that other policies besides right-to-work status are playing an important role in accounting for the differences in manufacturing activity at state borders.

Section VI also considers a second extension that looks at the effects of state policies on the size distribution of manufacturing establishments. Probusiness policies can be expected to have a disproportionate impact on large factories. Policies that weaken unions are more relevant to large establishments since they are more likely to be unionized. Low taxes on capital are more relevant to large establishments since they are more likely to be capital-intensive. The results are consistent with this hypothesis. The fraction of all employment that is in large manufacturing establishments increases abruptly when one crosses the border from an antibusiness state to a probusiness state.

E.   Some Relevant Literature

The method of this paper is in the spirit of the recent literature that uses data on identical twins to help resolve hard identification problems (e.g., Ashenfelter and Krueger 1994). There is some precedent in applying these ideas to a geographical context. Isserman and Rephann (1995) study the effects of the Appalachian Regional Commission. They match each county in Appalachia with a *twin* county outside of Appalachia with similar demographic and economic characteristics. The twin counties are viewed as a control group in the empirical analysis. Some authors have previously looked explicitly at state borders. Fox (1986) finds evidence that differences in sales tax rates between neighboring states affect retail sales in border counties. Card and Krueger (1994) consider the New Jersey–Pennsylvania border area to examine the effects of an increase in the minimum wage.

The rest of the paper is organized as follows. Section III is a brief theoretical section that makes a few points about what can happen at state borders. Section IV explains how I handle the geographic nature of the data. Section V is the main section of the paper. It examines what happens to manufacturing activity at the border between probusiness and antibusiness states. Section VI considers two extensions of the analysis. Section VII presents a conclusion.

III.   Theoretical Background

Before looking at the data, I find it useful to start with a theoretical model that lays out what can happen at state borders when adjacent states pursue different policies. This section presents a simple model and makes several points that will play a role in the later discussion. For example, this section discusses what an estimate of a policy's effect near the border can say about the policy's effect away from the border.

The economy is a line segment. Locations are indexed by $y \in [-1, 1]$. There are two political jurisdictions, or states, and $y = 0$ is the boundary. The locations with $y \leq 0$ are in a state called the South. The locations with $y > 0$ are in a state called the North. The South pursues a probusiness policy, and the North pursues an antibusiness policy.

At each location, there is a set of manufacturing entrepreneurs. Assume for now that the entrepreneurs are initially uniformly spread out through the economy. An entrepreneur initially located at a point y chooses whether to set up a factory at his or her initial location y or to set up no plant at all. As explained below, some entrepreneurs may have a third option of building a plant at an alternative location. Let q denote the productivity of a manufacturing entrepreneur. This equals the amount of the final good that is produced if a manufacturing agent of productivity q sets up a plant and employs a worker. Assume that q is uniformly distributed on the unit interval and that the distribution of q is independent of location.

Workers are perfectly mobile and homogeneous. The competitive wage w is constant across locations.

If a manufacturing entrepreneur sets up a factory in a location in the South, the entrepreneur's profit equals his or her productivity q less the competitive wage w paid to the single employee less any moving costs incurred. (Moving costs are described below.) If a manufacturing entrepreneur sets up in the North, an additional cost c is incurred. This cost arises because the North pursues the antibusiness policy. The cost c has a variety of interpretations. It can represent the cost of unions that emerge in the North because of pro-union policies. Alternatively, the cost can arise because of stringent regulations or high taxes in the North.

As mentioned above, some entrepreneurs have the option of moving to an alternative location. With probability p, an entrepreneur initially located at location $y > 0$ in the North has some alternative location $y' < 0$ in the South. Given that an entrepreneur has an alternative location, assume that this location y' is drawn from a uniform distribution over the set of locations $[-1, 0]$ in the South. Finally, assume that the cost of moving from y to y' is $t \cdot (y - y')$, that is, t dollars per unit of distance moved.

This simple formulation captures two intuitive ideas. One is that the farther one moves from his or her initial location, the higher the cost. The other is that an entrepreneur may not have the option of moving to the border point $y' = 0$ in the South to minimize moving costs. The initial location at y may have some specific geographic features that the entrepreneur needs, for example, access to a river or availability of a crucial raw material. The border point $y = 0$ may not have these crucial geographic features, but an interior location $y' < 0$ in the South may have them.

Let $M(y)$ denote the measure of manufacturing employment at location y. Since each factory hires one worker, $M(y)$ equals the measure of entrepreneurs initially at y who set up plants plus any entrepreneurs who move to y to set up a plant. It is straightforward to calculate $M(y)$, and its shape is illustrated in figure 2a. There exists a critical distance $\hat{y}$, defined by $t\hat{y} \equiv c$, such that the cost of moving this distance exactly equals the cost c of the antibusiness policy. Entrepreneurs at locations $y > \hat{y}$ in the North are so far from the border that it would never be worth moving to the South. The measure of manufacturing employment here (denote this m°) equals the measure of entrepreneurs initially there with a productivity level q above $w + c$. The analogous case of $y < -\hat{y}$ is so far in the interior of the South that no entrepreneur would move there. The measure of employment here, m', is the measure of entrepreneurs with productivity above w. Note that m' is higher than m° since the productivity threshold of w on the probusiness side of the border is lower than the productivity threshold of $w + c$ on the antibusiness side.

Now consider $y \in (0, \hat{y})$. Manufacturing entrepreneurs in this region may be lucky enough to obtain locations in the South that are worth moving to, that is, locations at which $t \cdot (y - y') < c$. The lower y is, the closer the initial location is to the border and the higher the probability is that the entrepreneur draws a southern location worth moving to. This accounts for why manufacturing employment $M(y)$ is lower, the lower y is. Right at the border at which the policy changes, there is a discontinuous increase in manufacturing employment as one crosses into the South. As one lowers y further and moves farther south, manufacturing employment $M(y)$ decreases. This follows because as one moves farther away from the border in the South, the pool of entrepreneurs who are willing to pay the moving cost to get there shrinks.

Think of the status quo as a case in which the policies are the same in both states. In particular, suppose that initially both states pursue the same antibusiness policy. In this case, employment equals m° at all locations. This is illustrated by the dotted line in figure 2a. Now consider what happens if the South adopts the probusiness policy. In this particular figure, the effect of the policy is very small at locations away from the border since m' is not much bigger than m°. However, the policy change has a big effect at the border, driven by the entrepreneurs initially located just north of the border, who make a small move to the area just south of the border. This example shows that finding a big effect at the border by no means implies that a policy has a big effect far from the border. The effect of a policy may fizzle out to virtually nothing when one moves away from the border.

But it is also possible for the effect of the policy *not* to fizzle out as one moves away from the border, as can be seen in the following

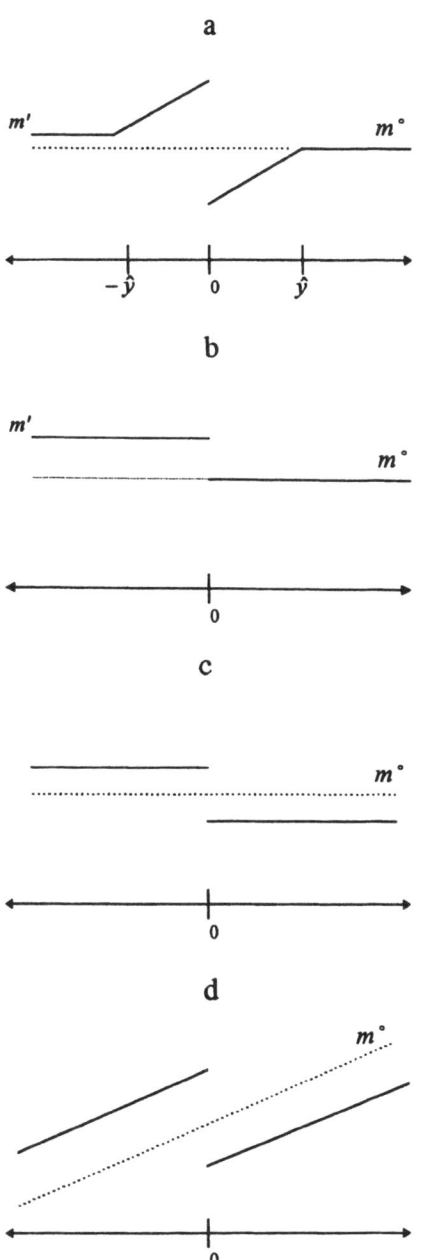

FIG. 2.—*a*, Effect at border fizzles out; *b*, *t* = ∞; *c*, *t* = 0; *d*, trend in manufacturing endowment and *t* = 0.

two examples. Suppose first that $t = \infty$, so that moving costs are infinite. This example is illustrated in figure 2b. Without the policy, all locations have employment of m°. If the probusiness policy is adopted in the South, employment in the South increases to m' because the productivity threshold decreases from $w + c$ to w. Employment in the North remains fixed because moving costs are too high for entrepreneurs to move.

In the second example, $t = 0$, so that moving costs are zero. This is illustrated in figure 2c. Assume also that c is close to zero. In the status quo, where the South does not adopt the policy, employment is m° everywhere. If the South adopts the policy, employment decreases in the North and increases in the South by virtually the same amount. The policy has virtually no effect on aggregate manufacturing employment since the cost of the policy is negligible. Even though the cost of the policy is negligible, any entrepreneur who has an opportunity to move to the South does so because the moving cost is zero.

Figures 2b and 2c illustrate that it is not possible to draw welfare conclusions from this border analysis. The two examples look exactly alike. Manufacturing employment is flat in the South, falls discontinuously at the border, and is flat in the North. However, these two examples are very different in terms of the welfare effects of the policy. In the case of figure 2b, the adoption of the probusiness policy by the South creates wealth in the South and has no effect in the North. Total employment and total welfare increase. In the case of figure 2c, adoption of the policy has a negligible effect on aggregate employment and welfare, but it does affect the distribution of employment.

Suppose that one were interested in determining the effect of the policy at locations far from the border. On the basis of the discussion so far, one might want to look at what happens to manufacturing employment as one moves away from the border. If, as in figure 2a, manufacturing employment in the South drops off quickly away from the border, one might think that the effects of the policy away from the border are not large. The final example illustrates that one should be careful about drawing such a conclusion.

Drop the assumption that the initial manufacturing endowments are uniformly distributed across the economy. Assume instead that the initial endowments are such that if policies were the same in the North and the South, the North would have a higher share of manufacturing activity. This is illustrated in figure 2d. The dotted line illustrates manufacturing employment in the status quo when the North and the South pursue the same antibusiness policy. In this case, manufacturing employment continuously increases as one moves in the direction of the North.

Suppose that the South adopts the probusiness policy. (One reason it might adopt a different policy from the North is that its manufacturing endowment is different.) Suppose that $t = 0$ as in figure 2c. The effect of the probusiness policy will look something like the solid line in figure 2d. The policy has a large effect on manufacturing activity at locations far from the border. However, the pattern near the border looks the same as in figure 2a, where the effects far from the border are small. So, one has to be careful not to confuse figure 2a with figure 2d. In principle, it might be possible to distinguish figure 2a from figure 2d by looking for the kinks $\hat{y}$ and $-\hat{y}$ in figure 2a. However, this would certainly be a tricky business, and I do not try to do it here.

In the empirical analysis, I shall look at what happens to manufacturing employment as a share of total employment. To tie the empirical work to the model, consider an extension of the model to allow for the existence of *service* entrepreneurs who are similar to the manufacturing entrepreneurs already described, with one difference: service entrepreneurs do not pay the cost c of the antibusiness policy in the North. The motivation for why state policies might have different effects for manufacturing and services is discussed in Section II*D*. Under the assumption that service entrepreneurs do not pay c, the differences in state policies will not affect the distribution of service employment. Suppose that I look at manufacturing's share of total employment (i.e., manufacturing plus services) and plot this as a function of distance from the border. Manufacturing's share as a function of distance from the border will be similar in shape to the plots in figures 2a–2d.

On the basis of the discussion in this section, I can draw several conclusions. First, if the policy makes a difference for manufacturing activity (i.e., if $c > 0$) but not for service activity, then there will be a discontinuous jump in manufacturing's share of total employment when one crosses the border into the probusiness state. Second, it is difficult to determine the effect of the policy far away from the border on the basis of what one sees close to the border. What I can say is that an estimate of the effect at the border places an upper bound on the effect far from the border. Third, it is difficult to draw welfare conclusions. Even if there is a large change in manufacturing activity at the border, the welfare effects of the policy might be small.

IV. The Treatment of the Geographic Data

This section describes the treatment of the geographic data. I start with a few definitions. States that currently have right- to-work laws (see fig. 1) are *probusiness* states, and those that do not are *antibusi-*

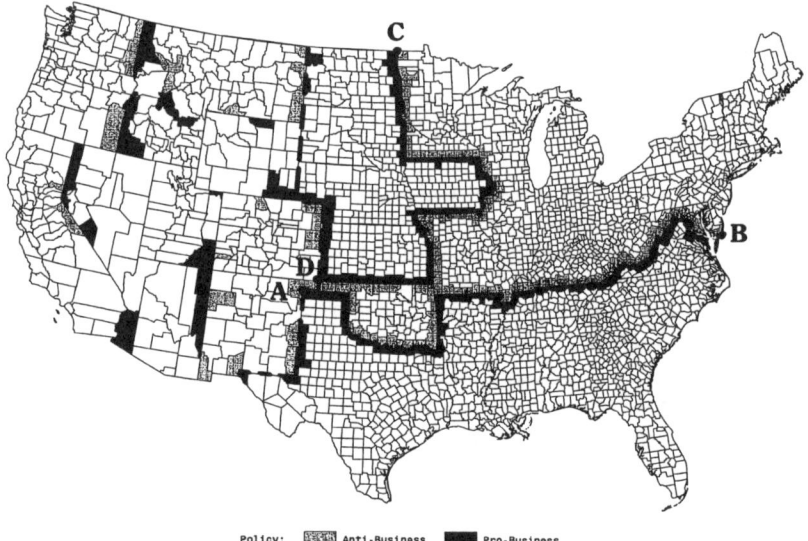

Policy: Anti-Business   Pro-Business

FIG. 3.—Counties within 25 miles of the policy change border

ness states. The *policy change border* is the set of state borders that separate probusiness states from antibusiness states.

The county is the geographic unit for this analysis. The county offers the finest level of detail for which comprehensive Census Bureau data are available. Figure 3 depicts the boundary lines of the 3,078 counties of the 48 contiguous states.[4]

I obtained the longitude and latitude coordinates of the population centroid of each county. Using these geographic coordinates, I calculated the minimum distance from the population centroid of the county to the policy change border and called this variable mindist$_i$. Figure 3 illustrates all the counties that are within 25 miles of the border, that is, the counties for which mindist$_i \leq 25$. Those on the probusiness side are dark gray, and those on the antibusiness side are light gray.

In Figure 3, a dashed line separates the western states (Montana, Wyoming, Colorado, New Mexico, and the states farther west) from the rest of the country. If one looks east of this dashed line, the counties 25 miles from the border nicely trace out the policy change border. These counties form a strip of land on both sides of the

---

[4] My definition of counties follows the Regional Economic Information System Program of the Bureau of Economic Analysis. This definition of counties merges the independent cities of Virginia into the counties that surround them. This makes the county structure in Virginia more like the structure in other states.

border of fairly uniform width. In contrast, the counties in the West that are 25 miles from the border make up what looks to be an odd assortment of counties. The reason for this difference is that counties in the West are so much bigger than counties outside of the West. Many counties in the West are larger than the state of New Jersey.

For most of the results I report in this paper, I exclude the western states from the analysis. My main reason for doing so is the large size of the counties in these states. A key step in my method is to accurately measure the distance of observed manufacturing activity from the policy change border. The coarseness of the geographic information in the western states makes accurate measurements of distance relatively difficult to make. A second reason is that by excluding the West, I avoid the awkward issue of how to classify Idaho, a state that only recently passed its right-to-work law (in 1986). Outside of the West, all states along the policy change border have had the same right-to-work policy since 1958. A third reason is that many of the counties in the western states are sparsely populated. There is likely to be a lot of noise in data from sparsely populated counties.

While the western states are excluded in the main analysis, I have redone the analysis with the western states included, and the estimates do not change much. This is discussed at the end of Section V.

Henceforth, exclude the states west of the dashed line. In the remaining states, the policy change border has two segments. Segment 1 begins at point *A*, at the western end of the Oklahoma-Texas border, and ends at point *B*, where the Maryland-Virginia border meets the Atlantic Ocean. I obtained the geographic coordinates of the line segments that make up this border. I mapped out the border and determined mile markers along the border analogous to something one might find on a highway. For example, the mile marker is zero at point *A*. The mile marker is 716 at the point at which the Oklahoma-Texas border ends and the Oklahoma-Arkansas border begins. The mile marker is 2,386 at the point at which segment 1 ends at the Atlantic Ocean.

Segment 2 of the policy change border begins at point *C*, where the Minnesota–North Dakota border intersects the boundary with Canada. It ends at point *D*, at the western end of the Oklahoma-Kansas border. Segment 2 is 1,891 miles long.

As discussed earlier, I determined the minimum distance, min-$dist_i$, of county *i* to the policy change border. I also kept track of the mile marker along the policy change border at which the minimum distance was attained. The geography of the actual policy change border is somewhat complicated because the border curves and bends. I found it useful to map the geographic information into a space in which the border is a straight line. Define two variables, y_i and x_i, for each county i. Set the absolute value of y_i equal to the distance between the center of the county and the border. Let y_i be positive if the county is in an antibusiness state, and negative otherwise. Formally, if county i is in an antibusiness state, then $y_i = $ mindist$_i$; if county i is in a probusiness state, then $y_i = -$mindist$_i$. The variable x_i is defined to be the point along the policy change border at which the minimum distance to the border is obtained. The point x_i specifies both the segment number and the mile marker of the closest point along the border. This procedure maps the complicated geographic data of the counties into a Cartesian space, where the policy change border is defined by the straight line $y = 0$. The counties with positive y are in the antibusiness region. The counties with negative y are in the probusiness region. The variable x provides a lateral dimension. A change in x at $y = 0$ is a movement along the policy change border.

V. The Effect on Manufacturing Activity

I now address the main question of this paper. Is there an abrupt change in manufacturing activity at the border at which policy changes?

Two measures of manufacturing activity are considered. One measure is manufacturing employment in a county as a percentage of total private nonagricultural employment in the county. The use of this measure is discussed at the end of Section III. I focus on the data from 1992, the most recent available when I began this project, but I also consider other years. I use County Business Patterns (CBP) data as well as data from the *Census of Manufactures*.[5] In the 1992 CBP data, employment of all U.S. manufacturing establishments is 18.2 million, and this represents 19.6 percent of total private employment that year.

The other measure is the growth rate in manufacturing employment over the postwar period from 1947 to 1992. I focus on the postwar period because this is the period during which the South made its great gains in economic development. The year 1947 also happens to be the year of the Taft-Hartley Act, which made it legal for states to enforce right-to-work laws, and states began passing these laws around that time. The growth rate in county i is defined as

---

[5] In a few cases, the employment figure for a particular county is withheld. In these cases, I use CBP data on cell counts of establishments by finely detailed employment size classes to estimate county employment.

LOCATION OF MANUFACTURING   683

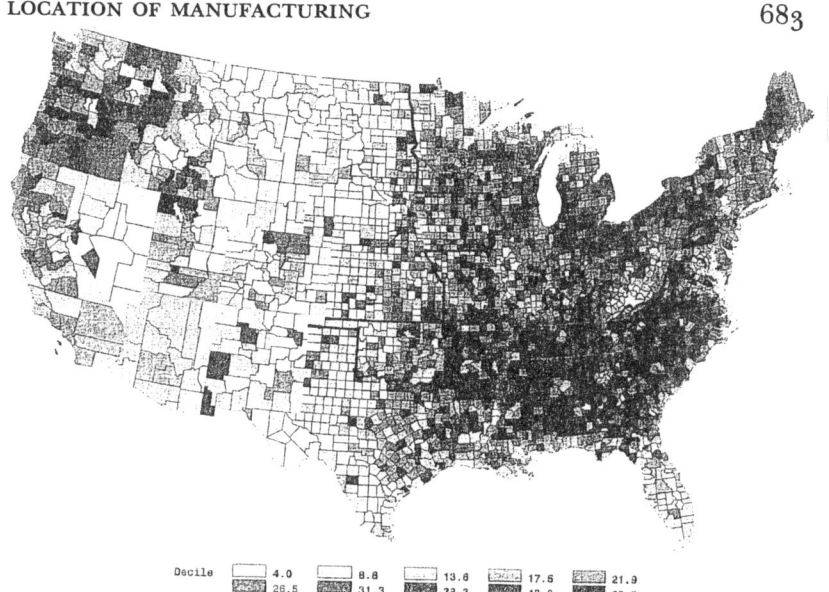

FIG. 4.—Distribution of 1992 manufacturing shares: county deciles

$$\text{growth}_i = 100 \times \frac{\text{emp}_{i,92} - \text{emp}_{i,47}}{.5\text{emp}_{i,47} + .5\text{emp}_{i,92}}, \tag{1}$$

where $\text{emp}_{i,47}$ and $\text{emp}_{i,92}$ are the levels of manufacturing employment. This measure of growth has a maximum value of 200, which is attained if a county had no employment in 1947 and positive employment in 1992. Analogously, the minimum value is -200. I choose this measure of growth because otherwise some counties would have infinite growth rates. Over the period from 1947 to 1992, total U.S. manufacturing employment grew at a rate of 24 percent as defined in equation (1).

Before I begin the statistical analysis, it is useful to look at a picture. Figure 4 illustrates the geographic distribution of the county manufacturing share deciles. The number to the right of the boxes at the bottom is the top share in the decile. For example, the first decile of counties consists of the counties with manufacturing shares between zero and 4.0. The counties in the first decile are indicated in white. The tenth decile consists of counties with shares between 48.0 and 88.8. They are indicated in black. The intermediate deciles are indicated by intermediate shades of gray. The two segments of the policy change border are noted in black, with the exception of the part of the border that involves Arkansas and Tennessee, where I use white to denote state borders.

A striking thing about figure 4 is the extent to which the top-decile counties (the ones marked in black) are concentrated in the South. Large sections of states such as Tennessee and Mississippi are marked in black. Consider segment 1 of the policy change border— the border that coincides with the border of the Confederacy. Begin with the Arkansas-Oklahoma portion of this border and head east along the northern border of Arkansas, Tennessee, and Virginia. It is clear in the figure that the counties on the probusiness side of this portion of the border tend to have higher manufacturing shares than the counties on the antibusiness side. But is the increase in manufacturing activity gradual from one region to the other, or is there an abrupt change at the border? It is hard to say. On one hand, to a striking extent, the shares begin to get high approximately at the border. The dark shades of gray in Arkansas appear to trace out the borders of Arkansas with Oklahoma and Missouri. (Even the heel of the boot in the southeastern corner of Missouri is visible.) On the other hand, at some places, the high manufacturing shares spill over into the antibusiness side of the border, as they do in parts of the Kentucky-Tennessee border. Of course, some noise is to be expected. The advantage of the statistical analysis to follow is that some of this noise can be averaged out.

Now consider segment 2 of the policy change border, the segment separating the Plains states from the industrial states of the Midwest. It is hard to pick up anything here at the border with the naked eye (with the exception, perhaps, of the relatively high frequency of first-decile counties in the Minnesota border area with the Dakotas).

One last comment about figure 4 concerns the white (i.e., first-decile) region in Kentucky and West Virginia near the border with Virginia. One of the main industries in this region is coal mining. There is a discontinuity in nature in terms of mountains and coal veins that coincides with state boundaries. Even if state policies made no difference, one would expect manufacturing shares to decline when one crosses the border into Kentucky and West Virginia, since the employment share in mining goes up. Therefore, in the statistical analysis to follow, I shall, for the most part, exclude the Kentucky-Virginia border and the West Virginia–Virginia border.

The statistical analysis is divided into two parts. The first part looks at some simple cross-tabulations of the data. The second part estimates a simple statistical model.

A. Cross-Tabulations of the Data

I begin by defining groups of counties on the basis of how far the counties are from the border and which side of the border they are on. Let the *antibusiness border layer* be the set of counties with $y_i \in (0, 25]$. In words, these are the counties in antibusiness states (since $y > 0$) that are within 25 miles of the policy change border (since $y_i \leq 25$). These counties are illustrated in figure 3 in light gray. There are 151 counties in this set. Note that this count does not include counties in the western states. The *probusiness border layer* is the set of counties with $y_i \in [-25, 0)$. There are 174 counties in this layer. I also define interior layers three deep on each side of the border. For example, for the antibusiness counties, the *first interior layer* consists of those counties in which the center is 25–50 miles from the border; that is, $y_i \in (25, 50]$. The *second interior layer* consists of those with $y_i \in (50, 75]$. The *third interior layer* consists of those with $y_i \in (75, 100]$. Analogously, there are three interior layers on the probusiness side. The number of counties in each of the six interior layers ranges from a low of 116 counties for the third antibusiness interior layer to a high of 149 counties for the first probusiness interior layer.

For each county, I determined the manufacturing share of total employment in the county and the manufacturing employment growth rate from 1947 to 1992. I then calculated simple unweighted means across counties. Column 1 of table 1 reports the mean cross-county share for the various border layers. Column 2 reports the mean cross-county growth. Columns 3 and 4 report the means when the coal region discussed earlier is excluded (i.e., the Kentucky-Virginia border and the West Virginia–Virginia border).

I begin the discussion by focusing on the border layers. Panel A presents the means for the antibusiness border layer and panel B the means for the probusiness border layer. The table shows that there are substantial differences in the mean shares between the two border layers. With the coal region included, the mean share is 21.0 percent on the antibusiness side and 28.6 percent on the probusiness side. With the coal region excluded, the shares are 22.1 on the antibusiness side and 27.9 on the probusiness side. In the remaining tables of this section, I exclude the coal region. As one might expect, all the estimates of differences at the border are bigger if I leave the coal region in.

Table 1 indicates that there is also a difference in the growth rates at the border. With the coal region included, the mean growth rate in the antibusiness border is 62.4. Just on the other side of the border, the mean growth rate is 100.7. These differences remain, even when the coal region is excluded.

To help assess the significance of the differences in the manufacturing shares and growth rates between the border layers, it is useful to consider how these variables change as one moves across the inte-

TABLE 1

MANUFACTURING EMPLOYMENT SHARES AND GROWTH RATES: CROSS-COUNTY
AVERAGES BY DISTANCE FROM BORDER AND SIDE OF BORDER

	COAL REGION INCLUDED		COAL REGION EXCLUDED	
MILES FROM BORDER	Share of 1992 Total (1)	Growth Rate, 1947–92 (2)	Share of 1992 Total (3)	Growth Rate, 1947–92 (4)
	A. Antibusiness Side of Border			
75–100	25.9	67.5	25.0	68.2
50–75	23.1	62.7	25.0	80.9
25–50	23.2	82.0	24.7	88.8
0–25	21.0	62.4	22.1	77.2
	B. Probusiness Side of Border			
0–25	28.6	100.7	27.9	104.2
25–50	26.7	89.1	25.5	88.3
50–75	26.7	92.9	24.5	90.1
75–100	25.4	91.8	23.1	93.5

rior of the probusiness side and the interior of the antibusiness side.
Suppose that one were to start at the probusiness layer 75–100 miles
from the border (call this pro:75–100). Consider a move into the
adjacent layer 50–75 miles from the border (pro:50–75). The manufacturing share goes from 23.1 at pro:75–100 to 24.5 at pro:50–75,
a change in share of 1.4. (I am using the data that exclude the coal
region here.) The change in share of 1.4 from this movement is
given in the last row of table 2. Analogously, if one moves from pro:
50–75 to pro:25–50, the share increases from 24.5 to 25.5, an in-

TABLE 2

TESTS OF EQUALITY OF MEANS OF ADJACENT LAYERS
(Coal Region Excluded)

	SHARE		GROWTH RATE	
ADJACENT COUNTY LAYERS	Change in Mean (1)	p-Value for Test of Equality (2)	Change in Mean (3)	p-Value for Test of Equality (4)
Anti:50–75 → anti:75–100	.0	.975	12.7	.259
Anti:25–50 → anti:50–75	.3	.880	−7.9	.463
Anti:0–25 → anti:25–50	2.6	.185	11.6	.283
Pro:0–25 → anti:0–25	−5.8	.003	−27.0	.008
Pro:25–50 → pro:0–25	2.4	.217	15.9	.104
Pro:50–75 → pro:25–50	1.0	.620	−1.8	.863
Pro:75–100 → pro:50–75	1.4	.517	−3.4	.742

crease of 1.0. The next step to the border layer pro:0–25 increases the share by 2.4. So far, all the movement has occurred within the probusiness side. In the next step, one crosses the border into anti: 0–25, and the share drops by 5.8. Once one is on the antibusiness side, the share starts going back up again as one crosses adjacent layers, with the changes equaling 2.6, 0.3, and 0.

There is an interesting pattern here: the share goes up gradually with a movement in the direction of the antibusiness layer, except for the big drop at the border. This pattern looks like what happens in figure 2a in the theoretical model and also like figure 2d. While this is intriguing, I want to put off for the moment what to make of this particular pattern. At this point, I am interested in establishing that the difference at the border is big in absolute value compared with the differences found in the interior. That is, the change in the share at the border is *abrupt* compared with the changes in the share within the interior. One way to make this point is to simply observe that the difference in share at the border of 5.8 is more than twice as large in absolute value as the differences of any of the other adjacent pairs. (The next highest is 2.6.) Another way to make the point is to use simple statistical methods. Consider a series of pairwise t-tests of null hypotheses that particular adjacent layers are drawn from the same distribution. Column 2 of table 2 gives the p-values for tests of these null hypotheses. For example, for the pro:75–100 and pro:50–75 adjacent layers, the p-value is .517; that is, under the null hypothesis of equality, with probability .517, the difference in means would be bigger in absolute value than the observed difference. The null hypothesis of equality cannot be rejected in this case. In contrast, the p-value for the adjacent border layers is .003, which is highly significant. What happens at the border sticks out as being very different from what happens between the other adjacent layers.

Similar results are obtained for the growth rate. Table 1 shows that the average growth rate is 104.2 percent for the probusiness border layer and 77.2 percent for the antibusiness border layer. This difference is bigger in absolute value than the differences of all the other adjacent layers. This difference is statistically significant (with a p-value of .008), and none of the other differences in growth rates between adjacent layers is statistically significant.

The results so far suggest that, on average, there is an abrupt increase in manufacturing shares and growth rates when one crosses the border into probusiness states. A natural question to ask is whether this difference is occurring throughout the policy change border. Or is it just happening for a few particular states?

Table 3 is a first step at addressing this issue. It is the same as table 1, except that it provides a breakdown by the two segments of the

TABLE 3

MANUFACTURING EMPLOYMENT SHARES AND GROWTH RATES BY SEGMENT AND
DISTANCE FROM BORDER

| MILES FROM BORDER | 1992 SHARE | | 1947–92 GROWTH | |
	Segment 1: Confederacy Border* (1)	Segment 2: Plains States Border (2)	Segment 1: Confederacy Border* (3)	Segment 2: Plains States Border (4)
	A. Antibusiness Side of Border			
75–100	25.4	24.4	75.9	58.3
50–75	23.0	26.7	97.7	67.5
25–50	28.5	21.1	101.8	76.5
0–25	26.6	17.7	99.1	54.7
	B. Probusiness Side of Border			
0–25	32.3	23.2	104.5	104.0
25–50	30.4	20.3	85.8	91.0
50–75	28.3	19.7	88.8	91.7
75–100	28.5	17.1	97.7	89.1

* Excludes coal region.

policy change border. That is, it distinguishes between counties that
are closest to segment 1 (the border segment that coincides with the
border between the Confederacy and the Union) and counties that
are closest to segment 2 (the border segment separating the Plains
states from the Midwest industrial states).

Consider first what happens to the manufacturing share. Table 3
shows that the big change in the manufacturing share that I found
with the combined data occurs in each of the separate segments.
For both segments, manufacturing shares increase by about 5.5
when one crosses the border into the probusiness side.

Notice that for the manufacturing shares of segment 2, with the
exception of the big drop at the border, there is a strong upward
trend as one moves up the column. This upward trend is not surprising. A movement up the column is a movement away from states
such as North and South Dakota to industrial states such as Minnesota, Wisconsin, and Illinois. If state policies had no effect on business location, I would expect, a priori, to find manufacturing shares
gradually increasing with a movement away from the Great Plains
toward the industrial heartland. If state policies did have an effect
on location, I might expect the share to gradually trend upward,
then fall at the border, and then gradually trend upward again, as
in figure 2d from the theoretical model. So the model in figure 2d
is one explanation for what is happening along segment 2.

As discussed in the theoretical section, there is another reason the share might trend upward with a movement across the border into the antibusiness side. This reason is that the effects of the policy may fizzle out as one moves away from the border. This is what happens in the model illustrated in figure 2a. So, in correspondence with figures 2a and 2d, I have two explanations for the trend found at segment 2: the effects of the policy fizzle out and the underlying geographic suitability for manufacturing gradually increases. The merits of these two explanations are hard to sort out, and I am not going to do so in this paper, except to make the following observation. The policy fizzling out model alone cannot account for the pattern in segment 2. In the policy fizzling out model illustrated in figure 2a, the manufacturing share far into the interior of the probusiness side is at least as high as the share far into the interior of the antibusiness side. But in the data for segment 2, the shares in the interior of the probusiness side of 19.7 and 17.1 are much lower than the shares of 24.4 and 26.7 in the interior of the antibusiness side. This suggests that some underlying trend in nonpolicy geographic factors plays some role in accounting for why the manufacturing share trends upward in segment 2 as one moves toward the antibusiness states.

Now consider what happens with the growth rates for the two segments. In segment 1, the average growth rate of the border layer is 104.5, and this is the highest growth rate over all the different layers. However, this is only negligibly higher than the average growth rate of the antibusiness layer. Hence, there is little difference at the border for segment 1. The story is very different for segment 2. There is a marked difference in average growth between the border layers: 54.7 on the antibusiness side and 104.0 on the probusiness side. But, in addition, the average growth rates of all the layers on the antibusiness side are quite small, whereas the growth rates of all the layers on the probusiness side are quite big. Something fundamental seems to be changing at the border here.

Table 4 takes a further step at examining the extent to which the effects found on the border as a whole are true for individual portions of the border. In this table, the policy change border is broken down into pairings of individual probusiness states with individual antibusiness states. Texas and Oklahoma are the first pairing, Arkansas and Oklahoma are the second pairing, and so forth. There are 17 pairs of individual states.[6] For each pair of bordering states, I calculated the mean share and growth for the counties in the border

---

[6] For the purposes of this table, the District of Columbia is combined with Maryland.

TABLE 4

MANUFACTURING EMPLOYMENT SHARES AND GROWTH RATES BY INDIVIDUAL BORDERS

Border States		1992 Share		Growth Rate, 1947–92	
Probusiness	Antibusiness	Probusiness (1)	Antibusiness (2)	Probusiness (3)	Antibusiness (4)
Texas	Oklahoma	17.3	16.1	29	54
Arkansas	Oklahoma	43.5	27.6	132	144
Arkansas	Missouri	40.7	30.1	158	125
Tennessee	Missouri	47.8	39.3	100	78
Tennessee	Kentucky	48.4	38.7	142	122
Virginia	Kentucky	17.7	3.4	143	-55
Virginia	West Virginia	31.7	20.1	59	5
Virginia	Maryland	16.3	8.5	89	84
North Dakota	Minnesota	16.2	6.3	137	20
South Dakota	Minnesota	16.2	11.1	138	27
Iowa	Minnesota	28.5	25.1	130	85
Iowa	Wisconsin	29.9	30.2	109	103
Iowa	Illinois	33.6	23.1	73	13
Iowa	Missouri	25.2	16.7	121	122
Nebraska	Missouri	13.8	10.0	69	167
Kansas	Missouri	21.1	22.6	78	96
Kansas	Oklahoma	19.5	11.2	80	-12

layers (the counties 25 miles from the border). Recall that over the entire border, the average share on the probusiness side is 28.6 and the average share on the antibusiness side is 21.0. Columns 1 and 2 of table 4 indicate that the share on the probusiness side is bigger than on the antibusiness side for virtually all the states along the border. There are only two exceptions out of the 17 pairwise comparisons (the numbers are printed in boldface). But in these two exceptions, the difference in shares between the bordering states is essentially zero. This table indicates that to a striking degree, the increase in manufacturing share on the probusiness side can be found throughout the policy change border.

Columns 3 and 4 look at average growth rates for each of the border state pairs. The results here are not quite as impressive as those for shares. Still, the growth rate is lower on the probusiness side in only five out of the 17 cases. The table indicates that the increase in growth on the probusiness side is widespread throughout the policy change border.

B.   A Simple Statistical Model

Table 4 shows that there are big changes in manufacturing shares as one moves *along* the policy change border, in addition to the changes that occur as one moves *across* the policy change border. On one hand, along the Texas-Oklahoma portion of the border, the shares are relatively low on both sides: 17.3 and 16.1. On the other hand, along the Tennessee-Kentucky portion of the border, the shares on both sides are relatively high: 48.4 and 38.7. This is also clearly evident in figure 3. This suggests that it might be useful to consider a statistical model that allows for the expected employment share in a county to vary *along* the border as well as *across* the border. This subsection considers such a model.

Suppose that the observed manufacturing share in county i in 1992 is represented by

$$\text{share}_i = \theta \text{probusinessdum}_i + \alpha(x_i) + \beta(x_i)y_i + \epsilon_i. \qquad (2)$$

The variable probusinessdum$_i$ is a dummy variable that equals one if county i is in a probusiness state and equals zero otherwise. The parameter θ is the effect of the probusiness policy on the manufacturing share. The functions $\alpha(\cdot)$ and $\beta(\cdot)$ are general continuous functions of x that allow manufacturing shares to vary across space in a general way. The variable ϵ_i is a classical measurement error.

To understand equation (2), consider the null hypothesis that state policies do not matter, that is, $\theta = 0$. Under equation (2), the expected share at a point along the border (i.e., $y = 0$) with mile marker x is given by the general function $\alpha(x)$. The expected share at a point away from the border is obtained by adding the trend term $\beta(x)y$ to $\alpha(x)$. Note the dichotomy here. If at $y = 0$ one moves in the x direction, the expected share varies in a general nonlinear way through $\alpha(x)$. If one moves in the y direction, the share varies in a linear way with slope $\beta(x)$. My motivation for this dichotomy is that movements in the y direction will be relatively small in the analysis: at most, 100 miles either way. Hence, a first-order (i.e., linear) approximation may be reasonable here. However, the movements in the x direction will cover a distance of 4,000 miles, so a first-order approximation would not be reasonable.

According to equation (2), the manufacturing share varies in a continuous and fairly general way across space with a discontinuous change of θ when one crosses the border into the probusiness side. My goal here is to estimate θ. To do so, I approximate the function $\alpha(\cdot)$ with a fourth-degree polynomial along border segment 1 and a second, different, fourth-degree polynomial along border segment 2. I do not report my estimates of the parameters of the $\alpha(\cdot)$ function because these parameters are of little interest in themselves. I consider four specifications for the trend function $\beta(\cdot)$. The first specification is no trend; that is, $\beta(x) = 0$ for all x. The second specification is a constant for the entire border; that is, $\beta(x) = \beta_0$ for all x. The third specification is a constant trend $\beta(x) = \beta_1$ for all x along segment 1 and a different constant trend, $\beta(x) = \beta_2$ for all x, along segment 2. The fourth specification is to allow $\beta(x)$ to be a different fourth-degree polynomial for each segment, analogous to what I do for $\alpha(x)$.

Panel A of table 5 presents the ordinary least squares estimates of θ for each of these four specifications. I restrict attention to counties within 100 miles of the border ($y \in [-100, 100]$). In specification 1 with no trend, the estimate of θ is 3.4 with a standard error of 0.9. In specification 2, which allows for a constant trend, the estimate of θ rises to 6.4 with a standard error of 1.6, and the estimate for this constant trend β_0 is 0.03. Given the existence of a positive trend, it is easy to see why the estimate of θ is higher in specification 2 than in specification 1. If there is a positive trend (but I do not allow for it), then my estimate of θ will be biased downward because locations on the probusiness side have low (negative) y's. Specification 3 allows a different constant trend for the two segments of the border. There is a large positive trend for segment 2 ($\beta_2 = 0.08$), the Plains states border. This is consistent with the earlier discussion of what happened in the cross-tabulation in table 3 for this border. Note that the estimated trend for segment 1 (the Confederacy border) is essentially zero. Specification 4 allows for the trend to vary in a gen-

LOCATION OF MANUFACTURING   693

TABLE 5

STATISTICAL MODEL

Parameter	Specification 1: No Trend, $\beta(x) = 0$ (1)	Specification 2: Constant Trend, $\beta(x) = \beta_0$ (2)	Specification 3: Different Constant for Each Segment, $\beta(x) \in \{\beta_1, \beta_2\}$ (3)	Specification 4: Trend $\beta(x)$ a General Function of x (4)
A. County Manufacturing Shares* ($N = 951$)				
θ	3.4 (.9)	6.4 (1.6)	6.5 (1.6)	6.6 (1.6)
β_0	...	.03 (.01)	...	...
β_1	...	...	−.01 (.02)	...
β_2	...	...	.08 (.02)	...
R^2	.306	.310	.330	.350
B. County Growth Rates* ($N = 892$)				
θ	19.1 (5.0)	21.2 (9.4)	21.2 (9.4)	23.1 (9.2)
β_0	...	.02 (.09)	...	...
β_1	...	...	.08 (.10)	...
β_2	...	...	−.04 (.10)	...
R^2	.118	.118	.120	.161

* Excludes coal region.

eral way, and the estimate of θ of 6.6 is approximately the same as in specifications 2 and 3. In conclusion, the results with this statistical model indicate that when one crosses the border into the probusiness side, the average increase in manufacturing share is approximately 6.6. This is an increase of about one-third since the average share is approximately 20 percent. This is similar to the difference found in the cross-tabulation in table 1. This difference has a t-statistic of over four, which has a high degree of statistical significance.

I considered a statistical model of county growth rates of the same form as (2), and the estimates of θ for the growth rates are in panel B of table 5. The estimates of θ are similar across the four specifications. The estimate of θ for specification 4, the most general case, is 23.1; that is, the expected manufacturing employment growth rate increases by 23.1 when one crosses into the probusiness side.

To place some perspective on these estimates of the shift parameter θ, I conducted a simple experiment. I considered a set of counties

TABLE 6

STATISTICAL MODEL: ESTIMATES OF SHIFT PARAMETER θ FOR
SIMULATED BORDERS, COUNTIES 50 MILES ABOVE AND BELOW
SIMULATED BORDER

Location of Simulated Border	1992 Share	1947–92 Growth Rate
$y = 100$	−.0	−20.9
	(2.7)	(15.8)
$y = 75$	1.8	−4.6
	(2.7)	(15.3)
$y = 50$	1.1	6.1
	(2.5)	(14.4)
$y = 0$ (true border)	9.1	39.9
	(2.1)	(13.0)
$y = -50$	−.9	4.4
	(2.2)	(12.9)
$y = -75$	−1.4	2.3
	(2.4)	(14.6)
$y = -100$	−3.3	−15.1
	(2.4)	(14.8)

all drawn from the same side of the policy change border. Within
this set of counties, I made up a simulated border and estimated the
statistical model (2). In order to be able to look at a variety of simulated borders, I estimated the model for counties 50 miles above and
below the border. Table 6 reports the results of this exercise.

The fourth row reports the case in which the simulated border is
$y = 0$. This is the case in which the simulated border coincides with
the actual border. The estimate of θ for manufacturing shares is 9.1
and for growth is 39.9. (I estimated the model under specification
4, where $\beta(x)$ is a general function.) These estimates are different
from the estimates of θ in table 5 because here only counties within
50 miles of the border are included, whereas in table 5, counties up
to 100 miles from the border are included. Nevertheless, the qualita-
tive story is the same. At the actual border, there are big changes in
manufacturing shares and growth rates that are highly statistically
significant.

Now consider the row labeled $y = 50$. For this row, counties with
y between zero and 100 were considered. All these counties are actually on the antibusiness side. But I estimated the statistical model
using $y = 50$ as a simulated border; that is, y's between zero and 50
were treated as though they were probusiness, and y's between 50
and 100 were treated as antibusiness. The estimate for θ is 1.1 for the
case of shares and 6.1 for the case of growth. Both of these figures are
small and not statistically significant. The same can be said for the
estimates of θ for the other simulated borders: the estimates are

LOCATION OF MANUFACTURING   695

TABLE 7

ESTIMATES OF SHIFT PARAMETER θ FOR ALTERNATIVE
SPECIFICATIONS AND YEARS
(Excludes Coal Region)

	Estimate of θ	Observations
Share of 1992 employment	6.6	951
(baseline case)	(1.6)	
Share of population:		
1992	2.5	951
	(.6)	
1987	2.0	951
	(.5)	
1982	1.8	951
	(.6)	
1972	1.2	723
	(.6)	
1963	1.3	917
	(.5)	
1954	.9	901
	(.5)	
1947	.4	895
	(.4)	
Manufacturing employ-		
ment growth:		
1947–92 (baseline)	23.1	892
	(9.2)	
1963–92	13.9	915
	(8.6)	
1982–92	11.1	948
	(6.0)	
Includes western states:		
1992 share	5.7	1,256
	(1.3)	
1947–92 growth	19.6	1,135
	(9.2)	

much smaller than those obtained at the true border, and the estimates are not statistically significant. Table 6 indicates that there is something special about the policy change border.

I conclude this section by discussing what happens when data from other years are considered and when the western states that so far have been excluded are incorporated into the analysis. Table 7 presents estimates for the shift parameter θ for these cases. For all these cases, the $\beta(\cdot)$ function is allowed to take the general form corresponding to specification 4 above. As in table 5, counties within 100 miles of the border are included. The first row of table 7 is the baseline case from table 5 for the effect on the 1992 manufacturing share. The estimate indicates that the average 1992 manufacturing share increases by 6.6 when one crosses the border into the probusiness side.

Data on manufacturing employment at the county level are available from the *Census of Manufactures* for a variety of years. However, I ran into problems collecting county-level data on total employment prior to 1964.[7] So, for this discussion, I look at manufacturing employment as a percentage of county population rather than total employment. Table 7 reports that the average 1992 manufacturing employment as a percentage of population increases by 2.5 when one crosses the border into the probusiness side. When I take into account that the 1992 U.S. population was 2.7 times total employment from the CBP data and that $2.5 \times 2.7 = 6.75$, this estimate of 2.5 percent of the total population is consistent with the previous estimate of 6.6 percent of total employment.

Table 7 reports the estimate of θ for various other census years before 1992. The estimate for 1947 is 0.4. Given the standard error of 0.4, this is not significantly different from zero in a statistical sense. Therefore, as of the beginning of the postwar period, there was not much of a difference at the border. The estimate for 1963 is 1.3, and this is significantly different from zero in a statistical sense. The estimate for 1987 is 2.0. It is interesting that the difference has grown from 2.0 to 2.5 over the period from 1987 to 1992. This suggests that there might be more at work here than the effects of right-to-work laws passed in the 1950s.

Table 7 also includes the results when all the western states are included in the analysis. Recall that I earlier excluded these states because the counties are so large and because Idaho changed its policy status in 1985. Table 7 shows that including these states makes little difference. The estimate of 5.7 on the effect on the manufacturing share is just a little below the estimate of 6.6 obtained when the western states are excluded.

VI. Two Extensions

This section considers two extensions of the analysis. One extension considers an alternative measure of policy. The other extension considers an alternative measure of industrial composition.

A. An Alternative Measure of State Policy

The analysis above uses a crude classification of state policies: a state is probusiness if it has a right-to-work law and antibusiness if it does

[7] The CBP program dates from 1947. However, before 1964, many counties were aggregated into larger reporting units. Data on the labor force by county are available from the *Census of Population*. However, this census reports employment by place of residence rather than place of employment.

LOCATION OF MANUFACTURING   697

not. In future work, it would be useful to extend the analysis to consider alternative measures of state policy. This subsection takes a first step in this direction by considering a well-known business climate ranking as an index of policy.

One can find rankings of state business climates in a variety of places. For this analysis, I choose the ranking constructed by Fantus Consulting in 1975.[8] Though dated, the Fantus index was constructed in a more comprehensive way than more recent alternatives. The ranking is based on 15 aspects of state policy, including labor market policies, workers' compensation policies, unemployment compensation taxes, corporate income taxes, and so forth. Table 8 presents the ranking of the states according to the overall score. At the bottom of this list are Massachusetts, California, and New York. The poor showings for these three states are certainly consistent with the conventional wisdom that these three states pursue policies that are relatively hostile to business.

Column 2 of table 8 reports whether or not the state currently has a right-to-work law. To a remarkable degree, the states that have right-to-work laws all have high Fantus rankings. This occurs even though right-to-work status counts for only one of the 15 criteria used to construct the index, and the 15 categories are equally weighted. This illustrates the point made in the Introduction that states with right-to-work laws tend to pursue other probusiness policies as well.

The previous analysis was limited to those state borders at which right-to-work status changed at the border. Unlike right-to-work status, the Fantus rankings change at all state borders. So here, policy varies at all state borders. To incorporate these additional state borders, I need to start over in the way I handle the geographic data.

This analysis considers the borders of all 48 contiguous states. (The results change very little if I exclude the western states or if I exclude the West Virginia and Kentucky coal region border.) There are 109 state border pairs: Alabama-Georgia, Alabama-Mississippi, and so forth. Let the borders be indexed by $b \in \{1, 2, \ldots, 109\}$. For each border pair b, classify the state that comes first in alphabetical order as state 1 for border b and the other state as state 2 for border b. A particular border is a *right-to-work border* if right-to-work status changes at the border. Otherwise it is a *non-right-to-work border*. There are 35 right-to-work borders and 74 non-right-to-work borders.

Consider a particular county i located in state s_i. I determine the

---

[8] Weinstein and Firestine (1978) present the results of this ranking and discuss how it was constructed.

TABLE 8

1975 FANTUS LEGISLATIVE BUSINESS CLIMATE RANKINGS

State	1975 Fantus Ranking	Does State Have a Right-to-Work Law Now?
Texas	1	yes
Alabama	2	yes
Virginia	3	yes
South Dakota	4	yes
South Carolina	5	yes
North Carolina	6	yes
Florida	7	yes
Arkansas	8	yes
Indiana	9	no (had a law, repealed in 1965)
Utah	10	yes
North Dakota	11	yes
Mississippi	12	yes
Georgia	13	yes
Iowa	14	yes
Tennessee	15	yes
Arizona	16	yes
Nebraska	17	yes
Colorado	18	no
Missouri	19	no
Kansas	20	yes
Oklahoma	21	no
Kentucky	22	no
New Mexico	23	no
Wyoming	24	yes
Idaho	25	yes (passed in 1985)
Louisiana	26	yes (passed in 1976)
Ohio	27	no
New Hampshire	28	no
West Virginia	29	no
Maine	30	no
Montana	31	no
Nevada	32	yes
Rhode Island	33	no
Wisconsin	34	no
Illinois	35	no
Maryland	36	no
New Jersey	37	no
Vermont	38	no
Washington	39	no
Oregon	40	no
Minnesota	41	no
Pennsylvania	42	no
Connecticut	43	no
Delaware	44	no
Michigan	45	no
Massachusetts	46	no
California	47	no
New York	48	no

SOURCE.—Weinstein and Firestine (1978).

LOCATION OF MANUFACTURING 699

TABLE 9

STATISTICAL MODEL FOR ALTERNATIVE POLICY VARIABLE

PARAMETER	JUST RIGHT-TO-WORK BORDERS (1)	JUST NON-RIGHT-TO-WORK BORDERS (2)	ALL BORDERS		
			(3)	(4)	(5)
A. County Manufacturing Shares					
ϕ (Fantus)	.38	.32	.35	$\cdots$	.28
	(.08)	(.09)	(.06)		(.07)
θ (right-to-work)	$\cdots$	$\cdots$	$\cdots$	7.40	3.19
				(1.47)	(1.85)
R^2	.516	.525	.546	.544	.547
Observations	923	1,837	2,760	2,760	2,760
B. County Growth Shares					
ϕ (Fantus)	2.28	1.56	1.96	$\cdots$	1.92
	(.53)	(.53)	(.37)		(.46)
θ (right-to-work)	$\cdots$	$\cdots$	$\cdots$	31.03	1.46
				(9.52)	(11.85)
R^2	.335	.362	.361	.356	.361
Observations	823	1,747	2,570	2,570	2,570

minimum distance, $mindist_i$, between county i and the closest bordering state. Let b_i denote the border that county i is closest to, and let x_i be the mile marker along the border at which the minimum distance is attained. If county i is in state 1 for border b, then let $y_i = mindist_i$. Otherwise, if county i is in state 2, let $y_i = -mindist_i$. In summary, each county i is associated with a border b_i, a point along the border x_i, and a point y_i that determines the distance and direction of county i from border b.

This subsection considers a statistical procedure that is analogous to that used in Section VB. Suppose that the manufacturing share in county i is determined by the following statistical model:

$$share_i = -\phi Fantus_i + \alpha_{b_i}(x_i) + \beta_{b_i}(x_i)y_i + \epsilon_i. \qquad (3)$$

The variable $Fantus_i$ denotes the Fantus ranking of the state that contains county i. A minus sign is included here because the higher $Fantus_i$ is, the lower the ranking. As in Section VB, for each border b, there are functions $\alpha_b(\cdot)$ and $\beta_b(\cdot)$ that allow for the component of $share_i$ that does not depend on policy to vary in a continuous way with x and y. Given the use of shift term $\alpha_{b_i}(x_i) + \beta_{b_i}(x_i)y_i$, the parameter ϕ measures how the average difference in manufacturing share at the border between two states varies with the difference in Fantus ranking between the two states.

Panel A of table 9 reports estimates of model (3) for various subsets of the data.[9] The first estimate is obtained by restricting the analysis to the subset of counties in which the closest border is a right-to-work border. For this subset of the data, the estimate of the Fantus coefficient ϕ is 0.38. The estimate implies that every one unit of difference in Fantus ranking at a state border is associated, on average, with a difference of 0.38 percentage points in the manufacturing share. A large estimate such as this is something that can be completely anticipated from the earlier results. As discussed above, there is a high correlation between the Fantus ranking and the presence of a right-to-work law. In fact, for the 35 right-to-work borders, the side with the right-to-work law has a higher Fantus ranking in all but three cases. (And in these three exceptions, the Fantus ranking is approximately the same on both sides.)[10] For these 35 borders, the Fantus ranking increases by an average of 14 places when one crosses the border into the right-to-work side. Given the estimate above of $\phi = 0.38$, a 14-place differential in Fantus ranking is associated with a $5.32 = 14 \times 0.38$ average difference in the manufacturing share at the border. This is close to the 6.6-percentage-point difference at the right-to-work border estimated in the baseline case in Section V*B*.

The second estimate is obtained by restricting the analysis to the non-right-to-work borders. I have no way of anticipating what the results will be here because the previous analysis did not consider any of these borders. The estimate of ϕ here is 0.32. It is remarkable how close this estimate is to the estimate of 0.38 for the other data subset of right-to-work borders. The key finding of the previous section is that differences in state policies are associated with differences in manufacturing activity at state borders. The estimate of ϕ here corroborates this finding with a completely new set of borders.

The third estimate is obtained by combining both sets of borders. The estimate of ϕ is 0.35, the average of the two estimates from the separate border sets.

The last two regressions in panel A of table 9 add to the statistical model (3) a dummy variable for whether or not the state has a right-to-work law. As in the previous section, let the parameter θ denote the coefficient on the right-to-work dummy. The regression in col-

---

[9] The procedure is analogous to that in Sec. V*B*. Only counties with mindist$_i \leq$ 100 are used in the estimation. For each *b*, a quadratic equation is used to approximate the function $\alpha_b(\cdot)$. (In Sec. V*B*, a quartic is used; in that case, there are two very long borders, whereas here there are 109 relatively short borders.) For each *b*, a constant is used to approximate $\beta_b(\cdot)$.

[10] The three exceptions are Kansas-Missouri, Colorado-Kansas, and Colorado-Wyoming, and the differences in Fantus rankings in these three cases are 1, 2, and 5, respectively.

umn 4 estimates θ under the constraint that the ϕ coefficient on the Fantus ranking is zero. The estimate for θ here is 7.4 with a standard error of about 1.5. This is approximately the same as the baseline estimate of 6.6 for θ in the previous section. The regression in column 5 allows both ϕ and θ to vary. The estimate for θ of 3.2 in this case is still a big number, but it is less than half of its value when ϕ is constrained to be zero. In addition, the standard error on the θ estimate rises to 1.9, which is high relative to the parameter estimate of 3.2. The story is different for the ϕ coefficient on the Fantus variable. The estimate of ϕ here is 0.28, which is 80 percent of the estimate of 0.35 for the case in which θ is constrained to be zero. The estimate of ϕ remains highly statistically significant. The Fantus variable, rather than the right-to-work variable, is the big story here.

Panel B of table 9 reports an analogous set of estimates for the case in which the manufacturing employment growth rate is the left-hand-side variable. The three key results in panel A for the share variable are also true in panel B for the growth variable. First, when I restrict the data set to include only the right-to-work borders, there is a large and significant coefficient on the Fantus variable. Given the high correlation between Fantus ranking and right-to-work status, this result, in essence, replicates the results in Section V concerning what happens to the growth variable at the right-to-work border. Second, when I restrict the data set to include only the non-right-to-work borders, there again is a large and significant coefficient on the Fantus variable. This is an entirely new set of data points, and the result corroborates the results from Section V that state policies matter. Third, when I include both the Fantus variable and the right-to-work variable in the regression, the Fantus variable is the main story.

B. An Alternative Measure of Industrial Composition

The analysis so far has focused on the effects of policy on the sectoral composition of a state's economy, that is, the fraction of employment in manufacturing. This subsection considers the effects of policy on the size distribution of establishments. As discussed in Section II, probusiness policies can be expected to have a disproportionate impact on large establishments. Large establishments are more likely to be unionized, so policies that weaken unions will matter more for them. Large establishments tend to be more capital-intensive, so lower taxes on capital will matter more for them.

Define an establishment with 100 or more employees to be a *large* establishment. In the 1992 CBP data, 44 percent of all employment is concentrated in large establishments. In the manufacturing sector by itself, 70 percent of employment is in large establishments. Outside of manufacturing, 38 percent of employment is in large establishments.

I estimated a statistical model for the share of employment in large establishments that is the analogue of the model above for the share of employment in manufacturing.[11] I used the same specification as in the previous subsection. (The results are essentially the same when I use the specification from Sec. V.) Table 10 reports the results. As in table 9, I consider the right-to-work variable by itself, the Fantus variable by itself, and the two variables together.

Consider first the case of all industries. In the case in which the right-to-work variable is by itself, the estimate of θ is 6.6. The interpretation is that, on average, the percentage of all employment in large establishments increases by 6.6 percentage points when one crosses the border into a right-to-work state. When the Fantus variable is by itself, the Fantus variable gets a large coefficient. When both variables are together, the right-to-work coefficient remains large and the Fantus coefficient falls by one-half. This is the opposite of what happens in table 9, where the right-to-work coefficient shrinks and the Fantus coefficient remains big.

Next consider the case of just manufacturing employment. The fraction of manufacturing employment in large establishments increases, on average, by 16.3 percentage points when one crosses a state border into a right-to-work state. This is a substantial effect.

Finally, consider the case of all industries besides manufacturing. For this case, crossing a state border into a probusiness state has essentially a zero effect on the size distribution of establishments. This is very different from what happens in the manufacturing sector. These results suggest that probusiness policies have a different effect on the manufacturing sector than on other sectors and that the fact that manufacturing establishments are larger than other establishments is not the explanation for this different effect.

VII. Conclusion

This paper starts out with a simple classification scheme: a state is defined as probusiness if it has a right-to-work law. The paper then examines the border areas between probusiness and antibusiness states. The differences in manufacturing activity at the border are surprisingly big. On average, the manufacturing share of total em-

---

[11] I estimated the amount of employment in large and small establishments by using the cell counts reported in the CBP data for the number of establishments in each of the various employment size classes.

TABLE 10

ESTIMATES OF STATISTICAL MODEL: SHARE OF EMPLOYMENT IN LARGE ESTABLISHMENTS

PARAMETER	ALL INDUSTRIES (N = 2,760)			MANUFACTURING (N = 2,728)			OTHER INDUSTRIES (N = 2,760)		
	(1)	(2)	(3)	(4)	(5)	(6)	(7)	(8)	(9)
φ (Fantus)	...	.24	.12	...	.60	.33	...	−.01	.07
		(.07)	(.09)		(.12)	(.15)		(.06)	(.07)
θ (right-to-work)	6.64	...	4.76	16.33	...	11.33	1.55	...	2.65
	(1.69)		(2.13)	(3.10)		(3.89)	(1.56)		(1.96)
R^2	.459	.458	.459	.434	.433	.435	.322	.322	.322

ployment in a county increases by about one-third when one crosses the border into the probusiness side. There is a lot of uncertainty and debate about whether or not state policies make much difference in the geographic distribution of industrial activity. The results of this paper suggest that state policies do matter.

It needs to be emphasized that the effect found here is an *overall* effect of state policy. The analysis does not identify the contribution to the overall effect of any one particular policy, for example, a right-to-work law. The next step is to quantify the roles of particular policies. The preliminary analysis in Section VI is a first step in this direction.

This paper develops a novel procedure for identifying whether policy matters, a procedure that may be applicable to other issues besides industry location. While the procedure is able to circumvent identification problems that have plagued previous work, it must be recognized that the procedure has its own limitations. Differences at state borders are not necessarily due to differences in state policies, since nature can have discontinuities. A good example is the coal veins and mountains that begin at the Kentucky-Virginia border. I excluded this coal region from the analysis, but there may be others I do not know about. And even if differences at the border are due to state policies, it may be policies from long ago that have nothing to do with a state's current policies toward business. For example, because Oklahoma was originally set up as an Indian territory more than 100 years ago, there remains today a sharp increase in the Native American population at the border between Arkansas and Oklahoma. Shifts in demographics at state borders can potentially be associated with shifts in the distribution of economic activities at state borders. These examples suggest the need for caution in ascribing the differences found at the border to differences in state policies toward business. I can take some comfort in the fact that the border considered consists of numerous pairs of adjacent states and is thousands of miles long. Over a long border, there can be some hope that extraneous factors will average out.

References

Ashenfelter, Orley, and Krueger, Alan B. "Estimates of the Economic Returns to Schooling from a New Sample of Twins." *A.E.R.* 84 (December 1994): 1157–73.
Bartik, Timothy J. *Who Benefits from State and Local Economic Development Policies?* Kalamazoo, Mich.: Upjohn Inst. Employment Res., 1991.
Card, David, and Krueger, Alan B. "Minimum Wages and Employment: A Case Study of the Fast-Food Industry in New Jersey and Pennsylvania." *A.E.R.* 84 (September 1994): 772–93.

Cobb, James C. *The Selling of the South: The Southern Crusade for Industrial Development, 1936–1990.* 2d ed. Urbana: Univ. Illinois Press, 1993.

Ellwood, David T., and Fine, Glenn. "The Impact of Right-to-Work Laws on Union Organizing." *J.P.E.* 95 (April 1987): 250–73.

Fox, William F. "Tax Structure and the Location of Economic Activity along State Borders." *Nat. Tax J.* 39 (December 1986): 387–401.

Fuchs, Victor R. *Changes in the Location of Manufacturing in the United States since 1929.* New Haven, Conn.: Yale Univ. Press, 1962.

Gall, Gilbert J. *The Politics of Right to Work: The Labor Federations as Special Interests, 1943–1979.* New York: Greenwood Press, 1988.

Ichniowski, Casey, and Zax, Jeffrey S. "Right-to-Work Laws, Free Riders, and Unionization in the Local Public Sector." *J. Labor Econ.* 9 (July 1991): 255–75.

Isserman, Andrew, and Rephann, Terance. "The Economic Effects of the Appalachian Regional Commission: An Empirical Assessment of 26 Years of Regional Development Planning." *J. American Planning Assoc.* 61 (Summer 1995): 345–64.

Minnesota Planning Division. *Border Cities Study: Border Cities and Interstate Competition for Jobs and Industry.* St. Paul: Minnesota Dept. Energy, Planning and Development, 1983.

Moore, William J., and Newman, Robert J. "The Effects of Right-to-Work Laws: A Review of the Literature." *Indus. and Labor Relations Rev.* 38 (July 1985): 571–85.

Newman, Robert J. "Industry Migration and Growth in the South." *Rev. Econ. and Statis.* 65 (February 1983): 76–86.

Olson, Mancur. *The Rise and Decline of Nations: Economic Growth, Stagflation, and Social Rigidities.* New Haven, Conn.: Yale Univ. Press, 1982.

Plaut, Thomas R., and Pluta, Joseph E. "Business Climate, Taxes and Expenditures, and State Industrial Growth in the United States." *Southern Econ. J.* 50 (July 1983): 99–119.

Wasylenko, Michael. "Empirical Evidence on Interregional Business Location Decisions and the Role of Fiscal Incentives in Economic Development." In *Industry Location and Public Policy,* edited by Henry W. Herzog, Jr. and Alan M. Schlottmann. Knoxville: Univ. Tennessee Press, 1991.

Weinstein, Bernard L., and Firestine, Robert E. *Regional Growth and Decline in the United States: The Rise of the Sunbelt and the Decline of the Northeast.* New York: Praeger, 1978.

Wheat, Leonard F. *Regional Growth and Industrial Location: An Empirical Viewpoint.* Lexington, Mass.: Lexington Books, 1973.

[6]

CAN LABOR REGULATION HINDER ECONOMIC PERFORMANCE? EVIDENCE FROM INDIA*

Timothy Besley and Robin Burgess

This paper investigates whether the industrial relations climate in Indian states has affected the pattern of manufacturing growth in the period 1958–1992. We show that states which amended the Industrial Disputes Act in a pro-worker direction experienced lowered output, employment, investment, and productivity in registered or formal manufacturing. In contrast, output in unregistered or informal manufacturing increased. Regulating in a pro-worker direction was also associated with increases in urban poverty. This suggests that attempts to redress the balance of power between capital and labor can end up hurting the poor.

I. Introduction

One of the key challenges of development economics is to identify policies that harm or hinder growth, along with an assessment of their effectiveness in poverty reduction. Traditional views of the growth process put development of manufacturing at center stage in the structural change accompanying economic development.[1] A casual look at the performance of some of the more successful Asian economies after 1960 adds credence to this view. For example, between 1960 and 1995 manufacturing as a share of GDP grew from 9 percent to 24 percent of GDP in Indonesia, 8 percent to 26 percent in Malaysia, and 12.5 percent to 28 percent in Thailand.[2] All of these countries had strong overall growth performances and saw significant falls in absolute poverty.

In contrast, the Indian economy did not experience a significant expansion of manufacturing as a share of national income. Manufacturing output constituted 13 percent of GDP in 1960 (ahead of the countries listed above) but grew to only 18 percent

* We are grateful to two anonymous referees, Daron Acemoglu, Roli Asthana, Abhijit Banerjee, Richard Blundell, Lawrence Katz, Stephen Nickell, Rohini Pande, Christopher Pissarides, Andrew Scott, Andrei Shleifer, Michael Smart, Christopher Udry, and a number of seminar and conference participants for useful comments and suggestions. Berta Esteve-Volart, Shira Klien, Silvia Pezzini, Marit Rehavi, Pataporn Sukontamarn, and Kamakshya Trivedi provided excellent research assistance. The first draft of the paper was written while Robin Burgess was visiting the Massachusetts Institute of Technology which he wishes to thank for support and encouragement. We thank STICERD for financial support.
    1. See, for example, Kaldor [1967] for an early forceful statement of this view.
    2. Figures on manufacturing shares come from various issues of the World Development Indicators, World Bank, Washington, DC.

The Quarterly Journal of Economics, February 2004

of GDP by 1995. India's overall growth over this period was also relatively modest, and it did not enjoy declines in absolute poverty on a scale witnessed elsewhere in Asia. While this pattern reflects a complex array of phenomena, a key issue is whether specific policy choices can be shown to have played a role.

This paper studies the role of labor market regulation in explaining manufacturing performance in Indian states between 1958 and 1992. Such regulation is frequently cited in explanations of India's poor growth performance over this period.[3] The charge is that granting excessive bargaining power to organized labor blunted investment incentives and gave India a generally unfavorable business climate. Our data on labor regulation come from looking at state amendments to the Industrial Disputes Act of 1947. While the act was passed at the central level, state governments were given the right to amend it under the Indian Constitution. The emphasis on central planning in India meant that state governments have had limited influence on industrial policy outside the area of industrial relations. We read the text of each amendment (113 in all) and classified each as pro-worker, pro-employer, or neutral. This gave a sense of whether workers or employers benefited or whether the legislation had no appreciable impact on either group. Regulation applies to a specific sector—formal manufacturing—smaller firms in informal manufacturing are not covered.

Between 1958 and 1992 registered manufacturing output per capita grew by 3.3 percent per annum in India as a whole. This, however, masks significant variations across states. For example, West Bengal, which had the highest level of registered manufacturing output per capita at the beginning of the period, had fallen to seventh in 1992—an average decline of 1.5 percent per annum. West Bengal also had the largest body of pro-worker labor regulation over the period. Its performance contrasts with Andhra Pradesh which grew at nearly 6 percent per year over the same period but which enacted pro-employer labor regulation.

We develop an econometric analysis of whether regulation can account for the cross-state pattern of manufacturing performance over time. Our results show that pro-worker labor regulation resulted in lower output, employment, investment, and productivity in the formal manufacturing sector. Output in the

---

3. See, for example, Stern [2001] and Sachs, Varshney, and Bajpai [1999].

informal sector increased. We also find that pro-worker labor regulation is associated with increases in urban poverty.

The paper illuminates long-standing debates about the role of the state in promoting or hindering economic development. While there is now an abundance of cross-country evidence on determinants of growth, relatively little of this identifies robust relationships with policy regimes (see Barro [1997]). Papers by Hall and Jones [1999] and Acemoglu, Johnson, and Robinson [2001] do suggest that the quality of government institutions matters for economic performance. Looking at policies directly, however, is notoriously difficult given that the details of government intervention differ across countries. Djankov, La Porta, Lopez-de-Silanes, and Shleifer [2002] looks at regulations governing the starting of businesses in a cross section of 85 countries. They find that countries with higher regulation of entry have less impressive performance across an array of social, political, and economic indicators.[4] They find, in particular that greater regulation expands the size of the unofficial economy. They argue that this is in line with a public choice view of regulation as being put in place by officials or insiders intent on extracting rents (see, for example, Stigler [1971], De Soto [1989], and Shleifer and Vishny [1998]).

Botero, Djankov, La Porta, Lopez-de-Silanes, and Shleifer [2003] code labor regulations in 85 countries, finding that heavier regulation of labor is associated with a larger unofficial economy, lower labor force participation, and higher unemployment. Labor regulations are often cited as a determinant of economic performance in OECD countries (see Freeman [1988], Blanchard [2003], and Nickell and Layard [2000]). Higher unemployment in Europe vis-à-vis North America, for example, is often attributed to more "rigid" labor institutions in the former [Nickell 1997]. For European countries, Nickell and Layard [2000] argue that labor-market institutions such as unions and social security systems are important drivers of economic performance with strict labor market regulations, employment protection and minimum wages playing a lesser role. Limited institutional change and the difficulty of controlling for other policies and conditions, however, hinders identification. A number of studies interact labor institutions with observable shocks [Blanchard and Wolfers 2000] or

---

4. India is close to average in this dimension—it is ranked as having less entry regulation than Indonesia and Japan.

technological change [Card, Kramarz, and Lemieux 1999] to explore dynamic effects.

Here, we utilize both time and cross-section variation in labor regulation. The relatively long time period (35 years) and the fact that so much of the policy environment is common to the Indian states makes it an ideal testing ground for the effects of regulation on economic performance and welfare. It adds to a growing body of subnational evidence that labor regulation affects economic performance. For example, Holmes [1998] uses comparisons across U. S. state borders to show that states which enacted pro-business right-to-work laws saw increases in manufacturing activity. Bertrand and Kramarz [2002] use time and regional variation in zoning board approvals to look at how these entry regulations affected employment growth in the French retail industry. Evidence from a variety of studies on Latin America also suggest the importance of labor regulation (see the collection of studies in Heckman and Pages [2003]).

The remainder of the paper is organized as follows. In Section II we examine how economic performance has varied across different states, trace the evolution of labor market regulation in India, detail how we capture the direction of regulatory change, and set out theoretical predictions on the impact of regulatory change on manufacturing performance. Section III contains the empirical analysis of the effect of labor regulation on manufacturing performance. Section IV turns to the welfare consequences of regulation in terms of poverty reduction, and Section V concludes.

II. BACKGROUND

Table I contains the descriptive statistics for the main variables that we use in our analysis. Manufacturing is comprised of two subsectors—an unregistered (informal) sector of small firms and a registered (formal) sector of larger firms.[5] During the period of our data, the latter makes up about 9 percent of state output, and the former 5 percent. Firms in the registered sector are covered by the Industrial Disputes Act and are included in the Annual Survey of Industries. This provides information on output, employment, wages, investment, and productivity at the

---

5. Specifically, firms are required to register if either (i) they have more than ten employees and electric power or (ii) they have more than twenty employees and do not use electric power.

TABLE I
DESCRIPTIVE STATISTICS: 1958–1992

	Mean	Standard deviation
Labor regulation	−0.148	0.925
Workdays lost to strikes per worker	4.350	11.90
Workdays lost to lockouts per worker	1.628	6.470
Log registered manufacturing output per capita	4.252	0.796
Log unregistered manufacturing output per capita	3.900	0.513
Log registered manufacturing employment	12.44	1.056
Log registered manufacturing fixed capital per capita	0.709	0.846
Log registered manufacturing value added per employee	−11.72	0.497
Urban poverty head count (percent)	43.14	12.76
Rural poverty head count (percent)	50.79	14.08
Log develop expenditure per capita	4.368	0.824
Log installed electricity capacity per capita	6.677	1.214
Log state population	10.31	0.727
Congress majority	12.95	7.767
Hard left majority	0.377	1.711
Janata majority	0.616	1.440
Regional majority	1.284	4.070

The data are for the sixteen main states for the period 1958–1992. Haryana split from the Punjab in 1965, and, after this date we include Haryana as a separate observation. We therefore have a total of 552 possible observations with deviations accounted for by missing data. See Appendix 1 for details on the construction and sources of the variables.

state level. Firms in the unregistered sector are not covered by labor regulations and are surveyed periodically in National Sample Surveys. Figure I shows how registered manufacturing output varies across states. Some states—Andhra Pradesh, Gujarat, Karnataka, Tamil Nadu, and Maharashtra—show striking growth, while states like Assam, Jammu, and Kashmir, and West Bengal stagnate (albeit from very different base levels). These patterns are similar if we look at employment.

A great deal of industrial regulation in India has been central. The centerpiece of the planning regime was the Industries (Regulation and Development) Act of 1951 which states that "it is expedient in the public interest that the Union should take under its control the industries in First Schedule" (this lists all the key manufacturing industries at that date). There have been no formal amendments to this act at the state level (see Malik [1997]). We therefore have a situation where industries in different states of India are subject to a common set of industrial policies except in the area of industrial relations. Entry regulation, via licensing

96   *QUARTERLY JOURNAL OF ECONOMICS*

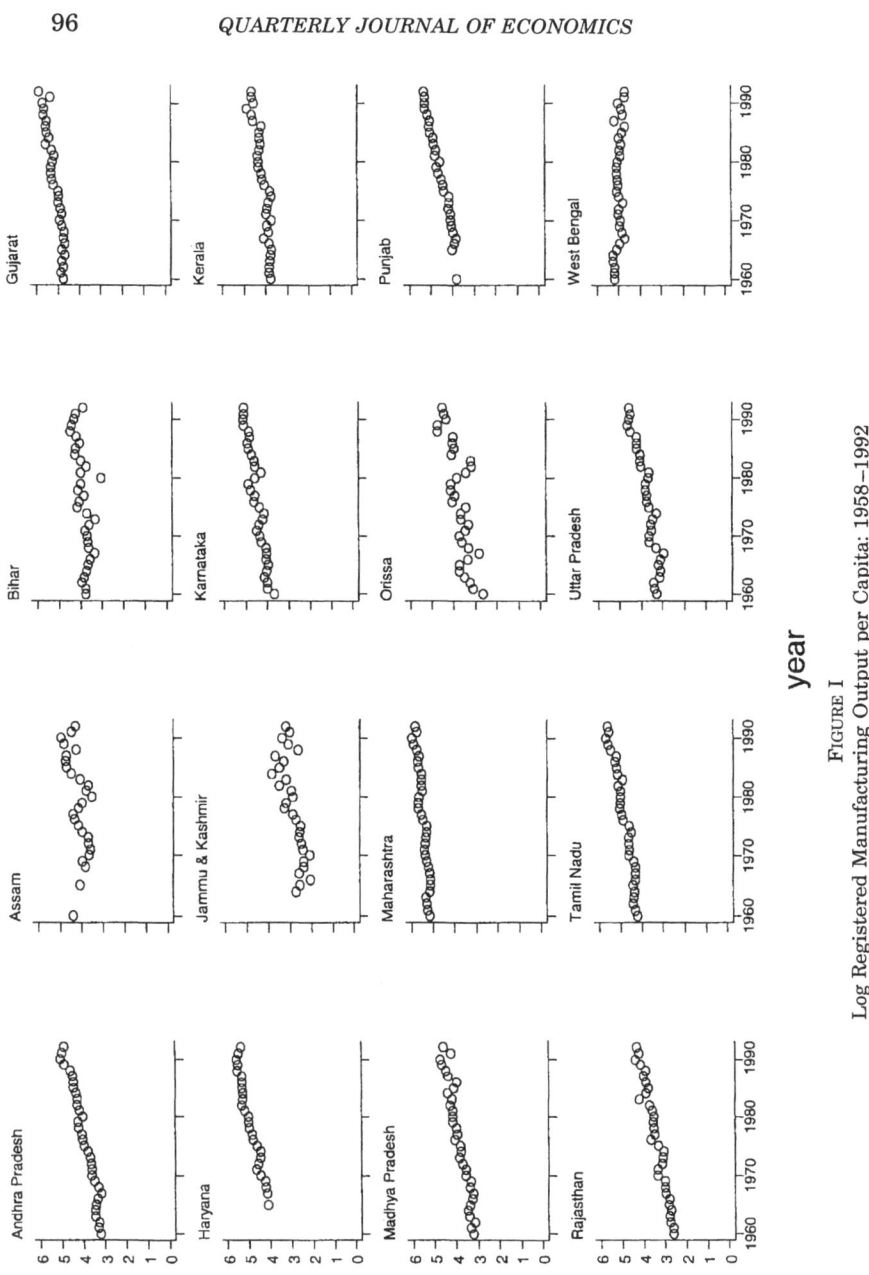

year

FIGURE I
Log Registered Manufacturing Output per Capita: 1958–1992

log registered manufacturing output per capita

and other instruments, for example, is completely controlled by central government.

There has been much concern about the impact of industrial licensing and the use of tariff and nontariff barriers. It is often suggested that this has led Indian manufacturing to perform poorly relative to other countries (see Singh [1964], Bhagwati and Desai [1970], and Bhagwati and Srinivasan [1975])—in particular, relative to countries in East Asia which experienced rapid manufacturing growth [World Bank 1993; Bhagwati 1998]. But it is not possible to relate its impact to the patterns of economic development found in Figure I.

Increasing attention is being paid to the spatial pattern of industrial development in India. A recent survey of about one thousand manufacturing establishments drawn from ten Indian states by Dollar, Iarossi, and Mengitsae [2001] suggests that productivity is 44 percent lower in states judged by managers to have poor business climates. Labor regulation is often singled out as an important element of business climate. Dollar, Iarossi, and Mengistae [2001] found that managers would be willing to lay off 16–17 percent of their workforce if there was greater labor market flexibility and that this measure of the cost of labor regulation had a significant negative impact on firm level productivity.

II.A. Labor Regulation

India is a federal democracy and under the Indian Constitution of 1949 industrial relations is a concurrent subject. This implies that central and state governments have joint jurisdiction over labor regulation legislation. The key piece of central legislation is the Industrial Disputes Act of 1947 which sets out the conciliation, arbitration, and adjudication procedures to be followed in the case of an industrial dispute. The Act was designed to offer workers in the organized sector some protection against exploitation by employers. The Act is comprised of seven chapters and forty sections, specifying the powers of government, courts and tribunals, unions and workers, and the exact procedures that have to be followed in resolving industrial disputes.[6] It has been extensively amended by state governments during the post-Independence

---

6. The seven chapters cover (I) definitions; (II) authorities under this Act; (III) reference of disputes to Boards, Courts, or Tribunals; (IV) procedures, powers, and duties of authorities; (V) strikes and lockouts, layoff and retrenchment, unfair labor practices; (VI) penalties; and (VII) miscellaneous (see Malik [1997]).

period. It is these amendments that we use to study the impact of labor market regulation on manufacturing performance and poverty.

We code legislation based on our reading of all state level amendments to the Industrial Disputes Act of 1947 from Malik [1997]. There were 113 such amendments since the Act was passed. Thus, although all states have the same starting point, they diverged from one another over time. Each amendment is coded as being either neutral, pro-worker, or pro-employer. While this method of classification required a number of judgment calls, we found surprisingly few cases of uncertainty.[7] For the purposes of quantitative analysis, we coded each pro-worker amendment as a one, each neutral amendment as a zero, and each pro-employer amendment as a minus one.

It is useful to give a couple of examples of this procedure. A sample pro-employer reform is from Andhra Pradesh in 1987. Our synopsis is:

> If in the opinion of the state government it is necessary or expedient for securing the public safety or the maintenance of public order or services or supplies essential to the life of the community or for maintaining employment or industrial peace in the industrial establishment it may issue an order which (i) requires employers and workers to observe the terms and conditions of an order and (ii) prohibits strikes and lockouts in connection with any industrial dispute.

This amendment gets a code of minus one in our data. A sample pro-worker reform is from West Bengal in 1980 where our synopsis is:

> The limit of 45 days for workers receiving 50% of their wages upon being laid off (if they worked for more than a year) is removed.

This gets coded as one in our data. Having obtained the direction of amendments in any given year, we cumulated the scores over time to give a quantitative picture of how the regulatory environment evolved over time. This is our basic regulatory measure used below.[8]

---

7. In each case, we based this on two independent assessments. Summaries of all amendments and their coding are available at http://econ.lse.ac.uk/staff/rburgess/wp.
8. In years in which there were multiple amendments, we use an indicator of the general direction of change. So, for example, if there were four pro-worker amendments in a given state and year, we would only code this as plus one rather than plus four. Coding in this manner gives us a total of nineteen changes in our period (see Figure II). In Appendix 2 we describe the individual state level amendments that lie behind each of these changes. These take a variety of forms covering limits on the ability to strike, changing the rules relating to layoff,

This method classifies states as either "treatment" or "control" states. The latter are states that do not experience any amendment activity in a pro-worker or pro-employer direction over the 1958–1992 period. There are six of these: Assam, Bihar, Haryana, Jammu and Kashmir, Punjab, and Uttar Pradesh. Among those that have passed amendments, our method classifies six states Andhra Pradesh, Karnataka, Kerala, Madhya Pradesh, Rajasthan and Tamil Nadu as "pro-employer." This leaves four "pro-worker" states: Gujarat, Maharastra, Orissa, and West Bengal. Figure II graphs the history of regulatory change across states over the period in question. For the most part, changes are monotonic although some states do move in different directions. We have both pro-worker and pro-employer states among the fast growers.

Pro-worker states on average had high per capita registered manufacturing output in 1960 relative to control states and pro-employer states. However, by 1990 there is no statistically significant difference between pro-worker and pro-employer states. Moreover, registered manufacturing output in the pro-employer states has overtaken that in the control states. This pattern is less pronounced when looking at overall output per capita. Other state characteristics such as total taxes per capita, development expenditure per capita, installed electricity per capita, and literacy show no significant difference between treatment and control states.

Before considering the impact of labor regulation on economic outcomes, we show that the regulation measure is related to the industrial relations climate in a state as measured by workdays lost to strikes and lockouts in the registered manufacturing sector.[9] This may be a key signal to potential investors. Table II shows that labor regulation is strongly positively correlated with workdays lost to strikes and lockouts per worker.[10]

---

retrenchment, and closure and giving workers or employers greater power in the procedures for resolving industrial disputes.

9. Strikes and lockouts are both important sources of lost working time. There are twice as many workdays lost to strikes than to lockouts. There is pronounced variation across states and time—West Bengal, for example, loses 25 times as many workdays to strikes per capita relative to Assam.

10. We run panel data regressions of the form,

$$y_{st} = \alpha_s + \beta_t + \mu r_{st-1} + \varepsilon_{st},$$

where y_{st} is workdays lost to strikes and lockouts per worker in the registered manufacturing sector, r_{st} is the regulatory measure, α_s is a state fixed effect, and β_t is a year effect. We cluster our standard errors by state to deal with concerns about serial correlation.

100   *QUARTERLY JOURNAL OF ECONOMICS*

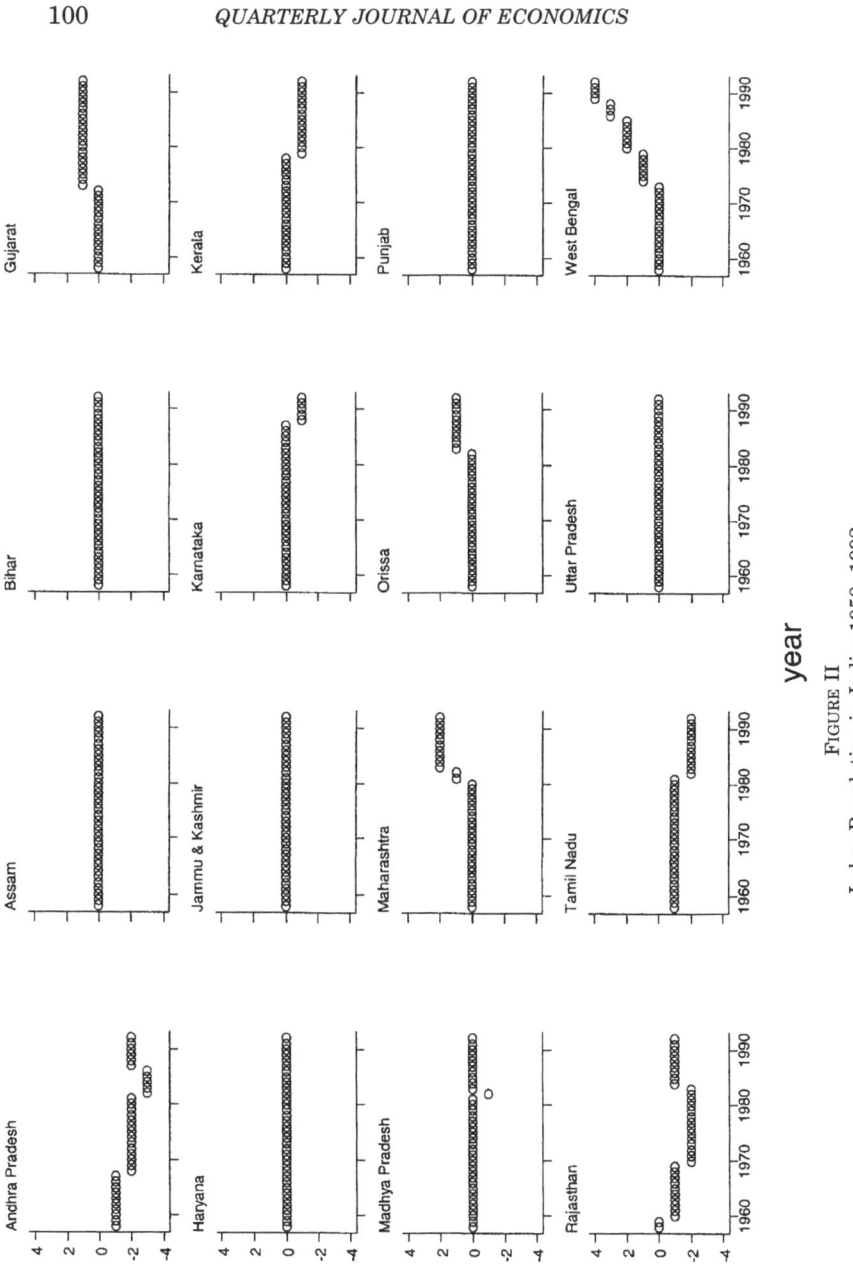

FIGURE II
Labor Regulation in India: 1958–1992

TABLE II
LABOR REGULATION AND INDUSTRIAL DISPUTES IN INDIA: 1958–1992

	(1)	(2)	(3)	(4)
	Workdays lost to strikes per worker	Workdays lost to strikes per worker	Workdays lost to lockouts per worker	Workdays lost to lockouts per worker
Method	OLS	OLS	OLS	OLS
Labor regulation	2.564**	1.732*	2.108**	0.965***
$[t-1]$	(2.55)	(1.87)	(2.32)	(3.57)
State effects	YES	YES	YES	YES
Year effects	YES	YES	YES	YES
State time trends	NO	YES	NO	YES
Adjusted R^2	0.08	0.07	0.14	0.15
Observations	547	547	514	514

Absolute t-statistics calculated using robust standard errors clustered at the state level are reported in parentheses, * significant at 10 percent, ** significant at 5 percent, *** significant at 1 percent. Data on workdays lost to strikes and lockouts are expressed on an annual basis, and we divide this by number of workers employed to get a per-worker measure. State amendments to the Industrial Disputes Act are coded 1 = pro-worker, 0 = neutral, −1 = pro-employer and then cumulated over the period to generate the labor regulation measure. The data are for the sixteen main states for the period 1958–1992. Haryana split from the Punjab in 1965, and, after this date, we include Haryana as a separate observation. We therefore have a total of 552 possible observations with deviations accounted for by missing data. See Appendix 1 for details on the construction and sources of the variables.

Columns (2) and (4) show this finding to be robust to including state-specific time trends. Thus, regulating in a pro-worker direction appears to be associated with greater disruption of production. This validates our measure as a representation of the industrial relations climate.

II.B. *Theoretical Considerations*

The defining difference between registered and unregistered firms is scale, with labor regulations affecting only registered firms. It is reasonable to suppose that all firms operate in a common set of factor markets whose prices they treat as parametric. For simplicity, suppose that firms all produce a common manufactured good. There are then two main routes via which labor regulation affects economic performance—a *relative price effect* and an *expropriation effect*. While intellectually distinct, they have similar implications for what we expect to find in the data.

The relative price effect is relevant if the effect of labor regulation is to raise the (fixed or marginal) cost of employing laborers. Labor regulation will typically create adjustment costs in hiring and firing labor and in making adjustments in the

102   QUARTERLY JOURNAL OF ECONOMICS

organization of production. We would expect firms in the registered sector to substitute away from labor (reducing employment)
toward other labor saving inputs (including capital if labor and
capital are substitutes). Regulation also lowers the firm's optimal
output level since it raises the marginal cost of production. We
would also expect regulation to affect the decision to register. In
states where regulations raise labor costs, firms will (other things
being equal) resist becoming registered by remaining small.
Thus, we would expect to find fewer registered firms along with a
higher level of production in the unregistered sector in states that
legislate in a pro-worker direction.

The expropriation effect refers to the dynamic implications of
labor regulation. By increasing the bargaining power of workers,
labor regulation can increase the importance of holdup problems
in investment.[11] Suppose that firms which invest in anticipation
of earning a particular return may face a problem if workers can
expropriate part of that return once the capital is sunk. This will
serve to discourage investment, even if labor and capital are
substitutes. This has similar predictions in terms of output, employment, and the decision to register as the relative price effect.
However, it strengthens the presumption that capital stocks will
also be lower. This effect shows why pro-worker labor regulation
is similar to insecure property rights for owners of capital as their
sunk investments are subject to worker expropriation.

Whether workers benefit from labor regulation is not clear-
cut. If labor costs rise because firms put in more worker-friendly
work practices, then it will depend on how these are paid for in
terms of lower wages or lower employment. There may also be
differential effects on insiders and outsiders. If there is a holdup
problem, then workers should realize that if they have too much
bargaining power, they will reduce investment to their own detriment (especially if labor and capital are complements). Whether
wages rise or fall is also not clear-cut.

III. METHOD AND RESULTS

Our econometric analysis is based on panel data regressions
of the form,

---

11. Grout [1984] developed one of the first models along these lines. Caballero
and Hammour [1998] draw out macroeconomic implications.

$$y_{st} = \alpha_s + \beta_t + \mu r_{st-1} + \xi x_{st} + \varepsilon_{st},$$

where y_{st} is a (logged) outcome variable in state s at time t, r_{st} is the regulatory measure (which we lag one period to capture the gap between enactment and implementation),[12] x_{st} are other exogenous variables, α_s is a state fixed effect, and β_t is a year fixed effect. We cluster our standard errors by state to deal with concerns with serial correlation [Bertrand, Duflo, and Mullainathan [2004].[13]

The state fixed effect captures state-specific factors such as culture and geography. The year effects capture common shocks such as central government amendments to the Industrial Disputes Act which took place in 1976 and 1982 (see Fallon [1987] and Fallon and Lucas [1993]) as well as other centrally implemented policies.

III.A. Basic Results

Table III looks at measures of output per capita and their link to labor regulation. The left-hand-side variable in column (1) is total state output per capita which does not appear to be correlated with the labor regulation regime. This is reasonable since labor regulation is sector-specific and registered manufacturing represents a fairly small part of the Indian economy. Above all, this suggests that labor regulation is not simply a proxy for generally poor government policy. Column (2) looks at agricultural output. A negative effect here would also suggest that our labor regulation is really proxying for other policies. In fact, there is a weak positive effect suggesting that discouraging manufacturing may encourage agricultural production. In contrast, nonagricultural output—which includes manufacturing—is negatively correlated with labor regulation (column (3)). Column (4) shows that there is no effect on output in the construction sector, another sector where labor regulation is not applied.[14]

Turning to manufacturing, column (5) shows that the point estimate becomes larger and more significant when focusing on

12. Our results are robust to imposing different lags. Our reading of the literature suggests that amendments come into force roughly one year after they are passed.
13. We conducted some stationarity tests for panel data of the kind suggested by Madalla and Wu [1999]. These suggested no difficulty in assuming stationarity.
14. Over our period construction accounts for 5 percent of total state output and 10 percent of nonagricultural output.

TABLE III

LABOR REGULATION AND OUTPUT IN INDIA: 1958–1992

	(1)	(2)	(3)	(4)	(5)	(6)	(7)
	Log state output per capita	Log state agricultural output per capita	Log state nonagricultural output per capita	Log state construction output per capita	Log total manufacturing output per capita	Log registered manufacturing output per capita	Log unregistered manufacturing output per capita
Method	OLS	OLS	OLS	OLS	OLS	OLS	OLS
Labor regulation [$t - 1$]	-0.002	0.019*	-0.034*	-0.019	-0.073**	-0.186***	0.086**
	(0.14)	(1.81)	(1.69)	(0.29)	(2.05)	(2.90)	(2.46)
State effects	YES	YES	YES	YES	YES	YES	YES
Year effects	YES	YES	YES	YES	YES	YES	YES
Adjusted R^2	0.93	0.84	0.95	0.76	0.93	0.93	0.75
Observations	509	509	509	509	509	508	509

Absolute t-statistics calculated using robust standard errors clustered at the state level are reported in parentheses, * significant at 10 percent, ** significant at 5 percent, *** significant at 1 percent. Total, nonagricultural, agricultural, total manufacturing, registered manufacturing, and unregistered manufacturing output figures are all components of state domestic product and are expressed in log real per capita terms. State amendments to the Industrial Disputes Act are coded 1 = pro-worker, 0 = neutral, −1 = pro-employer and then cumulated over the period to generate the labor regulation measure. The data are for the sixteen main states for the period 1958–1992. Haryana split from the Punjab in 1965, and, after this date, we include Haryana as a separate observation. We therefore have a total of 552 possible observations with deviations accounted for by missing data. See Appendix 1 for details on the construction and sources of the variables.

total manufacturing output. Breaking this into registered and unregistered sectors as in columns (6) and (7) of Table III provides further confirmation that the effect at work is specific to registered manufacturing. There is now a larger and more significant negative effect on registered manufacturing in column (6). Moreover, for unregistered manufacturing in column (7), we get the opposite sign—high levels of pro-worker labor regulation have a positive impact on output in this sector.[15] Thus, labor regulation seems to deter formal registration, encouraging firms to remain in the informal sector.

These results make sense. Labor regulation is affecting only that sector where we should expect to see an effect. Since labor regulations are the main regulatory instrument in registered manufacturing under state control, this finding is compelling. Our next tasks are to check the robustness of these findings to a number of other specifications and to expand the set of registered manufacturing performance measures beyond just output.

Table IV assesses the robustness of the finding that registered manufacturing responds negatively to pro-worker labor regulation. Column (1) replicates the basic result from Table III. In column (2) we add a number of controls. These are the log of real development expenditure per capita which includes spending on health, education, infrastructure, and administration. This helps crudely to measure differences in human capital and infrastructure due to government activities. We also include the log of installed electrical capacity per capita, measured in kilowatts, to capture the capacity of states to generate electricity. It may also be a reasonable proxy for the general state of infrastructure and is positively associated with registered manufacturing output. Finally, the log of the state population is also included as a crude measure of changing labor market conditions within a state. Column (2) shows that the coefficient on labor regulation remains negative and significant when we include these controls.

While these results help to deal with the concern that labor regulation is a proxy for other state level policies, it is possible that some aspects of the policy environment are difficult to measure. As a further robustness check, we therefore add in controls for the political complexion of states on the grounds that policies toward the registered manufacturing sector are likely to be cor-

---

15. The idea that firms migrate to the informal sector to escape regulation is widespread: see, for example, Schneider and Enste [2000].

TABLE IV
LABOR REGULATION AND MANUFACTURING PERFORMANCE IN INDIA: 1958–1992

	(1)	(2)	(3)	(4)	(5)	(6)
	Log registered manufacturing output per capita	Log registered manufacturing output per capita	Log registered manufacturing output per capita	Log registered manufacturing output per capita	Log registered manufacturing output per capita	Log unregistered manufacturing output per capita
Method	OLS	OLS	OLS	OLS [state time trends]	OLS [no West Bengal]	OLS [no West Bengal]
Labor regulation [$t-1$]	-0.186*** (2.90)	-0.185*** (3.65)	-0.104*** (2.67)	0.0002 (0.01)	-0.105*** (2.59)	0.077** (2.25)
Log development expenditure per capita		0.240* (1.88)	0.184 (1.55)	0.241** (2.28)	0.208 (1.69)*	0.492*** (3.39)
Log installed electricity capacity per capita		0.089 (1.47)	0.082 (1.51)	0.023 (0.69)	0.053 (1.21)	-0.070 (1.11)
Log state population		0.720 (0.75)	0.310 (0.26)	-1.419 (0.61)	0.629 (0.53)	-3.724*** (3.18)
Congress majority			-0.0009 (0.09)	0.020** (2.08)	-0.002 (0.27)	0.017 (0.95)

continued overleaf

Hard left majority		$-0.050{*}{*}{*}$	-0.007	$-0.073{*}$	$0.154{*}$
		(2.97)	(0.77)	(1.72)	(1.84)
Janata majority		0.008	-0.020	0.004	$0.090{*}{*}$
		(0.34)	(0.60)	(0.15)	(2.20)
Regional majority		0.006	0.026	0.003	0.002
		(0.70)	(1.11)	(0.32)	(0.18)
State effects	YES	YES	YES	YES	YES
Year effects	YES	YES	YES	YES	YES
State time trends	NO	NO	YES	NO	YES
Adjusted R^2	0.93	0.94	0.95	0.94	0.80
Observations	508	491	491	459	459

Absolute t-statistics calculated using robust standard errors clustered at the state level are reported in parentheses, * significant at 10 percent, ** significant at 5 percent, *** significant at 1 percent. Registered and unregistered manufacturing output are in log real per capita terms. State amendments to the Industrial Disputes Act are coded 1 = pro-worker, 0 = neutral, −1 = pro-employer and then cumulated over the period to generate the labor regulation measure. Log of installed electrical capacity is measured in kilowatts, and log development expenditure is real per capita state spending on social and economic services. Congress, hard left, Janata, and regional majority are counts of the number of years for which these political groupings held a majority of the seats in the state legislatures. The data are for the sixteen main states for the period 1958–1992. Haryana split from the Punjab in 1965, and, after this date, we include Haryana as a separate observation. We therefore have a total of 552 possible observations with deviations accounted for by missing data. See Appendix 1 for details on the construction and sources of the variables.

related with political outcomes. To this end, we assemble a picture of each state's "political history" as measured by the number
of years during our data period that particular political groupings
have held a majority of the seats in the state legislature. The
relevant groupings for this exercise are the Congress party, the
Janata parties, hard left parties, and regional parties. The results
are in column (3). They show that greater hard left control of the
state legislature depresses growth in registered manufacturing.
The coefficient on labor regulation does, however, remain negative and significant, even though it is smaller in absolute size.
The result is consistent with the notion that there are antibusiness policies which hard left governments introduce. Nonetheless, the effect of labor regulation remains.

In column (4) we add state-specific time trends. In this case,
the identification of the effects of labor regulations comes from
whether such law changes lead to deviations from preexisting
state-specific trends. The effect of labor regulation is no longer
apparent. Thus, states with similar patterns of labor regulation
also have similar long-term trends. Labor regulation therefore
appears to be driving differences in these trends. But this does
raise the issue of whether it is possible to separate out effects of
labor regulations per se from impacts due to the climate of labor
relations such as union power and labor/management hostility
which manifest themselves in the trend growth rate. We return to
this issue below.

Column (5) addresses the sensitivity of the results to the
inclusion of West Bengal. This state is an important case for our
analysis since it passed the largest number of pro-worker amendments and has had a declining manufacturing base. However, as
column (5) shows, the results hold up even if we exclude it from
the regression.[16] In column (6) we show that the result on unregistered manufacturing is robust to including our control variables
and excluding West Bengal.

Table V looks at the effect for a variety of other performance
measures in registered manufacturing. We report this for a specification that includes the full set of controls. In columns (1) and
(2) we look at two measures of manufacturing employment. The
first, reported in column (1), is the log of total employees taken
from the Annual Survey of Industries. This covers both produc-

---

16. We carried out further checks by excluding each of the states, and in all
cases the coefficient on labor regulation remained negative and significant.

tion workers and those in supervisory or managerial positions. We find that states with more pro-worker legislation have lower levels of employment in registered manufacturing. This parallels our findings for output.[17] Column (2) examines daily employment defined as total worker attendances over a year divided by the total number of days worked by the factory. This measure, which captures the intensity of labor usage, is based on returns submitted by registered manufacturing firms and comes from a separate data source, the Indian Labor Yearbook.[18] Here again we find a negative and significant impact of labor regulation. Comparing columns (1) and (2) suggests that there is greater adjustment in the intensity of labor usage as opposed to in aggregate employment levels which may be connected to constraints on firing workers and closing down firms [Fallon and Lucas 1993].

Column (3) of Table V considers how earnings per worker are affected by labor regulation. The measure is obtained by dividing the total factory wage bill (which includes all monetary payments to workers) by the number of workers. We find that there is no significant effect of regulation on payments to workers.[19] This lines up with the fact that theory does not give any clear-cut predictions for wages. The bottom line is that workers do not appear to be gaining from pro-worker amendments.

In column (4) of Table V we examine fixed capital formation. Labor regulations that increase worker bargaining power are likely to reduce capital formation. The coefficient on labor regulation is consistent with this story. Column (5) shows that the number of registered manufacturing factories is negatively related to pro-worker labor regulation.[20] Column (6) looks at firm efficiency in the form of value added per employee. Value added in firms is lower in which there is more labor regulation. This is

---

17. It is also consistent with Fallon [1987] and Fallon and Lucas [1993] who found that strengthening job security regulations via the 1976 and 1982 central government amendments to the Industrial Disputes Act was associated with a reduction in labor demand in firms covered by the regulation but not in small firms uncovered by job security regulations.

18. As they are based on submissions, these figures are likely to be less reliable than those based on the Annual Survey of Industries. They nonetheless serve as a useful robustness check.

19. In an earlier version of the paper, we found that is also true for a number of different measures of earnings drawn from both the Annual Survey of Industries and the Indian Labor Yearbook (see Besley and Burgess [2002]).

20. This variable captures the net flow of firms in the registered manufacturing sector. It shows that the number of firms is significantly lower in states with more pro-worker regulation, suggesting that pro-worker regulation is either acting as a deterrent to new firms or to firms dying at a faster rate.

TABLE V

LABOR REGULATION AND EMPLOYMENT, INVESTMENT, AND PRODUCTIVITY IN REGISTERED MANUFACTURING IN INDIA: 1958–1992

	(1)	(2)	(3)	(4)	(5)	(6)
	Log registered manufacturing employment	Log daily employment in registered manufacturing	Log earnings per worker in registered manufacturing	Log fixed capital per capita	Log number of factories per capita	Log value added per employee
Method	OLS	OLS	OLS	OLS	OLS	OLS
Labor regulation	−0.072*	−0.285***	0.008	−0.120**	−0.234***	−0.127**
$[t-1]$	(1.70)	(3.48)	(0.09)	(2.49)	(3.44)	(2.16)
Log development expenditure per capita	0.076	0.327*	0.207	0.594***	0.229	0.262**
	(0.64)	(1.82)	(1.52)	(2.93)	(1.50)	(2.09)
Log installed electricity capacity per capita	0.073	0.111	0.019	0.232*	0.037	−0.034
	(1.34)	(1.51)	(0.34)	(1.82)	(0.95)	(0.45)
Log state population	−0.099	2.122	1.116	−1.130	1.18	−1.19
	(0.09)	(1.14)	(0.93)	(0.61)	(0.42)	(0.81)
Congress majority	0.008	−0.009	−0.037*	0.008	−0.006	0.009
	(0.61)	(0.39)	(1.66)	(0.43)	(0.36)	(0.73)
Hard left majority	−0.028	−0.124***	0.0004	0.001	−0.044*	0.019
	(1.43)	(3.93)	(0.01)	(0.05)	(1.81)	(0.90)

continued overleaf

Janata	0.050*	−0.024	−0.002	0.001	0.028	−0.003
	(1.67)	(0.59)	(0.04)	(0.04)	(0.66)	(0.10)
Majority						
Regional majority	0.007	0.018	−0.003	0.0002	−0.032	−0.0001
	(0.31)	(0.69)	(0.34)	(0.02)	(1.49)	(0.02)
State effects	YES	YES	YES	YES	YES	YES
Year effects	YES	YES	YES	YES	YES	YES
Adjusted R^2	0.98	0.91	0.75	0.80	0.90	0.64
Observations	516	459	513	515	460	435

Absolute *t*-statistics calculated using robust standard errors clustered at the state level are reported in parentheses, * significant at 10 percent, ** significant at 5 percent, *** significant at 1 percent. Registered manufacturing employment refers to total employment in factories, and daily employment is defined as total worker attendances over a year divided by the total number of days worked by the factory. Earnings per worker is obtained by dividing total annual remuneration by the number of workers. Fixed capital represents the depreciated value of fixed assets owned by the factory on the closing date of the accounting year. The number of factories refers to the number in the registered manufacturing sector in each state where adjustments are made for deregistration and new entrants. Value-added per employee is obtained by deducting the value of total inputs and depreciations from the value of output and dividing this by the number of employees in a factory. State amendments to the Industrial Disputes Act are coded 1 = pro-worker, 0 = neutral, −1 = pro-employer and then cumulated over the period to generate the labor regulation measure. Installed electrical capacity is measured in kilowatts, and development expenditure is real per capita state spending on social and economic services. Congress, hard left, Janata, and regional majority are counts of the number of years for which these political groupings held a majority of the seats in the state legislatures. The data are for the sixteen main states for the period 1958–1992. Haryana split from the Punjab in 1965, and after this date, we include Haryana as a separate observation. We therefore have a total of 552 possible observations with deviations accounted for by missing data. See Appendix 1 for details on the construction and sources of the variables.

consistent with an expropriation effect whereby blunting investment incentives leads to labor regulations being associated with
lower productivity in the registered manufacturing sector.[21]

To gauge the economic significance of these findings we look
at two extreme cases: Andhra Pradesh as a pro-employer state,
and West Bengal as a pro-worker state. The coefficients from the
basic specifications in Tables IV and V imply that without their
pro-employer reforms, Andhra Pradesh would have registered
manufacturing output which was 72 percent of its actual 1990
level and manufacturing employment that was 73 percent of its
1990 level. If West Bengal had not passed any pro-worker amendments, it would have enjoyed a registered manufacturing output
that was 24 percent higher than its 1990 level and employment
that was 23 percent higher.[22] Thus, the implied economic magnitudes are sizable.

Collectively these results paint a consistent picture.[23] Across
the board, our labor regulation measure is correlated with poor
economic performance in the registered manufacturing sector. It
also leads to a larger informal sector.

21. The results in Table V are robust to excluding West Bengal. However, in
common with the output results, they are not robust to including state-specific
time trends.
22. Though inclusion of the full set of political and economic controls does
reduce the magnitudes of these effects, they remain economically important.
23. As a further control for omitted variables, we have collected information
on the efficiency of state high courts in India as measured by annual pendency
rates. The pendency rate is constructed by adding the number of cases pending at
the beginning of the year to cases filed in the year and dividing this by cases
resolved during the year. This measure, which is available only for a shorter time
period, 1971–1996, may be a determinant of the property rights regime in force in
the state. In contrast with our labor regulation measure, it has a significantly
negative impact on log agricultural output per capita (the coefficient is -0.105
with a robust t-statistic, adjusted for clustering on state, of 2.57). It also has
significant and negative association with nonagricultural output as a whole.
Within manufacturing it is negatively correlated with the log of unregistered
manufacturing output per capita (the coefficient is -0.458 with a robust t-statis-
tic, adjusted for clustering on state, of 1.69)—the opposite sign from labor regulation variable (the coefficient is 0.098 with a robust t-statistic, adjusted for
clustering on state, of 2.35). Thus, court inefficiency is correlated with lower
informal sector manufacturing. Unlike labor regulation this efficiency measure is
not significantly negatively correlated with the log of output per capita in registered manufacturing. The picture that emerges therefore is one where court
efficiency adversely affects economic activity in a wide range of sectors, in particular in the large informal sectors where problems of property rights and law
and contract enforcement may be acute. In contrast, labor regulations only negatively affect the sector to which they apply and encourage economic activity in
unregistered manufacturing and agriculture. These results help to increase our
confidence that our amendments measure is picking up the impact of labor
regulation as opposed to other antibusiness policies. The question of how courts
work in India and affect economic performance is an important issue for further
research.

III.B. Endogeneity

A remaining concern is that states with larger vested interests in manufacturing at the beginning of the period may have
experienced greater pressure to pass pro-worker amendments
and may, as a consequence, have experienced slower growth.
Indeed, theoretical arguments along these lines have been developed in the political economy of development literature. For example, Krusell and Rios-Rull [1996] model the idea that political
insiders can see development as a threat to their rents and hence
lobby for protection. In an Indian context, workers would lobby
for stricter labor regulation as a means of extracting a greater
share of the surplus from existing investments even though this
may deter future investment. Thus, the negative correlation between output and performance is consistent with reverse causation. We now develop two ways of addressing this concern
empirically.

As our measure of the extent of vested interests, we take the
average level of union membership (union members divided by
population) before 1977.[24] We first use these data to match states
that experience labor market reforms (pro-worker or pro-employer) with control states based on the level of unionization.[25]
We then regress labor regulation on the difference between registered manufacturing in a "treatment" state and that in its
matched "control" state while also including match dummies in
the regression.

The results are in columns (1)–(3) of Table VI. They confirm
the effects on registered and unregistered manufacturing output
per capita and employment in registered manufacturing per capita that we have found throughout. They add credibility to the
findings since they guard against the concern that there is something in the initial condition, rather than the subsequent policy
experience, which is driving subsequent performance.

An extension of this idea can also yield an instrumental
variable for labor regulation. Looking at Figure II, it is striking
that most of the labor regulation changes take place after 1977.
This is no coincidence. Following Prime Minister Indira Gandhi's
declaration of a state of emergency (suspending democratic insti-

---

24. The data on union membership are patchy. For example there are no
usable data for Jammu and Kashmir. Moreover, there are often gaps in the series.
We choose the pre-1977 average to get a better sense of the level of unionization.
25. See Appendix 1 for details on state matches. We also matched based on
initial registered manufacturing output per capita, obtaining similar results.

TABLE VI
LABOR REGULATION AND INDUSTRIAL PERFORMANCE: DEALING WITH ENDOGENEITY CONCERNS

	(1)	(2)	(3)	(4)	(5)	(6)	(7)
	Log registered manufacturing output difference	Log unregistered manufacturing output difference	Log registered manufacturing employment difference	Log registered manufacturing output	Log unregistered manufacturing output	Log registered man employ	Labor regulation
Method	OLS on matched differences	OLS on matched differences	OLS on matched differences	2SLS	2SLS	2SLS	OLS
Labor regulation difference	-0.132*** (5.50)	0.310*** (8.20)	-0.064** (2.30)				
Labor regulation $[t-1]$				-0.399*** (4.02)	0.117* (1.80)	-0.370*** (3.50)	
Mean unionization *post 1977 dummy							0.095*** (3.52)
Mean nonlandlord *post 1977 dummy							-1.422** (2.48)
Match dummies	YES	YES	YES	NO	NO	NO	NO

continued overleaf

State effects	NO	NO	NO	YES	YES	YES	YES
Year effects	YES	YES	YES	YES	YES	YES	YES
Overidentification test p-value				0.98	0.99	0.78	
F-test instruments(Prob $> F$)							7.46 (0.006)
Adjusted R^2	0.84	0.77	0.96	0.88	0.79	0.90	0.79
Observations	283	283	300	480	480	517	525

Absolute t-statistics calculated using robust standard errors are reported in parentheses. * significant at 10 percent, ** significant at 5 percent, *** significant at 1 percent. For columns (1)–(3) we average the level of union membership (union members divided by population) before 1977 and use these data to match states that experience labor market reforms (pro-worker or pro-employer) with control states based on the level of unionization. We then regress labor regulation on the difference between registered manufacturing in a "treatment" state and that in its matched "control" state while also including match dummies in the regression. Standard errors in columns (4)–(6) are clustered at the state level. The two instruments for our lagged [$t - 1$] labor regulation measure are (i) the pre-1977 unionization measure interacted with a post-1997 dummy and (ii) the proportion of constituent districts of modern states which operated nonlandlord land revenue systems in British India interacted with a post-1977 dummy. The overidentification test we employ is due to Sargan [1958]. The number of observations times the R^2 from the regression of the stage two residuals on the instruments is distributed $\chi^2 (T + 1)$, where T is the number of instruments. State amendments to the Industrial Disputes Act are coded $1 =$ pro-worker, $0 =$ neutral, $-1 =$ pro-employer, and then cumulated over the period to generate the labor regulation measure. Installed electrical capacity is measured in kilowatts and log development expenditure is real per capita state spending on social and economic services. The data are for the sixteen main states for the period 1958–1992. Haryana split from the Punjab in 1965, and after this date we include Haryana as a separate observation. We therefore have a total of 552 possible observations with deviations accounted for by missing data. See Appendix 1 for details on the construction and sources of the variables.

116   *QUARTERLY JOURNAL OF ECONOMICS*

tutions), the political power of her party (Congress) was significantly and permanently diminished.[26] There were a number of switches in political control with Congress losing its majority in half of our states between 1975 and 1978. The most notable example was the Left Front which gained a majority in West Bengal in 1977 and has remained the majority coalition ever since. The 1947 Industrial Disputes Act represented a piece of Congress legislation which was largely kept intact pre-1977 by Congress-dominated state governments. Post-1977 state deviations are likely in part to be a result of changes in political control. And the direction that post-1977 amendments took would depend, in part, on the importance of the initial vested interests (as proxied by union membership). This suggests that the union membership variable interacted with a dummy which equals one after 1977 may pick up the time path of labor regulation.

In addition to union membership, we also use historical patterns of land tenure to develop a further instrument.[27] The main difference is between those areas in India where land revenue was collected through landlords or not. Banerjee and Iyer [2002] show that these measures have an impact on contemporary patterns of development, particularly agricultural productivity and public good provision. Our motivation for using this variable is the possibility that it is correlated with contemporary patterns of political development. In confirmation of this, we find that areas dominated by nonlandlord-based revenue collection have larger concentrations of regional parties today, i.e., those that do not have a large role in other states or in the national legislature. In many cases, these parties were the main competitor to the Congress party and hence benefited politically from the state of emergency. Hence, our instrument interacts the fraction of districts in each state that had nonlandlord based revenue collection systems with a dummy variable which equals one after 1977 to mark the persistent shift in political control after the state of emergency.

---

26. Declaration of a state of emergency was a response to calls for her resignation after she was found guilty of using illegal practices during the prior election campaign. Between 1975, when emergency was declared, and 1978, when fresh elections were called, the share of congress votes in state assemblies dropped from 60 percent to 38 percent.

27. We are grateful to Abhijit Banerjee and Lakshmi Iyer for providing these data. For each modern state, the variable that we use is the mean number of constituent districts in British India that had nonlandlord-based land revenue systems. Its construction is described in detail in Appendix 1.

Column (7) of Table VI confirms that both of our instruments are correlated with labor regulation (F-statistic $=$ 7.46). The union variable is positively correlated with labor regulation while the variable based on the proportion of districts under the non-landlord based agricultural tax system is negatively correlated with labor regulation.[28] In columns (4), (5), and (6), we report two-stage least squares estimates of the effect of labor regulation on output and employment using these two variables as instruments. Our results are robust to this instrumentation. Moreover, the Sargan test of overidentification passes comfortably.[29]

The effects in the instrumental variables case are uniformly larger in absolute size. This suggests that, if anything, biases could be due to high levels of economic performance generating demand for protecting workers.[30] Overall, these results increase our confidence that poor performance in registered manufacturing was a consequence rather than a cause of labor regulations.

III.C. Disaggregated Evidence

The evidence presented so far aggregates all registered manufacturing industries together. But Indian states have quite different manufacturing bases. Hence, there might be a suspicion that patterns of specialization affect the direction of regulation in ways that could bias our results. For example, early industrializing states might specialize in slow growing labor-intensive industries which spawn stronger vested interests, thereby inducing a negative correlation between pro-worker regulations and manufacturing performance.

In response to such concerns, we present results on disaggregated data which look at the impact of labor regulation at the

---

28. As we discussed above, the second of these is explained by the correlation between this variable and regional party development.
29. The results are not robust to including state-specific time trends. Thus, we cannot rule out the possibility that the *trends* in manufacturing output prior to our data period were important in the subsequent pattern of manufacturing development.
30. This is consistent with our efforts to investigate whether changes in labor regulations were timed around deviations in manufacturing output changes from their trend. We constructed a measure of "recessions" classified as periods in which output growth falls below trend for two consecutive years. No clear pattern emerged. Recessions actually accompanied pro-firm regulatory changes in five of our eighteen reforms (Andhra Pradesh in 1968, Karnataka in 1988, Madhya Pradesh in 1982, Rajasthan in 1970, and Tamil Nadu in 1982). By contrast, it accompanied pro-worker changes in only three cases (Maharastra in 1974, Orissa in 1983, and West Bengal in 1974).

three-digit industry level for the period 1980–1997.[31] In line with
the analysis above, we investigate the link between performance
and labor regulation by running panel regressions of the form,

$$y_{ist} = \alpha_{is} + \beta_t + \delta_i t + \mu r_{st-1} + \varepsilon_{ist},$$

where y_{ist} is a (logged) three-digit industry outcome variable,
r_{st-1} is the labor regulation measure measured at the state level
and lagged one period, α_{is} is a state-industry fixed effect, β_t is a
year effect, δ_i is a dummy variable which is equal to one for
industry i, and t is a time trend. We cluster our standard errors
by state-industry grouping to deal with concerns about serial
correlation. Inclusion of the state-industry fixed effect allows us
to control for unobserved, time-invariant factors that affect performance at the state three-digit industry level. Thus, identification is now coming from within state-industry variation. The
inclusion of three-digit industry time trends in the regressions
also helps to control for the possibility that industries experience
different rates of technological change.

Column (1) in Table VII confirms the basic result above
showing that regulating in a pro-worker direction has a significant and negative impact on registered manufacturing output.
Column (2) shows that the results for employment also mirror
those for state level analysis—employment growth within three-
digit industries is lower in states which regulated in a pro-worker
direction. Column (3) confirms our result on fixed capital—investment in fixed capital is lower in pro-worker versus pro-employer
states. Moreover, the magnitude of the coefficients we observe in
columns (1)–(3) of Table VII is similar to those in Tables IV, V,
and VI. Column (4), which looks at the number of registered firms
in a three-digit industry, lines up with the investment effect in
column (3) by suggesting that there is greater entry/lower exit in
states that regulate in a pro-employer direction. Column (5)
shows that regulating in a pro-worker direction is correlated with

31. The data form an unbalanced panel. Our analysis retains state industries
that remain in the panel for at least ten years, and within these industries we
restrict our attention to firms that employ more than a hundred workers to get
around the problem of smaller firms being excluded from the sample to maintain
confidentiality. Using this definition, we have a total of 101 three-digit industries
in our panel with an average of 68 in each state. The results we obtain are robust
to using a balanced panel (i.e., only retaining state three-digit industries that
remain in the panel over the whole 1980–1997 period).

TABLE VII

LABOR REGULATION AND INDUSTRIAL PERFORMANCE IN INDIA: INDUSTRY LEVEL
ANALYSIS 1980–1997

	(1)	(2)	(3)	(4)	(5)
	Log registered manufacturing output	Log registered manufacturing employment	Log registered fixed capital	Log number factories	Log value added per employee
Method	OLS	OLS	OLS	OLS	OLS
Labor regulation	−0.087***	−0.060***	−0.063*	−0.041***	−0.026**
[t − 1]	(3.68)	(3.19)	(1.86)	(2.86)	(2.07)
State *industry effects	YES	YES	YES	YES	YES
Year effects	YES	YES	YES	YES	YES
Industry time trends	YES	YES	YES	YES	YES
Adjusted R^2	0.90	0.90	0.81	0.92	0.74
Observations	21323	21323	20539	21206	21254

Absolute *t*-statistics calculated using robust standard errors clustered at the state-industry level are reported in parentheses, * significant at 10 percent, ** significant at 5 percent, *** significant at 1 percent. The data used in the regressions are a panel data set on three-digit registered manufacturing industries across the sixteen main states of India for the period 1980–1997. The data form an unbalanced panel. Our analysis retains state industries that remain in the panel for at least ten years, and within these industries we restrict our attention to firms that employ more than a hundred workers to get around the problem of smaller firms being excluded from the sample to maintain confidentiality. Using this definition, we have a total of 101 three-digit industries in our panel with an average of 68 in each state. State amendments to the Industrial Disputes Act are coded 1 = pro-worker, 0 = neutral, −1 = pro-employer and then cumulated over the period to generate the labor regulation measure. The regressions include three-digit industry time trends to help control for the possibility that industries experience different rates of technological change. See Appendix 1 for details on the construction and sources of the variables.

lower productivity at the three-digit industry level as measured by value-added per employee.[32]

While available only for a shorter time period, these results are very similar to those found for the aggregate data for the period 1958–1992. They allay any fears that our results are an artefact of patterns of specialization or technological change in registered manufacturing across Indian states.

IV. WELFARE CONSEQUENCES

We turn finally to the effect of labor regulation on poverty. This is important for a number of reasons, not least because it may give a sense of where the burden of the effects identified in the last section have been felt. To assess this, we use poverty data

32. Although we are allowing for industry-specific time trends, the results do not hold up with state-specific trends.

120   QUARTERLY JOURNAL OF ECONOMICS

from Ozler, Datt, and Ravallion [1996]. We focus on urban and rural head counts which measure the percentage of the population below the Indian urban and rural poverty lines. The econometric specification we use is the same as for manufacturing performance.

We expect the direct effect on poverty to depend on the extent to which the earnings of the poor are derived from registered manufacturing. While we have no direct quantitative estimate of this, it is instructive to consider the correlation between poverty rates and different components of state output in India. To do so, we disaggregated state output into agricultural, registered manufacturing, unregistered manufacturing, and "other" (nonagricultural/nonmanufacturing).[33] We find that for urban poverty, the largest coefficient is on registered manufacturing and "other."[34] Agricultural output and unregistered manufacturing are not significantly correlated with urban poverty. For rural poverty, there is a significant negative correlation between unregistered manufacturing and poverty, and no significant correlation with registered manufacturing. These findings square with the fact that registered manufacturing firms are located mainly in urban areas whereas unregistered manufacturing firms are located in both rural and urban areas.

Given this pattern of correlations, our presumption is that pro-worker regulation is positively correlated with poverty in urban areas—with an effect operating through lowered registered manufacturing output and employment. There is no reason to expect a correlation with rural poverty. Table VIII shows that this is indeed the case. In column (1) we see that labor regulation has no effect on overall poverty. This lines up with our result for overall output. Regulating in a pro-worker direction, however, is associated with higher urban poverty (columns (2)). In column (3) we see that, in line with our expectations, there is no significant effect on rural poverty. This is consistent with the majority of registered manufacturing firms being in urban locations. In column (4) we find that the results hold up when we add economic

33. Specifically, we run

$$p_{st} = \alpha_s + \beta_t + \gamma y_{st} + \varepsilon_{st},$$

where y_{st} is a vector of disaggregated income measures and p_{st} is a poverty head count measure.

34. We cannot reject the hypothesis that the coefficients on these two output sources are equal.

controls to our basic specification from column (2). The labor regulation variable continues to exert a significant positive influence on the urban head count. It is interesting to note that Congress control and hard left control are associated with higher levels of urban poverty.

Column (5) adds state-specific time trends. Once again, this wipes out the effect of labor regulation. This underlines the need to exercise caution in attributing the effects observed in columns (2) and (4) to labor regulations as opposed to interactions of underlying differences in the industrial relations climate with regulations.

In column (6) we see that the effects remain when we run the regression only for years when NSS surveys were carried out. This shows that the result in column (6) is not sensitive to interpolating poverty statistics between years. In column (7) we exclude West Bengal from the regression and continue to observe a positive and significant link between pro-worker labor regulation and urban poverty. The coefficient on labor regulation in urban head count regressions remains highly stable across the full range of specifications (barring column (5)) in Table VIII.[35]

The economic significance of these effects can be gauged by examining what urban poverty would have been in 1990 if states had not passed pro-worker or pro-employer amendments using the coefficient from column (2) in Table VIII. Our empirical model predicts that, without their pro-employer reforms, then Andhra Pradesh would have urban poverty that was 112 percent of its 1990 level. Similarly, if West Bengal had not passed any pro-worker amendments, it would have had urban poverty that was 11 percent lower in 1990. This comparison starkly brings out how the direction of regulatory change matters. According to our estimates, there would have been around 640 thousand more urban poor in Andhra Pradesh in 1990 and around 520 thousand fewer

---

35. To check whether the coefficients in Table VIII are consistent with the entire effect on poverty reduction coming through the effect on registered manufacturing output, we regressed urban poverty on registered manufacturing. This yields a coefficient of -3.4. The size of the effect implied in Table III is 0.8 compared with a coefficient in Table VIII of 2.3. However, despite the apparently larger reduced-form effect, these two estimates do lie within the 95 percent confidence interval for the compound effect of labor regulation. Nonetheless, the results are suggestive of the possibility of a direct effect of labor regulation on poverty beyond the effect operating through falls in registered manufacturing output. For example, regulations could make it easier for nonpoor insiders to exclude poor outsiders from access to jobs in the registered sector.

TABLE VIII
LABOR REGULATION AND POVERTY IN INDIA: 1958–1992

	(1)	(2)	(3)	(4)	(5)	(6)	(7)
	Overall head count	Urban head count	Rural head count	Urban head count	Urban head count	Urban head count	Urban head count
Method	OLS	OLS	OLS	OLS	OLS [state time trends]	OLS [survey years only]	OLS [no West Bengal]
Labor regulation [$t - 1$]	−0.008	2.288***	−0.821	2.070**	−0.270	2.251**	1.916**
	(0.01)	(3.31)	(0.48)	(2.52)	(0.30)	(2.52)	(1.99)
Log development expenditure per capita				−3.468	−0.983	−2.900	−4.044
				(0.82)	(0.32)	(0.79)	(0.94)
Log installed electricity capacity per capita				0.242	1.260	1.058	0.875
				(0.28)	(1.60)	(1.02)	(1.27)
Log state population				−5.448	38.74	−3.717	−10.42
				(0.29)	(1.28)	(0.19)	(0.56)
Congress majority				0.418**	0.206	0.464**	0.452**
				(1.98)	(0.63)	(2.36)	(1.99)

continued overleaf

Hard left majority			0.508*	−0.083	0.501	0.306
			(1.76)	(0.21)	(1.46)	(0.39)
Janata majority			0.518	0.819	0.326	0.557
			(1.14)	(1.28)	(0.73)	(1.19)
Regional majority			0.463***	0.439	0.504***	0.487***
			(2.86)	(0.90)	(2.76)	(2.86)
State effects	YES	YES	YES	YES	YES	YES
Year effects	YES	YES	YES	YES	YES	YES
Adjusted R^2	0.83	0.88	0.89	0.91	0.87	0.89
Observations	547	547	518	518	311	485

Absolute *t*-statistics calculated using robust standard errors clustered at the state level are reported in parentheses. * significant at 10 percent, ** significant at 5 percent, *** significant at 1 percent. Poverty head count is the percentage of the population below the official Indian poverty lines which are separately defined for rural and urban areas. In column (4) the rural-urban poverty difference is the difference between the rural and urban head count measures for each state. In column (7) we include data only for years when National Sample Surveys were carried out. State amendments to the Industrial Disputes Act are coded 1 = pro-worker, 0 = neutral, −1 = pro-employer and then cumulated over the period to generate the labor regulation measure. Installed electrical capacity is measured in kilowatts, and development expenditure is real per capita state spending on social and economic services. Congress, hard left, Janata, and regional majority are counts of the number of years for which these political groupings held a majority of the seats in the state legislatures. The data are for the sixteen main states for the period 1958–1992. Haryana split from the Punjab in 1965, and after this date we include Haryana as a separate observation. We therefore have a total of 552 possible observations with deviations accounted for by missing data. See Appendix 1 for details on the construction and sources of the variables.

124   *QUARTERLY JOURNAL OF ECONOMICS*

urban poor in West Bengal if these states had not amended the Industrial Disputes Act.[36]

These welfare results are striking. The battle cry of labor market regulation is often that pro-worker labor market policies redress the unfavorable balance of power between capital and labor, leading to a progressive effect on income distribution. We find no evidence of this here—indeed the distributional effects appear to have worked against the poor.

V. Conclusions

This paper has examined the link between regulation and long-run development. The evidence amassed in the paper points to the direction of labor regulation as a key factor in the pattern of manufacturing development in India. Regulating in a pro-worker direction was associated with lower levels of investment, employment, productivity, and output in registered manufacturing. It also increased informal sector activity.

The results leave little doubt that regulation of labor disputes in India has had quantitatively significant effects. In India, the hand of government has been at least as important as the invisible hand in determining resource allocation. This has provoked heated debate about which aspects of this role have constituted a brake on development. It is apparent that much of the reasoning behind labor regulation was wrong-headed and led to outcomes that were antithetical to their original objectives.

The paper finds little evidence that pro-worker labor market regulations have actually promoted the interests of labor and, more worryingly, that they have been a constraint on growth and poverty alleviation. Our results have not been able thus far to find any gainers except for the extent to which there may have been capital and labor flows across Indian states in response to policy disparities as they have developed. Our finding that regulating in a pro-worker direction was associated with increases in urban poverty are particularly striking as they suggest that attempts to redress the balance of power between capital and labor can end up hurting the poor.

---

36. The urban population of Andhra Pradesh and West Bengal were 17.15 and 18.15 million, respectively, in 1990.

The fact that our results are not robust to state-specific time trends does raise the question of whether the effects that we are picking up are those due to labor regulations per se or the consequences of a poor climate of labor relations—union power and labor/management hostility—which affect the trend rate of growth within a state. This goes to interpretation of the finding. But either way, the analysis suggests that labor market institutions in India have had an important impact on manufacturing development.

The analysis reinforces the growing sentiment that government regulations in developing countries have not always promoted social welfare. The example that we have studied here is highly specific and it is clear that it cannot be used to promote a generalized pro- or antiregulation stance. Future progress will likely rest on improving our knowledge of specific regulatory policies. Research involving particular country experiences will be an important component of this. Only then can the right balance between the helping and hindering hands of government be found.

APPENDIX 1: DATA

The data used in the paper come from a wide variety of sources.[37] They cover the sixteen main Indian states listed in Figure I and refer mainly to the period 1958–1992. Haryana split from the state of Punjab in 1965. After this date on, we include separate observations for Punjab and Haryana. Variables expressed in real terms are deflated using the **Consumer Price Index for Agricultural Laborers** (CPIAL) and **Consumer Price Index for Industrial Workers** (CPIIW). These are drawn from a number of Government of India publications which include Indian Labour Handbook, the Indian Labour Journal, the Indian Labour Gazette and the Reserve Bank of India Report on Currency and Finance. Ozler, Datt, and Ravallion [1996] have further corrected CPIAL and CPIIW to take account of interstate

---

37. Our data sets builds on Ozler, Datt, and Ravallion [1996] which collects published data on poverty, output, wages, price indices, and population to construct a consistent panel data set on Indian states for the period 1958 to 1992. We are grateful to Martin Ravallion for providing us with these data and to Guarav Datt for answering various queries. To these data, we have added information on labor regulation, manufacturing performance, political representation, infrastructure, and public finances of Indian states.

126   *QUARTERLY JOURNAL OF ECONOMICS*

cost of living differentials and have also adjusted CPIAL to take account of rising firewood prices. The reference period for the deflator is October 1973–March 1974. State **population** data used to express magnitudes in per capita terms and as a control come from the 1951, 1961, 1971, 1981, and 1991 censuses [Census of India, Registrar General and Census Commissioner, Government of India] and has been interpolated between census years. Separate series are available for urban and rural areas.

The **labor regulation** variable comes from state-specific text amendments to the Industrial Disputes Act of 1947 as reported in Malik [1997]. We decided to code each change in the following way: a 1 denotes a change that is pro-worker or anti-employer, a 0 denotes a change that we judged not to affect the bargaining power of either workers or employers, and a −1 denotes a change which we regard to be anti-worker or pro-employer. There were 113 state-specific amendments coded in this manner. Where there was more than one amendment in a year, we collapsed this information into a single directional measure. Thus, reforms in the regulatory climate are restricted to taking a value of 1, 0, −1 in any given state and year. To use these data, we then construct cumulated variables that map the entire history of each state beginning from 1947—the date of enactment of the Industrial Disputes Act.

Data on **annual workdays lost to strikes and lockouts** come from various issues of the Indian Labour Yearbook, Labour Bureau, Ministry of Labour, Government of India. We divide this by number of workers employed from the Annual Survey of Industries data to get a per-worker measure.

State output comes from Estimates of State Domestic Product published by Department of Statistics, Ministry of Planning, Government of India. Output variables are deflated and expressed in log per capita terms. The breakdown of total output into agricultural, nonagricultural, and manufacturing output is done under the National Industrial Classification System (NIC) which conforms with the International Standard Industrial Classification System (ISIC). Within manufacturing—registered manufacturing is defined by the Factories Act of 1948 to refer to firms with ten or more employees with power or twenty or more employees without power. Unregistered manufacturing refers to firms below these cutoffs, and the size of this sector is appraised by sample surveys carried out by the Department of Statistics.

Figures on **employees and workers** come from the Annual Survey of Industries, Central Statistical Office (Industrial Statistics Wing), Department of Statistics, Ministry of Planning and Programme Implementation, Government of India. Workers are defined as to include all persons employed directly or through any agency whether for wages or not and engaged in any manufacturing process or in any other kind of work incidental to or connected to the manufacturing process. Employees include all workers and persons receiving wages and holding supervisory or managerial positions engaged in administrative office, store keeping section and welfare section, sales department as also those engaged in purchase of raw materials, etc. or purchase of fixed assets for the factory and watch and ward staff. **Daily employment** figures are from returns submitted from firms under the Factories Act of 1948 which have been analyzed and collated in the Indian Labour Yearbook, Labour Bureau, Ministry of Labour, Government of India. They are obtained by dividing total worker (defined as above) attendances in a year by the number of days worked by the factory.

Earnings are defined to include all remunerations capable of being expressed in monetary terms and also payable more or less regularly in each pay period to workers. It includes (a) direct wages and salary payments, (b) remuneration for period not worked, (c) bonuses and ex gratia payments paid both at regular and at less frequent intervals. It excludes (a) layoff payments that are made from trust or other social funds set up expressly for this purpose, imputed value of the benefits in kind, (b) employer's contribution to the old age benefits and other social security charges, direct expenditure on maternity benefits and crèches and other group benefits, (c) traveling and other expenditure incurred for the business purpose, are reimbursed by the employer are excluded. Earnings are expressed in terms of gross value, i.e., before deduction for fines, damages, taxes, provident funds, employee's state insurance contribution, etc. They come from the Annual Survey of Industries and are expressed in real per worker terms.

Value-added in the registered manufacturing sector is the increment to the value of goods and services that is contributed by the factory and is obtained by deducting the value of total inputs and depreciations from the value of output. The **number of factories** variable comes from the list maintained by the Chief

Inspector of Factories in each state that is updated to take into account both deregistration of firms and new entrants. It thus captures the net flow of firms in the registered manufacturing sector. **Fixed capital** represents the depreciated value of fixed assets owned by the factory on the closing date of the accounting year. Fixed assets are those that have a normal productive life of more than one year. Fixed capital covers all types of assets new or used or own constructed, deployed for production, transportation, living or recreational activities, hospitals, schools, etc for factory personnel. All these measures come from the Annual Survey of Industries.

Total **installed electrical capacity** of electrical generation plants is measured in thousand kilowatts and come from various issues of the Statistical Abstracts of India, Central Statistical Office, Department of Statistics, Ministry of Planning, Government of India. It is expressed in log per capita terms. **Development expenditure** refers to state spending on economic services (agriculture, rural development, special area programs, irrigation and flood control, energy, industry and minerals, transport and communications, science, technology, and environment) and social services (education, medical and public health, family welfare, water supply and sanitation, housing, urban development, labor and labor welfare, social security and welfare, nutrition and relief). The primary source is an annual publication, Public Finance Statistics (Ministry of Finance, Government of India). This information is also collated in the Reserve Bank of India's annual publication Report on Currency and Finance.

The data on **political histories** come from Butler, Lahiri, and Roy [1991]. These primary data are aggregated into four political groupings which are defined in the text and expressed as shares of the total number of seats in state legislatures. State political configurations are held constant between elections. Political history is measured by the number if years during our data period that particular political groupings have held a majority of the seats in the legislature. In our data period, the relevant groupings are the Congress party, the Janata parties, hard left parties, and regional parties. These groupings contain the following parties: (i) Congress Party (Indian National Congress + Indian Congress Socialist + Indian National Congress Urs + Indian National Congress Organization), (ii) Janata parties (Lok Dal + Janata + Janata Dal), (iii) a hard left grouping (Commu-

nist Party of India + Communist Party of India Marxist), and a
(iv) grouping made up of regional parties.

For our measure of **unionization** we use the number of
union members in a state divided by the state population and
averaged over the pre-1977 period. The source of these data is the
Indian Labour Yearbook, Labour Bureau, Ministry of Labour,
Government of India. For the matched estimation we rank states
by this variable and then match treatment states to control states
with the closest level of pre-1977 unionization. The treatment-
control matches are as follows: Andhra Pradesh-Uttar Pradesh,
Gujarat-Bihar, Karnataka-Haryana, Kerala-Bihar, Madhya
Pradesh-Uttar Pradesh, Maharashtra-Assam, Orissa-Uttar
Pradesh, Rajasthan-Uttar Pradesh, Tamil Nadu-Assam, and
West Bengal-Assam. For our historical **land tenure** measure we
used data from Banerjee and Iyer [2002] who classified the land
revenue system imposed in each district of British India as land-
lord or nonlandlord based. To construct our state measure, we
took the mean value for constituent districts of modern states
weighting each by land area of the district.

Our **disaggregated registered manufacturing data**
come from the Annual Survey of Industries which reports information on production activity in the registered manufacturing
sector across the sixteen main Indian states for more than 100
three-digit industries during 1980–1997.

The **poverty** figures we use for the rural and urban areas of
India's sixteen major states, spanning 1957–1958 to 1991–1992
were put together by Ozler, Datt, and Ravallion [1996]. These
measures are based on 22 rounds of the National Sample Survey
(NSS) which span this period. The NSS rounds are not evenly
spaced: the average interval between the midpoints of the surveys ranges from 0.9 to 5.5 years. Surveys were carried out in the
following years 1958, 1959, 1960, 1961, 1962, 1963, 1965, 1966,
1967, 1968, 1969, 1970, 1971, 1973, 1974, 1978, 1983, 1987, 1988,
1990, 1991, and 1992. Because other data are typically available
on a yearly basis, weighted interpolation has been used to generate poverty measures for years where there was no NSS survey.
The poverty lines used are those recommended by the Planning
Commission [1993]. The head count measures are estimated from
the grouped distributions of per capita expenditure published by
the NSS, using parameterized Lorenz curves using a methodology detailed in Datt and Ravallion [1992].

130   *QUARTERLY JOURNAL OF ECONOMICS*

APPENDIX 2: REGULATORY CHANGE IN INDIA: 1958–1992

State	Change year	Amendments and codes	Overall code
Andhra Pradesh	1968	Limits strikes and lockouts in designated public utilities [−1].	Pro-employer
	1982	Facilitates settlement of industrial disputes in labor courts [−1].	Pro-employer
	1987	Prohibits strikes and lockouts when in the public interest [−1]. Workers have to be paid before closing down firm [1]. Prior workers given preference when rehiring [1]. Dismissed workers paid from reinstatement not rehiring date [1]. Imposes penalty for not complying with order prohibiting industrial disputes [−1]. Individual workers can apply to labor court for adjudication [1]. Widens judicial powers to recover money owed to workers by employer [1]. Lengthens the notice employer must give worker about change in conditions of service [1].	Pro-worker
Gujarat	1973	Imposes penalty on employer for not nominating representatives to councils within firms [1].	Pro-worker
Karnataka	1988	Individual workers can apply to labor court for adjudication [1]. Enforces attendance at industrial dispute hearings [−1]. Empowers state governments to transfer disputes across tribunals to facilitate settlement [−1]. Prohibits strikes and lockouts when in the public interest [−1]. Extends rules for layoff, retrenchment, and closure to smaller firms [1].	Pro-employer
Kerala	1979	Prohibits strikes and lockouts when in the public interest [−1]. Imposes penalty for not complying with order prohibiting industrial disputes [−1].	Pro-employer
Madhya Pradesh	1982	Extends powers of labor courts to settle industrial disputes [−1]. Facilitates settlement of industrial disputes in labor courts [−1]	Pro-employer
	1983	Applies closure rules to previously uncovered undertakings [1].	Pro-worker

Appendix 2
(CONTINUED)

State	Change year	Amendments and codes	Overall code
Maharashtra	1981	Compensation now received for closure due to layoff [1]. Workers receive 100 percent as opposed to 50 percent of wages for layoff due to electricity problems [1]. Extends rules for layoff, retrenchment, and closure to smaller firms [1].	Pro-worker
	1983	Gives power of appeal to workers to overturn decision to close down firm [1].	Pro-worker
Orissa	1983	Extends rules for layoff, retrenchment, and closure to smaller firms [1]. Gives power of appeal to workers to overturn decision to close down firm [1].	Pro-worker
Rajasthan	1960	Exact criteria for being union member defined [−1]. Defines employers in firms subcontracted to industry as employers for industrial disputes purposes [1]. Defines who is allowed to be involved in bargaining processes on behalf of unions [−1]. Gives definition of what a union is in an industrial dispute [−1]. Definition of worker for industrial disputes purposes extends to those subcontracted with an industry [1].	Pro-employer
	1970	Empowers the states to refer industrial disputes to industrial tribunals when it is in the public interest [−1]. Prohibits strikes and lockouts when in the public interest [−1]. Imposes penalty for not complying with order prohibiting industrial disputes [−1]. Widens judicial powers to recover money owed to workers by employer [1]. Defines union registration rules to prevent multiple representation [−1].	Pro-employer
	1984	Extends rules for layoff, retrenchment, and closure to smaller firms [1]. Can continue layoffs due to natural disasters for more than 30 days without permission [−1]. Union representative has to be involved in negotiations concerning retrenchment of workers [1]. Applies closure rules to previously uncovered undertakings [1]. Increases penalty for unauthorized layoff and retrenchment of workers [1]. Extends rules for layoff, retrenchment, and closure to smaller firms [1].	Pro-worker

Appendix 2
(CONTINUED)

State	Change year	Amendments and codes	Overall code
Tamil Nadu	1982	Prohibits strikes and lockouts when in the public interest [−1]. Imposes penalty for not complying with order prohibiting industrial disputes [−1].	Pro-employer
West Bengal	1974	Prohibits layoff of worker given employment on same day [1].	Pro-worker
	1980	Includes workers involved in sales in definition of worker [1]. Retrenchment does include workers terminated on grounds of ill health [1]. Extends period within which report of conciliation proceedings must be submitted [1]. Extends date at which conciliation proceedings are deemed to have started [1]. Facilitates settlement of industrial disputes in labor courts [−1]. Facilitates the making of awards by labor courts [1]. Limit on the number of days laid-off workers receive 50 percent of their wages is removed [1]. Laid-off worker only have to present themselves once a week at the plant if layoff extends for more than seven days [1]. Workers have to be paid before closing down firm [1]. Prior workers given preference when rehiring [1]. Dismissed workers paid from reinstatement not rehiring date [1]. Extends rules for layoff, retrenchment, and closure to smaller firms [1]. Extends period after which employer can commence layoff [1]. Widens judicial powers to recover money owed to workers by employer [1]. Lengthens the notice employer must give worker about change in conditions of service [1].	Pro-worker
	1986	Makes transparent the award procedures to be followed and relief to be given to discharged, dismissed, or retrenched workers [1].	Pro-worker
	1989	Individual workers can apply directly to conciliation officer and labor court for adjudication [1]. Employers have to demonstrate ability to pay compensation to workers before closing down firm [1]. Refusal of employment is grounds for an individual worker to enter into an industrial dispute [1].	Pro-worker

Coding of text of amendments is from Malik [1997]. Fuller summaries of all amendments and their coding are available at http://econ.lse.ac.uk/staff/rburgess/wp.

DEPARTMENT OF ECONOMICS AND STICERD,
LONDON SCHOOL OF ECONOMICS

REFERENCES

Acemoglu, Daron, Simon Johnson, and James A. Robinson, "The Colonial Origins of Comparative Development: An Empirical Investigation," *American Economic Review*, XCI (2001), 1369–1401.

Banerjee, Abhijit, and Lakshmi Iyer, "History, Institutions and Economic Performance: The Legacy of Colonial Land Tenure Systems in India," available at http://econ-www.mit.edu/faculty/download_pdf.php?id=517, 2003.

Barro, Robert, *Determinants of Economic Growth: A Cross-Country Empirical Study* (Cambridge: MIT Press, 1997).

Besley, Timothy, and Robin Burgess, "Can Labor Regulation Hinder Economic Performance? Evidence from India," CEPR Discussion Paper No. 3260, 2002.

Bertrand, Marianne, and Francis Kramarz, "Does Entry Regulation Hinder Job Creation? Evidence from the French Retail Industry," *Quarterly Journal of Economics*, CXVII (2002), 1369–1413.

Bertrand, Marianne, Esther Duflo and Sendhil Mullainathan, "How Much Should We Trust Differences-in-Differences Estimates?" *Quarterly Journal of Economics*, CXIX (2004), 249–275.

Bhagwati, Jagdish, "The Design of Indian Development," in Isher Alhuwalia and Ian Little, eds. *India's Economic Reforms and Development: Essays for Manmohan Singh* (Delhi: Oxford University Press, 1998).

Bhagwati, Jagdish, and Padma Desai, *India: Planning for Industrialization* (Delhi: Oxford University Press, 1970).

Bhagwati, Jagdish, and T. N. Srinivasan, *Foreign Trade Regimes and Economic Development* (Delhi: Mcmillan, 1975).

Blanchard, Olivier, and Justin Wolfers, "The Role of Shocks and Institutions in the Rise of European Unemployment: The Aggregate Evidence," *Economic Journal*, CX (2000), C1–C33.

Blanchard, Olivier, "Rents, Product and Labor Market Regulation, and Unemployment," Lecture 2 in *The Economics of Unemployment: Shocks, Institutions, and Interactions* (Cambridge, MA: MIT Press, 2003).

Botero, Juan, Simeon Djankov, Rafael La Porta, Florencio Lopez-de-Silanes, and Andrei Shleifer, "The Regulation of Labor," typescript, available at http://rru.worldbank.org/DoingBusiness/Downloads/LaborRegulations/flopslabor.3.pdf, 2003.

Butler, David, Ashok Lahiri, and Prannoy Roy, *India Decides: Elections 1952–1991* (New Delhi: Aroom Purie for Living Media India, 1991).

Caballero, Ricardo J., and Mohamad L. Hammour, "The Macroeconomics of Specificity," *Journal of Political Economy*, CVI (1998), 724–767.

Card, David, Francis Kramarz, and Thomas Lemieux, "Changes in the Relative Structure of Wages and Employment: A Comparison of the United States, Canada and France," *Canadian Journal of Economics*, XXXII (1999), 843–877.

De Soto, Hernando, *The Other Path: The Invisible Revolution in the Third World* (New York: Harper & Row, 1989).

Djankov, Simeon, Rafael La Porta, Florencio Lopez-de-Silanes, and Andrei Shleifer, "The Regulation of Entry," *Quarterly Journal of Economics*, CXVII (2002), 1–37.

Datt, Gaurav, and Martin Ravallion, "Growth and Redistribution Components of Changes in Poverty Measures: A Decomposition with Applications to Brazil and India in the 1980s," *Journal of Development Economics*, XXXVIII (1992), 275–295.

Dollar, David, Giuseppe Iarossi, and Taye Mengistae, "Investment Climate and Economic Performance: Some Firm Level Evidence from India," mimeo, World Bank, 2001.

Fallon, Peter, "The Effects of Labor Regulation upon Industrial Employment in India," World Bank Research Department Discussion Paper No. 287, 1987.

Fallon, Peter, and Robert E. B. Lucas, "Job Security Regulations and the Dynamic Demand for Labor in India and Zimbabwe," *Journal of Development Economics,* XL (1993), 241–275.

Freeman, Richard, "Labor Market Institutions and Economic Performance," *Economic Policy,* VI (1988), 64–80.

Grout, Paul, "Investment and Wages in the Absence of Binding Contracts: A Nash Bargaining Approach," *Econometrica,* LII (1984), 449–460.

Hall, Robert E., and Charles I. Jones, "Why Do Some Countries Produce So Much More Output per Worker Than Others?" *Quarterly Journal of Economics,* CXIV (1999), 83–116.

Heckman, James, and Carmen Pagés, ed., *Law and Employment: Lessons from Latin American and the Caribbean* (Chicago: The University of Chicago Press for the NBER, 2003).

Holmes, Thomas J., "The Effect of State Policies on the Location of Manufacturing: Evidence from State Borders," *Journal of Political Economy,* CVI (1998), 667–705.

Kaldor, Nicholas, *Strategic Factors in Economic Development* (Ithaca, NY: Cornell University Press, 1967).

Krusell, Per, and Jose-Victor Rios-Rull, "Vested Interests in a Positive Theory of Stagnation and Growth," *Review of Economic Studies,* LXIII (1996), 301–321.

Maddala, G. S., and Shaowen Wu, "A Comparative Study of Unit Root Tests with Panel Data and a New Simple Test," *Oxford Bulletin of Economics and Statistics,* LXI (1999), 631–652.

Malik, P. L., *Industrial Law* (Lucknow: Eastern Book Company, 1997).

Nickell, Stephen, "Unemployment and Labor Market Rigidities: Europe versus North America," *Journal of Economic Perspectives,* XI (1997), 55–74.

Nickell, Stephen, and Richard Layard, "Labor Market Institutions and Economic Performance," in Orley Ashenfelter and David Card, eds., *Handbook of Labor Economics* (Amsterdam: North-Holland, 2000).

Ozler, Berk, Guarav Datt, and Martin Ravallion, "A Data Base on Poverty and Growth in India," mimeo, World Bank, 1996.

Planning Commission, *Report on the Expert Group on the Estimation of the Proportion and Number of Poor* (New Delhi: Government of India, 1993).

Sachs, Jeffrey, A. Varshney, and N. Bajpai, eds., *India in the Era of Economic Reforms* (Delhi: Oxford University Press, 1999).

Sargan, John D., "The Estimation of Economic Relationships Using Instrumental Variables," *Econometrica,* XXVI (1958), 393–415.

Schneider, Friedrich, and Dominic Enste, "Shadow Economies: Sizes, Causes and Consequences," *Journal of Economic Literature,* XXXVII (2000), 77–114.

Shleifer, Andrei, and Robert Vishny, *The Grabbing Hand: Government Pathologies and Their Cures* (Cambridge: Harvard University Press, 1998).

Singh, Manmohan, *India's Export Trends* (Oxford: Clarendon Press, 1964).

Stern, Nicholas, *A Strategy for Development* (Washington, DC: World Bank, 2001).

Stigler, George, "The Theory of Economic Regulation," *Bell Journal of Economics,* II, (1971), 3–21.

World Bank, *The East Asian Miracle* (Oxford, UK: Oxford University Press, 1993).

Journal of Economic Perspectives—Volume 12, Number 3—Summer 1998—Pages 111–130

Deregulation and the Labor Market

James Peoples

D
eregulation, specifically the removal of government rate regulations and restrictions on entry, has been one of the most significant economic policy changes of the last few decades. The effects of such policy changes are not limited to the product market, as stepped-up competition in an industry can easily place greater downward pressure on labor earnings. This article focuses on employment, earnings, and unionization patterns in the deregulated trucking, railroad, airline and telecommunications industry, as an approach for examining the influence of deregulation on the labor market. This set of industries represents many of the primary targets of deregulation in the late 1970s and early 1980s, as they have moved toward a business environment in which government policies place greater emphasis on allowing the market to set prices and determine successful entry. The time that has elapsed since these policy changes provides a long enough observation period to allow for detecting patterns in these industries.

One way to visualize quickly the relationship between economic regulation and the labor market is to consider the relationship between regulated industries and unions. Regulation that restricts entry of potential competitors allows for relative ease of unionization, because the per worker cost of organizing employees is low in industries consisting of a few large firms. Moreover, successfully organizing a large proportion of the industry work force enhances the bargaining advantage of unions, since they possess the power to severely disrupt operations during a labor strike. Indeed, before deregulation, unions in the trucking, railroad, airline and telecommunications industries negotiated wages for their members that were at least 14 percent higher than the wages received by their counterparts in other industries (Hendricks, 1994). Rate regulation that allowed carriers in these indus-

■ *James Peoples is Associate Professor of Economics, University of Wisconsin-Milwaukee, Milwaukee, Wisconsin.*

tries to pass on costs to costumers also contributed to their unions receiving high wages for their members (Annable 1973; Ehrenberg, 1979; Moore, 1986). The movement towards deregulation and enhanced competition thus presents a challenge to unions, since new and typically non-union firms are now able to take advantage of the removal of entry restrictions.

The following section presents an overview of the employment and unionization patterns in the four industries considered here over time. The next section then tells the story, one industry at a time, of how the relationship developed between a regulated industry and its workers. The article then examines patterns of labor earnings following deregulation in these industry sectors. Finally, some concluding remarks are offered.

Industry Unionization, Employment and Earnings Trends

Table 1 presents information on the size of the work force in trucking, railroads, airlines and telecommunications from the early 1970s to the 1990s, along with the weekly earnings of workers and percentage of workers in each industry belonging to a union. The sample years from 1978 to 1996 should be taken to cover the post-deregulation period for trucking, railroads, and airlines. The years 1983 to 1996 encompass the post-deregulation period for telecommunications, following the break-up of AT&T in 1984. The summary results in the table show some similarities and differences across the industries.

For example, the findings on trucking suggest an appreciable reduction of the union membership rate of 46 to 23 percent over the deregulation period from 1978 to 1996. Apparently this is not the continuation of a trend in this industry, given that unionization was falling only mildly, by 3 percentage points, from 1973 to 1978. The union membership pattern is consistent with the notion that the trucking industry has relatively low barriers to entry, which meant that deregulation allowed non-trivial entry of non-union carriers. The trucking employment pattern reveals further evidence suggesting the ease of entry into this industry. After a pre-deregulation period of relatively low employment growth, from 977,000 in 1973 to 1,111,000 in 1978, the number of workers employed in trucking dramatically increased to 1,907,000 in 1996. Together, the union membership rate and industry employment trends suggest a tremendous loss of labor bargaining power following deregulation. This loss is further supported by the findings in Table 1 that show workers in this industry experiencing their real weekly earnings falling from $491 in 1978 to $353 in 1996.

In contrast to the trucking industry, the findings on railroad workers do not reveal any especially substantial effect of deregulation on the union membership rate in this industry; as shown in Table 1, the percentage of railroad workers belonging to a union only fell from 79 to 74 percent over the 1978 to 1996 observation period. This pattern reflects the difficulties of non-union entry in an industry which is often characterized as naturally oligopolistic. However, while a high percentage of union membership suggests that railroad unions

Table 1

Unionization, Employment and Labor Earnings Patterns in Transportation and Telecommunications Industries

Industry	1973	1978	1983	1988	1991	1996
Trucking						
Union Membership Rate	49%	46%	38%	25%	25%	23%
Work Force Size (×1,000)	997	1,111	1,117	1,544	1,617	1,907
Weekly Earnings (1983/84 dollars)	$499	$491	$404	$386	$405	$353
Railroad						
Union Membership Rate	83%	79%	83%	81%	78%	74%
Work Force Size (×1,000)	587	580	428	363	286	282
Weekly Earnings (1983/84 dollars)	$475	$491	$507	$490	$494	$470
Airlines						
Union Membership Rate	46%	45%	43%	42%	37%	36%
Work Force Size (×1,000)	368	465	464	683	696	800
Weekly Earnings (1983/84 dollars)	$499	$498	$455	$420	$443	$435
Telecommunications						
Union Membership Rate	59%	55%	55%	44%	42%	29%
Work Force Size (×1,000)	949	1,075	1,060	1,114	1,107	1,126
Weekly Earnings (1983/84 dollars)	$399	$442	$457	$447	$458	$488
All Other Industries						
Union Membership Rate	23%	22%	19%	16%	15%	14%
Work Force Size (×1,000)	72,619	81,737	85,220	97,704	99,080	107,844
Weekly Earnings (1983/84 dollars)	$399	$363	$301	$310	$322	$334

Source: Information on union membership rates and industry work force sizes were provided by Barry Hirsch and David Macpherson. Information on labor earnings for the 1973–1991 sample period are taken from Current Population Survey Files and the 1996 earnings are taken from Hirsch and Macpherson's Union Membership and Earnings Data Book (1997a). The sample years from 1978 to 1996 cover the post-deregulation period for trucking, railroads and airlines. The years 1983–1996 cover the post-divestiture period for telecommunications.

retained their bargaining power following deregulation, the employment decline reported in Table 1 suggests otherwise. The number of workers employed in this industry fell by more than half from 1978 to 1996. This employment pattern certainly suggests that carriers had some ability to consolidate services and negotiate more efficient work rules. Despite increased joblessness in this industry, railroad unions were able to avoid the earnings losses experienced in trucking. Rather, by 1996 the real mean labor earnings of $470 was only $21 below the level attained in 1978.

The profile of airline workers is similar to the trucking example, but in a less extreme way. Union membership rates in this industry are declining; in Table 1, the percentage of unionized airline members fell from 45 percent to 36 percent between 1978 and 1996. As opposed to trucking, the airline industry has retained a highly concentrated market structure since deregulation. Moreover, the dramatic expansion in the number of people flying—driven in part by the lower prices due to deregulation—has led to appreciable employment gains in this industry. This growth in an industry dominated by a few large carriers enhances the ability of unions to increase their membership roles. Indeed, taking the product of the annual union membership rates and employment levels suggests the number of union members in this industry increased from 209,250 to 288,000 from 1978 to 1996, respectively. The reduction of the percentage of workers belonging to the union may still indicate some loss of bargaining power, as real labor earnings did decline from $498 in 1978 to $435 in 1996. Nonetheless, this decline is much less than for trucking.

Telecommunications workers showed declining union membership rates over the 1973–1996 observation period. This is most pronounced following the 1984 break-up of AT&T and the deregulation of long-distance services. The findings in Table 1 show that the union membership rate fell by 26 percentage points from 1983 to 1996, which is the largest post-deregulation decline of the four industries examined here. The introduction of labor saving technology into the production process most likely contributed to this reduction in the percentage of union members. The findings in Table 1 reveal that this drop in percentage membership occurred during a period of moderate employment growth of 66,000 workers from 1983 to 1996. While these trends might signal the erosion of union bargaining advantage, the findings in Table 1 reveal real weekly earnings gains for telecommunications workers of $457 to $488 covering the 1983 to 1996 post-divestiture/deregulation observation period. This earnings trend is a continuation of gains occurring before regulatory reform. An explanation of such a trend is that the introduction of new technology throughout the 1970s, '80s and '90s requires the employment of highly skilled workers who command high wages.

The summary figures in Table 1 offer some evidence that the bargaining power of labor declined in all four of these industries following deregulation. This evidence is consistent with the observation that entry by non-union firms weakens unions' control over the industry labor supply, and that the shift from rate regulation toward competitive pricing makes it unprofitable for carriers to pass on higher union wages that are not justified by higher productivity. Nonetheless, it is also interesting that the percentage of workers represented by unions in these industries continues to exceed by far the national average. The bottom rows of Table 1 shows that *outside* of the four industries specifically listed in Table 1, only 14 percent of the workers belonged to a union in 1996. It is possible then that while unions in deregulated industries face greater difficulties, they may still retain some bargaining power to negotiate advantageous wage and benefit packages. This seems to be the case for rail, airlines and telecommunications, given the findings in Table 1 that show workers in these industries continuing to experience a substantial earnings advantage over their counterparts in other industries. Only workers in trucking faced a marked erosion of their mean earnings premium.

Regulation, Deregulation, and Labor Relations: Four Industry Stories

Regulation of prices and entry was applied somewhat differently in each of these industries. The conditions of deregulation, like what barriers to entry remained, differed as well. The industries have some inherent differences, and labor laws differ across these industries. The combination of these differences can help to explain the different patterns of labor market outcomes in the trucking, railroad, airline and telecommunications industries.

Trucking

Of the industries examined here, trucking might seem the one that comes closest to satisfying the conditions for competition. Most sectors of this industry are characterized by low capital and entry costs to carriers and because worker skills are acquired quickly, the supply of labor to the industry is elastic (Hirsch and Macpherson, 1997b). However, this industry had long faced severe entry and rate restrictions. The Motor Carrier Act of 1935 gave the Interstate Commerce Commission (ICC) authority to the "for-hire" part of the trucking industry, which consisted of restricting entry and setting rates for truck companies or owner-operators who could be hired to provide long-haul service for intercity and interstate carriage service. "Private" carriers—the non-trucking companies who are limited to transporting their own products—were not similarly restricted, and thus provide a useful comparison group.

Entry and rate regulation had a profound effect on labor relations in the trucking industry. Entry restrictions supported the development of high concentration along long-haul routes and across major U.S. regions that are serviced by for-hire carriers. The low per worker cost of organizing employees that is associated with this type of market structure allows ease of unionization in this industry. Indeed, following the enactment of the Motor Carrier Act of 1935, the International Brotherhood of Teamsters (IBT) organized a large segment of the trucking sector. IBT's membership in trucking grew from 75,000 in 1933 to 370,000 by 1939 (Perry, 1986, p. 41), and reached 920,000 by 1948. The IBT's presence was most pronounced in intercity carriage, where the percentage of truckers under union contract grew from essentially none in 1933 to 80 percent by the mid-1940s. While regulatory legislation enacted in 1935 surely helped create an industrial relations environment conducive to union growth, the concurrent passage of the 1935 National Labor Relations Act also contributed to conditions that are favorable to union membership gains. Nonetheless, the IBT did take advantage of this favorable environment. This opportunistic behavior is further depicted by this union augmenting their bargaining advantage by instituting the National Master Freight Agreement in 1964 as a framework for negotiating concurrently with major carriers.

Uniform shipping rates along entry-regulated routes that were determined by using mark-up pricing methods influenced industrial relations in this industry by allowing carriers to partly pass on labor costs (Annable, 1973; Moore, 1978). While

most researchers agree that this type of regulation allowed for-hire carriers to capture significant rents, there is also some argument suggesting that shippers received
better quality service in the form of superior on-time performance and low probability of cargo damage (Alexis, 1997). Engaging in such non-price competition
influences labor market outcomes by increasing the demand for better qualified
drivers who command high wages.

   Labor and product market conditions in trucking were significantly altered by
deregulation. The ICC made some initial policy changes in 1978, leading to a record
number of applications from new and existing carriers for routes (Rose, 1987;
Hirsch, 1988). Congress then legislated these changes with the approval of the 1980
Motor Carrier Act, which further facilitated the influx of low-cost, non-union carriers in the for-hire sector. This increased availability of alternative low-cost carriers
following deregulation certainly weakened the bargaining advantage of the
Teamsters.

Railroads

   The railroad industry did not much resemble a competitive industry prior to
regulation. In fact, one of the primary economic rationales for regulating this industry was that it was an oligopolistic market characterized by economies of scale
and high sunk costs, and thus potentially subject to fits of "destructive" competition, where the existence of sunk costs would lead to very low prices and cycles of
bust and boom (Perelman, 1994). Probably the most significant reason for imple-
menting rate and entry regulation was to enhance the financial performance of this
industry (Grimm and Windle, 1997). Nonetheless, railroads were plagued with financial problems following the implementation of regulation in the 1920s. The
problem was a combination of excess capacity in the railroad industry and the
emerging alternative modes of transportation, mainly trucking. Regulatory rules
enacted to help carriers in the railroad industry ironically also contributed to the
poor performance of railroad carriers. For instance, the setting of minimum rates
above competitive levels heightened railroad carriers' vulnerability to intermodal
competition from trucking. Regulations stipulating that these carriers service low
density, unprofitable lines further reduced their ability to compete successfully.

   This sort of product market environment does not suggest that regulation generated much rent to share with workers. Instead, high labor costs might arise from
the additional demand for workers to service poorly performing routes.

   Consistent with the notion that concentrated industries are easier to organize,
railroad unions represented nearly all non-management workers during the pre-
deregulation period of restricted entry. The development of railroad unionization
was heavily influenced by the labor law guidelines of the 1926 Railroad Labor Act
that prohibited unions representing different occupational group of workers employed by the same carrier. As a result, rather than the emergence of a single
dominant union representing the work force, the majority of union rail workers
belonged to three unions: the United Transportation Union; the Brotherhood of
Maintenance of Way Employees; and the Transportation Communications Union
(Talley and Schwarz-Miller, 1997). Fragmenting union representation in this man-

ner could shift the bargaining advantage in favor of carriers. If these unions were unable to coordinate their negotiations, then carriers could use the strategy of targeting the weakest union and trying to use that settlement as a pattern for successful negotiations with other carriers. However, railroad unions addressed this problem in 1973 by negotiating industrywide agreements as a group with the representative of the major railroad carriers belonging to the National Railway Labor Conference (which had been established in 1963).

Railroad negotiations during the period of regulation were characterized by the unions' emphasis on work-rules. The outcome of focusing on this issue, in part, was defining a work day based on mileage covered. Sustaining this requirement over time allowed rail workers to take advantage of this rule as an approach towards increasing their earnings, since improvements in train speed permitted them to work extra shifts without markedly increasing their weekly hours worked (Talley and Schwarz-Miller, 1997; MacDonald and Cavalluzzo, 1996). Railroad unions also negotiated work rules that defined appropriate crew sizes to consist typically of an engineer, conductor and two brakemen, and sometimes included an extra brakeman and fireman. While such a requirement might have helped to create employment for workers, it introduced inefficiencies when carriers converted from steam to diesel engines, and automated switching operations, since these changes eliminated the need for firemen and extra brakemen (Talley and Schwarz-Miller, 1997).

Railroad deregulation drastically changed the business and labor relations environment. Following the 1976 Railroad Revitalization Reform Act and the 1980 Staggers Act, railroad carriers were provided the latitude to charge competitive shipping rates, abandon unprofitable routes and consolidate operations (Grimm and Windle, 1997). Carriers also emphasized labor costs reduction as an approach for improving their financial performance, as evidenced by the post-deregulation negotiation of work-rule changes that reduced required crew sizes and lengthened the minimum daily mileage constituting a basic work day (MacDonald and Cavalluzzo, 1996).[1] This declining demand for rail workers was further facilitated by the industry's adoption of labor-saving technologies, like electronic-based communications and information systems, which made it possible to automate almost every phase of traffic control: signaling, car management, train dispatching, and train movement (Talley and Schwarz-Miller, 1997). In sum, these labor market changes clearly indicate an erosion of the bargaining advantage of railroad unions following the deregulation of this industry.

Airlines

The airline industry was characterized by the dominance of four major trunk carriers by the 1930s: American Airlines, Eastern Airlines, Trans World Airlines and United Airlines. While this type of market structure might foster the non-competitive behavior that is targeted by price regulators, it was actually once again

---

[1] Talley and Schwarz-Miller (1997) argue that federal recommendations during the early 1980s by the Presidential Emergency Board gave railroads the leverage to make subsequent crew-reduction agreements possible.

the potential for "destructive" competition that led to the introduction of economic regulation through the 1938 Civil Aeronautics Act. As in the case of railroads, the fear was that an industry with large sunk costs could be susceptible to outbreaks of price-slashing that would lead to harmful boom and bust cycles. This market structure did not change appreciably following regulation; after 1938, potential entrants were prohibited from competing with incumbent trunk carriers, and after 1952 new entry did not occur in the local carrier sector (Keeler, 1981). In an attempt to avoid destructive pricing behavior, uniform rates were set for carriers as a mark-up over costs. The regulated companies competed along non-price dimensions by offering more frequent flights (Douglas and Miller, 1974; DeVany, 1975), and on other elements like using more modern aircraft, providing more comfortable seating and the like (Card, 1997). The overall extent of this type of competition was probably strong, given the relatively low levels of airline profitability during this period of regulation (Card, 1997), which suggest that this industry was not generating substantial regulatory rents to share with labor.

Union membership in the airline industry reached relatively high levels during the period of restricted entry and non-price competition. As was the case in the railroad industry, airline carriers and their unions were covered by the 1926 Railroad Labor Act. Under the administration of this act's provisions in the airline industry, labor relations were characterized by the proliferation of over 100 bargaining unions across carriers (Hendricks et al., 1980) and by a lack of inter-union cooperation.[2] Indeed, Cappelli (1987) observes that it was common for unions to cross each other's picket lines, and Craypo (1986) and Cremieux (1996) argue that certain contract provisions had the effect of making it illegal for one union to engage in sympathetic job actions in support of other airline unions. Clearly, this type of union behavior enhanced the bargaining power of carriers. Airline carriers also acted to cooperate and to bolster their bargaining advantage through the 1958 establishment of the Mutual Aid Pact, which put in place a strike insurance system that provided grounded carriers with a portion of the extra revenue earned by their competitors during the strike (Card, 1997). Overall, when compared to the pre-deregulation labor relations environment in trucking, it seems that airline unions should have experienced greater difficulty receiving rent for their members. Nonetheless, past research suggests that unionized workers employed in the airlines industry did receive an earnings premium (Card, 1986, 1997; Hirsch and Macpherson, 1995; Hendricks, 1994). Airline unions may have been able to retain bargaining power for their employees partly because they represented workers such as pilots and mechanics who are vital to carrier operations and who are difficult to replace quickly during strikes (Cremieux, 1996; Peoples, 1990a).

Deregulation had an immediate impact on labor relations in the airline industry. Card (1997) reports that the number of certified carriers tripled from 1977 to 1983, reaching a total of 93, and then reached a high of 106 carriers in 1985.

---

[2] Walsh (1995) observes that while intra-carrier union coalitions were highly uncommon, there was a history of union interaction at the national level among AFL-CIO-affiliated airline unions.

This influx of non-union and low-cost carriers challenged the bargaining advantage of airline unions, and many incumbent carriers were able to negotiate major wage concessions from their unions (Cappelli, 1985). However, the extent to which deregulation influenced these wage changes is not obvious, since stepped-up competition in this industry in the late 1970s and early 1980s coincides with an increase in oil prices during the late 1970s and business cycle downturn in the early 1980s. By the end of the 1980s, airline industry conditions had evolved in a way that was much more favorable to the enhancement of union bargaining power. By that time, the introduction of the hub-and-spoke distribution system and the dominance of a few computer reservation systems again created a competitive advantage for a few major union carriers. However, even the bargaining advantage of these carriers is challenged due to the 1978 elimination of the MAP strike insurance program. Many of these large union carriers had contributed to this source before deregulation and were able to draw from it to support continued operations during a labor strike. Without this funding these carriers must now finance their own operations when faced with a strike. Despite the development of these favorable union bargaining conditions, the switch from non-price to price competition in this industry suggests post-deregulation carrier resistance to union wage demands.

Telecommunications

At the turn of the century, the telecommunications industry was essentially an integrated monopoly. AT&T was the dominant long-distance and short-haul voice transmission carrier, as well as the primary supplier of telecommunications equipment. In accordance with the guidelines of the 1910 Mann-Elkins Act, the industry was regulated to ensure that AT&T provided affordable and universal service. However, it was not until the passage of the 1934 Federal Communications Commission Act that the FCC was established to oversee competitive entry and set interstate rates in this industry. State public utility commissions enforced these regulations for intrastate communications services, and entry was prohibited into the local interstate sector. Regulation of entry was less restrictive in the long-haul sector, as certificates of operation were granted to specialized carriers starting in 1960. Nonetheless, AT&T accounted for over 90 percent of the market sales in this sector prior to its breakup in 1984.

Up until the break-up of AT&T, regulators addressed the possibility of AT&T exercising its monopoly power by setting a maximum rate of return on AT&T's net investment. It has been observed that this type of regulation presents less of an incentive to contain costs, when compared to the alternative of setting a price cap (Hendricks, 1994). Ehrenberg (1979) observes that rate-of-return regulation might have contributed to reducing AT&T's resistance to union wage demands since the regulatory commission did not seriously consider labor costs when setting rates.

Union organizing was tremendously successful in this industry during the period of entry restriction, thanks in part to the absence of significant entry by non-AT&T carriers. The industry's largest union, the Communications Workers of America (CWA), represented more than 550,000 construction, maintenance, switchboard, and clerical workers throughout the Bell system. The second largest union, the International Brotherhood of Electrical Workers (IBEW), represented more than 100,000 telephone linemen, cable splicers, installers and draftsmen. These unions have been successful in taking advantage of the labor market environment; past research reveals telecommunication labor earnings premiums of 22 percent (Peoples, 1990b; Hendricks, 1994). The introduction of labor saving technology, however, has eroded the bargaining advantage of these unions even before regulatory change in this industry. Most vulnerable were telephone operators whose job responsibilities were rapidly replaced by new transmission equipment.

The 1984 breakup of AT&T and the differing application of regulation across states radically altered labor relations in the telecommunication industry. The changes stipulated by the U.S. Department of Justice required AT&T to divest itself of 22 Bell operating companies represented by seven regional Bell operating companies. After this, the CWA and IBEW faced separate negotiations with AT&T and the regional operating companies and their subdivisions. Bargaining separately with multiple employers stretches union resources and reduces union leverage. This erosion of bargaining power is compounded by the continued displacement of members by new labor saving technology and the increased share of non-union supervisory personnel in craft and clerical occupations (Keefe and Boroff, 1994).

Although competition in telecommunications is still gaining momentum, the competition that does exist has already placed downward pressure on costs. For instance, AT&T now competes with non-union rivals in long distance and manufacturing. In addition, by entering non-traditional telecommunication markets, it now faces new domestic and foreign competition (Smith, 1989). Even though the regional Bell operating companies dominate local and regional markets, they have also encountered greater pressure to lower costs. For instance, by 1995 more than half of the state public utility commissions instituted rate regulation, such as price caps, that promoted profit enhancement through cost savings. Furthermore, the introduction of fiber optic cables allowed new entrants to compete for the lucrative metropolitan area service. Despite this increased pressure to contain costs, the generally strong financial performance of AT&T and the regional Bell operating companies following divestiture suggests some potential for rent sharing with labor, at least in the near term. Continuing policy changes in this industry might further affect labor relations. An example is the 1996 telecommunications bill that allows long-distance carriers to compete in local exchange markets; allows regional Bell operating companies to compete in the long-distance market and allows cable companies to compete for telephone service (Harris and Kraft, 1997; Pal, 1997).

Labor Earnings and Rent Sharing

To this point, the focus of the discussion has been primarily on the institutional legislative and regulatory details of how deregulation has affected the labor market in these four industries. While there have been mention of earnings premiums for union workers in these industries, the discussion of earnings has not, to this point, offered much detail. This section will analyze earnings figures from several perspectives.[3]

Non-Management Earnings Patterns

In a deregulated industry, enhanced industry emphasis on cost savings and declining union control over the labor supply reduce the likelihood of workers receiving high earnings. This earnings effect is not necessarily limited to union workers, especially if the union set the standard industry wage before deregulation. This would occur if non-union employers matched union wages in an attempt to avoid unionization of their work force. Past research tests the deregulation-wage effect hypothesis by estimating pre- and post-deregulation labor earning premiums. Any erosion of these premiums is interpreted to suggest that pre-deregulation earnings advantages partly reflect workers having received economic rents in the past. The possibility of increased labor demand arising from stepped-up competition suggests the potential for a countervailing effect following deregulation. Hence, earnings premium outcomes are not certain, a priori. This section reports past findings and uses individual worker information from Current Population Survey files to estimate weekly earnings premiums on non-management workers employed in the deregulated trucking, railroad, transportation and telecommunications industries.[4] This set of non-supervisory workers is comprised of union and non-union employees. These workers represent over 90 percent of their respective industry's workforce prior to deregulation. Past research indicates that telecommunications is the only one of the industry groups considered here in which non-management workers experienced a substantial reduction in their share of industry employment following deregulation (Peoples, 1997). On average, 91 percent of telecommunications workers were employed in non-management positions from 1973 to 1985; this fell to an average of 86 percent over the succeeding six years. The earnings premiums of these workers are derived by separately estimating earnings equations for each observation year. The equation is specified such that the log of earnings is the dependent variable. The explanatory variables include for individual workers their years of education and work experience; race, sex and marital status; standard metropolitan statistical area (SMSA) and regional residential status; and the individuals' occupation and (log of) "usual" weekly hours worked. A dummy variable indicating employment in a particular deregulated industry is also included as an explanatory variable, and the estimated coefficient on the dummy variable repre-

---

[3] Tables with the complete results presented in this section are available from the author upon request.
[4] To be more specific, the samples used in Figures 1–4 that follow are based on information taken from the 1973 to 1977 May CPS files and from CPS outgoing rotation group files of the 168 monthly surveys conducted between January 1987 and December 1991. Full-time employees between the ages of 16 and 65 who reported non-zero weekly earnings is used as the selection criterion for individuals employed in non-trucking industries. Only individuals employed as truck drivers who satisfy the selection criterion are used in the trucking sample. This restriction yields a sample of 835,770 for all industries and 18,863, 6,395, 6,988, and 16,054 for trucking, railroad, airlines and telecommunications, respectively.

Figure 1

Non-Management Percentage Earnings Differential of Truck Drivers in the For-hire Sector (Comparison Group: Non-Transportation Operatives)

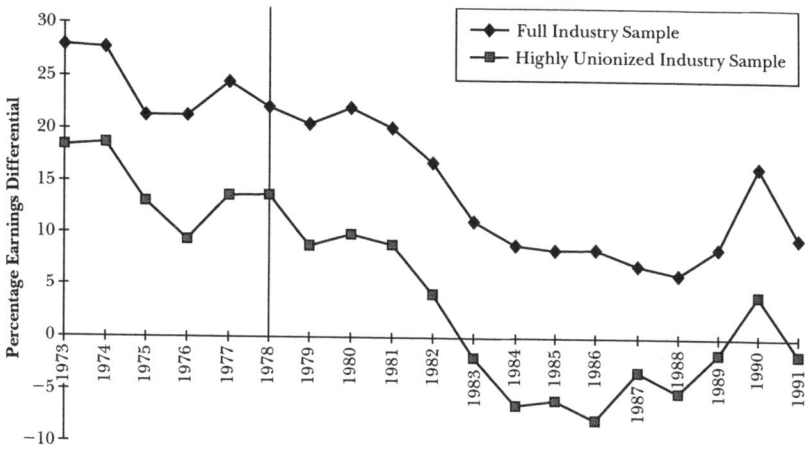

sents the earnings differential of deregulated industries.[5] Two sets of estimates for each deregulated industry are reported in Figures 1–4: one set of estimates uses the sample population of workers employed in all U.S. industries; the other uses the sample of workers employed in highly unionized industries. Additional vertical lines in these figures distinguish the dates of changes in regulatory regimes. In trucking, 1978 depicts the beginning of deregulation, since this is the year in which entry and rate restrictions were substantially reduced by the ICC. In rail, 1976 and 1980 depict the years when the Railroad Revitalization Reform Act and Staggers Act were passed to deregulate this industry. In airlines, 1978 depicts the year of the airline deregulation act. In telecommunications, 1986 depicts the initial year of labor negotiations following the 1984 break-up of AT&T.

Let us again begin with the trucking industry. Past research has found that for-hire truck drivers received an earnings premium that declined after the industry was deregulated. For instance, Hirsch and Macpherson (1997b) report truck drivers' earnings advantage over their non-truck driver counterparts employed in other industries declining from 22 percent in 1977–78 to less than 2 percent by 1995 (see also Rose, 1987; Hendricks, 1994). Figure 1 presents the results of the earnings equation estimated for truck drivers. The vertical axis reveals the gap in earnings for truck drivers as revealed by the dummy variable in the earnings equation, after adjusting for other characteristics, as compared to highly unioned non-

---

[5] This is converted into percentage differentials by exponentiating the estimated coefficient, subtracting one, and then multiplying this difference by 100.

Figure 2

Non-Management Percentage Earnings Differential of Workers in the Railroad Industry (Comparison Group: Workers in Non-Transportation and Non-Telecommunications Industries)

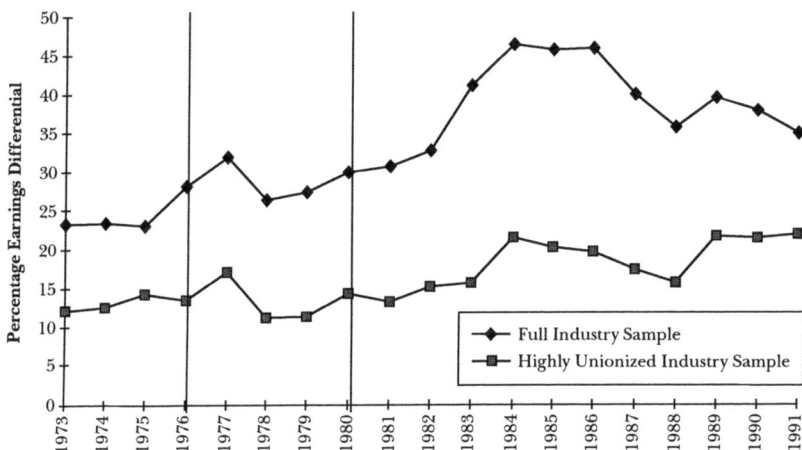

transportation operatives in other industries.[6] The findings suggest a noticeable drop of this earnings gap beginning by 1982. This corresponds with post-deregulation contract negotiations stipulating no wage gains from 1982 to 1984. Apparently, before deregulation, truckers were not only able to earn a premium compared to workers in other industries, they were also able to earn a premium compared to workers in other highly unionized industries. Soon after deregulation, the premium relative to other highly unionized industries disappeared, although a lesser earnings premium relative to other workers remained.

The findings on railroad earnings do not uncover any obvious evidence that earnings premiums declined after deregulation, whether the date of deregulation is taken as the 1976 Railroad Revitalization Reform Act or as the 1980 Staggers Act. Figure 2 shows that in comparison with all other workers, after adjusting for the characteristics in the earnings equation, the wage premium for railroad workers rose from 30 percent in 1980 to 45 percent in 1986, and then declined to 35 percent

---

[6] Following Hirsch (1988) the earnings of for-hire truck drivers are compared to non-transportation operatives. This choice avoids that possibility of comparing the earnings of these drivers to a set of workers whose wages are also likely to be influenced by deregulation. This might occur when using truck drivers outside the for-hire sector as the comparison group. Truck drivers are chosen as the representative group for this industry because they comprise such a large share of the work force. This restriction is not applied to the other transportation and telecommunications industries because they employ workers in a much more varied set of occupations; for those industries, the comparison group is all workers in non-transportation and non-telecommunications industries.

Figure 3
Non-Management Percentage Earnings Differential of Workers in the Airline Industry (Comparison Group: Non-Transportation and Non-Telecommunications Industries)

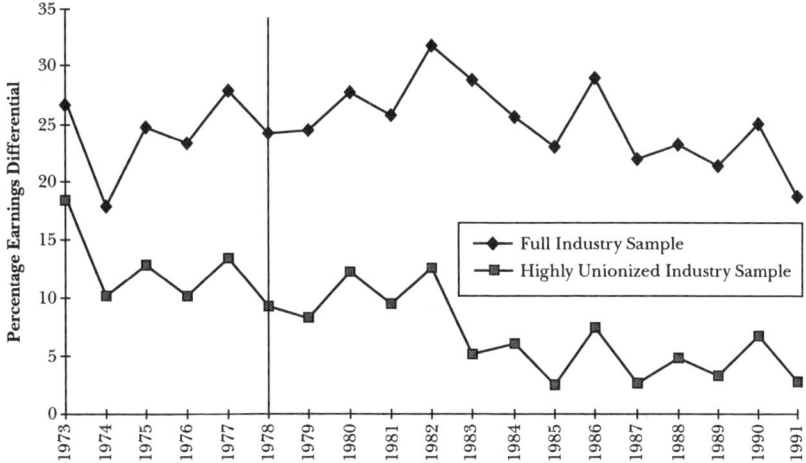

by 1991. However, the lower premiums do not fall below their pre-deregulation level. The earnings premium compared to other highly unionized industries is smaller, but it does not decline after deregulation. The earnings premium for workers in the railroad industry over their counterparts in other highly unionized industries actually rises over the initial years following regulatory reform, peaks in the mid-1980s and declines thereafter. Studies by Talley and Schwarz-Miller (1997) and MacDonald and Cavalluzzo (1996) confirm this overall pattern of earnings in the railroad industry.

In the airline industry, for the full industry sample, airline labor premiums in Figure 3 rose slightly after deregulation and peaked at 32 percent by 1982, before falling to 18 percent in 1991. In comparison, airline workers' earnings advantage over workers in other highly organized industries peaked at 13 percent by 1982 and fell to less than 3 percent by 1991. Past findings on earnings in the airline industry using a similar methodology have also indicated that labor earnings premiums following deregulation of 10 percentage points (Card, 1997; Hirsch and Macpherson, 1995). Using a simulation methodology, Cremieux (1996) found a larger drop. However, airline workers continued to receive markedly higher post-deregulation earnings than their non-airline counterparts employed in industries with a small percentage of the workers belonging to a union. This evidence supports the possibility of continued rent-sharing in this industry despite greater competition. Past research on wage dispersion complements this observation. While theory suggests that the law of one price should hold in a competitive market, Card (1997) reports

Figure 4

Non-Management Percentage Earnings Differential of Workers in the Telecommunications Industry (Comparison Group: Non-Transportation and Non-Telecommunications Industries)

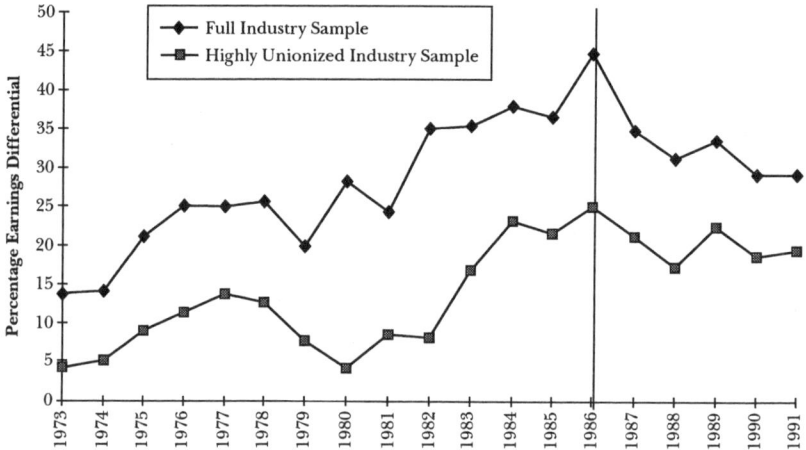

greater wage dispersion for homogenous workers within the airline sector following deregulation. Further, Fortin and Lemieux (1997) find a sizeable deregulation effect on wage dispersion for unionized men in transportation and telecommunications.

In telecommunications, Figure 4 reveals that earnings differentials were climbing in this industry up to 1986, which is the initial year of separate regional and local labor negotiations following the 1984 break-up of AT&T. When using the full industry sample, telecommunications earnings premiums rose from 14 percent in 1973 to a high of 45 percent in 1986. This is consistent with the notion that the continuous pre-divestiture introduction of new labor-saving technology required the payment of high wages to employ the highly skilled workers needed to operate such equipment. However, after the breakup of AT&T, these premiums fall to 29 percent by 1991. Still, on average over this time horizon, post-divestiture earnings differentials for telecommunications workers are on average slightly higher than the pre-divesture findings (Hendricks, 1994; Peoples, 1990b). In comparison with other highly unionized industries, the pattern is similar, although the wage premium is lower. Hendricks (1994) finds a similar pattern of earnings premiums for telecommunications workers. Since deregulation in telecommunications is still gathering momentum, it may be that the declining premiums reported for the relatively short time period following divestiture will signal the beginning of longer term erosion of telecommunications earnings advantage.

Taken as a whole, what do the findings on earnings differentials in these four industries tell us? Non-management workers in all four industries continue to receive an earnings premium after deregulation; however, in three of the four industries (railroads excepted), that premium declined after deregulation. The largest decline in earnings premium was in trucking, which seems to be the industry which has moved closest to full competition, and suggests that less competitive industries will have higher profits and pay higher wages to workers. In the case of railroads, deregulation almost certainly helped profits by giving carriers in this industry the flexibility to change outmoded labor practices. Remember that all four industries also are relatively highly unionized, which has surely helped in maintaining their earnings premiums. It is also possible, however, that the earnings equations did not include all the possible characteristics that may be affecting earnings differentials, and there may be unobserved factors about the industry or the workers which are affecting the earnings differentials over time.

Management Earnings Patterns

The opportunity for sharing the rents of regulated industries was not just available to workers in these industries—it was available to managers as well. Since managers are prohibited from joining a union, estimating earnings for this set of employees allows for investigating whether rent sharing is a more general phenomenon that only occurs in unionized environments. Here, separate earnings equations were estimated for the pre- and post-deregulation observation periods, again using Current Population Survey files. The dependent variable was the log of weekly earnings, and excluding occupational dummies, the independent variables were the same as those used to specify the non-management earnings equation. The occupational dummies were not needed when estimating the management earnings equation, since the sample population consist solely of managers from all industries.[7] It is not productive here to use this data to estimate annual figures, because the small annual sample size of managers for most of the deregulated industries means that such estimates are not very precise. However, comparing the coefficient on the dummy industry variable for the pre- and post-deregulation period is revealing.

These results uncover earnings patterns that parallel those reported on non-management employees. In trucking, management earnings premiums declined markedly in trucking following deregulation, falling from a 13 percentage point earnings premium in the pre-deregulation years to a "premium" of −2 percent in the post-deregulation years. The earnings premium for railroad managers barely budged; it was 20 percentage points before deregulation, and 19 percentage points after. The earnings premiums for airline and telecommunications managers fell slightly with deregulation: from 10 to 7 percentage points for airline managers, and from 31 percentage to 25 percentage points for telecommunications managers.

---

[7] Restricting this sample to managers allows for the earnings comparison of workers with similar job responsibilities. Non-transportation and non-telecommunications industries are chosen as the comparison group to avoid earnings distortion that arise from including other deregulated industries as part of this group.

Notably the earnings premiums for telecommunications managers stayed relatively high, similar to the high premiums received by workers in that industry. Similar results on the pattern of management earnings in deregulated industries are found by Belzer (1997) in railroads, Card (1997) in airlines, and Hendricks (1997) in telecommunications.

In sum, not only did workers receive high earnings before deregulation, but managers did as well. The way in which these earnings premiums for managers eroded as a result of deregulation is similar to the way the premiums eroded for workers.

Relative Earnings Loss Following Job Displacement

Workers in all four of these industries continued to receive relatively high earnings following deregulation. This was especially the case for railroad and telecommunications workers. One possible explanation here is that these industries were not yet competitive, and substantial rents remained to be shared. Another related possibility is that a highly organized work force contributed to higher non-management earnings. However, an alternative explanation is that employers in these industries hired highly valued workers who would command high earnings even if they were not employed in a regulated, unionized, lower competition industry. Conventional inter-industry earnings comparisons do not allow for testing this possibility, because detailed individual data on the relevant worker characteristics such as reliability, promptness, being painstaking, and so on does not exist. However, Alexis (1997) argues that the non-price competition that developed during regulation created a business environment that encouraged the employment of such workers. This pre-deregulation focus on employing highly valued workers might have set the precedence for hiring standards that continued even with the switch to competitive pricing.

The experience of displaced workers offers one method for identifying the relative market value of individual workers' characteristics, as suggested by Krueger and Summers (1988). Such an approach assumes that the demand for workers exhibiting highly valued characteristics will reduce their earnings loss following job displacement, all else equal. Evidence on the experience of displaced workers is available through the biannual Displaced Worker Survey.[8] The specification of the earnings change equation follows that used by Card (1997) and Hirsch and Macpherson (1997b). The dependent variable is the difference of the log of earnings, both pre- and post-displacement, in real dollars. Explanatory variables include measures of the pre-displacement characteristics of workers such as age, experience, years of schooling, sex, race, and marital status. Other explanatory variables include

---

[8] The samples used when estimating earnings changes of displaced workers are taken from the 1984, 1986, 1988, 1990, 1992, and 1994 displaced worker supplement to the CPS. These sources provide information on a random sample of individuals who reported losing a job any time during a 5 year span prior to the respective survey year (previous 3 years in 1994). Displaced individuals between the ages of 16 and 65 who are re-employed full-time is used as the selection criterion for individuals employed in non-trucking industries. Only individuals employed as truck drivers who satisfy the selection criterion are used in the trucking sample. This yields a sample of 21,463 individuals for all industries and 475, 97, 194, and 132 for trucking, railroad, airlines and telecommunications, respectively.

dummy variables indicating the displacement year, whether the displacement was caused by plant closing, whether the worker received early notification of displacement, the pre- and post-displacement occupation, and the post-displacement industry. The key explanatory variable is an added dummy variable identifying whether the industry had been deregulated. This is intended to reveal whether the experience of workers displaced in deregulated industries differs from that of others. This calculation is carried out separately for each of the four industries, which allows for different dates at which deregulation occurred. The comparison groups are the same as those used earlier when examining earnings differentials.

The results of these calculations are that workers displaced from the trucking and airline industries experienced very similar earnings changes to workers displaced from other industries; the coefficient on the industry dummy variable in these cases was less than 2 percentage points and lacked statistical significance. An interpretation of these results is that the market demand for the re-employed trucking and airline workers is strong enough for them to avoid relatively high earnings losses—remember, employment overall is growing in these industries. Of course, this does not mean that displaced trucking and airline workers did not suffer losses, only that their losses were no different than those of displaced workers from other industries.

In contrast, workers displaced from the railroad and telecommunications industries experienced markedly higher earning losses than workers displaced from other industries: 20 percentage points higher for railroads and 15 percentage points higher for telecommunications. This may reflect the strong possibility that industry-specific skills attained in these industries are not in high demand by other employers. It also fits with the observation that increased use of labor saving technology in railroad and telecommunications has lowered the demand for workers with skills specific to these industries.

Concluding Remarks

Deregulation has radically altered labor relations in the trucking, railroad, airline, and telecommunications industries, but what is interesting is the differing approaches to reducing labor costs that were used in each industry. For example, industry labor earnings premiums fell sharply in trucking, somewhat in airlines, slightly in telecommunications, and barely in railroads. It is perhaps no coincidence that the size of the workforce dramatically increased in trucking and airlines, held roughly steady in telecommunications, and fell dramatically in railroads—a pattern roughly the opposite of the changes in earnings.

Finding declining per worker labor costs following deregulation reveals an important source of consumer welfare gains in transportation and telecommunications. Indeed, taking the product of the earnings premium changes reported in this article from the time before deregulation and labor's total annual compensation in 1991 indicates worker losses in current dollars up to $5.7 billion in trucking, $1.2 billion in railroads, $3.4 billion in airlines, and $5.1 billion in telecommunications.[9] Of course, these quick calculations should be taken only as illustrating the order of magnitude of losses to labor. But to place these figures in context, the annual consumer welfare gains from deregulation have been roughly estimated at $50 billion for a not exactly comparable group of industries in the accompanying paper by Clifford Winston in this issue. This indicates that worker surplus losses do represent a sizeable share of consumer welfare gains from deregulation. Moreover, the losses to labor are greater than just the erosion of worker wages. The declining percentage of workers belonging to a union following deregulation raises other labor market concerns. For instance, unions can serve a positive economic role by helping employers to identify and address workers concern over issues such as working conditions, promotional practices, job security and labor compensation. A healthy interaction between unions and employers can lead to a healthier work environment, which in turn can enhance worker productivity. However, deregulation has had the expected labor market effect of reducing the bargaining advantage of unions in transportation and telecommunications.

■ *This article has greatly benefitted from the comments and suggestions of Jacqueline Agesa, Marcus Alexis, John Bitzan, Bradford De Long, David Card, Wallace Hendricks, Barry Hirsch, Kaye Husbands, Alan Krueger, David Macpherson, Sharon P. Smith and Timothy Taylor. The author is also grateful for the assistance received while on leave at the Kellogg Graduate School of Management at Northwestern University.*

[9] The base years used to calculate the change in earnings premiums for rail and airlines are 1985, and 1982, respectively. These choices reflect the peak years for these premiums. 1978 and 1986 are the base years for trucking and telecommunications, respectively. For trucking, this represents the year that the ICC removed entry and rate restriction and for telecommunications, this represents the initial year of labor negotiations following the break-up of AT&T.

References

Alexis, Marcus, "Commentary on Earnings and Employment in Trucking: Deregulating a Naturally Competitive Industry." In James Peoples, ed. *Regulatory Reform and Labor Markets.* Boston, Massachusetts: Kluwer Academic Publishers, 1997.

Annable, James, "The ICC and the Cartelization of the American Trucking Industry," *Quarterly Review of Economics and Business,* Summer 1973, *13,* 13–47.

Belzer, Michael, "Collective Bargaining After Deregulation: Do the Teamsters Still Count?" *Industrial and Labor Relations Review,* July 1995, *48,* 636–55.

Belzer, Michael, "Commentary on Railroad Deregulation and Union Labor Earnings." In James Peoples, ed. *Regulatory Reform and Labor Markets.* Boston, Massachusetts: Kluwer Academic Publishers, 1997.

Cappelli, Peter, "Airlines." In David Lipsky and Clifford Donn, eds. *Collective Bargaining in American Industry.* Lexington, Massachusetts: Lexington Books, 1987.

Cappelli, Peter, "Competitive Pressures and Labor Relations in the Airline Industry." *Industrial Relations,* Fall 1985, *24,* 316–38.

Card, David, "Deregulation and Labor Earnings in the Airline Industry." In James Peoples, ed. *Regulatory Reform and Labor Markets.* Boston, Massachusetts: Kluwer Academic Publishers, 1997.

Card, David, "The Impact of Deregulation on the Employment and Wages of Airline Mechanics," *Industrial and Labor Relations Review,* July 1986, *39,* 527–38.

Craypo, Charles, *The Economics of Collective Bargaining.* Washington, D.C.: Bureau of National Affairs, 1986.

Cremieux, Pierre-Yves, "The Effect of Deregulation on Employee Earnings: Pilots, Flight Attendants, and Mechanics, 1959–1992," *Industrial and Labor Relations Review,* July 1996, *49,* 223–42.

DeVany, Arthur, "The Effect of Price and Entry Regulation on Airline Output Capacity and Efficiency," *Bell Journal of Economics,* Spring 1975, *6,* 327–35.

Douglas, George, and James Miller, "Quality Competition, Industry Equilibrium, and Efficiency in the Price Constrained Airline Market," *American Economic Review,* September 1974, *64,* 657–69.

Ehrenberg, Ronald, *The Regulatory Process and Labor Earnings.* New York: Academic Press, 1979.

Fortin, Nicole, M., and Thomas Lemieux, "Institutional Changes and Rising Wage Inequality: Is There a Linkage?" *Journal of Economic Perspectives,* Spring 1997, *11:2,* 75–96.

Grimm, Curtis, and Robert Windle, "Regulation and Deregulation in Surface Freight, Airlines and Telecommunications." In James Peoples, ed. *Regulatory Reform and Labor Markets.* Boston, Massachusetts: Kluwer Academic Publishers, 1997.

Harris, Robert, G., and C. Jeffrey Kraft, "Meddling Through: Regulating Local Telephone Competition in the United States," *Journal of Economic Perspectives,* Fall 1997, *11:4,* 93–112.

Hendricks, Wallace, "Deregulation and Labor Earnings," *Journal of Labor Research,* Summer 1994, *15,* 207–34.

Hendricks, Wallace, "Labor Negotiations with Regional Monopolies: The Telecommunications Industry." In James Peoples, ed. *Regulatory Reform and Labor Markets.* Boston, Massachusetts: Kluwer Academic Publishers, 1997.

Hendricks, Wallace, Peter Feuille, and Carol Szersen, "Regulation, Deregulation, and Collective Bargaining in Airlines," *Industrial and Labor Relations Review,* October 1980, *34,* 67–81.

Hirsch, Barry, "Trucking Regulation, Unionization, and Labor Earnings: 1973–85," *Journal of Human Resources,* Summer 1988, *23,* 296–319.

Hirsch, Barry, and David Macpherson, "Earnings and Employment in Trucking: Deregulating a Naturally Competitive Industry." In James Peoples, ed. *Regulatory Reform and Labor Markets.* Boston, Massachusetts: Kluwer Academic Publishers, 1997b.

Hirsch, Barry, and David Macpherson, " Earnings, Rents, and Competition in the Airline Labor Market," Florida State University Economics Working Paper 94-12-1, December 1995.

Hirsch, Barry, and David Macpherson, *Union Membership and Earnings Data Book 1996: Compilations from the Current Population Survey.* Washington, D.C.: Bureau of National Affairs, 1997a.

Keefe, Jeffrey, and Karen Boroff, "Telecommunications Labor-Management Relations After Divestiture." In Paula Voos, ed. *Contemporary Collective Bar-*

gaining in the Private Sector. Madison, Wisconsin: Industrial Relations Research Association, 1994.

Keeler, Theodore, "The Revolution in Airline Regulation." In Leonard Weiss and Michael Klass, eds. *Case Studies in Regulation: Revolution and Reform.* Boston, Massachusetts: Little, Brown, 1981.

Krueger, Alan B., and Lawrence H. Summers, "Efficiency Wages and the Inter-Industry Wage Structure," *Econometrica,* March 1988, *56,* 259–93.

MacDonald, James, and Linda Cavalluzzo, "Railroad Deregulation: Pricing Behavior, Shipper Responses, and the Effects on Labor," *Industrial and Labor Relations Review,* July 1996, *50,* 80–91.

Moore, Thomas Gale, "The Beneficiaries of Trucking Regulation," *Journal of Law and Economics,* October 1978, *21,* 327–43.

Moore, Thomas Gale, "U.S. Airline Deregulation: Its Effects on Passengers, Capital and Labor," *Journal of Law and Economics,* April 1986, *24,* 1–28.

Pal, Debashis, "Commentary on Labor Negotiations with Regional Monopolies: The Telecommunications Industry." In James Peoples, ed. *Regulatory Reform and Labor Markets.* Boston, Massachusetts: Kluwer Academic Publishers, 1997.

Peoples, James, "Airline Deregulation and Industry Wage Levels," *Eastern Economic Journal,* January–March 1990a, *16,* 49–58.

Peoples, James, "Concluding Observations." In James Peoples, ed. *Regulatory Reform and Labor Markets.* Boston, Massachusetts: Kluwer Academic Publishers, 1997.

Peoples, James, "Wage Outcomes Following the Divestiture of AT&T," *Information Economics and Policy Journal,* 1990b, *4,* 105–26.

Perelman, Michael, "Fixed Capital, Railroad Economics and the Critique of the Market," *Journal of Economic Perspectives,* Summer 1994, *8,* 189–95.

Perry, Charles, *Deregulation and the Decline of the Unionized Trucking Industry.* Philadelphia, Pennsylvania: Wharton School's Industrial Research Unit, 1986.

Rose, Nancy, "Labor Rent-Sharing and Regulation: Evidence from the Trucking Industry," *Journal of Political Economy,* December 1987, *95,* 1146–8.

Smith, Sharon P., "Bargaining Realities: Responding to a Changing World." In Wei-Chiao Huang, ed. *Organized Labor at the Crossroads.* Kalamazoo, Michigan: W. E. Upjohn Institute for Employment Research, 1989.

Talley, Wayne, and Ann Schwarz-Miller, "Railroad Deregulation and Union Labor Earnings." In James Peoples, ed. *Regulatory Reform and Labor Markets.* Boston, Massachusetts: Kluwer Academic Publishers, 1997.

Walsh, David, "Toward a 'Seamless' Workforce? Interunion Cooperation in the Airline Industry." In Peter Cappelli, ed. *Airline Labor Relations in the Global Era.* Ithaca, New York: Industrial and Labor Relation Press, 1995.

Name Index

Abodeely, J.E. 156
Abowd, J.M. 90, 128, 129
Abraham, K.G. 181
Acemoglu, D. 284
Adams, W. 123
Addison, J.T. 77, 80, 81, 82, 83, 85, 89, 90, 92, 93, 94, 95, 105, 106, 108, 109, 111, 125, 126, 127, 130, 132, 135
Adler, D. 206
Akerlof, G.A. 181
Alchian, A.A. 50, 84
Alesina, A. 34
Alexis, M. 331, 342
Alstott, A.L. 201
Alvarez, M. 14
Annable, J. 327, 330
Aoki, M. 131
Ashenfelter, O.C. 54, 80, 89, 93, 94, 95, 96, 129
Atleson, J.B. 76
Autor, D. 11
Axelrod, R.M. 77, 140
Ayres, I. 195

Babcock, L. 195
Bajpai, N. 283
Baldwin, C.Y. 84
Banerjee, A. 320
Barenberg, M. 221
Barro, R. 16, 21, 284
Bartik, T.J. 243
Beck, T. 14, 21
Becker, G.S. 7, 81, 162
Belzer, M. 342
Benello, C.G. 142
Berkowitz, M. 94
Bertola, G. 11
Bertrand, M. 285, 294
Besley, T. 5, 39, 300
Bewley, T.F. 170, 182, 189, 190, 206, 218, 235
Bhagwati, J. 288
Blades, L.E. 175, 200
Blanchard, O. 284
Blanchflower, D. 42
Blanpain, R. 12
Block, M.K. 123
Bloom, D.E. 54

Boeri, T. 11
Bonanno, C.D. 157
Bork, R.H. 144
Boroff, K. 335
Botero, J. 284
Boylaud, O. 5
Briggs, V. 50, 54
Brock, J.W. 123
Brown, C. 61
Brown, J.N. 89, 93, 129
Buchanan, J. 8
Burgess, R. 5, 39, 300
Butler, D. 319

Caballero, R.J. 293
Calabresi, G. 172
Campbell, T.J. 87, 111, 112, 114, 124, 128
Cappelli, P. 333, 334
Card, D. 95, 129, 250, 285, 333, 339, 342
Cavalluzzo, L. 332, 339
Cazes, S. 11
Chamberlain, N.W. 154
Chammah, A.M. 139–40
Charness, G. 182
Chidzero, A.-M. 15
Clabault, J.M. 123
Clark, K.B. 89, 90, 94, 127, 128, 129, 132, 135, 136, 137
Coase, R.H. 77, 184
Cobb, J.C. 249
Cohen, G.M. 85, 86, 96, 149, 154, 156, 174
Cohen, M.A. 136
Coleman, J.L. 98, 139, 140
Cooter, R. 77, 98, 131, 140
Cox, A. 75, 76, 117, 124, 157
Cox, T. 12
Cramton, P.C. 96, 132
Craypo, C. 333
Cremieux, P.-Y. 333, 339
Curme, M.A. 125

Dahlby, B.G. 110
Datt, G. 311, 316, 320
Dau-Schmidt, K.G. 138
Davey, H.W. 108, 109, 110
De Soto, H. 284

Economic Approaches to Law

1. Law and Economic Development
    Hans-Bernd Schäfer and Angara V. Raja

2. Economics of Family Law (Volumes I and II)
    Margaret F. Brinig

3. The Evolution of Efficient Common Law
    Paul H. Rubin

4. Social Norms, Nonlegal Sanctions, and the Law
    Eric A. Posner

5. Economics of Contract Law
    Douglas G. Baird

6. Public Choice and Public Law
    Daniel A. Farber

7. Economics of Federalism
    (Volumes I and II)
    Bruce H. Kobayashi and Larry E. Ribstein

8. Economics of European Union Law
    Paul B. Stephan

9. Economics of Property Law
    Richard A. Epstein

10. Economics of Conflict of Laws
    (Volumes I and II)
    Erin A. O'Hara

11. Economics of Tort Law
    (Volumes I and II)
    Alan O. Sykes

12. Economics of Labor and Employment Law
    (Volumes I and II)
    John J. Donohue III

13. Economics of Evidence, Procedure, and Litigation
    (Volumes I and II)
    Chris W. Sanchirico

Future titles will include:

Economics of Antitrust Law
Benjamin Klein and Andres V. Lerner

Economics of Administrative Law
Susan Rose-Ackerman

Game Theory and the Law
Eric B. Rasmusen

Economics of Criminal Law
Steven D. Levitt and Thomas J. Miles

Jeremiah 31: 35-36

Thus says the Lord
who gives the sun for a light
by day,
the ordinances of the moon
and the stars for a light
by night,
who disturbs the sea
and its waves roar
(The Lord of hosts is His name):

"If these ordinances depart
from before Me, says the Lord,
then the seed of Israel
shall also cease from being
a nation before Me forever."

To David
from Anna